BELA LUGOSI
IN PERSON

Bill Kaffenberger
Gary D. Rhodes

Foreword by Ann Croft

Designed by Michael Kronenberg

Printed in the United States

Published by BearManor Media
P. O. Box 71426
Albany, GA 31708
books@benohmart.com

Unless otherwise noted, all photographs come from the collections of Gary D. Rhodes and Bill Kaffenberger.

Library of Congress Cataloguing-in-Publication Data
Rhodes, Gary D. and Bill Kaffenberger
Bela Lugosi in Person / Bill Kaffenberger and Gary D. Rhodes
p.cm.
Includes bibliographical references and index
ISBN 978-1-62933-316-8
1. Lugosi, Bela, 1882-1956. 2. Motion Picture Actors and Actresses–United States–Biography. I. Rhodes, Gary D. II. Kaffenberger, Bill. III. Title.
PN2859.H86L836

Authors' Notes: Some images chosen for this book are of an imperfect quality, but they are reproduced herein due to their rarity and their importance to the narrative.

Also, for the sake of internal consistency, "theatre" has been used as the spelling of choice in this book, even in those cases when the original spelling was "theater."

For Kristin Dewey
- G.D.R.

and

In loving memory of my Dad, Mom, and brother David.
I miss all of you every day!
- B.K.

Foreword

By Ann Croft

My contact with Bela Lugosi was to understudy the actress portraying Lucy in his 1951 British tour of *Dracula* onstage, to be the effects manager, and to be prepared to scream and/or faint in the audience during the show.

I didn't get off to a very good start. At the first cast meeting when I was due to meet Bela, he spotted me across the room, his face lit up, and he came towards me hands outstretched saying "How wonderful, my ideal Lucy." Naturally this didn't make me very popular with the rest of the cast, even though they were a very delightful bunch of people.

Suffice to say when I next went out on tour, the theatre managers remembered me burning the stages and causing small fires because of my inexperience with the smoke gun in *Dracula*. This was used to herald Bela's appearance with a puff of smoke placed under his cloak. I managed to scorch three of his magnificent cloaks that even then cost £300 each, but he forgave me each time. He was a lovely man, very courteous and generous.

On one occasion (I think we were playing Lewisham Hippodrome), the Stage Director announced we only had three people in the audience in a theatre seating 3,000. Bela looked a little disconcerted, and then asked if the punters had paid for their seats. On hearing that they had, he decided to go ahead with the show as if there was a full house. The only difference was I didn't have to scream.

Bela's wife Lillian was a lovely lady who made sure he was well looked after, and was very kind to me. He was an absolute gentleman who always

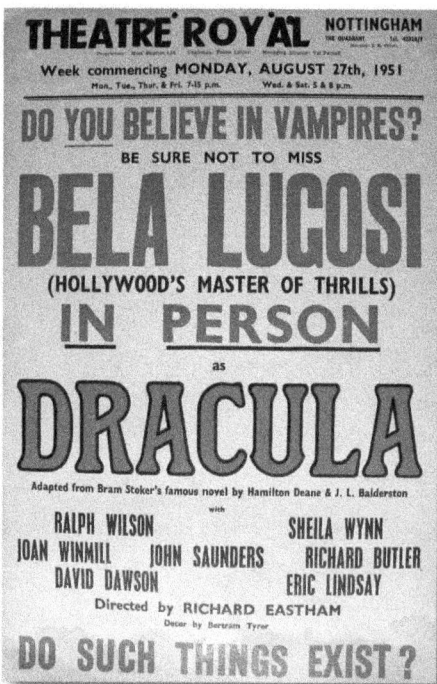

A poster used during Lugosi's 1951 tour of Great Britain and Northern Ireland.

Actress Ann Croft.
(Courtesy of Ann Croft)

said "thank you" to the stage crews after each performance, unlike some other stars that I could mention. When I was sacked for drinking in the bar at the Golders Green Hippodrome on my way back from screaming (I was teetotal at the time), Bela felt that perhaps the management had been a little harsh, so he arranged a farewell party for me and gave me a book signed by all the cast, including himself and Lillian, and of course a signed photograph for remembrance. The few months I spent with them was educational, interesting, and a fantastic introduction to the theatre and the meaning of a true star.

As a footnote, whilst on the tour I bought a beautiful little puppy that I called Bela, and the real Bela was delighted. There were many memorable incidents, including opening night, when the bats I was throwing on wires wrapped around Lucy's four poster bed and had to hang there until the interval, much to Lillian's amusement.

Bela was wonderful with the cast and with his fans on the tour, and I am grateful to Gary D. Rhodes and Bill Kaffenberger for bringing back to me such wonderful memories and humorous times. I hope the book gets the recognition it deserves, as it is so beautifully researched.

Publicity still of Bela Lugosi for *Dracula* (1931), autographed to a fan. *(Courtesy of David Wentink)*

Introduction

Crowds sporting scary T-shirts and even scarier monster makeup gather at convention centers, cash in hand, waiting impatiently until the minute hand strikes the hour and guards open the doors. Once inside, the mob forms into lines, one after another. Some lead to actors with magic markers in hand, ready to inscribe 8x10 glossies to blushing admirers. Others lead to a photographer's camera and lights, with fans quickly replacing one another at an actor's side, each getting a quick "hello" or even a lucky handshake when they have their picture taken.

These paths cost money, but they lead directly to horror film stars. The two-dimensional figure once threateningly colossal on a theatre screen – or made miniature on a tablet or smart phone – now stands there in person, usually smiling, though not always, so that the movie fan can see him or her live and in the flesh.

The scene is not uncommon in the 21st century. Horror film conventions and autograph shows allow fans to meet and even mingle with Those Who Were There, with Those Who Were in the Film. Of course many of these persons are stars only in the sense that their onscreen characters have become popular. The hockey mask is famous; those who wore it are not, outside of a small coterie of devoted followers.

The notion of the film star making a personal appearance has existed for over a century. In St. Louis in 1910, during a period in which the slang term "movie" was just coming into common usage, moviegoers flocked to see "The Girl of a Thousand Faces" in person. She was Florence Lawrence, the "Biograph Girl" who was finally billed with her real name after being hired by Carl Laemmle, Sr., the mogul who started Universal Pictures.

In a cunning publicity stunt, Laemmle had anonymously announced that Lawrence had died, and then – to generate even more publicity – declared the first report was false. Lawrence's health was never better; in fact, her new Laemmle-produced films were coming soon to a theatre near you.

When the assemblage in St. Louis laid eyes on Lawrence, they could hardly contain themselves. There she stood, both alive and live: overexcited fans allegedly rushed the stage and tore at her clothes. A trade publication reported that she had been met with the kind of "enthusiasm" hitherto reserved only for presidential candidates and prizefighters.[1]

The everyday person's longing to see and even possibly meet the famous has deep historical roots, ranging from those who wanted to glimpse royalty in past centuries to those who gawked at Jesse James' corpse in 1882. And collecting autographs was common during the nineteenth century, even before the advent of the cinema.[2]

But movie stars have exuded a unique allure, in part because they are so regularly present through their own absence. Unlike other kinds of celebrities during the classical Hollywood era, the film star – thanks to his or her illuminated reproduction at movie theatres – appeared in large cities and small towns on a regular basis. Fans came to "know" stars that they had never seen in person, let alone met.

The rise of the feature film resulted in more and more stars making personal appearances, whether acting in stage plays or promoting their films. During the twenties and thirties, an increasing number of stars also created vaudeville acts. As *Variety* reported in 1930: "The theory appears to be that the stars will do for a one-time appearance anyway, [even if they are] unable to do more than look pleasant on the stage."[3] Sinews in venues, ready to smile and perhaps even shake one's hand after the big show was over.

In some cases, personal appearances meant stars not only excited their fans, but also gained what *Billboard* called a "stronger foothold in their respective studios," their employers learning just how popular they were.[4] And for those stars whose bright lights were dimming, working in vaudeville or summer stock provided much-needed income.

All that said, the personal appearance could cause stars a degree of stress, whether having their clothes pawed in public or having to travel hundreds or even thousands of miles to cities and towns that did not stand in the shadow of a sign regally announcing "Hollywoodland."

At least some movie fans sympathized with the rigors that stars experienced when pressing the flesh. The topic surfaced in interviews published in movie magazines and even on the screen thanks to *In Person* (1935) with Ginger Rogers. In it, she plays a movie star who wears "almost a femme Frankenstein getup" in public so as to avoid all the many fans who want to meet her.[5]

The much-storied career of Bela Lugosi represents a tale that is both unique and common: sui generis and yet also generic. Like most movie stars dating back to Florence Lawrence (who committed suicide in 1938), his Hollywood career followed a typical trajectory: he climbed to film fame, and then – punctuated by one major comeback – he fell into increasing obscurity. Such is the gravity of being famous in Hollywood.

Other aspects of Lugosi's career are distinctive, particularly in that, thanks to the 1931 film version of *Dracula*, he became the very first horror film star. Such a claim is certain to raise a few eyebrows, and yet it is very definitely the case, so much so that it is surprising that it hasn't been more widely discussed in the myriad books and articles written about both him and the horror film.

To be sure, actors dating all the way back to Georges Méliès (the famous producer-director who appeared in the majority of his own films at the turn of the twentieth century) have portrayed horrific characters onscreen. During the silent film era, various persons did so on a repeated basis, including Paul Wegener, Conrad Veidt, and Lon Chaney. They were film stars, to be sure, but their stardom was founded on far more than bizarre characters and fantastical

Lugosi signs an autograph for a fan in England in August 1935 while his wife stands beside him.
(Courtesy of D'Arcy More)

storylines. In a trio of books, for example, Michael F. Blake has expertly dissected Chaney's filmography, illustrating that he was much more than a star in a small number of what we might now call horror films.[6]

The term "horror film" (or, by extension, "horror movie") did not even concretize as a name for a distinct genre of cinema until the spring and summer of 1931. While that adjective was occasionally used in earlier periods to describe certain films or scenes within them, it was not until 1931 that "horror film" became used and understood in the film industry and American popular culture in the same way that one might say "western" or "musical."

Here again we can invoke Bela Lugosi, as it was the release of *Dracula*, his most famous film, which propelled the term "horror film" into popular culture. In a fascinating disavowal of Universal Pictures' publicity materials, critics and audiences across the United States eschewed romance and mystery taglines prepared for them and instead adopted the term "horror," which would be repeatedly applied to similar films during the rest of 1931, throughout 1932, and in every single year since.

Lugosi was thus the first horror film star, his name and face and persona reaching stardom as a direct result of the newly termed cycle of films that *Dracula* initiated. He became famous for horror, rather than being a famous actor who played a few horrific roles. And the orbit he occupied was far higher than an unknown actor in a Michael Myers mask could ever hope to reach.

During his heyday, Lugosi's fans not only wanted to see his films, but also to see him, up close and in person: to meet him, to get an autograph, to converse with him, or – hope of hopes – to befriend him, or even marry him (as Lugosi fan Hope Lininger did in 1955). While he had acted onstage at least as early as 1902, Lugosi's live appearances after the release of the film *Dracula* were different. He was no longer a theatre actor, or even a notable Broadway actor, or – for that matter – a featured film player, as he had been in Hungary, Germany, and America.

A TRIBUTE

To Carl Laemmle..the pioneer..the builder.. the fighter. The grand old man of the motion picture industry.. in the gloaming of whose life comes the great honor of presenting to all women .. to all lovers .. the finest drama of human emotions ever produced .. the John M. Stahl Production

TONIGHT

The premiere of this great picture has been dedicated to Carl Laemmle..the famous and the great of Hollywood will gather to pay tribute to him

Genevieve Tobin
Lois Wilson
Will Hays
Ruth Chatterton
John M. Stahl
Lawrence Tibbett
Gloria Swanson
Cecil B. De Mille
George Baker
Mayor of Portland, Ore.
Carl Laemmle Jr.
Lilyan Tashman
Helen Twelvetrees
Walter Huston
Sue Carol
Ina Claire
Bela Lugosi
Jean Harlow
Charles Rogers
Bette Davis
Ralph Forbes
Laura La Plante
Charlie Murray
Thelma Todd
Neil Hamilton
Lola Lane
Frances Dade
Helen Parrish
Edmund Breese
Rose Hobart
Helen Chandler
Lew Ayres
Alice Joyce
Fifi Dorsay
George Brent
May Robson
Natalee Moorhead
Vera Gordon
June Collyer
Mervyn LeRoy

Conrad Nagel
Master of Ceremonies

Tom Terris
and
George Brent
at the Microphone

SEED

By
CHARLES G.
NORRIS

CARL LAEMMLE PRESENTS
A UNIVERSAL PICTURE

JOHN BOLES
GENEVIEVE TOBIN
LOIS WILSON

A CARL LAEMMLE JR. PRODUCTION
DIRECTED BY
JOHN M. STAHL

ABE LYMAN AND HIS BAND

CARTHAY CIRCLE

DIRECTION FOX WEST COAST THEATRES

After February 1931, he was a movie star, and so when he made public appearances in theatre, vaudeville, or otherwise, he not only had to modulate his performance in the manner all actors must when they go back and forth between stage and screen, but he also had to maintain a certain kind of presence. A star is more than an actor. A star brings with him or her certain expectations as well as histories, meaning their famous films and roles. For better or worse, he was Bela "Dracula" Lugosi.

That was the case from February 1931 onward. And Lugosi's personal appearances were many in number and varied in type. In 1932, he was back on the legitimate stage in *Murdered Alive*, and was as a result the first horror film star to headline a three-act play. Later that same year, he revived *Dracula–The Vampire Play*, making him the first horror film star to appear onstage in a role that he had already played onscreen.

In 1933, thanks to Earl Carroll's *Murder at the Vanities*, Lugosi became the first horror film star to play Broadway. Only months later, he became the first horror film star to appear in vaudeville.[7]

And Lugosi in the flesh was something to behold. Consider what his fourth wife Lillian Arch said in an interview: "I never got tired of watching him, because even without the makeup and all that he could be so charming. He'd charm anybody off their feet. And then when the beast [Dracula] came out of him, he looked so vicious."[8]

Many persons who saw Lugosi onstage remarked upon the power and intensity of

Lugosi's first known advertised personal appearance after the release of *Dracula* in February 1931. Published in the *Los Angeles Times* of April 17, 1931.

his portrayals, which were informed by his screen persona and underpinned by his decades of experience in the theatre. Likewise, those who met him offstage regularly expressed surprise at how different he was in "real life," even if real life in most of these cases meant public encounters that lasted for mere minutes or seconds.

And yet meeting Lugosi, even just shaking his hand, often left an indelible impression, becoming an important and unforgettable event. That was true not only of his legion of fans, but also of some of his fellow performers.

Even Elaine Stritch, Broadway's grand dame, seemed to glow when speaking of Lugosi. As if to position herself closer to him, she shared an improbable anecdote, claiming he downed seventeen Scotch whiskeys when the two were together at a bar, and then – after the bartender refused to sell him more alcohol – successfully pulled a tablecloth out from under all the dishes and glasses resting atop it. From there, he sought more whisky elsewhere.[9]

Bela Lugosi Crime Report

The "Veiled Woman" sat in the "Thirteenth Chair" and dined with the "Prisoners." She cried, "Oh, For a Man!" not knowing "Such Men Are Dangerous." The "Renegades" were "Broadminded" about taking "Dracula" with them on their "Black Camel" to visit "Women of All Nations." "The White Zombie" with the aid of "Chandu, the Magician," committed "Murders in the Rue Morgue" on "The Island of Lost Souls" by means of "The Death Kiss."

(*Continued on page* 95)

(*Continued*

"The Mysterious Mr. Wong" spent a "Night of Terror" at the "International House" after "The Return of Chandu." "The Whispering Shadow" was satisfied that the "Black Cat" received "The Mark of the Vampire" for chasing "The Raven" because he knew that "The Best Man Wins."—Hope Lininger, Johnstown, Pa.

Fan letter from Lugosi's future wife, published in *Modern Screen* in December 1935.*(Courtesy of Kristin Dewey)*

Lugosi live could be larger than life, larger even than his own real life.

It is true that the caliber of Lugosi's personal appearances devolved during his 25 years as a horror film star in America. His very first after the release of *Dracula* seems to have been an advertised appearance at a Los Angeles film premiere in April 1931; his last was apparently a short publicity tour for *The Black Sleep* (1956), a horror movie in which he played a minor role.

In prior literature, Lugosi's films have usually commanded the most attention, and with good reason, given that he was first and foremost a movie star, certainly in America. But many of his live appearances from 1931 to 1945 ran parallel to when his Hollywood career was (in varying measures) at its peak.

Aside from scant paragraphs here and there, these live appearances have merited relatively little attention. Indeed, some of the dozen we cover at length in this study are unknown outside of his most dedicated fans.

The impetus of this book is thus two-fold. For one, we see intrinsic value in surveying these personal appearances, bringing to them a level of depth that has been absent in prior texts. The details of these performances, their critical reception, and their position in Lugosi's life and career are important. Lost and forgotten histories deserve to be reclaimed.

Secondly, we believe the era under review does indeed constitute the most important in Lugosi's Hollywood film career. Production histories of those movies have been described on many occasions, whether in books specifically about him, as in Richard Bojarski's *The Films of Bela Lugosi* (Citadel, 1980), or in the context of the horror genre, such as Tom Weaver's *Poverty Row Horrors!* (McFarland, 1993). An increasing number of theoretical perspectives are being brought to bear on Lugosi films as well, as evidenced by texts like *Recovering 1940s Horror Cinema: Traces of a Lost Decade* (Lexington, 2015), edited by Mario Degiglio-Bellemare, Charlie Ellbé, and Kristopher Woofter.

For decades, the films of Hollywood stars have regularly been analyzed using these kinds of approaches, and rightly so. Investigating films using production information, censorship data, critical reviews, and even surviving fan letters can reveal important insights into a star's career.

By contrast, the personal appearance has seldom been used as a lens through which historians have examined an actor's film career. Indeed, at first such a notion might well seem contradictory, as examining stage roles or vaudeville acts is arguably a matter apart from scrutinizing a film career.

However, that is in fact the second key purpose of this book: to present new perspectives on Lugosi's film career by examining his work "in the flesh." In many respects, these personal appearances speak directly to his film career, both its periods of success (as in his attendance at a film premiere) or its periods of decline (as in appearing at a reissue screening of *Dracula* when no new film roles were on offer).

The varied content of these "in person" events was also directly involved in a dialogue with Lugosi's screen persona. For example, their content sometimes reflected roles he had portrayed onscreen, like Dracula of course, as well as roles that stage producers hoped he would eventually portray onscreen, if their plays became successful enough to be purchased by Hollywood studios. Such interactions between the two media can be distilled with one example: Lugosi would get laughs in live performances of *Arsenic and Old Lace* in 1943 and 1944 by revealing that he killed a victim because he said he "looked like Bela Lugosi." The joke only worked because it drew upon Lugosi's screen persona.

Put another way, Bela Lugosi's film career was refracted through these live shows. "Bela Lugosi in Person" can teach us much new about Bela Lugosi on the screen, as well as the fans who enjoyed his movies. It is here that we hope to augment not only our understanding of Bela Lugosi, but also to propose a fresh approach to star studies, one that can be used to examine a Hollywood actor's film career anew. Much can be learned about the cinema and its stars by an examination of these kinds of live appearances.

As in our prior book, *No Traveler Returns: The Lost Years of Bela Lugosi* (BearManor Media, 2012), as well as in Rhodes' earlier books on Lugosi and his films, we rely herein on a New Film History methodology that attempts to engage as rigorously as possible with primary sources.[10] While digitized archival materials have been extremely helpful, so too have the yellowing, one-of-a-kind pages that are buried at given libraries, historical societies, and museums. For the first time anywhere, for example, we present hitherto unknown

To my friend
Alex
in remembrance

Bela Lugosi

Portrait of Lugosi autographed
for his friend, Alex Gordon.
(Courtesy of David Wentink)

information from declassified OSS files, as well as previously undocumented information about the long-forgotten television program *Murder and Bela Lugosi* (1950). As an addendum, we also provide a timeline of Lugosi's personal appearances from the release of *Dracula* in 1931 until his death in 1956.

As part of this process, we have likewise attempted to recover and present relevant and in some cases previously unpublished illustrations. Some are stunning images, such as the one that adorns our book cover. Others survive only in crumbling newspaper pages or damaged microfilm. However, despite their poor quality, we believe it worthwhile from a historical perspective to include them, as they otherwise would languish unseen, lost to time.

Both of us believe our work represents an important intervention into an ongoing conversation about one of the most fascinating and important Hollywood film stars of the 20th century. As much as we have uncovered, more work remains. Definitive books on subjects do not exist, as the research continues.

As a result, we do not profess that the present volume records every single personal appearance Lugosi made, any more than we claim to have unlocked all of the mysteries of Lugosi's Hollywood career.

However, we do hope this book represents an important exploration of "Bela Lugosi in Person," ranging from his initial fame in the months following the release of *Dracula* in 1931 to the end of World War II in 1945. Here is an overlooked facet of Lugosi's famous career, one that we are very pleased to share.

Gary D. Rhodes
Belfast, Northern Ireland

Bill Kaffenberger
Hanover, Virginia

(Endnotes)

1   "Ovation for Film Star in St. Louis." *Billboard* 9 Apr. 1910.
2   See, for example: "Autograph Collecting." *Christian Advocate* 26 Apr. 1883.
3   "More Circuits Using Film Stars in Person for Theatre Stages." *Variety* 2 July 1930.
4   Schultz, John A. "The Value of Personal Appearances to Film Player [*sic*]." *Billboard* 29 Aug. 1936.
5   "In Person." *Variety* 18 Dec. 1935.
6   Blake, Michael F. *Lon Chaney: The Man Behind the Thousand Faces* (New York: Vestal Press, 1990); Blake, Michael F. *A Thousand Faces: Lon Chaney's Unique Artistry in Motion Pictures* (New York: Vestal Press, 1995); Blake, Michael. *The Films of Lon Chaney* (New York: Vestal, 1998).
7   Here we would underscore that we are speaking of Lugosi the horror film star. Certainly Lugosi, Boris Karloff, and others had been onstage *prior* to becoming horror film stars.
8   D'Arc, James V. "Oral History Interview Donlevy, Lillian Lugosi." 20 May 1976. Available at L. Tom Perry Special Collections, Harold B. Lee Library, Brigham Young University, Provo, Utah.
9   Stritch, Elaine. *Dracula Meets Elaine Stritch*. Filmed interview excerpt from Theater Talk's *Elaine Stritch Birthday Bash*. Available at: https://www.youtube.com/watch?v=MqN-vao_de0. Posted 13 Feb. 2013. Accessed 25 Jan. 2015.
10   Rhodes' other books on the subject include *Lugosi* (Jefferson, NC: McFarland, 1997), *White Zombie: Anatomy of a Horror Film* (Jefferson, NC: McFarland, 2002), *Bela Lugosi, Dreams and Nightmares* (Narberth, PA: Collectables, 2007), and *Tod Browning's Dracula* (Sheffield, England: Tomahawk, 2014).

BELA
LUGOSI
IN PERSON

Bill Kaffenberger
Gary D. Rhodes

Foreword by Ann Croft

Bela Lugosi in a publicity still for *Dracula* (1931).

Chapter 1

The Wine of Anubis

During his sideshow lecture, Dr. Mirakle unveils a caged ape and informs the frightened crowd: "Here is the story of man. In the slime of chaos, there was the seed, which rose and grew into the tree of life. Life was motion." Evolution permitted a "four-legged thing" to stand upright and walk, and for an ape to become human. Mirakle's arresting doctrine was little more than a recapitulation of Charles Darwin's.

The famous carnival scene in Robert Florey's film *Murders in the Rue Morgue* (1932) remains one of Bela Lugosi's most memorable. With curly hair and nineteenth-century dress, Dr. Mirakle looks none-too-different than surviving photographs of Edgar Allan Poe, who in 1841 published the short story on which the film was based.

But the film's script was quite different than Poe's story. After all, Darwin did not publish *On the Origin of Species* until 1859, and the character Dr. Mirakle does not even appear in Poe. *Murders in the Rue Morgue* had changed, in part from screenwriters reworking the Poe story and integrating elements of *The Cabinet of Dr. Caligari* (1920). Two stories grew and merged, thus creating a third. The result was *Murders in the Rue Morgue*, but a different *Rue Morgue*, a new *Rue Morgue*.

Here was evolution, even if not quite of a Darwinian type. Perhaps it was closer to what philosopher and politician Edmund Burke expressed in the eighteenth century: "We must all obey the great law of change. It is the most powerful law of nature." Or perhaps other terms are better suited to describe a phenomenon of change that involves literary and artistic homage, appropriation, growth, and metamorphosis.

At any rate, *Murders in the Rue Morgue* was hardly the first time that Lugosi interacted with such change. Bram Stoker's novel *Dracula* transformed considerably to become the 1927 Hamilton Deane-John L. Balderston Broadway play. Abbreviating the novel for the stage resulted in the elimination of all scenes set in Transylvania, as well as numerous important characters. The novel and the play were both *Dracula*, but they were not the same

Dracula. The limitations of the stage – and the artistic input from writers other than Stoker – necessitated variations.

The same was true when Universal Pictures transformed *Dracula* into the 1931 film. It reinstated some aspects of the novel, drew upon certain elements of the stage play, and – thanks to the involvement of a number of screenwriters – introduced several new ideas. Once again, *Dracula* changed. So did Lugosi's performance, as he himself realized. Playing Dracula onscreen was different than playing Dracula on the stage.

In a way, *Dracula* evolved even prior to Stoker's novel, not merely in the shifting historical depictions of Vlad the Impaler, but also in vampire folklore. The same was true of vampire literature, from Polidori's *The Vampyre, A Tale* (1819) to Le Fanu's *Carmilla* (1871), as well as to the vampire onstage, from Planché's *The Vampire; or, The Bride of the Isles* (1820) to Boucicault's *The Vampire* (1852, aka *The Phantom*).

Much like Deane-Balderston's Count Dracula, for example, Polidori's Lord Ruthven appears in England without initially arousing the suspicions of those who fall prey to his bloodlust. Likewise, Boucicault's Rees is a wise elder not unlike Stoker's Van Helsing, or – for that matter – the Van Helsing of Broadway in 1927 and of Hollywood in 1931. Put another way, the origins of Stoker's *Dracula* predate his authorship of the novel.

Change also abounded in the nascent horror film of the early 1930s. After *Dracula*'s success, Universal initially considered a trio of possible sequels to it, but then quickly shifted its attentions from the supernatural to the natural. In the spring and summer of 1931, the studio debated over which story should be next on its agenda: Shelley's *Frankenstein* or Poe's *Murders in the Rue Morgue*. In the end, *Frankenstein* came first, hitting theatres in November 1931, followed by *Rue Morgue*, released in February 1932.

But discussing the order of their release distracts from the larger point: both films featured mad scientist storylines, a major change from the supernatural vampires of *Dracula*. And while Lugosi famously did not appear in *Frankenstein*, he did portray Dr. Mirakle, a mad scientist who attempts to fuse the blood of a woman with that of an ape.

Lugosi's evolution from Dracula to Mirakle was important, given the large number of times he would subsequently play mad scientists onscreen. It is also significant biographically, given that he was hoping to escape the horror genre: *Rue Morgue* transformed him from one kind of horror character into another.

That transition would also impact upon Lugosi's return to the stage in 1932, his first major live appearance after becoming a Hollywood star in 1931. By the time that *Rue Morgue* was released in February 1932, a stage play called *The Black Tower* was surviving, even if not flourishing, on Broadway. When its New York run ended in March of that year, its reincarnation under the new title *Murdered Alive* was slowly coming to life on the West Coast. And that version would star Lugosi as yet another mad scientist.

The *Los Angeles Herald and Express* remarked that *Murdered Alive* was "the first stage appearance of Bela Lugosi since his footlight creation of the male vampire in *Dracula*."[1] For the *San Francisco Examiner*, *Murdered Alive* meant, importantly, "Lugosi in Person."[2] He was onstage, and ticket-buyers could sit nearby and watch him, just as Mirakle's audience does in *Murders in the Rue Morgue*.

Publicity for *Murders in the Rue Morgue* (1932). *(Courtesy of Kristin Dewey)*

As for Lugosi, *Murdered Alive* proved to be a fascinating albeit minor component in his ongoing transition into horror movie stardom. And for Hollywood, the play became another brick in the foundation of the mad scientist genre, its influence extending beyond the sphere of any single actor or even the confines of the stage.

The Wine of Anubis (1913)

"'Tut! Tut!' The old man smiled in good humor. 'Drink the wine. It will heal all your pain. You've got to drink it, you know. You can't help yourself. It will be much pleasanter not to be forced. Don't you see how stiff you are? You can hardly raise your hand. Drink it!'"

So wrote Crittenden Marriott in his short story *The Wine of Anubis*, published in America in *The Blue Book Magazine* in January 1913.

Born in Baltimore in 1867, Marriott was an author of some repute in the late nineteenth and early twentieth centuries, his work encompassing newspaper journalism, magazine articles, short stories, and novels. Best known among them was likely *The Isle of the Dead Ships*, a 1909 novel that merited a reprint in 1925.[3] By the time Marriott died in 1932, it had twice been adapted for the silver screen: Maurice Tourneur's *The Isle of Lost Ships* (1923, with Anna Q. Nilsson), and Irvin Willat's *The Isle of Lost Ships* (1929, with Virginia Valli).[4]

By contrast, Marriott's story *The Wine of Anubis* was not very well known. In it, reporter Tom Harkaway attempts to travel around the world in six months relying only on money that he earns during his journey. In order to generate much-needed cash, Tom accepts a job as a model from a sculptor named Winslow. But Winslow imprisons Tom, who soon realizes that his body is growing weaker and stiffer with each passing day. Winslow is not talented, at least in the field of art; he

The *Wine of Anubis* was published in *The Blue Book Magazine* in January 1913.

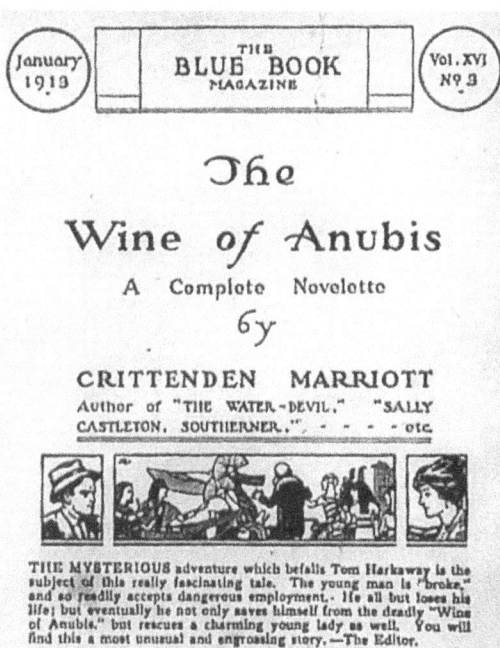

From *The Blue Book Magazine* of January 1913.

creates his lifelike sculptures by inducing victims to drink a potion that slowly turns them to stone.

His serum is thus the "wine of Anubis," a reference to the jackal-headed Egyptian god who protected graves and who helped Isis to embalm Osiris. Anubis guided souls to the afterlife and was commonly linked to mummification.

Thanks to Winslow's niece Vera, Tom ingests an antidote and regains his health. He kills Winslow's servant and flees with Vera. In retaliation, Winslow blows up his own home.

The tale represents something of an inverse of Greek myths like that of Pygmalion, in which a sculptor breathes life into his own statue. In his study "From Hephaistos to the Silver Screen," Vito Adriaensens notes that:

> Classical Greek sculpture embraced movement to the extent that it sought to blur the lines between bronze and flesh. The illusion of life that exudes from these idealized frozen bodies was sometimes even complemented by an open mouth that not only fit a narrative context in which the subjects spoke or sang to one another, but could also indicate the process of breath.[5]

For Marriott, life became stone, not the other way around; for him, Winslow was something of a gorgon-like mad scientist.

Though it never seems to have been reprinted or anthologized, *The Wine of Anubis* somehow managed to survive the yellowing pages of *The Blue Book Magazine* and adapt into a new form, one that would initially not star Bela Lugosi.

The Black Tower (1932)

In December 1931, newspapers announced that Ralph Murphy – who had written *Sh, the Octopus* (1928) – had at long last found backing for *Murdered Alive*, a three-act play that he had written some two years earlier.[6] One newspaper account claimed, "Producers have been afraid to bring it to the boards, considering it too much of a thriller, but since the sensational success of the horror film, *Frankenstein*, they have changed their minds."[7]

In this case, the producer in question was Ben Stein, who had earlier brought *The Jade God* (1929) to Broadway. Stolen from an Eastern temple, the jade artifact curses all of those who come into possession of it. Perkins (played by Margaret Wycherly, who starred opposite Lugosi in the 1929 film *The Thirteenth Chair*) spoke "enigmatic lines in a sepulchral tone of voice" and walked "about in a prescient daze that resembles the somnambulism of Lady Macbeth."[8] Though not a major success, *The Jade God* made Stein money, enough so that he saw possibilities in *Murdered Alive*.

A "highly unusual character," according to one journalist, Ben Stein was well known for making money in the theatre. "He knows more angles about speculators and seat sales than Kate Smith has pounds," the *Syracuse Journal* once joked.[9] Those angles included retitling *Murdered Alive*; for Broadway, it became *The Black Tower*.

The reason for the name change is difficult to determine, but what is clear is that Murphy's play drew upon *The Wine of Anubis*, a fact that did not go unnoticed in 1931. Marriott did

The *Black Tower* on Broadway
(Courtesy of the New York Public Library, Billy Rose Theatre Division)

not receive credit from Murphy or Stein, which may be why some publicity tried to claim *The Black Tower* was actually based on "one of the most unusual cases in European criminology." But while Marriott's story was clearly a key influence, Murphy's play was in some respects unique, and perhaps made more so due to Lora Baxter's involvement in its rewrites.[10]

For the play, Marriott's Winslow character became not merely an artist, but also a man of science, Dr. Eugene Ludlow. His confederates include a large, African-American henchman (not unlike a character in *The Wine of Anubis*), and also a fellow scientist, Professor Steiffitz, who concocts the statue-inducing potion. Here seems to be the influence of *Frankenstein* (1931) and *Dr. Jekyll and Mr. Hyde* (1931), with Ludlow being depicted as much or more of a mad scientist as he is an artist. Likewise, those films – as well as *Dracula* (1931) and others – may have prompted the play to focus not on a male victim, as Marriott had, but instead on a female character. Evolutions abounded.

Set in New York, *The Black Tower* begins at midnight in a "lonely spot in Central Park." Acts II and III unfold in the "Tower Room" of Dr. Ludlow's country house, "far up the Hudson." Its laboratory features all manner of secret doors, sliding panels, and elevators. It is also hermetically sealed and "artificially oxygenized."

Using a mixture of formaldehyde and other drugs, Ludlow forges his life-like statues as monuments to both art and science, at least until the authorities rescue the kidnapped woman and put an end to his evil-doings.

Sidney Salkow staged *The Black Tower*, which starred Walter Kingsford as Dr. Ludlow. After a tryout in Newark, opening night came at the Sam H. Harris Theatre on January 11, 1932, with the initial performances attended by "capacity crowds."[11] However, by the middle of February,

ACE O' HORRORS

"Murdered Alive," opening to-morrow night at the Carthay Circle, has for its leading character Bela Lugosi, the human refrigerator.

Published in the *Los Angeles Herald and Express* on April 1, 1932.

the show moved to the Ambassador.[12] By that point, its Broadway competition included Kenneth Webb's *Zombie*, one of the inspirations for the Lugosi film *White Zombie* (1932).

Reviewing *The Black Tower*, the *New York Evening Post* wrote, "with the exception of one or two short-lived and uncomfortable moments, it remains a thriller which does not thrill. … Their play is as feeble and puerile an attempt at horrific claptrap as any one could ask for."[13] The *Sun* was equally harsh, telling readers, "*Black Tower* brazenly violates every rule.

It introduces insanity for motive, which is rightly forbidden: it gives away everything at the start; it relies entirely on physical action."[14]

By contrast, the *World-Telegram* was somewhat kinder, noting, "it looks like a fair-to-middling hair-raiser." But the newspaper still felt compelled to report that it was "neither as exciting as *The Bat* or *The Thirteenth Chair*, nor as enervating as *The Ghost Train* or *The Gorilla*."[15]

All that said, the *Syracuse Journal* conveyed its belief that "the chief complaint seems to be that *Black Tower*, which was announced as a mystery thriller, turned out to be a mystery thriller. It made people in the audience shrink; it even made one woman faint."[16] Another review doubled that number, claiming two ladies lost consciousness during opening night.[17]

Other journalists saw in *The Black Tower* something akin to what Ben Stein had seen. The *Daily News* drew comparisons to the films *Frankenstein* and *Dr. Jekyll and Mr. Hyde*, and the

Sinister, Ah! Ha!

BELA LUGOSI— Seen in 'Murdered Alive' at Carthay Circle on April 6. This will be a stage production. Henry Goode drew the sketch.

From the *Illustrated Daily News* (Los Angeles) of March 29, 1932.

The marquee reads:

WORLD PREMIERE "REBOUND" — INA CLAIRE
ROBT. AMES — MYRNA LOY — ROBT. WILLIAMS

EDW. H. GRIFFITH'S "REBOUND" RKO PATHE
SMARTEST COMEDY IN TWENTY YEARS

The Carthay Circle Theatre.

Daily Mirror praised the play's horrific scenery.[18] But perhaps the most memorable description appeared in the *Herald-Tribune*: at a "critical juncture of the play you are permitted to see one of the doctor's subjects in a state of near-decomposition, resembling something prematurely arisen from the tomb."[19]

As for the villainous Dr. Ludlow, Walter Kingsford's portrayal brought him a modicum of acclaim. One newspaper bestowed on him the description of "a cool, calculating villain."[20] Another called him "quietly insane."[21] His character was mad, but his portrayal was not maniacal.

When *The Black Tower* closed in March 1932, the cast had given 72 performances. It had not quite achieved the longevity of *The Jade God* (which appeared 96 times on Broadway), in some measure because it had never really found an audience.

But there had also been interpersonal problems early in its production, specifically between Ben Stein and Ralph Murphy. Together with Lora Baxter, Murphy brought charges against Stein while *The Black Tower* was still at the Sam H. Harris Theatre. By that time, Murphy was on RKO's payroll on the West Coast, but was not so far away to not hear that Stein had the entire third act rewritten without his permission or involvement, apparently to save money on the construction of another set.[22] Stein confessed to making the changes, but argued Murphy's original ending would have jeopardized the lives of the actors and proven "obnoxious to the audience."[23] Relations between the producer and writers never improved.

Los Angeles

Reading a billboard that advertised Bela Lugosi in the play *Murdered Alive*, child star Jackie Cooper complained, "Huh, there's no sense to that. He couldn't be murdered dead, could he? He'd have to be alive to be murdered." *Photoplay* magazine agreed, adding that Cooper had used "pretty good logic."[24]

While not responding directly to Jackie Cooper, the *Los Angeles Times* claimed that Lugosi onstage would "settle" that very question. The paper added, "Masterminds of science and criminology may not concur with Lugosi in his theory that it is possible to be alive though murdered. However, the actor will stake his reputation as the stage and screen's foremost doer of diabolical deeds that he will accomplish the feat before the audience."[25]

Having regained the full rights to *Murdered Alive* from Ben Stein, Ralph Murphy and Lora Baxter enlisted a new producer on the West Coast. Arthur Greville Collins agreed to produce and direct the play, with the coauthors likely as interested in using performances as a platform to sell their story to a film studio as anything else. Along with the tradition of Hollywood adapting such plays as *The Bat* (1920), *The Cat and the Canary* (1922), *The Monster* (1922), *The Gorilla* (1925), *Dracula* (1927), and others, Warner Bros. had purchased the rights to *Doctor X* (1931) in January 1932.[26]

Jack Stuart Knapp published his one-act *The Horror Walks* in 1931, and Charles Champion struggled unsuccessfully to get a new mystery play onto the stage in early 1932. All of this was to capitalize on what *Variety* called the "horror fad" in the movies.[27] Whereas the horror

Published in the *Los Angeles Times* on March 31, 1932.

From the *Los Angeles Times* of April 1, 1932.

play had once influenced American cinema, the two media were now engaged in a dialogue with one another, and Ralph Murphy definitely wanted to join the conversation.

According to *Variety*, news of *The Black Tower*'s reincarnation brought forth a laugh from Ben Stein.[28] Perhaps he chuckled because Collins' entire outlay for the production was only $200, an incredibly small amount of cash to stage a three-act play in Los Angeles with a major film star.

How had he managed it? The Fox-West Coast chain furnished the theatre and the stage crew on a 50-50 gamble. Out of Collins' half, various percentages would go to the authors and cast. Lugosi signed for ten percent, with the other actors getting two percent and no guarantee. That meant Collins spent the entire $200 on advertisements.[29]

Collins reverted to Murphy and Baxter's original title, as well as to their original third act. Not surprisingly, Lugosi potrayed Dr. Ludlow, though the character was renamed Orloff, presumably to better match Lugosi's perceived foreign persona. In short, the play was changing yet again.

Betty Ross Clarke – who had just costarred with Lugosi in *Murders in the Rue Morgue* – assumed the female lead of Sylvia Knight; Bruce Craden appeared as glassy-eyed and stiff-limbed victim Strickland, who is nearly embalmed when the play begins.

The rest of the cast included Everett Brown (as the mute henchman Fangh), W. E. Watts (as

A lit billboard promotes *Murdered Alive* in Los Angeles. *(Courtesy of Bill Chase)*

the scarred Professor Steiffitz), Eily Malyon (as Mona, Orloff's dope-fiend confederate), Lew Kelly (as Inspector Quirk), David Callas (as Duffy, the "dumb cop"), and Rodney McLennan (as the "hero" Nicholas Rumsey, who is in love with Sylvia Knight).

Collins originally hoped to open the play in Los Angeles on March 26, but delays occurred, perhaps due to Lugosi's work on the *White Zombie* film set.[30] Rehearsals were in progress by March 24, if not sooner, and the play finally premiered at the Carthay Circle Theatre (1,500 seats) on April 2, 1932.[31] The theatre – which at times had screened movies and at times presented stage plays – had been dark in the weeks before *Murdered Alive* opened.[32]

Elsewhere in the city, however, the lights were bright. Thurston, Paderewski, Joe E. Brown, Ted Lewis, and even the infamous comedian Fatty Arbuckle were onstage in Los Angeles during *Murdered Alive*'s run. Lionel Atwill appeared in person as master of ceremonies for the premiere of *It's Tough to Be Famous* (1932), and Lugosi's friend Ervin Nyíergyházi won applause for a Los Angeles piano concert.[33]

Ads for *Murdered Alive* promoted "Bela Lugosi Himself" at prices that ranged from fifty cents to a dollar for evening tickets and only 25 to 75 cents for matinees.[34] The *Los Angeles Times* hinted that opening night would find celebrities in the audience, and the *Illustrated Daily News* even tried to convince readers to buy tickets based upon the theatre's "ample free parking."[35]

Varied publicity stories included Lugosi's argument that horror plays gave audiences the "thrill of witnessing something entirely foreign to their normal lives that stirs the senses and leaves them with the feeling of having really been entertained."[36] The *Los Angeles Record* – while incorrectly reporting that Lugosi had attended the finest schools in Hungary – promised readers that in real life he was actually a pleasant person. As for tales like *Dracula* and *Murdered Alive*, Lugosi's philosophy (at least for the sake of publicity) was, "It's a killing business, but I love it."[37]

COOLS CUTICLE

Cuticle will freeze and goose-flesh flourish at the Carthay Circle tonight, where Bela Lugosi is being starred in "Murdered Alive."

Published in the *Los Angeles Herald and Express* on April 2, 1932.

The Los Angeles-area newspapers reacted more positively than their Broadway counterparts had:

Lugosi is magnificent in the role ... A large audience greeted the opening on Saturday night and the company took some six curtain calls following the last act.

– *Los Angeles Examiner*[38]

Much horror is produced ... when the mad doctor, on the verge of discovery, decapitates his subject and the head rolls on the stage to stare at the audience.

– *Los Angeles Herald and Express*[39]

There was a fair-sized audience at Carthay Circle last night, some professionals from Hollywood and a number of college students. The production, which needs speeding up in tempo, seems to be eerie enough to satisfy the fan seeking sensational thrillers.

– *Illustrated Daily News*[40]

The piece is acted admirably throughout with particular praise due Lugosi and Watts. ... The play's chief fault is in its dialogue, which is pedestrian throughout.

– *Hollywood Citizen-News*[41]

Likewise, even while complaining of "infantile" dialogue and Lugosi's occasionally "inaudible" dialogue, the *Los Angeles Times* praised the "Lugosi personality" and believed the play's "essential idea" to be "quite grand."[42]

Critics from at least two industry trade publications attended the LA show as well. *Variety* labeled the cast "professionally capable," but complained the storyline was:

From the *Los Angeles Times* of April 3, 1932.

BELA LUGOSI IN PERSON

… unusually unpleasant. It goes a bit too far in its ghastly realism. Few persons not clinical cases themselves will fancy the sight of two scientific maniacs punching hypodermics into the flesh of victims selected at random from the flotsam of a public park and shanghaied into a chamber of horrors.[43]

The *Hollywood Filmograph* was more kind, enthusing that it was "just a bit more thrilling" than anything Lugosi had "done in the past." The trade also heaped praise on costars Lew Kelly and Eily Malyon.[44] (Kelly later appeared onscreen with Lugosi in *Bowery at Midnight* in 1942. Malyon later appeared onscreen in *The Hound of the Baskervilles* in 1939 *and She-Wolf of London* in 1946.)

Aside from reviews, the play's key publicity resulted from an injury Lugosi sustained on April 4. An "error of backstage mechanics" at the end of Act II caused him to fall sixteen feet. Though he had broken three ribs and an attending physician warned him not to continue, Lugosi forged ahead onstage only twenty minutes after the accident occurred.[45] In addition to getting local publicity, the story also appeared in *Billboard*, which was hardly sympathetic to the play, having apparently sided with Ben Stein over Ralph Murphy.[46]

Alma Whitaker of the *Los*

Playbill to *Murdered Alive* at the Carthay Circle. *(Courtesy of Dennis Phelps, as preserved in one of Bela Lugosi's personal scrapbooks)*

From the interior of the Carthay Circle playbill. *(Courtesy of Dennis Phelps, as preserved in one of Bela Lugosi's personal scrapbooks)*

HERE'S LURKING AT YOU!

By Troy Orr

♦

Looking under one's bed before retiring isn't confined to spinsters anymore!

No, dear reader, nearly all of us are "bed-looker-unders" nowadays. For, who can tell—Bela Lugosi may be lurking there, and when Lugosi lurks you may be assured that something terrifying will happen shortly—f'rinstance murder!

There are murders and then there are murders. The last named is to be said in a hushed voice denoting terror and, preferably, with that expression described as "wide-eyed."

It is the latter variety that Lugosi specializes in. This diabolical actor has put color into the killing business. His orgies of destruction are far from being prosaic—as you will testify after seeing "Murdered Alive."

When authors figure out better ways of exterminating the human race you can wager your last kopec that they will call upon Lugosi to do the dirty work.

It is really to be considered a pleasure to be murdered by such a skilled performer. Furthermore, it adds distinction to your demise. And then, too, consider the delightful suspense of wondering whether he will blow you to atoms or secrete scorpions in your tapioca.

BELA LUGOSI

Whatever your end may be you can rest assured it'll be simply killing, my dear, if Lugosi handles the case.

However, away from his fiendish footlight fancies you will find Bela Lugosi a most delightful person—with nary a murder concealed on his person.

To judge from the characters he portrays on stage and screen one might be inclined to think Bela was reared in a slaughter-house, with time out to get his degree in poisoning.

As a matter of fact he attended the finest schools in his native Hungary and his home life is as routine as yours and mine—well, I don't know about yours.

And he wouldn't think of murdering anyone away from the theatre. A kindlier nature you never contacted. Even brush salesmen don't annoy him, he just smiles resignedly and buys one.

His whole philosophy can be summed up in Mr. Lugosi's own words: "It's a killing business—but I love it"

— 12 —

Betty Ross Clarke

Angeles Times later reported that, despite "the direst of pain, [Lugosi] finished that third act in the best traditions of a first-class trouper." She added, "I interviewed him in bed at his home [the] next morning, all strapped up and forbidden to move," but nevertheless he appeared in the next performance and all that followed. Lugosi also told Whitaker that three studios were vying for the play as "picture material."[47]

Lugosi's dedication to *Murdered Alive* may well have been stronger than some of his audiences'. After its first week, *Variety* reported that the play "failed to get any attention" in Los Angeles, and that it had been a "mistake" staging it at the Carthay Circle. The trade added that its "take of $4,500 was considerable [*sic*] under the nut."[48]

Murdered Alive concluded the LA run on April 16, its second week generating only $2,600. Translation: a "total loss," blamed on the theatre being "too far from the center of town to be a successful pop-priced mystery house."[49] Given their shared financial stake in the grosses, Lugosi and his costars were likely disappointed. That feeling was not shared in New York, however, where Ben Stein's supporters "failed to weep."[50]

San Francisco

Arthur Collins produced his next version of *Murdered Alive* at the RKO Orpheum (2,900 seats) in San Francisco, budgeting the show at approximately $2,700.[51] The cast remained the same, as did the play, at least according to accounts that claimed it was presented in its "complete" form.

Artwork of Lugosi as Dracula used to publicize *Murdered Alive*. (Courtesy of Dennis Phelps, as preserved in one of Bela Lugosi's personal scrapbooks)

San Franciscans saw *Murdered Alive* in three acts and with a prologue; however, the timing of the daily performances and the rest of the bill – which included Universal's movie *The Cohens and Kellys in Hollywood* (1932) – suggest the play had in fact been abbreviated.

Advertisements heralded the Orpheum program as a "triumph in motion picture theatre history," meaning a chance to see a stage play at far less than the $3 ticket prices in Manhattan, as well as its pairing with a new feature film. The Orpheum presented four shows daily, at 1:20PM, 3:45PM, 7:00PM, and 9:30PM, with shows before 5:00PM priced at 35 cents and those after at 60 cents. The theatre also promoted a one-time "spook show" performance at 11:30PM on Saturday, April 23.[52]

The *San Francisco Chronicle* warned readers that *Murdered Alive* "makes *Dracula* seem like a child's bedtime story," and celebrated Lugosi for imbuing the Orloff role with "fascinating mystery and weird power."[53] The paper's review added that exhibitors everywhere would be watching to see the results of the unique pairing of a three-act play with a feature film.

While admitting that it was not "holeproof," the *San Francisco Examiner* of April 23, 1932 generally commended the play:

Satan himself couldn't think of anything more horrible. *Dracula* and *Frankenstein* pale by comparison. They are positively naïve when held up to the light with *Murdered Alive*.

Producer Arthur Collins has directed it with a swiftly-moving tempo … He has likewise cast it capably and wisely – what menace, I ask you, could impersonate the demented surgeon who petrifies human beings into statues, half so well, as Bela Lugosi, who originated the role of *Dracula* on the Broadway stage? His performance is skilled and smooth.

STARTLING ANNOUNCEMENT
2 TREMENDOUS ATTRACTIONS

BELA (DRACULA) LUGOSI
ON THE STAGE IN
THE BLOOD-CHILLING MURDER MYSTERY
"Murdered Alive"
Three-Act Drama—Big Cast
IN ADDITION TO
THE SCREEN'S LATEST LAUGH RIOT
"THE COHENS AND KELLYS IN HOLLYWOOD"
NOW PLAYING
At the RKO-Orpheum Theater
HERE'S HOW TO WIN:

In between today's classified ads are a number of sentences pertaining to Bela Lugosi. Find these sentences, write them and then send them to the Classified Advertising Manager, Dept H, together with a clipping of what you consider the best written and most attractive classified advertisement, and a few words telling why you selected this particular advertisement. Letters must reach our office not later than 4 p m the following day. Write as many sets of answers and essays as you like. Complete every day.

WEDNESDAY WINNERS
FIRST PRIZE, 6 GUEST TICKETS:
Miss Fanny Roth, 2233 Divisadero st.
SECOND PRIZE, 4 GUEST TICKETS:
Edgar Colton, 3505 Jackson st.
NEXT FOUR WILL RECEIVE 2 GUEST TICKETS EACH:
V. Braun, 252 Castro st.
Wallace Mark, 20 Adele Court, Apt. 453.
Edith Leonard, 2418 35th ave.
George Edwards, 890 Eddy st., Apt. 6.
TICKETS WILL BE MAILED.

From the *San Francisco News* of April 23, 1932.

The paper also praised W. E. Watts and Betty Ross Clarke (who had earlier appeared onstage in a San Francisco production of *Death Takes a Holiday*).

The *San Francisco News* reacted quite differently, so much so that it seems hard to believe its critic witnessed the same play:

The stage play is a routine horror drama. With great care it takes in all the stock chills that have accumulated since dramatists first discovered that goose pimples can be golden. And with great care it avoids the slightest semblance of originality.

Murdered Alive fails to gain distinction even by the presence of Bela Lugosi … The audience laughed at his lines. But that was no singular slight to Mr. Lugosi alone. It laughed at practically everybody else's, including Betty Ross Clarke's screams.[54]

Unhappy with the Cohens and Kellys film, this review ended by declaring the double bill "combined the worst features of stage and screen."

Lugosi sculpting a bust of himself in a publicity photo for *Murdered Alive*.

Another image of Lugosi sculpting a bust of himself for *Murdered Alive.* *(Courtesy of D'Arcy More)*

Initial estimates were that the Orpheum bill would gross an "extremely bad $8,500."[55] By the end of the week, *Variety* reported something even worse: an "unsatisfactory" $8,000.[56] *Murdered Alive* had failed as badly in San Francisco as it had in Los Angeles.

Reappearances

With little aplomb, *Murdered Alive* returned to Los Angeles, opening at the RKO Orpheum (2,000 seats) on April 30, 1932. Here was a shortened version of the play, paired once again with *The Cohens and Kellys in Hollywood.* As in the case of San Francisco, Lugosi and the cast gave performances four times daily, with the shows starting at 1:15PM, 4:00PM, 7:00PM, and 9:30PM.[57]

Having reviewed the play only weeks earlier, the press paid little attention to it, save for the *Illustrated Daily News*, which wrote, "Betty Ross Clarke's blonde beauty enhances the somber surroundings and a capable cast makes the production worthwhile."[58]

Whether or not they enjoyed the play or film, audiences in Los Angeles would have witnessed fascinating contrasts at the Orpheum. The horror play contrasted sharply with the ethnic humor of the Cohens and the Kellys, which apparently followed *Murdered Alive* on the bill, thus providing

Published in the *San Francisco Examiner* on April 22, 1932.

comic relief.

But then there was another contrast, one that was not likely lost on Lugosi, even if some members of the audience hardly noticed. The Cohens and the Kellys film included a cameo appearance by Boris Karloff, who had become famous thanks to the 1931 version of *Frankenstein*. Here Lugosi towered high in the theatre's advertisements: he was a movie star onstage and in the flesh. Karloff was seen only briefly, uncredited in the film, and yet his projected image loomed large onscreen at every show. (While the change of Ludlow's character name to Orloff in *Murdered Alive* was to suit Lugosi's foreign persona, the precise choice of "Orloff" – as opposed to any other foreign-sounding name – might well have been an effort to arouse thoughts of Karloff.)

From the *Los Angeles Herald and Express* of April 29, 1932.

Murdered Alive ended its second run in Los Angeles on May 5, 1932, having given 24 performances over six days, rather than the planned 28 in seven. The stated reason for closing one day early: to keep an "engagement in the Northwest," the extra day allowing the cast "more time to travel."[59]

But the cast did not travel to the Northwest. The real reason for the early closure was likely financial. *Variety* reported that *Murdered Alive*'s box-office receipts at the Orpheum were "disappointing"; the trade later described the stage-screen combo as a "slaughter," adding, "the horror thing is washed up locally."[60]

Conclusion

Even though Bela Lugosi hoped to avoid the horror genre in 1931 and 1932, he simultaneously embraced it, starring not only in *Murders in the Rue Morgue*, but also in *White Zombie*, and, immediately thereafter, in *Murdered Alive*. The reasons may have been many, though it's likely that financial concerns bested all others. *White Zombie* meant quick cash for roughly eleven days of work, and *Murdered Alive* held the potential of pocketing ten percent from a successful play.

However, the play proved even less of a success on the West Coast than it had been on Broadway, despite reverting to its original title and original third act. Lugosi had thus made his big return to the stage in a failure that likely brought him little financial compensation.

Murphy and Baxter's dreams of selling *Murdered Alive* to a Hollywood studio did not transpire, perhaps because it fared so poorly in Los Angeles and San Francisco. But that

Published in the *Los Angeles Herald and Express* **on May 2, 1932.**

hardly meant the play died.[61] Rather, it evolved. It mutated.

In February 1933, Warner Bros. released Michael Curtiz's Technicolor horror film *Mystery of the Wax Museum* with Lionel Atwill and Fay Wray. It was something of an outgrowth of the same studio's *Doctor X* (1932), meaning another color horror film directed by Curtiz that starred Atwill and Wray.

Mystery of the Wax Museum drew upon various sources. Glenda Farrell's fast-talking reporter certainly seems influenced not only by Lee Tracy's role in *Doctor X*, but also by the 1928 stage play and 1931 film *The Front Page*.

Officially, Warner Bros. based the film on Charles Belden's *The Wax Works*, which it purchased in July 1932. Belden had not published his short story, though he had allegedly registered it in January 1932. Then, in February 1932, independent producer Charles Rogers had optioned Belden's unproduced play *The Wax Museum*; given its title, it presumably bore some resemblance to his short story.[62]

Rogers never exercised his option on *The Wax Museum* specifically because he and his attorneys had determined that Belden's work was likely an infringement upon *The Black Tower*. Likewise, Warner Bros. carefully compared their shooting script for *Mystery of the Wax Museum* to *The Black Tower*, and with good reason.[63]

Mystery of the Wax Museum resounds with echoes of *Murdered Alive*. In the film, Atwill plays a sculptor named Ivan Igor whose preferred medium is wax rather than stone. Unlike Dr. Ludlow/Dr. Orloff, Igor has talent, but he loses the ability to use it after becoming disfigured in a fire. Thanks to a drug-addled assistant (who is something of a combination of Steiffitz and Mona) and a mute sculptor (not unlike Fangh), Igor uses corpses as the basis for his waxworks. As he explains to Fay Wray's character, being encased in wax bestows "immortality" on his victims. As Adriaensens has noted, the film features the "reverse Pygmalion motif."[64] Put another way, Igor's victims are murdered alive.

Surprisingly, Ralph Murphy did not sue the studio, nor is there any evidence that he tried to wrangle money from them. But the similarities between his play and their film are definitely there, having evolved, as they would continue to do in two remakes of *Mystery of the Wax Museum*.[65] Life is motion, just as Dr. Mirakle had said it was.

In fact, Bela Lugosi attended the premiere of one of those remakes, Andre de Toth's *House of Wax* (1953), starring Vincent Price. He entered the theatre dressed as Dracula, accompanied by a man in a gorilla costume who looked not unlike Mirakle's ape.

Publicity still for *Murdered Alive* depicting Orloff (Lugosi) and Fangh (Everett Brown).

A newsreel cameraman captured Lugosi's arrival on film while fans beamed at the aging star, who was live and in person. According to his friend Alex Gordon, Lugosi did not stay to watch all of *House of Wax*. Whether he saw enough to recognize its similarity to *Murdered Alive* is unknown, but the similarity is there. The story had evolved, but its earlier form can still be detected.

(Endnotes)

1   "Lugosi Is Fiend Ace." *Los Angeles Herald and Express* 2 Apr. 1932.
2   "Lugosi in Person for Orpheum." *San Francisco Examiner* 20 Apr. 1932.
3   "Crittenden Marriott." *New York Times* 30 Mar. 1932. The 1925 edition of *The Isle of Dead Ships* was a conventional reprint, rather than being a movie tie-in edition.
4   An entry on the 1923 version of *The Isle of Lost Ships* appears in Soister, John T., Nicolella, Henry, et al. *American Silent Horror, Science Fiction, and Fantasy Feature Films, Volume 1* (Jefferson, NC: McFarland, 2012).
5   Adriaensens, Vito. "From Hephaistos to the Silver Screen: Living Statues, Antiquity and Cinema." *Cineaction* Spring 2013.
6   Murphy's play *Sh, the Octopus* would be later adapted into the film *Sh! The Octopus* (1937). The exclamation point appears only in the title of the film version.
7   "Murphy's Thriller." *The Standard Union* (Brooklyn, NY) 26 Dec. 1931.
8   Atkinson, J. Brooks. "The Play." *New York Times* 14 May 1929.
9   Hellinger, Mark. "All in a Day." *Syracuse Journal* 23 Jan. 1932.
10   At times, the press referred to Lora Baxter as Helen Baxter, and also occasionally spelled her name Laura.
11   Kayton, Alvin J. "In the Theatres on Broadway." *Brooklyn Daily Star* 16 Jan. 1932.
12   "*Black Tower* Moves." *Brooklyn Eagle* 13 Feb. 1932.
13   Brown, John Mason. "The Play." *New York Evening Post* 12 Jan. 1932.
14   Lockridge, Richard. "Detective Wanted." *New York Sun* 18 Jan. 1932.
15   Garland, Robert. "Cast and Miscast." *New York World-Telegram* 12 Jan. 1932.
16   Vadeboncoeur, E. R. "Intellectual Mania Hits at Theatre." *Syracuse Journal* 17 Jan. 1932.
17   "Fainting Ladies in Audience Add to Drama's Thrills." *New York Daily News* 12 Jan. 1932.
18   Ibid; Mortimer, Lee. "The Ladies Shriek When *Black Tower* Terrors Stalk Out." *New York Daily Mirror* 12 Jan. 1932.
19   Hammond, Percy. "The Theatres." *New York Herald Tribune* 12 Jan. 1932.
20   Washburn, Charles. "Stage Villain for the First Time Is Villainous Offstage." *Brooklyn Eagle* 7 Feb. 1932.
21   Lockridge, Richard. "Routine Hocus-Pocus." *New York Sun* 12 Jan. 1932.
22   "*Black Tower* Spoiled by Economy, Is Claim." *Variety* 9 Feb. 1932.
23   Mehler, Jack. "Stage Whispers." *Billboard* 23 Apr. 1932.
24   Untitled. *Photoplay* June 1932.
25   "Lugosi Will Settle Issue." *Los Angeles Times* 28 Mar. 1932.
26   "Warners Buys *Dr.* [sic] *X*; Kicks on *Society* Sale." *Variety* 19 Jan. 1932.
27   Knapp, Jack Stuart. *The Horror Walks* (Boston: Walter H. Baker, 1931); "Horror Fad Hits Stage." *Variety* 12 Jan. 1932.
28   "Broadway." *Variety* 19 Apr. 1932.
29   "$200 Legit Outlay." *Variety* 5 Apr. 1932.
30   Crow, Jim. *Hollywood Citizen News* 14 Mar. 1932.
31   Babcock, Muriel. "Whispers in the Wings." *Los Angeles Times* 24 Mar. 1932.
32   "How Fares the Stage in Cinema Land?" *New York Times* 3 Apr. 1932.
33   See, for example: Advertisement. *Los Angeles Examiner* 1 Apr. 1932; Advertisement. *Illustrated Daily News* (Los Angeles) 6 Apr. 1932; Advertisement. *Los Angeles Herald and Express* 2 Apr. 1932; Advertisement. *Illustrated Daily News* 6 Apr. 1932; "Lionel Atwill Is Ceremony Master for Fairbanks Jr." *Illustrated Daily News* 6 Apr. 1932; "Nyiregyhazi [sic] Is Unusual Pianist of Rare Ability." *Illustrated Daily News* 15 Apr. 1932.
34   Advertisement. *Los Angeles Times* 1 Apr. 1932.
35   "Auto Park Aids Carthay Patrons." *Illustrated Daily News* 9 Apr. 1932.

36   "Happy Mood Prevails in Stage Realm." *Los Angeles Examiner* 3 Apr. 1932.
37   "Lugosi Likes Murder." *Los Angeles Record* 9 Apr. 1932.
38   Lawrence, Florence. "Bela Lugosi, Betty Ross Clarke, Maxine Castleton, Maud Adams, Doug \ Fairbanks Jr." *Los Angeles Examiner* 4 Apr. 1932.
39   Oliver, W. E. "Horror Is At Circle." *Los Angeles Herald and Express* 4 Apr. 1932.
40   Barnes, Eleanor. "Mystery Thriller at Carthay." *Illustrated Daily News* 4 Apr. 1932.
41   Crow, Jim. "Thrill Drama on Boards at Carthay House." *Hollywood Citizen-News* 4 Apr. 1932.
42   Schallert, Edwin. "Shivery Show Enjoyed." *Los Angeles Times* 5 Apr. 1932.
43   "*Murdered Alive.*" *Variety* 12 Apr. 1932.
44   "Bela Lugosi Thrills Audiences at Carthay Circle." *Hollywood Filmograph* 9 Apr. 1932.
45   "Star Continues in Play Despite Painful Injuries." *Los Angeles Times* 7 Apr. 1932.
46   See, for example: Mehler, Jack. "Stage Whispers." *Billboard* 23 Apr. 1932.
47   Whitaker, Alma. "Show Goes on Despite Broken Ribs." *Los Angeles Times* 10 Apr. 1932.
48   "Grace George, $6,000, Tops L.A.; Maude Adams, Three Days, $5,200." *Variety* 12 Apr. 1932.
49   "$2,600 for Mystery Play at Carthay Circle, L.A." *Variety* 19 Apr. 1932.
50   Mehler, "Stage Whispers."
51   "Hollywood." *Variety* 19 Apr. 1932.
52   Advertisement. *San Francisco Chronicle* 22 Apr. 1932.
53   Warren, George C. "Orpheum Has Bill of Many Thrills." *San Francisco Chronicle* 23 Apr. 1932.
54   Sontheimer, Morton. "Orpheum Has Movie, Drama on Same Bill." *San Francisco News* 23 Apr. 1932.
55   "Frisco's 2 Tabs." *Variety* 26 Apr. 1932.
56   "Frisco Frisky with Big $19,000 on *Scarface*; *Crowd Roars* $13,000." *Variety* 3 May 1932.
57   Advertisement. *Los Angeles Herald and Express* 29 Apr. 1932.
58   Barnes, Eleanor. "Creepy Show at Orpheum." *Illustrated Daily News* 2 May 1932.
59   "*Girl Crazy* Will Begin Run Friday." *Los Angeles Times* 4 May 1932.
60   "*Hotel* at Chinese Looks $35,000; *Crowd Stars* in L.A. at $18,000; *Scarface* $19,000, Maybe 3d Wk." *Variety* 3 May 1932; "*Hotel* $32,000 in Chinese 2d Wk.; RKO's Nice $10,000 with Indie; Rest of Los Angeles in Rut." *Variety* 10 May 1932.
61   The title *Murdered Alive* was reused as well. Samuel French published Wilbur Braun's three-act play *Murdered Alive!* (the title featuring an exclamation mark) in 1934. Despite the fact it was a mystery, the main similarity between the new play and old was the use of the same title.
62   Koszarski, Richard. *Mystery of the Wax Museum* (Madison, WI: University of Wisconsin Press, 1979).
63   Ibid.
64   Adriaensens, p. 43.
65   Here we are referring to *House of Wax* (1953) and *House of Wax* (2005).

Bela Lugosi in a classic publicity
still from *Dracula* (1931).

Chapter 2

Long Live Decay

Bela Lugosi was typecast in the United States long before he ever played the role of Dracula.

From his earliest English-language appearance on the American stage, he became the exotic foreigner, his dark features and thick accent transforming him into the Other. Though the storylines and exact nature of the roles would vary, Lugosi the Foreigner appeared before American audiences in such plays as *The Red Poppy* (1922), *Arabesque* (1925), *Open House* (1925), and *The Devil in the Cheese* (1926). The same was true of silent films like *The Silent Command* (1923), *The Rejected Woman* (1924), and *Daughters Who Pay* (1926).[1]

The dawn of the talkie further positioned Lugosi as the Foreigner, with moviegoers finally able to hear the voice that Broadway knew all too well. He could be vaguely coded as Indian (*The Thirteenth Chair* of 1929), Arab (*Renegades* in 1930), or Italian (*Oh, for a Man* in 1930). Depending on the role, Lugosi was from Far Away, or even Further Away. He was not American. It was nothing to do with citizenship or politics. Rather, it was typecasting. It was a kind of role, even if it manifested in different forms in different films and plays.

Once *Dracula* (1931) transformed him into a movie star, Lugosi became typecast again, with Hollywood situating him into what became six different roles. There were many films and many characters, but only six basic roles, over and over again, for the space of a quarter century. The boundaries between the six could be porous, but that only further tied him to them.

Lugosi the Foreigner arguably appeared in nearly all of his American films, but that category would certainly describe the parts he played in *Women of All Nations* (1931), *Broadminded* (1931), and *International House* (1933). American audiences had little trouble accepting him as Middle Eastern or Russian or almost any other kind of Other. Occasionally Lugosi the Foreigner could be heroic or sympathetic; *The Black Cat* (1934), *The Return of Chandu* (1934), and *The Invisible Ray* (1936) are examples. Or he could be cold and unfeeling,

Lugosi the Foreigner.
From *Women of All Nations* (1931).

as in *Ninotchka* (1939), or even horrifying, as in *Island of Lost Souls* (1932), with his accent being so foreign as to make him spokesman for the "Beast Men" (as the film's pressbook calls them).[2] Or Lugosi could represent both paradigms, as in his portrayal of Bela the Gypsy in *The Wolf Man* (1941).

Lugosi the Red Herring quickly became another of the six roles in question, his association with the horror genre making him automatically suspicious in post-*Dracula* films. Guilty until proven innocent: that was Lugosi in *The Black Camel* (1931), *The Death Kiss* (1933), *Night of Terror* (1933), *The Whispering Shadow* (1933), *The Gorilla* (1939), *Spooks Run Wild* (1941), *Night Monster* (1942), and *Scared to Death* (1947).

But then there were the times when He Did Do It. Lugosi the Criminal, who stole, murdered, and occasionally pillaged. Here was the scofflaw side of Lugosi the Foreigner, with his roles including not only workaday bandits and criminal masterminds, but also Asian villains and Nazi fifth columnists. Murder, mail fraud, and more can be found in: *The Best Man Wins* (1935), *Mysterious Mr. Wong* (1935), *Postal Inspector* (1936), *SOS Coast Guard* (1937), *Black Friday* (1940), *The Saint's Double Trouble* (1940), *You'll Find Out* (1940), *Black Dragons* (1942), *Bowery at Midnight* (1942), *Ghosts on the Loose* (1943), and *Genius at Work* (1946). In short, Lugosi could handle a gun, or even a tommy gun.

Jeanette Loff, who says Portland is always her first choice of home towns, is to play the feminine lead in a dreadful play, "Dracula." It isn't my idea of a role for the lovely and talented Loff lady. She is another Norma Shearer in dramatic ability. And one of these days she'll have a big play that proves it.

From the *Oregonian* (Portland) of September 14, 1930.

The more maniacal side of Lugosi the Foreigner was the Mad Scientist, trying to create new life, keep old life alive, take over another life, or just cause general chaos, domestically or globally. Here are the many doctors of *Murders in the Rue Morgue* (1932), *The Raven* (1935), *The Phantom Creeps* (1939), *The Devil Bat* (1940), *The Corpse Vanishes* (1942), *The Ape Man* (1943), *Return of the Ape Man* (1944), *Voodoo Man* (1944), *Zombies on Broadway* (1945), *Bela Lugosi Meets a Brooklyn Gorilla* (1952), and *Bride of the Monster* (1955).

Much in the same way that Lon Chaney, Jr. regularly portrayed variations of his famous role Lennie in *Of Mice and Men* (1939), Lugosi would at times repeat his characterization of Ygor, the fifth category of the six. Creating the role in *Son of Frankenstein* (1939), he played Ygor again in *The Ghost of Frankenstein* (1942) and – at least in the shooting script, insofar as Ygor's brain was inside the Monster's body – in *Frankenstein Meets the Wolf Man* (1943). Other Lugosi roles recalled Ygor to greater or lesser degrees, particularly those in *The Black Cat* (1941), *The Body Snatcher* (1945), and *The Black Sleep* (1956). Lugosi the Henchman, so to speak.

To be sure, there was overlap between these five categories. Lugosi's dual roles allowed him to be both heroic and villainous in *Murder by Television* (1935). Lugosi was both a red herring and a would-be criminal in *One Body Too Many* (1944). And his presence as the Foreigner was felt even when a given character's name ill-suited him. Filmmakers like Tod Browning and playwrights like Ralph Murphy rewrote characters names to better match his background, but some producers were not as discriminating, meaning that Lugosi the Other was surprisingly named Peters in *The Gorilla*, Dr. Brewster in *The Ape Man*, Dr. Marlowe in *Voodoo Man*, and Professor Dexter in *Return of the Ape Man*.[3]

And while he is certainly a foreign presence in *White Zombie* (1932) and *Glen or Glenda* (1953), it is admittedly difficult to categorize his characters in those two films. In the former, he is foreign, even to the Haitian landscape, but whether he is truly supernatural (as his ability to command others hypnotically even when he is not in the same room with them suggests) or not (he has to rely on a smoke bomb in an effort to escape the heroes) is hard to determine. The same is true in *Glen or Glenda*, as he seems on the one hand to be an omniscient narrator who exists above the storyline and has special access to the audience (speaking as he does, directly into the camera lens), but on the other hand, he seems to keep something of a cheap mad scientist laboratory, just in case of, well, we never really learn why.

With all of their similarities and differences, these categories total only five roles. The sixth, of course, is Lugosi the Vampire. One can certainly quibble about how many times he played vampires onscreen. *Dracula* (1931), *The Return of the Vampire* (1944), and *Abbott and Costello Meet Frankenstein* (1948) come to mind immediately, though these too overlap with the aforementioned kinds of roles, not only being that the vampires are themselves Lugosi the (Supernatural) Foreigner, but because Dracula in the Abbott and Costello film is also something of a would-be mad scientist.

El Capitan

11th and Morrison
ATwater 6424

Last Times Saturday

William Collier Jr.
(in person) in

"Blessed Event"

MAT. SAT.—25c, 35c, 50c, 75c
NIGHTS—25c, 50c, 75c, $1, $1.25

Shock Week Starts SUN.

BELA LUGOSI
Star of Stage and Screen in

"DRACULA"

Published in the *Oregonian* on February 26, 1931.

In a short subject called *Hollywood on Parade* (1933), Lugosi bites Betty Boop (Mae Questel) while wearing his Dracula costume, though strictly speaking he does not portray Dracula; he portrays "Bela Lugosi as Dracula," a wax figure of himself come to life. And then there is Count Mora in *Mark of the Vampire* (1935), the atmospheric Tod Browning film in which the supernatural is explained away at the story's conclusion. Arguments can easily be mounted in both directions as to whether these "vampires" count.

But whether one totals Lugosi's vampire roles in Hollywood as three, four, or – to be generous – five, the fact is that he portrayed the supernatural creature fewer times than he did *any* of the other five roles described herein. Put another way, Lugosi was far more often a mad scientist or workaday crook in Hollywood than he ever was a vampire.

And so here is a moment where numbers might lie, or at least mislead. Even if he had played a vampire only once in Hollywood, meaning in *Dracula* (1931), Lugosi would likely still be remembered more for that role than any other. Power and presence and personality in a single film trumped the mad doctor incarnations and the red herring butlers. After the 1931 film, he became "Bela (Dracula) Lugosi," at least according to studio publicity.

Here was not merely a screen role, but also a persona, one larger than any single film, larger than the characters of all of Lugosi's other films combined. And it was a persona that grew and flourished

Lugosi the Red Herring. From
The Whispering Shadow (1933).

long after the 1931 movie was released. Its voracious appetite was something that at times Lugosi tried to starve, and that at times he tried to feed, even if grudgingly so. After all, even though he rarely appeared as Dracula or vampires in the movies, he regularly did so at live appearances and stage revivals. He also riffed on the character for many radio and television programs.

Folklore and literature generally suggest that vampiric bodies do not decay, but one can chart Lugosi's aging process in Dracula photographs that span the distance of nearly three decades, including those of him at rest in August 1956.

Thus Lugosi reneged on a promise to himself, one that he shared with a fan magazine even prior to the original *Dracula*'s screen release: his pledge to never play the role again after the film's production came to an end. But he did, and the first occasion came in the unexpected location of Portland, Oregon in 1932.

Just three weeks after completing the run of *Murdered Alive* at Los Angeles' Orpheum theatre, Lugosi arrived in Portland on May 26 to prepare for a new stage production of *Dracula–The Vampire Play*.[4]

Between the two plays, Lugosi guest-starred on a special radio program at station KHJ, broadcast over 35 Columbia networks on May 22, and then relayed to 105 other countries. The purpose was to invite Europeans to the summer Olympics in Los Angeles. Speakers included Marlene Dietrich (who invited the Germans), Claudette Colbert (who invited the French), Maureen O'Sullivan (who invited the Irish), Olga Baclanova (who invited the Russians), Laurel and Hardy (who invited the British), and Lugosi, who – not unexpectedly – invited his fellow Hungarians.[5]

BELA LUGOSI

Stage and screen star, who arrived in Portland yesterday for title role in "Dracula" next week at the El Capitan theater.

From the *Oregonian* of May 27, 1932.

But when Lugosi spoke to Americans, at least through his screen persona, he did not discuss sports. Shortly before his appearance in Portland, one newspaper journalist described how moviegoers beheld their mysterious Dracula of stage and screen:

Imaginative minds will visualize him as sleeping at night in a purple velvet coffin, drinking his after dinner coffee while blue lights burn and a string orchestra [plays] Sibelius' *Valse trieste* or Grieg's *Hall of the Mountain Kings*.

[By contrast,] Lugosi lives on a hilltop with his dogs, his books, and his music. He reads histories, modern essays on economics and sociology and biographies. He plays the piano and even sings a little, his native folk songs preferably. He indulges in no showy sports, but takes long walks on the hills back of his Hollywoodland home.

Lugosi the Criminal. From
SOS Coast Guard (1937).

422-26

Lugosi the Mad Scientist.
From *Murders in the Rue
Morgue* (1932).

… Right now Lugosi has one great ambition. He wants to accumulate a moderate fortune to give him an income of $50 a week.

'On $50 a week a man can be happy,' says the actor, who is also a philosopher. 'On $500 a week he can be miserable. With the smaller sum, he lives the simple life. He keeps close to nature.'[6]

This journalist reported what so many others would in the years that followed: Lugosi the Man was not at all similar to Lugosi the Vampire, or – for that matter – Lugosi the Red Herring, the Criminal, or the Mad Scientist.

And yet he *was* Lugosi the Vampire in Portland, at least for those fans who bought tickets during the height of the Great Depression to see him in person.

The City of Roses

Dracula and Portland shared a history together prior to the 1932 stage production, though it was marked more by near misses than anything else. One journalist claimed *Dracula–The Vampire Play* would appear on the Portland stage in 1928, but such was not to be. Then, in September 1930, actress Jeanette Loff – who called Portland her "first choice of home towns," even though she was actually born in Cronno, Idaho – was announced as the "feminine lead" in Universal's *Dracula* (1931).[7] But Loff wrangled her way out of her studio contract, and so the role in question ended up going to Helen Chandler.

By contrast, Universal's *Dracula* did make a major splash in the City of Roses in 1931. It made its local premiere during the last weekend of February at the RKO Orpheum alongside a vaudeville bill that

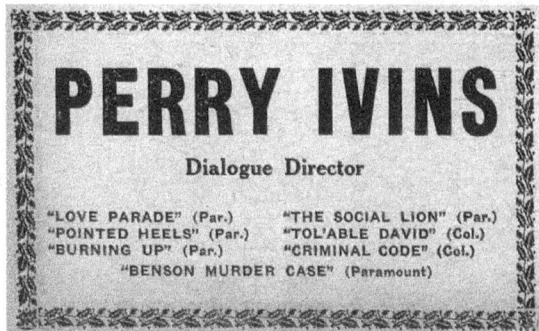

PERRY IVINS

Dialogue Director

"LOVE PARADE" (Par.) "THE SOCIAL LION" (Par.)
"POINTED HEELS" (Par.) "TOL'ABLE DAVID" (Col.)
"BURNING UP" (Par.) "CRIMINAL CODE" (Col.)
"BENSON MURDER CASE" (Paramount)

From *Variety* of December 31, 1930.

included a comic singer, five female jugglers, and a harpist.[8] The local censor board required one cut from the film, though the specifics of the offending footage are unknown. At any rate, it hardly seems to have hampered audience response.

As *The Oregonian* wrote, "as soon as the last curtain falls [on the vaudeville show], you get to thinking again about that darned *Dracula*."[9] The *Oregon Daily Journal* called the film a "big picture," praising both its visual and aural effects.[10] Along with *Reaching for the Moon* (1931), *Dracula* was one of the two "big winners" in the city that week, the vampire grossing around "$15,000," a marked increase over the previous week's $11,500 with *Millie* (1931).[11]

And then, finally, there was *Dracula* onstage in 1932. At long last, the play arrived in Portland, featuring not Bela Lugosi the Broadway actor, but Bela Lugosi, the Hollywood star. Surviving primary sources do not detail the names of the financial backers, but it is clear that

Perry Ivins directed the show; he also assumed the role of Renfield. Born in Trenton, New Jersey in 1894, Ivins had worked as a journalist in the 1920s, then as an actor (including on Broadway), and finally as a stage director.

In 1927, only months before *Dracula* opened on Broadway, Ivins authored his ironically titled poem *Long Live Decay!* Its sentiment hardly predicted his eventual association with the vampire play:

"Dracula" Will Be Staged at El Capitan This Week.

Bela Lugosi Plays Star Role in Famous "Shocker" Drama.

"DRACULA," the horror play that Portland playgoers have been hoping to see for the last three seasons, has at last come to the playhouse at Eleventh and Morrison, where Bela Lugosi, star of both the stage and screen versions of the play, will make his first appearance on a Portland stage in the role that made him famous, that of Count Dracula.

"Dracula" has been described by critics as a play for people that like their coffee strong. There is no mistake about this thriller being of the type that will shock the staunchest of playgoers who like thrilling plays. It deals with the supernatural and there is no awkward explanation at its conclu-

Bela Lugosi.

From the *Oregonian* of May 29, 1933.

I love these dear decadent days,
For I'm securely pure.
Go be abnormal as you please,
I'll stick to the moralities.
And will they pay me? Sure!

We witness that the newer plays
Inevitably deal
With too-voracious mother-love
Or subtle variations of
The so-called sex appeal.

But I'll depict instead of these
In any play of mine
A girl who's primitively chaste,
A mother safe to be embraced,
And a hero masculine.

Then, when the man has won the maid,
And–after that–they've kissed,
There shall be dancing in the street
And grateful cheers from the effete:
'At last, a novel twist!'[12]

No, in early 1927, horror did not seem to be that which Ivins sought, but his brush with the genre occurred long before *Dracula* in Portland. Only months after publishing *Long Live Decay!*, he acted in a stage version of Sax Rohmer's *Fu Manchu* in Cincinnati.[13]

In the same way that the talkies wrecked many Hollywood careers, they propelled others. Ivins became a film actor in 1929, and then divided his time between the cinema and the theatre. He also notably worked as a dialogue director, including on such films as *The Benson Murder Case* (1930) and *The Criminal Code* (1931). And in May 1932, he directed Lugosi the Vampire at Portland's El Capitan Theatre.

Publicity for *Dracula* played up the horror and film star angle, stating "SHOCK WEEK Starts Matinee Today" and "The Original Dracula of Stage and Screen Fame in Person as

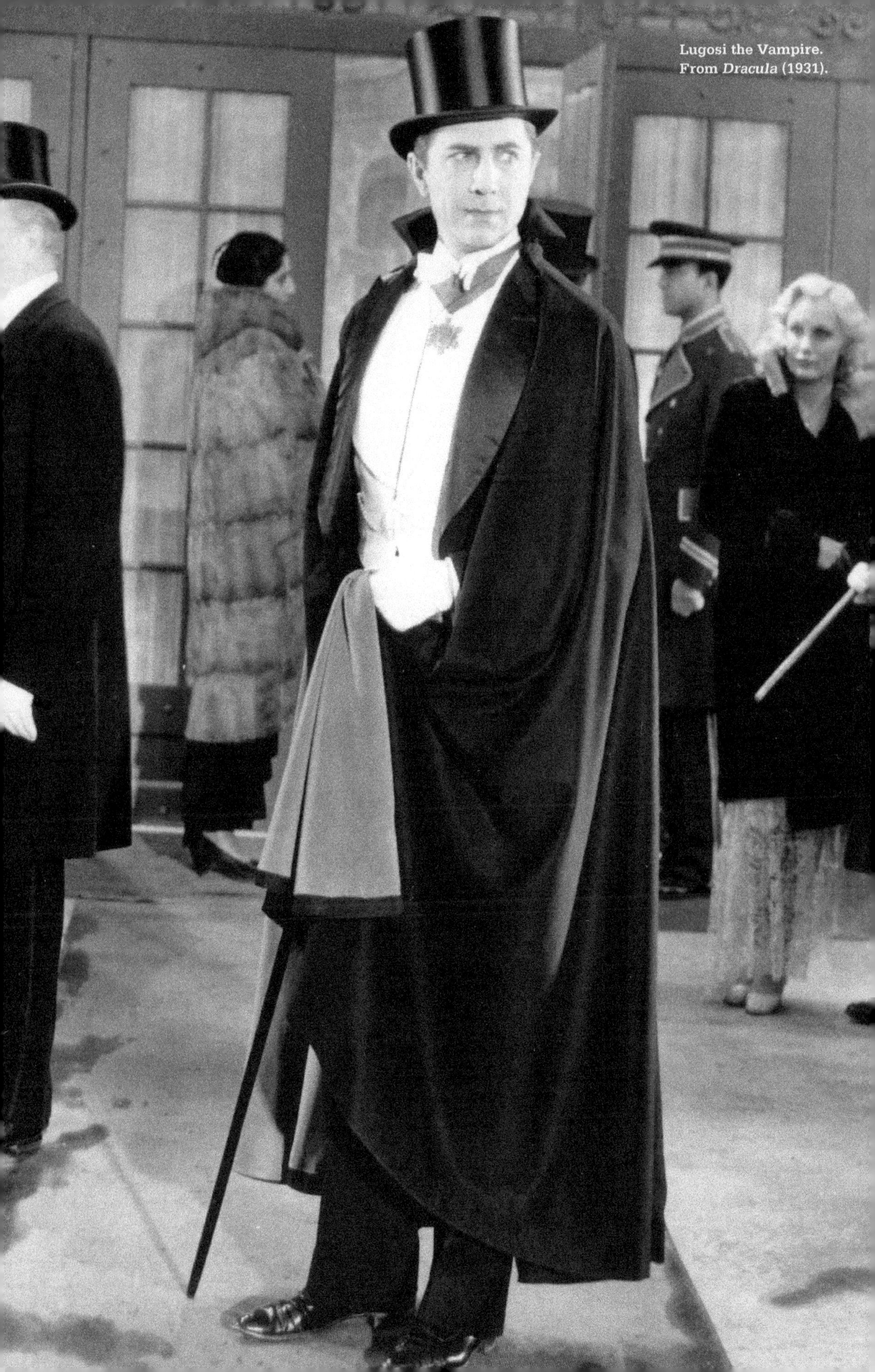

Lugosi the Vampire.
From *Dracula* (1931).

Lugosi engaging in one of the hobbies
he described to the press in 1932.

Guest with the El Capitan Players."[14] Heralding Lugosi's first stage appearance in the city, one journalist described *Dracula* as "a play for people that like their coffee strong. There is no mistake about this thriller being of a type that will shock the staunchest of playgoers...."[15]

Being interviewed in Portland about having won the title role in Universal's film version of *Dracula*, Lugosi recalled:

'I was never more pleasantly surprised in my life,' Mr. Lugosi exclaimed yesterday after he had made an exit from an imaginary stage in the lounge of El Capitan theatre and the rehearsal went on for a few minutes without him. 'Here is Perry Ivins as director, the same Perry who was dialogue director for the film, *Murders in the Rue Morgue*, in which I was the eccentric villain. Here is Leon Waycoff [as Harker], who played the lead in that picture. Here are Henry Hall [as Dr. Seward] and Norman [Feusier, as Van Helsing] and Morry Foster [as Butterworth], who all have played in *Dracula* on the stage. It is a fine company, and we are going to give a great performance - you'll see.'

Either Lugosi did not mention or the journalist did not record the fact that British actress Marion Clayton portrayed Lucy in Portland; she had earlier played Anna Baumer in *All Quiet on the Western Front* (1930) and would later appear in *Mutiny on the Bounty* (1935). Ruth Lee was cast as Miss Wells, and Matt Lermer was in charge of the "scenic effects."[16]

Published in the *News-Telegram* (Portland, OR) on May 29, 1932.

The same journalist then patiently waited on Lugosi, who was called back to the El Capitan stage in the middle of their interview:

Mr. Lugosi's presence was needed again for the rehearsal. A bit of business was not to his liking, so he and another player went over it and over again for ten minutes until each step, each gesture, each turn of the body, was placed and timed to perfection. The incident may be symbolic of the kind of precision the audience will see when *Dracula* takes the stage next week. Presently he was free again...

'It is not generally realized in the rest of the world,' he said, 'that Hungary plays more Shakespeare than any other country, including England. For 30 years the national theatre in Budapest has had a minimum of one Shakespearean play a week, and sometimes two or three. The national theatre is operated by the government to give the people good literature in the form of drama and it does not depend upon the box office.'

Mr. Lugosi played in motion pictures in Europe, but he dismisses that portion of his career with a gesture. 'It was just experimental,' he explained....[17]

Waxing nostalgic, Lugosi not only remembered his work on the Hungarian stage, as he would do with much regularity in America, but he also curiously dismissed the value of his Hungarian and German films.

Another attendant at the rehearsals also spoke about Lugosi's penchant for perfectionism and his directorial advice:

… preliminary to the widely advertised production, [Lugosi] was regally entertaining. As a matter of course, he knew his part to perfection. It was not really necessary for him to rehearse, but he wanted every member of the cast letter perfect and would go through all the motions, even of the other performers; he'd lead them through the scenes, suggest that this player face the footlights at 'just this angle,' and that that actor 'turn just so, please.' Then he'd propose … 'a bite to eat.'[18]

Audience Acclaims Hungarian

By HARRY STEINFELD

LONG, tall, gaunt Bela Lugosi, with eye of steel and those dreadfully tapered fingers, brought Count Dracula back to the stage last night at the El Capitan, and it'll be a long time before those who were there forget it.

The play itself is weird, almost ghastly, but when in the lead role it has Lugosi, it becomes almost ghostly.

The man should know the role.

From the *News-Telegram* (Portland, OR) of May 30, 1932.

Even though Lugosi and the cast and crew seem to have worked well together, the same may not have been true of his interactions with the backers.

Unsubstantiated rumors persisted for years afterwards that Lugosi forced a welching producer to pay the Portland actors before opening night or he would himself inform the audience that there would be no show.[19] While unverifiable, the tale seems plausible in the wake of the percentage deals given to the cast of *Murdered Alive*, deals that likely brought them little or no cash.

What is certain is that during his stay in Portland, Lugosi guest-starred on a radio show called *The Breakfast Club*; making a "saturnine speech;" he "gesticulated like one cheating you out of a pound of flesh, but only said it was early for him to be up."[20] If he groused, it was perhaps because opening night had already come and gone. Lugosi the Vampire preferred to work after dark.

Almost Ghostly

The Portland premiere occurred on Sunday, May 29, 1932.[21] The El Capitan Theatre offered Wednesday and Saturday matinees for *Dracula*, with tickets priced at 25, 35, 50 and 75 cents. Seats at the evening shows were scaled from 35¢ to $1.25.[22]

In at least two of those seats sat critics from the local newspapers. *The Oregonian* later enthused:

Publicity portrait of Lugosi, photographed by Freulich in 1932.

Dracula... has had many distinguished performances on stage and screen, but it is doubtful that it ever has been presented better than at El Capitan theatre in Portland in the week's engagement that started yesterday. Bela Lugosi... heads the cast as guest star with his own characterization of the vampire. His is one of the most finished performances ever given here by any actor in any role. Every tone of his voice, every gesture and every attitude is invested with a depth of meaning, and it is chiefly to his credit that such an impossible character seems for two hours very real.

Excellent work in support is contributed by every one of the seven other members of the cast.

The review added that much of the play's success was due to an "eerie atmosphere ... created by ingenious lighting, or lack of lighting, and to off-stage effects."[23]

The Portland *News-Telegram* was equally impressed, admitting that any version of the play would be "weird" and "almost ghastly," but went on to say:

...when in the lead role it has Lugosi, it becomes almost ghostly. The man should know

Ballyhoo for Lugosi's film *White Zombie* (1932), which opened some two months after the Portland version of *Dracula–The Vampire Play*. *(Courtesy of D'Arcy More)*

the role. He created it. The stage and screen portrayals brought him fame, and justly. He's a magnificent actor, and in *Dracula* at his best.

Lugosi is admirably supported by an excellent cast. ... [Perry] Ivins, who is the company's director, is a marvelous performer – so good, in fact, that this reviewer, who happens to know him well, couldn't for the life of him recognize him on the stage. There wasn't a feature about him, the slightest mannerism, familiar.

The *News-Telegram* lobbied readers to buy tickets, because, after all, "A Bela Lugosi isn't in Portland every day."[24] And he was not there for long, either. The show closed as planned on June 4, 1932. By that time, Lugosi and company had given nine performances.

Regrettably, no audience reactions seem to have been recorded. One wonders if Lugosi's Hollywood star power added to his stage presence, and if viewing the film only months earlier might have caused Portland theatregoers to be even more impressed by seeing him in the flesh.

Perhaps a few were intrigued or confused by the fact that the play and film are quite different, more than even most modern historians seem to understand, to the degree that, for example, Mina is the lead female character in the film, but she is already dead by the time the play's narrative begins.

Regardless, audiences at those nine performances witnessed something special. Not only did they mark Lugosi's initial return to the role Dracula after Universal's film version, but they also became his only appearance in the full, three-act play until 1943, and even then – as Chapter 7 will detail – the length of the 1943 version seems have to been trimmed, at least to a minor degree.

Conclusion

Lugosi did not forget the City of Roses. Perhaps he recalled it in 1933, when his stage costar Norman Feusier made a brief appearance in his serial *The Whispering Shadow*. Or when Perry Ivins portrayed Fritz in *Son of Frankenstein* in 1939. Or, for that matter, on the four different occasions between 1934 and 1944 that he costarred in films and serials with Henry Hall.[25] Perhaps.

At any rate, he definitely recalled his brief tenure in Portland in 1936, telling a reporter:

I had a wonderful time there, going for rides in motorboats and being fed fresh salmon. ... I brought back a box of smoked salmon with me, and forgot it on the train. I went back to the Pullman to get him, but each one of the crew had part of my fishes and was starting home for a nice meal. I had to go to the porter and the conductor and brakeman and get a piece of my salmon from each man, who didn't want to give him up. But I get mad, and so I get my fish.[26]

Lugosi Broke, with Furniture Main Asset

OCT 2 8-1933

ngeles, Oct. 24.

Bankruptcy petition of Bela Lugosi, filed in U. S. District court here, lists $2,965 in liabilities and $600 worth of possible assets. Largest debt was the $1,000 clothing bill owed Alexander and Oviatt.

Lugosi listed four suits of clothes valued at $100 and a $500 equity in furniture as his assets.

Lugosi not only got his fish, but he also got his paycheck for one week in *Dracula*. How much it tallied is unknown, but it was likely a good deal more than the $50 per week that he once claimed could please him.

Happily or not, Lugosi had broken his promise about never playing the vampire again, relenting for the El Capitan. Was it because he changed his mind and embraced the role in 1932? Was it because he so desired to visit Portland? Or, was it to redeem himself on the stage after the failure of *Murdered Alive*? "Perhaps" must again be the word of choice.

In all likelihood, *Dracula*'s overwhelming lure for Lugosi in 1932 was financial. His profit sharing in *Murdered Alive* probably netted him little cash, and he was not a man who managed the money he did make very well. Even if he personally could have been happy with $50 per week, his creditors would have felt otherwise.

And regrettably for all of them, even Dracula could not save Lugosi from his debts in 1932. By Halloween of that year, the press reported that he was broke, his main asset being furniture.[27] Filing bankruptcy meant his debts became public information. Dating back

BANKRUPT'S PETITION FOR DISCHARGE AND ORDER THEREON

IN THE DISTRICT COURT OF THE UNITED STATES

For the Southern District of California—Central Division

In the Matter of

.... BELA LUGOSI ....

Bankrupt.

No. 19639-H

IN BANKRUPTCY

To the Honorable Judge of the District Court of the United States,
For the Southern District of California—Central Division

.... Bela Lugosi .... of .... Los Angeles

(Name of Bankrupt)   (City)

in the County of Los Angeles and State of California in said District, respectfully represents:

That on the .... 17th .... day of .... October, 1932 .... last past .... was duly adjudged bankrupt under the Acts of Congress relating to bankruptcy; that .... he .... has .... duly surrendered all .... his property and rights of property, and has fully complied with all the requirements of said Acts and of the orders of the Court touching said bankruptcy.

WHEREFORE .... he PRAYS that .... he .... may be decreed by the Court to have a full discharge from all debts provable against .... his estate under said Bankruptcy Act, except such debts as are excepted by law from such discharge.

Dated this .... 9th .... day of .... November .... A.D., 1933

Bela Lugosi

Bankrupt

ORDER OF NOTICE THEREON

as far as 1926, they included personal loans, room rent, transportation, dentistry, clothes, groceries, tobacco, as well as unspecified "goods, wares, and merchandise."[28] Some of them were incurred during the weeks spent working on *Murdered Alive* and on the Portland *Dracula*, among them advertisements Lugosi published for himself.

Lugosi crossed the Rubicon in Portland, reuniting with Dracula for the very first time, despite his earlier vow, and from there, Dracula hovered ever near him until his death, far more so than any red-herring butler or wild-eyed mad scientist. Real vampires, were they to exist, do not decompose. But the fortunes of Lugosi and Dracula decayed during 1932 and over so many of the long years that followed until his death, when the actor was buried in one of his vampire capes.

(Endnotes)

1   As an addendum to this discussion, it is worth noting that a number of producers and critics in Germany also perceived Lugosi's Otherness, as is evident in some of the roles he played and reviews of the same.

2   The pressbook for *Island of Lost Souls* alternates between the terms "Beast Men" and "Beast-Men."

3   Here we refer to *The Thirteenth Chair* (1929). In the Broadway play, the character's name was Inspector Donahue; for the film, the same role became Inspector Delzante, presumably to better suit Lugosi. With regard to the mention of Ralph Murphy, Chapter 1 of this book notes that the role of Ludlow in *The Black Tower* was changed to Orloff in *Murdered Alive*.

4   "Bela Lugosi Here to Play Dracula Role." *The Oregonian* (Portland, OR) 27 May 1932.
5   Palmer, Zuma. "Radio." *Hollywood Citizen-News* 21 May 1932; "Radio, Once Taboo, Now Vaudeville's Stand-by." *Los Angeles Times* 22 May 1932.
6   Lawrence, Florence. "Another Shiver Drama by Bela Lugosi." *Los Angeles Examiner* 27 Mar. 1932.
7   "Play Contest Stringed." *The Sunday Oregonian* (Portland, OR) 14 Sept. 1930.
8   Advertisement. *The Oregonian* 26 Feb. 1931.
9   Truebridge, John K. "Picture at RKO Orpheum Sets Record as Thriller." *The Oregonian* 27 Feb. 1931.
10   "*Dracula* Found Fascinating Thriller." *The Oregon Daily Journal* (Portland, OR) 27 Feb. 1931.
11   "P'tland Doing Well, 3 Are Beating $12,000." *Variety* 4 Mar. 1931: 10. [In the 18 Mar. 1931 issue of *Variety*, a survey of February grosses claimed *Dracula* grossed only $13,000 during its week at the Orpheum.]
12   Ivins, Perry. "Long Live Decay!" *Life* 24 Mar. 1927.
13   "Cincinnati Premiere." *Billboard* 3 Sept. 1927.
14   "*Dracula* Will Be Staged at the El Capitan This Week." *The Oregonian* (Portland, OR) 29 May 1932.
15   Ibid.
16   "Bela Lugosi Here to Play Dracula Role." *The Oregonian* 27 May 1932.
17   Ibid.
18   "Lugosi's Playing On Local Stage Recalled by Film." *The Oregonian* 20 Sept. 1938.
19   A book dealer conveyed this rumor to film collector Lynn Naron.
20   Moyes, William. "Behind The Mike." *The Oregonian* 1 June 1932.
21   Steinfeld, Harry. "Cine Matters." *The News-Telegram* (Portland, OR) 28 May 1932.
22   Advertisement. *The Oregonian* 31 May 1932.
23   "Lugosi Gives Weird Drama Tense Touch." *The Oregonian* 30 May 1932.
24   Steinfeld, Harry. "Audience Acclaims Hungarian." *The News-Telegram* 30 May 1932.
25   Hall appeared four times in films and serials that starred Lugosi: *The Return of Chandu* (1934), *Shadow of Chinatown* (1936), *The Ape Man* (1943), and *Voodoo Man* (1944).
26   Hazen, David W. "Bela Lugosi Famous in Hungary As Actor Before Entering Movies." *The Oregonian* 17 Feb. 1936.
27   "Lugosi Broke, with Furniture Main Asset." *Variety* 28 Oct. 1932.
28   This data, and the quotation regarding "goods, wares, and merchandise," stem from surviving court paperwork approving Lugosi's bankruptcy, filed in the Southern District Court of California, Central Division in 1932, and assigned number 19639-H.

A publicity portrait of Bela Lugosi for *Murder at the Vanities* (1933).

Chapter 3

The Phantom of Broadway

"Look! You want to see? See! Feast your eyes, glut your soul on my cursed ugliness! Look at Erik's face! Now you know the face of the voice! You were not content to hear me, eh? You wanted to know what I looked like? Oh, you women are so inquisitive! Well, are you satisfied? I'm a good-looking fellow, eh?"

Gaston Leroux wrote that dialogue for the title character of his 1910 French novel *The Phantom of the Opera*, the tale of a disfigured impresario who inspires fear thanks to his ghostly backstage presence.[1] Describing himself as good-looking was, of course, sarcasm that follows the famous moment when he is unmasked. Similar dialogue appears in Universal's 1925 film adaptation, which starred Lon Chaney in the title role. Subsequent actors like Claude Rains, Herbert Lom, Maximilian Schell, and Charles Dance portrayed the character in films and on television, but it was not until 1988 that the story became a Broadway play.

At least that is one version of history. Another view would be that Bela Lugosi played the Phantom of the Opera – or, more accurately, a loose variation of him – on the New York stage in 1933, over five decades before the Andrew Lloyd Webber musical took the theatre world by storm.

For Lugosi, 1933 marked a period of transition. In January, he married Lillian Arch. He was 50; she was 21. The two eloped to Las Vegas after sharing "moments stolen at dances and parties" at the Magyar Athletic Club.[2] Lugosi had been married thrice before, but the unions were brief. The first lasted less than two years, the second less than one month, and the third less than a week. By contrast, Lugosi and Lillian would spend some two decades together.

Lugosi's career was also transforming in 1933, though not for the better. Despite his financial troubles in 1932, he was still a major star that year, playing, for example, the lead role in Universal's (relatively) big-budget horror movie *Murders in the Rue Morgue*. By the end of 1932, he was but a featured player under heavy makeup in *Island of Lost Souls* (1932),

Lon Chaney as *The*
Phantom of the Opera
(1925). *(Courtesy of Bill Chase)*

Lugosi in test makeup for *Island of Lost Souls* (1932). *(Courtesy of Richard Sheffield)*

which starred not Lugosi, but Charles Laughton, Richard Arlen, and Leila Hyams. In 1933, he received star billing in low-budget independent films, but played only supporting roles at the major studios.

Of course the type of roles he played did not change. More than anything else, it was the year of the red herring. Lugosi fell under suspicion of murder in *The Death Kiss* (1933) and *Night of Terror* (1933), but was innocent in both, despite his mysterious presence and – in the case of the latter movie – an equally mysterious turban, not unlike the one he wore as the villainous Roxor in *Chandu the Magician* (1932).

His two other feature films found him playing Lugosi the Foreigner, one being his small role in *The Devil's in Love* (1933) at Fox, and the other being a featured, but still supporting role as a Russian in Paramount's comedy *International House* (1933), which sported an impressive cast that included everyone from George Burns and Gracie Allen to Cab Calloway and Rudy Vallee. But the film's lead players were W. C. Fields and Peggy Hopkins Joyce. Of

Earl Carroll and some of his *Vanities* chorus girls in 1928.

Lugosi, Fields would later quip:

> 'Funny thing about me in full dress,' he remarked. 'Everybody thinks I look like Dracula when I get into one – I mean like Bela Lugosi when he's Dracula. One time when I was playing in Philadelphia, Lugosi was playing there and I went backstage to see if I really did look like him. I talked Hungarian to him and he was real friendly. He looked like me all right, only older, so I figure I must look like him when he was playing Dracula....'[3]

Fields remains an iconic figure, of course, but Peggy Hopkins Joyce – though famous in her day and sometimes considered one of the most notable American women of the first half of the twentieth century – is now largely forgotten.

A sometimes-dancer, sometimes-model, and sometimes-actress, Joyce was best known for her scandalous affairs, engagements, a half dozen marriages, and five divorces, most of them with wealthy men who added to her famous wealth and equally famous collection of diamonds and furs. Anita Loos immortalized Joyce's exploits by patterning the Lorelei Lee character in *Gentleman Prefer Blondes* after her. For that matter, Lugosi's role in *International House* as Joyce's divorced Russian husband was based in part on Joyce's second marital

Lugosi and Peggy Hopkins Joyce in the 1933 film *International House*.

partner, the Swedish Count Gosta Morner.

Among Joyce's many paramours in the 1920s was famed Broadway producer Earl Carroll, the "body merchant" who attempted to compete with Florenz Ziegfeld's annual *Follies*. Carroll's *Vanities* (which started in 1923) proved successful in part due to their opulence, but also because the "troubadour of the nude" (as he was also called) glorified the American girl even more than Ziegfeld, at least if her degree of undress was used as the metric. "Through these portals pass the most beautiful girls in the world," Carroll would say of the *Vanities*.

Born in 1893, Earl Carroll was an ambitious, risk-taking businessman who pursued Peggy Hopkins Joyce sexually with the same tenacity as he would W. C. Fields professionally. Both appeared in his *Vanities* during the Roaring Twenties, a period in which Carroll's personal life became as infamous as any nudity he put on stage.[4] After a 1926 party featuring a bathtub brimming with illegal booze and a nude female model made the press, Carroll was sentenced to six months in the Atlanta penitentiary.[5]

Jail hardly ended Carroll's career; in fact, some even believed his scandals provided free publicity for the *Vanities*, which returned to the stage in 1928, 1930, 1931, and 1932 (with 1929 not being a break, but rather the introduction of his similar revue, *Earl Carroll's Sketch*

Book). What Carroll wanted, he usually got. And by 1933, that included Bela Lugosi. Despite Lugosi's Hollywood standing being somewhat diminished, he remained a big name, and certainly one of the biggest when it came to horror.

And so, in 1933, Lugosi not only met W. C. Fields and Peggy Hopkins Joyce, but also Earl Carroll. And for Carroll, Lugosi would become an unofficial Erik the Phantom, a Phantom not of the Opera, but of Broadway, of the *Vanities*.

The Vanities Murder

As early as January of 1933, Earl Carroll was already in the planning stages for his eleventh edition of the *Vanities*. The *New York Evening Post* reported:

> Earl Carroll, who has been strangely quiet since the closing of the recent *Vanities*, is thinking of producing a mystery play, according to his representative. The locale is backstage during a *Vanities* performance and a large revue cast would be required as well as the regular actors. It may be called *The Murder at the Vanities* he adds. And may we add that *The Vanities Murder* might be less unwieldy?[6]

About a week later, Rufus King was hard at work developing the book for *Murder at the Vanities*, with Carroll humorously "threatening to produce it."[7] At the time, King was well known for such mystery novels as *Murder by the Clock* (1929), which had become a Paramount horror movie in 1931.

Murder at the Vanities was not Carroll's first brush with horror. His 1932 edition of *Vanities* included a comedy sketch called *The Cabinet of Doctor X*; it also featured Harriet Hoctor's dance *The Raven*, a precursor to the one performed in the 1935 Lugosi film of the same name. Reviewing her act, *Variety* claimed it should have been titled *The Bat*, *The Vampire*, or even *Dracula*, given the dark wings on Hoctor's costume and – at least for its pre-*Vanities* incarnation – a stage full of other vampires clad in black.[8]

The 1932 edition of the *Vanities* proved to be a financial disaster for Earl Carroll, which meant funding for the Rufus King book did not come easily. At times, trade publications reported that Paramount Pictures financed *Murder at the Vanities* so as to be able to make a film version of it after its Broadway run. And to be sure, Carroll and King did have their eyes on Hollywood from the very start.

The final agreement between Paramount and

Harriet Hoctor in her "Raven Dance" costume for Carroll's 1932 edition of the *Vanities*.

Artwork of James Rennie used to publicize _Murder at the Vanities_.

Carroll was more convoluted than some press accounts described. The studio's initial involvement – which seems to have been for $100,000 – guaranteed them the first chance to bid on the picture rights, the price dictated by how long the show lasted on Broadway. The agreement also required Carroll to supervise the film personally.[9] Here is likely why Carroll sought Hollywood stars rather than Broadway actors; he was after an "all picture cast."[10]

And from the very start, Carroll wanted Lugosi to play the villain, or at least a villainous red herring. He signed Lugosi in April 1933, making it the first key role to be filled.[11] Soon thereafter, Carroll initiated another of his famous searches for chorus girls, holding auditions at the Forty-Fourth Street Theatre.[12] They had to be, at least according to his eyes, the "most beautiful girls in the world."

In May, in an apparent effort to keep generating free publicity, Carroll leaked a bit more of King's plot to the press:

[It] will be about a _Vanities_ chorus girl who is put 'on the spot' by gangsters... they murder her during a performance of the _Vanities_ – thus enabling Carroll to combine the best features of a _Vanities_ show with an exciting murder mystery in which the entire audience participates....[13]

Such a story combined the musical, gangster, and mystery genres, with – of course – the requisite "nudism" for which Carroll was by equal turns famous and infamous.

But the plot of _Murder at the Vanities_ went through various incarnations, presumably due to the narrative challenge of successfully fusing scary murders with what was in essence a "girlie show." For example, one journalist witnessed rehearsals that were greatly at odds with the final storyline:

I sat up until 2 a.m ... watching Earl Carroll rehearse _Vanities_. Carroll labored on one scene particularly. It revealed the murder method. Bela Lugosi tossed red acid onto his victim during a number under red spotlights.

But when I dropped in at the New Amsterdam again the other night I found that Lugosi committed no murders and that the red acid and the red spotlights were no longer in the show. The whole thing had been greatly altered....[14]

The alterations also meant that – despite Carroll's earlier suggestion – the final book did not feature the audience actively "participating" in the show.

In fact, *Murder at the Vanities* continued to evolve even after its premiere. In its final form, the show unfolded as a backstage murder mystery punctuated with typical *Vanities*-style acts, including comedians Mackie and La Vallee in a sketch called *The Drunks*. That was in addition to a number of new songs and of course the expected display of female flesh. During Act I, for example, four rows of blondes performed a fan dance that supposedly broke "all the records for Broadway nudism."[15]

As for the mystery, the plot opened with a murdered chorus girl discovered on some piping suspended above the stage. Hence the arrival of handsome, dinner jacket-wearing Inspector Ellery, who orders the theatre doors to be locked so that he can conduct his investigation. Suspicion immediately falls on the mysterious Siebenkase (Lugosi), who sneaks around in a green spotlight. His face is horribly scarred from acid hurled on him when he was a child.

Some plot summaries would later suggest that the first murder turns out not to be a murder, but just the result of an accidental broken neck. But a real murder closes Act I when the Blue Blade (as the anonymous villain is known) stabs one of the girls with twelve-inch shears jammed through a hole in the floor. Here again the plot thickened, as one surviving synopsis notes the murderer kills the wrong person. At least two or more murders – and/or near-murders, depending on the plot summary one reads – take place before an innocent girl is cleared of suspicion and the real culprit is caught: a wardrobe mistress bumping off starlets so as to clear the way for her own daughter's ascent to stardom.

Lugosi the Red Herring had more reasons to bring suspicion down upon himself than his hideous appearance. One article claimed that Siebenkase was a "German character actor"; another said he skulked "around the stage in a Lexington Avenue Swami's costume. He has a dagger that he uses every once in a while in a black-out."[16] An old stage trick, the "black-out" meant turning off all the lights at a particularly scary moment, with the villain sometimes even making his way from the stage and into the audience. Moreover, though plot synopses make it difficult to know why, another account claimed that there was also a "dummy" of Lugosi's Siebenkase on the stage at one point as well.[17] Whatever the reason, the key to his character was – in a

A portrait of Jean Adair photographed not long after she appeared in *Murder at the Vanities*.

Two publicity shots of Lugosi for *Murder at the Vanities* that apparently tried to conceal exactly how he would appear onstage in the play. *(Courtesy of Randy Nesseler)*

narrative echo that did not go unheard in 1933 – a re-cooked version of Erik the Phantom, served with a side dish of red herring.

While casting Lugosi and finding the chorus girls came first, Carroll searched at length for a handsome actor to play Inspector Ellery. In late July, having apparently given up on persuading a Hollywood star, he signed James Rennie. Rennie had been a Broadway regular since 1919, serving as leading man to such actresses as Katharine Cornell and Ruth Chatterton.[18] Jean Adair – who would later play opposite Boris Karloff on Broadway in *Arsenic and Old Lace* (1941), as well as opposite Lugosi in a tour of the same play in 1944 – took on the role of the wardrobe mistress. Billy House – who would later appear in Val Lewton's *Bedlam* (1946) – assumed the part of a comical assistant stage manager.[19] And, in what seems to have been the final key role to be cast, there was also Russian actress Olga Baclanova, who had recently appeared in Tod Browning's *Freaks* (1932).[20]

To join the others in time for rehearsals, Lugosi and wife Lillian left California during the last week of July 1933, briefly visiting Provo, Utah on July 26, and then arriving in New York City around August 1.[21] On the way, they also stopped in Pennsylvania to visit Comerford Theatre executive Harry Spiegel. According to the press, the two spent "several hours" together discussing the film industry.[22]

Rehearsals began in early August.[23] Actress Pauline Moore, who was cast as the young ingénue, later told film historian Gregory William Mank, "Earl Carroll was right in there at rehearsals, and all the way through – he had his finger in everything. He really liked to talk, to get to know the different people in the company."[24]

From the *Philadelphia Inquirer* of August 20, 1933.

Carroll also tried to get to know Hollywood. Before the show opened, the press continued to speak about the forthcoming film adaptation:

> Bela Lugosi, selected for an outstanding role in the production, is already in New York, and various other cast members are being assembled. Carroll was very eager to get picture people for the more important parts, but was unable to secure just the ones he wanted. The film version will, of course, be held in abeyance until after the stage show has been produced, but it is practically assured that Lugosi will do the same role on the screen as he is playing on the stage....[25]

The prevalence of these stories leads one to think that, while the Broadway show was important, it was secondary to the proposed film.

Originally the press claimed there would be a "try-out tour" for *Murder at the Vanities*.[26] In the end, the tryout was limited to just one city. But that was in and of itself something of a victory for Carroll, who was embroiled in a two-front war. For one, producer Jed Harris made a claim against *Murder at the Vanities*, arguing its plot was essentially the same as *Little Baby Blue*, an unproduced Jack McGowan play. Having paid McGowan a $2,000 advance, Harris was upset at seeing the rights he controlled become useless. At the time, McGowan was in California writing for Paramount; the studio's desire to avoid trouble with their pending *Vanities* film meant Harris got his money back.[27]

Artwork depicting one of the first scenes in *Murder at the Vanities*.

Carroll's bigger problem came from Manhattan's Local 829 of the Scenic Artists Union. They forbade their members from building the new sets because of unpaid bills on his 1932 version of *Vanities*.[28] Carroll contested the union's claims on the basis that two different corporations owned the two shows and so one had nothing to do with the other. He sought a court injunction against the union, and even tried to enlist President Roosevelt's help in the matter, arguing that the union's recalcitrance was hampering employment during the Great Depression.[29]

In the meantime, Carroll had to proceed with scenery as best he could in order to avoid jeopardizing his deal with Paramount. Initially, he told the press he would use a European process that "projected scenery" onto a screen. Invented by Max Tauber, the system could "reflect scenery from the front, the back or the sides and can do it in colors...."[30]

But in the end, it seems Carroll relied on physical sets, even if they were austere in comparison to his prior shows. He obtained props in New York, but – in an effort to bypass Local 829 – he arranged for all technical construction to be done by firms in Philadelphia.[31] *Murder at the Vanities* would be particularly reliant on a "double revolving stage" that helped the play move from its "onstage" setting to its "backstage" mystery.[32]

'MURDER AT THE VANITIES'

Published in the _Brooklyn Eagle_ on September 3, 1933.

By August 12, 1933, the conflict with Local 829 was resolved in the union's favor, with Carroll ordered to pay them some $6,500.[33] The embattled show went ahead.

The City of Brotherly Love

The curtain first raised on _Murder at the Vanities_ at the Garrick Theatre in Philadelphia. Originally scheduled to open on August 24, the premiere was delayed due to the "necessity to install a new stage floor and revolving stages to work the show."[34] The new date was set as August 28, but that too had to change, with the opening finally taking place on August 30, 1933.[35]

Ticket prices for the evening performances were set as high as $3.30 for orchestra seats and as low as $1.10 for the gallery. Carroll also scheduled Wednesday and Saturday matinees at cheaper prices. Advertisements gave Lugosi third-billing.[36]

Critical response was uniformly poor, with the reviewers pulling no punches as they rushed to their typewriters:

Carroll had a bag of tricks up that voluminous tux sleeve, but experienced considerable difficulty in getting them out. And this mysterious background, which savors of the old-time thrillers, was hackneyed and trite.[37] [The production], as it is presently constituted, suffers from an overdose of plot, which has the same effect upon it as several quarts of [the barbiturate sleeping aid] Veronal.[38]

– Philadelphia Daily News

The original mystery intended by the plot thickened almost too thoroughly as beauteous maidens stumbled over strange revolving stages, important properties refused to work

Earl Carroll will present his "Murder at the Vanities" at the New Amsterdam Theater tonight. He is part-author, sharing the honors with Rufus King, who conceived the combination of murder mystery and musical show which this edition of the "Vanities" is heralded as being. The revue section has been contrived by Edward Heyman, Richard Myers, Eugene Conrad and Stuart C. Whitman. Chester Hale has staged the dances and there will be projected scenery by Max Teuber. The principal actors will include Olga Baclanova, James Rennie, Billy House, Bela Lugosi, Jean Adair, Beryl Wallace and Ben Lackland.

From the *New York Herald-Tribune* of September 12, 1933.

at the right time, lines of dialogue vanished into thin air and other ludicrous and pathetic mishaps marred the evening....[39]

–*Philadelphia Public-Ledger*

At present the show is in its travail of preparation, and a sardonic jinx must have hovered over the first presentation, because many of the simpler and elementary things went wrong – lights that would not turn off when they were expected to, cues missed, formations scrambled. In addition no apparent attempt has been made to bring it within proper playing time. The faint promise of the first act ... was dispelled during the second when the mechanics of the play fell to pieces literally, and the whole thing ended in a burlesque with even the participants apparently giving up hope of retrieving anything from the wreck of this initial performance. It is seldom that such an utter rout has been witnessed on the local stage.[40]

–*Philadelphia Inquirer*

News travelled fast, including to Manhattan, where *New York Times* and the *New York Evening Post* published similar reviews.[41]

Whatever problems stemmed from the book, others may have been the result of sabotage; the rotating stage failed to turn during at least one performance. Blaming the Scenic Artists Union, Carroll's publicist later claimed that the stage's ball bearings had been intentionally encased in paper. Carroll's crew also accused union members of trying to block the departure of props from New York.[42]

Nevertheless, Carroll immediately went to work on rectifying the problems, lobbying critics to review the show a second time. The *Inquirer* soon reported:

Murder at the Vanities ... has been so transformed that there is difficulty in recognizing it as the formless, chaotic production it was on its initial performance. There is still work to be done on it, it is true, but the presentation last night, when it began its final week in this city, was such an improvement over the original show....

Many patrons who attended the opening performance went to the theatre last evening full of doubt that anything could be done with it, and skeptical that anything had been done. But the first scene, a new set with a new number, immediately brought back suggestions of the old *Vanities*, and when it was run off with dash and confidence, hope for the production was revived. This feeling was emphasized as it progressed. The drama and the revue have been dovetailed more expertly and some semblance of sanity has been worked into the muddled murder story as it was originally given.

New and fresh costumes have spruced up the spectacular features, but the lack of tuneful music in the song numbers was still evident. In addition, the projection of songs through a loud-speaker [sic] proved a terrible irritation.[43]

To this account, the *Public-Ledger* added that the new version moved with "more clarity ... its finish has been entirely changed."[44] By contrast, the *Philadelphia News* bluntly said, "even after it was 'fixed up,' it was just about as engaging as a prohibition lecture."[45]

The Garrick tryout ended on September 6, 1933. Despite efforts to improve it, *Variety* concluded that the show had "died miserably" in Philadelphia.[46]

IN TONIGHT'S NEW PLAY

Artwork of Lugosi published in the *Brooklyn Eagle* on September 12, 1933.

At the same time, the trade argued the show was "worth saving," and that it could be rescued by a "closing of several weeks for rewrites and alterations."[47]

Carroll – who admitted that more revisions were needed – had originally hoped to open the show on Broadway on September 8. But he did not have weeks to spare. Too much depended on a September premiere, particularly his deal with Paramount. After only four days of "intensive rehearsal periods" (and the rapid purchase of a new song for the show), *Murder at the Vanities* made its New York debut.[48]

The Great White Way

While Earl Carroll touted his show's cutting-edge marriage of musical and mystery, the *New York Herald-Tribune* conjured tales of the old Broadway traditions. The New Amsterdam Theatre had stood for nearly three decades when *Murder at the Vanities* opened, its stage having been trod by everyone from Irene and Vernon Castle to Will Rogers and Bert Williams. Carroll had himself rented it for his 1930 edition of *Vanities*.[49]

Situated across the street from the opulent, art nouveau New Amsterdam was Billy Minsky's Republic. To counter Carroll's play, Minsky's place hung a sign labeling its own show *Slaughter at the Republic*.[50] But Minsky ran burlesque shows, whereas Carroll produced opulent stage productions in the field of legitimate theatre, and he wanted the world to know it.

Daily Variety touted *Murder at the Vanities'* "swank" premiere on September 12, but first-nighters watching the "backstage" story had no knowledge of the problems transpiring in

Paul Garrits, who appeared on roller skates in *Murder at the Vanities*.

the real backstage.[51] Only two hours before the curtain rose, the comedy team of Shaw and Lea walked out, angry that they were not signed to a "run-of-the-play contract and billing," but that their agreement instead featured a two-week cancellation clause, the notice controlled by Carroll. Carroll reassured them that the entire cast had such clauses in their contracts, but the duo still quit.[52]

The bigger trouble came from those judges appointed to the theatrical bench. Perhaps the New York critics were poised to attack *Murder at the Vanities* because they considered Carroll to be lowbrow. Or perhaps it was because they smelled blood in the water after the show's rocky beginnings in Pennsylvania. Whatever the reason, they represent a parade as long as any line of showgirls that Carroll had ever put on the stage:

As displayed at the New Amsterdam, the result is not triumphant. ... As is the case with oil and water, Scotch and ginger ale, and alcohol and gasoline, murder and music don't get along so well together. Let alone corpses and comedy.[53]

–*New York World-Telegram*

Murder at the Vanities is just that. It murders two good ideas... and the hybrid achieves nothing beyond mediocrity. It's neither fish, flesh nor good red-herring.[54]

–*Variety*

..the revue bogs up the mystery meller and the mystery meller would bog up the revue if that hadn't already been done sufficiently by the revue itself. It is slow-moving, with not a single sock specialty, and only a couple of reasonably attractive spectacle scenes to enliven the monotony.[55]

–*Billboard*

Earl Carroll tries to mix a murder show and a revue, and produces a mongrel.[56]

–*Life*

It's *Broadway* and *The Phantom of the Opera* combined and ruined.[57]

–*Motion Picture Herald*

The fault in the *Vanities*, however, isn't so much the way its ingredients have been mixed as their quality.[58] Only recommended to anatomy students.[59]

–*New Yorker*

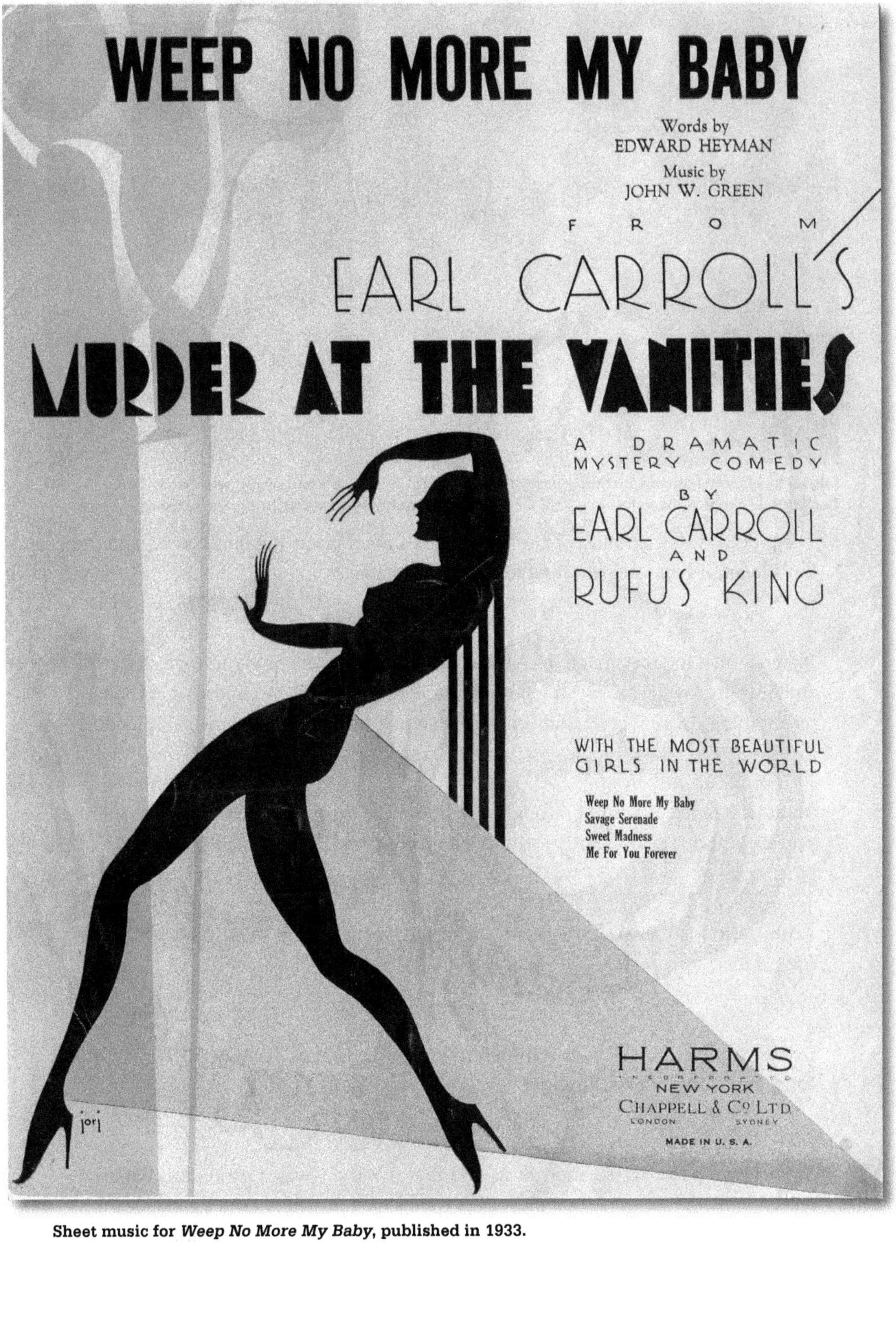

Sheet music for *Weep No More My Baby*, published in 1933.

Lugosi at Mickey Mouse's birthday party with (from far left), Joe Penner and wife, and Olga Baclanova. From right to left are Paul Garrits and an unknown woman. *(Courtesy of George Chastain)*

The plot ... is slow and heavy, the vaudeville commonplace, the music sickly and the movement, if I may be permitted to say so, is lethargic.[60]

–New York Herald-Tribune

It merely goes to prove that in its murder plot, the show is about as routine as it is in its anatomy displays, all of which follow the tradition, since it seems nobody has thought up anything else for big set numbers except getting the girls on, and their clothes off.[61]

–New York Evening Journal

Amid its frazzled strivings nothing really stood firm excepting Mr. Carroll's unfailing year-in, year-out preoccupation with the franker aspects of the female anatomy.[62]

–New York American

...Mr. Carroll is the wizard bereft of his magic. *Murder at the Vanities* lacks the regal Carroll touch.[63]

– New York Times

I could not stay to see who really did the murder. I know anyway. So far as I am concerned, his name is Carroll.[64]

–New York Daily News

... for better or for worse, most of us said that it was anyway a good idea. Weekend reflection makes me think that most of us were wrong. It wasn't even a good idea.[65]

–Syracuse American

[It] proved poor entertainment. Partly because Carroll did not have the money to do things in his usual lavish way, partly because he was just plain dumb in what he did do.[66]

–Springfield Union and Republican

Though a small degree of variation can be detected in their notices, these critics generally agreed that the show's songs were weak, just as – in an isolated act of generosity – some of them mustered praise for Paul Garrits, who performed a dance on roller skates.[67]

Largely uniform though the reaction was, a small number of reviewers defended the play, even if only in minor respects:

It is an evening which is far too long for its own good. But for the most part it is different enough and sufficiently varied to achieve its double purpose of holding the attention while Mr. Carroll, in his generous way, is filling the eye.[68]

–New York Evening Post

Lugosi at an unknown event with Ben Lyon (center). *(Courtesy of Bill Chase)*

From the *New Yorker* of October 7, 1933.

There are a great many theatregoers who will enjoy the varied attractions of *Murder at the Vanities*. Probably when it has run a week it will be tightened, given more point and somehow vivified. It is pretty, and it is earnest.[69]

–*Brooklyn Eagle*

It is not by any means Mr. Carroll's most lavish revue, and certainly it is far from Mr. King's best mystery, but the two ingredients support each other admirably, and in combination display virtues which neither possesses alone. … *Murder at the Vanities* is herewith recommended.[70]

–*New York Sun*

The union of melodrama and musical comedy is quite adroitly managed.[71]

–*Wall Street Journal*

…a fairly good mystery story was used as the rack on which to hang a revue.[72]

–*Theatre Arts Monthly*

And yet these meekly positive comments are in some ways misleading when excised from the rest of their text, as these same critics also found much to complain about.

A writer for *Stage* magazine published his sixteen-year-old son's reaction to the show, which was also somewhat favorable. The teen thought the mystery plot was "hooey," but liked a few of the songs, particularly *Me for You Forever*. He commended the lighting and found the bare legs worthwhile, though the scandalous fan dance was "child's play" compared to what he could see at Minsky's burlesque shows. More than anything else, the boy hoped he could get his father to arrange for him to meet Pauline Moore.[73]

Beset with troubles ranging from financial to critical, Carroll was not without a small degree of good fortune. The New York License Commissioner "showed his teeth" in October as part of an effort to rid the city of "indecent" shows. Inexplicably, *Murder at the Vanities* somehow evaded his

Artwork published in the *New York Post* on October 16, 1933.

wrath, its chorus girls proceeding, as one account noted, "as undraped as ever."[74]

Carroll could also take heart in the fact that his critics and his audiences viewed the show differently. During its first month, *Murder at the Vanities* usually played to near-capacity crowds; its first week grossed $23,000 and its second $25,000.[75] Orchestra seating was sold out nearly every night. *Billboard* tallied 67 audience laughs at a single performance.[76] The same trade reported its box-office success was a sign that playgoers had a hunger for musicals.[77] In response, *Stage* magazine sarcastically announced, "New York and its guests from Montana like it."[78]

One newspaper reported that ten "prominent" residents of Charlotte, North Carolina flew 565 miles just to spend an evening at Carroll's show.[79] They also might have seen stars sitting in audience seats nearby. Maurice Chevalier, Al Jolson, Ruby Keeler, Rudy Vallee, and Paul Whiteman were among the play's famous ticket-buyers.[80]

What such celebrities thought of Lugosi is unknown. In fact, most critics didn't bother reviewing Lugosi's performance at all.[81] Those who did were generally positive, certainly more so than they were to the overall production:

> Among the actors you will be pleased to observe... while you tremble to your boots, [is] Mr. Lugosi.[82]
>
> –*New York Sun*

Advertisement published in the *New York Post* on October 21, 1933.

Playbill to *Murder at the Vanities*, published after its move to the Majestic Theatre.

From the interior of the *Murder at the Vanities* playbill.

...with Bela Lugosi stalking around ominously under a green spotlight as an unpleasant character, it has its interludes of tension, and in general forces an audience to listen quietly and with interest....[83]

–New York Post

Bela Lugosi spends the evening sauntering about the stage in different awe-inspiring costumes and being very enigmatic and menacing.[84]

–Brooklyn Eagle

..Bela Lugosi goes growling around in his best Dracular [*sic*] manner.[85]

–Wall Street Journal

Lugosi and Lisa Silbert were a sinister pair....[86]

–Variety

The *New Yorker* referenced Lugosi's "hypnotic" work onstage, but worried that audiences might find its power diminished thanks to being juxtaposed with a parade of beautiful women singing about murder.[87]

Few specific audience reactions were recorded, but the crowds kept buying tickets in good numbers during October and November 1933. Along with the standard newspaper ads, Carroll had the cast promote the show wherever possible. On October 12, Lugosi and a few of his costars presented a sketch from *Vanities* on the *Rudy Vallee Hour* at 8PM EST.[88] A few weeks later, the lead players (who presumably included Lugosi, though he wasn't specifically named) made a Halloween night appearance at the Hotel Towers' new supper club, the Don Pedro Room.[89] Quite appropriately, the cast was introduced at midnight.[90] Then, on November 17, Lugosi, James Rennie, Minnie Dupree, Naomi Ray and Olga Baclanova promoted *Vanities* on WEAF's radio show *The Theatre Presents*.[91] The ensemble presented its sketch at 12:15AM EST.[92]

For a play that had undergone numerous evolutions, change ironically continued to be a constant. *Murder at the Vanities* moved to the Majestic Theatre on November 6, 1933. According to *Billboard*, the decision was wise: grosses moved upwards to $20,000 during its first week there, after having been around $18,500 a week prior to the move.[93] By contrast,

Variety reported a gross of only $15,000, reporting that profits before and after the move were roughly the same.[94]

As for behind-the-scenes stories, few have emerged. Speaking about the cast in later years, Pauline Moore recalled Lugosi and his young wife Lillian:

> She cooked for him – and with a lot of garlic. So, when he hypnotized you on stage, you knew what he had for dinner! I had come from a Pennsylvania Dutch background, so there was no such thing as garlic in my experience – but I was quite aware of it in Lugosi's experience! He and his wife ate together, and spent all their time together, and sometimes, I think, she'd cook for him in his dressing room.[95]

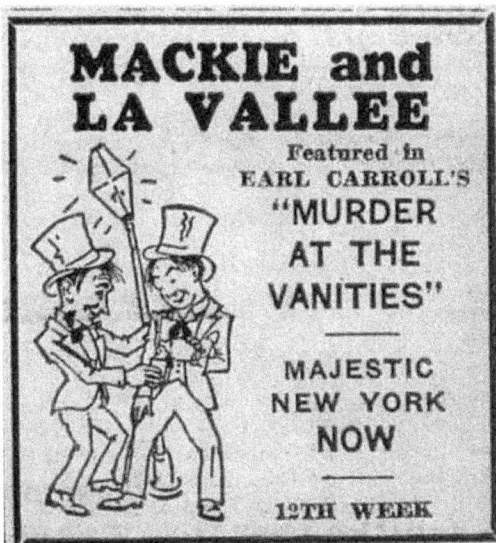

MACKIE and LA VALLEE

Featured in EARL CARROLL'S "MURDER AT THE VANITIES"

MAJESTIC NEW YORK NOW

12TH WEEK

Published in *Variety* on November 28, 1933.

Moore also remembered that comedian Billy House allegedly suffered a heart attack one night, and "every minute he wasn't onstage he was sitting there, the sweat just running off him. But the minute his time came for an entrance – on he went!"

Other anecdotes largely involve the cast comings-and-goings. After just two weeks or so on Broadway, Minnie Dupree took over for Jean Adair, because Adair left for Hollywood.[96] Showgirl Eunice Coleman travelled to the same destination after signing a contract with Fox.[97] And then, on November 13, James Rennie flew to Cleveland only to be trapped there due to fog.[98] An unhappy Carroll had Louis Eccles fill in for him that night; Rennie was back onstage by the following evening.[99]

There were also more troubles with the Scenic Artists Union. In late September, Carroll charged two Local 829 officials of being involved in a conspiracy against him. Carroll even charged one of the two men with coercion. Both officials were arrested, but the magistrate released them almost immediately, given that he believed the row was essentially a "civil matter."[100]

As for Lugosi, the press covered his attendance at city restaurants. One journalist wrote:

> [Lugosi stands] up frequently when the white beam searches among the tables and glitters on the swizzle sticks. Bela startled the professionally modest folk at an opening the other night when he frankly admitted that he had been out of the public eye for some time and was getting around now to get himself remembered all over again.[101]

Foremost among his local appearances was Mickey Mouse's birthday party held at

This advertisement was published in both *Variety* and the *New Yorker* just after Lugosi left the production.

the Hollywood Restaurant. Adorned with photos of movie stars, the famous Manhattan nightspot found Lugosi rubbing shoulders with the likes of Buster Keaton, Inez Courtney, Bert Lahr, and *Vanities* costars Rennie and Baclanova. Famous guests that night would "only nibble at the food in the accepted Mickey Mouse manner"; dancing would be "on and under the tables."[102]

Lugosi also impressed local press with the stark difference between his character on stage and in the films and his personality away from the footlights: "I was prepared for a fiery-eyed, foreign-looking gent when my host introduced me to Bela Lugosi. Instead, I found a faultlessly groomed gentleman, who might be president of a small city's rotary club. He likes, of all things, gardening."[103]

But Lugosi's most unexpected reception came not at a nightclub, but instead at an area hospital:

Dracula stalked through the emergency ward of St. John's Hospital [in Elmhurst, Queens Borough, New York] but didn't frighten anyone. Ambulance Surgeon Pterno, nurses and the human vampire met professionally. The hospital physician attended Dracula and his beautiful wife for injuries suffered in an automobile accident. The patients in real life are Bela Lugosi, Hungarian screen star and Dracula in reel life and his wife. Mrs. Lugosi was the more seriously injured. She suffered abrasions and cuts of the forehead and nose and a hemorrhage of the nose. Her husband was bruised on the forehead. They were injured when their automobile was in collision with another car near the Queens Plaza.

After thanking the ambulance surgeon and nurses, Lugosi invited them to attend *Murder at the Vanities*.[104] Whether he gave them complimentary tickets or not is unknown.

Conclusion

As the year 1933 ended, Earl Carroll enjoyed greater and greater fortune. In December, he had something of a minor victory over his foes when the President and Business Manager for the Scenic Artists' Union were finally on trial for charges of conspiracy and extortion.[105] *Murder at the Vanities* forged ahead at the Majestic Theatre, where it would end its successful run on March 10, 1934 after 207 performances. And, most importantly, the film adaptation of his revue was moving into production at Paramount.

In January 1934, Carroll travelled to Hollywood to supervise the film, taking with him eleven of his showgirls.[106] Seven would remain in Hollywood after the production wrapped.[107] And they did actually appear in the movie, unlike, say, James Rennie or Olga Baclanova or Pauline Moore, who was involved in some film shorts by the end of January 1934.[108]

In fact, Paramount made so many changes to the storyline of *Murder at the Vanities* that anyone who saw it on Broadway must have been more baffled by the changes in the film version than they were by its whodunit tale. A delightful pre-Code mystery-musical, the film does depict murders backstage while the *Vanities* show proceeds onstage. Carroll's signature showgirl numbers are present, though the models reveal less skin than they had on Broadway. And there is a rotating stage set that echoes the one used in Philadelphia and New York.

But the changes are monumental. None of the Broadway songs appear (even though they had already been published as sheet music), their replacements being performed by the likes of Duke Ellington and his orchestra. Victor McLaglen plays a detective, but the character name Ellery was switched to the backstage manager, here played by Jack Oakie. Rather than open the show, the first murder doesn't occur until some 35 minutes into the 89-minute film. The first murder weapon is a long pin; the second is a gun. The two are committed by different murderers, neither of whom is the wardrobe mistress (played here by Jessie Ralph).

Suspicion falls on only three people: the show's lead star (played by Carl Brisson), the wardrobe mistress (who is now the lead star's mother), and a particularly hammy actor (played by Charles Middleton). All of them are proven innocent. Acid appears briefly, but it is not used in a murder.

Most notably, there is no Siebenkase and there is no Bela Lugosi. Months earlier, a trade publication wrote, "the summer dog-day worries were how to release Lugosi for the film version, if the stage production became a hit and kept the show overly long in New York."[109] He was, after all, the man whom Carroll had specifically pursued for the revue. But not only was Lugosi absent from the Paramount film, he was also absent from the last four months of the Broadway run.

The *New York Times* announced that William Balfour, who had been playing the small role

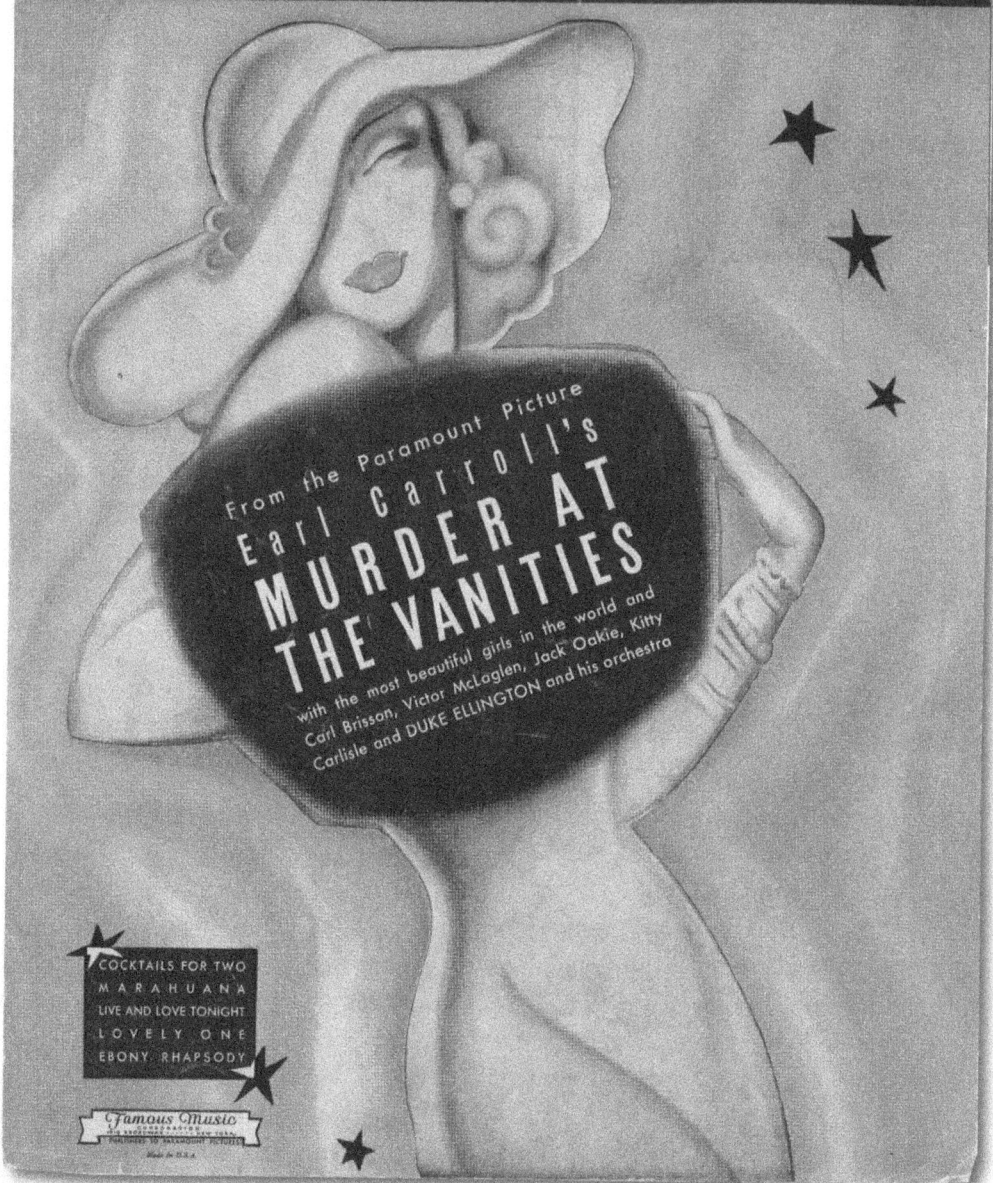

Sheet music promoting the film version of *Murder at the Vanities* (1934). The song *Cocktails for Two* was not featured in the stage version

of the night watchman, would replace Lugosi during the third week of November.[110] But Lugosi changed his mind, sticking with Siebenkase a little longer, until December 3, 1933, only two days before he headlined a new vaudeville act.[111]

One day after Balfour took over for Lugosi onstage, a news report indicated that Victor McLaglen would replace Bela Lugosi as the lead player in the film version of *Murder at the Vanities* (1934).[112]   But that was not finally accurate, as McLaglen essayed a role that was much the same as James Rennie's on Broadway. Siebenkase simply did not appear in the film version, not even under another name. In the movie, there is no suspicious red herring with a disfigured face. There is no mysterious "actor" whose face is green. There is no Erik the Phantom, or an unofficial variation of him.

Lugosi had opted to leave the Broadway play. Whether the same was true of the film, or whether Paramount (for whom he'd recently completed two films) no longer needed him due to script changes is unknown.

What is clear is that Lugosi played the Phantom of Broadway once more after leaving *Murder at the Vanities*, at least in a sense. Following a performance on December 3, 1933, Lugosi never again appeared on the Great White Way. He was conspicuously absent from Broadway for the rest of his career, despite his repeated efforts to mount a comeback. As Leroux wrote of Erik the Phantom, "He doesn't often come this way."

(Endnotes)

1   Here we opt to date Leroux's novel as 1910, given that it was first published in book form that year. It had earlier been serialized during the autumn of 1909 and the spring of 1910.
2   "Bela Lugosi Weds in Vegas." *Reno Evening Gazette* (Reno, NV) 1 Feb. 1933.
3   "High Juggler." *New Yorker* 11 Aug. 1945.
4   Joyce appeared in the 1923 edition of *Vanities*; Fields in the 1928 edition.
5   For more information on Carroll, see: Murray, Ken. *The Body Merchant* (Pasadena, CA: Ward Ritchie, 1976).
6   Waldorf, Wilella. "Forecasts and Postscripts." *New York Evening Post* 28 Jan. 1933.
7   Waldorf, Wilella. "Forecasts and Postscripts." *New York Evening Post* 4 Feb. 1933.
8   "Harriet Hoctor and Co." *Variety* 13 May 1931.
9   "Inside Stuff–Legit." *Variety* 1 Aug. 1933; "Jed Harris Will Get Royalty Refund from Par on *Vanities* Deal." *Variety* 8 Aug. 1933.
10   "Carroll After Pic Names for *Murder at Vanities*." *Variety* 21 Mar. 1933.
11   "Mr. Carroll's Plans." *Brooklyn Eagle* 27 Apr. 1933.
12   Waldorf, Wilella. "Forecasts and Postscripts." *New York Evening Post* 11 May 1933.
13   Arthur, Art. "Reverting to Type - Shreds and Patches." *Brooklyn Eagle* 12 May 1933.
14   Arthur, Art. "Reverting to Type." *Brooklyn Eagle* 23 Oct. 1933.
15   Hammond, Percy. "The Theatres." *New York Herald-Tribune* 13 Sept. 1933.
16   Harrison, Paul. "There's Murder In The Airs [*sic*] At Carroll's New *Vanities*." *Indiana Evening Gazette* (Indiana, PA) 28 Sep. 1933; De Casseres, Benjamin. "Plays That Hit The Picture Idea." *Motion Picture Herald* 14 Oct. 1933.
17   "New Earl Carroll Show." *Philadelphia Bulletin. Murder at the Vanities* File, Rare Book Department, Free Library of Philadelphia.
18   Morehouse, Ward. "Broadway After Dark." *New York Sun* 28 July 1933.
19   Morehouse, Ward. "Broadway After Dark." *New York Sun* 31 July 1933.
20   "Engagements." *Variety* 8 Aug. 1933.
21   "20 Years Ago." *Sunday Herald* (Provo, UT) 26 July 1953.
22   "Star of *Dracula* Visitor at Family." *Scranton Republican* (Scranton, PA) 1 Aug. 1935.
23   Morehouse, Ward. "Broadway After Dark." *New York Sun* 26 July 1933.
24   Mank, Gregory William. "The Hollywood Adventures of Pauline Moore." *Films in Review* July-Aug. 1994.
25   Kingsley, Grace. "Hollywood in Review." *New Orleans Times-Picayune* 4 Aug. 1933.
26   King, William G. "Summer Plays and Players." *New York Evening Post* 3 Aug. 1933.
27   "Jed Harris Will Get Royalty Refund From Par on *Vanities* Deal." *Variety* 8 Aug. 1933.
28   "New Carroll Show Halted By Union." *New York Times* 26 July 1933.
29   Ibid.
30   "Tries Phantom Scenery." *New York Times* 16 Aug. 1933.

31   "Theatre Work for Philadelphia." *Philadelphia Inquirer* 3 Aug. 1933.
32   "Double Revolving Stage Used in *Murder at the Vanities*." *New York Evening Post* 9 Sept. 1933.
33   "Scenic Artists Upheld." *New York Times* 12 Aug. 1933.
34   "Show Opening Delayed." *Philadelphia Inquirer* 21 Aug. 1933.
35   "Rennie's Cool Restraint in a Police Inspector Part." *Philadelphia Inquirer* 27 Aug. 1933; "Earl Carroll to Open the Season." *Philadelphia Inquirer* 20 Aug. 1933.
36   Advertisement. *Philadelphia Inquirer* 20 Aug. 1933.
37   P. K. "*Murder at Vanities* Proves Disappointing." *Philadelphia Daily News* 31 Aug. 1933.
38   Keen, J. H. "Observations." *Philadelphia Daily* News 31 Aug. 1933.
39   Qtd. in "*Murder at the Vanities* Opens Philadelphia Theatrical Season – Earl Carroll's Latest Production, En Route to Broadway, Combines Mystery Melodrama and Musical Review." *New York Evening Post* 31 Aug. 1933.
40   "*Vanities* Linked With Murder Story – Combination of Drama and Revue Has Rough Going on First Night." *Philadelphia Inquirer* 31 Aug. 1933.
41   "Earl Carroll's Novelty." *New York Times* 31 Aug. 1933; Waldorf, Willela. "Forecasts and Postscripts." *New York Evening Post* 7 Sept. 1933.
42   "Unionists Held for Trial in Carroll Case." *Variety* 19 Dec. 1933.
43   "Carroll Play Now Has Greater Promise." *Philadelphia Inquirer* 5 Sept. 1933.
44   Hauser, Odell. "Carroll Piece Is Seen In New and Revised Version – "*Murder at the Vanities* Now More a Mystery and Less a Revue." *Philadelphia Public Ledger, Murder at the Vanities* File, Rare Book Department, Free Library of Philadelphia.
45   Keen, J. H. "*Murder at Vanities* May Be Another *Abie's Irish Rose*." *Philadelphia Daily News* 7 Oct. 1933.
46   "*Murder* Gives Philly Poor Start." *Variety* 5 Sept. 1933. The quotation "died miserably" can be found in: "*Cheer*, $24,000, First Click in Philly." *Variety* 19 Sept. 1933.
47   Waters. "*Murder at the Vanities*." *Variety* 5 Sept. 1933.
48   "Carroll Show Coming." *New York Evening Post* 1 Sept. 1933; Waldorf, Willela. "Forecasts and Postscripts." *New York Evening Post* 5 Sept. 1933; Waldorf, Willela. "Forecasts and Postscripts." *New York Evening Post* 8 Sept. 1933; "Air Briefs." *Billboard* 2 Sept. 1933. The new song Carroll purchased was called *Sweet Madness*.
49   "*Vanities* Premiere Recalls Theatre's Opening in 1903." *New York Herald-Tribune* 10 Sept. 1933.
50   "More than Murder Now." *Billboard* 23 Sept. 1933.
51   "*Murder* Swank Gotham Premier." *Daily Variety* 13 Sept. 1933.
52   "Act Quits *Murder* on One-Way Notice Terms." *Variety* 19 Sept. 1933.
53   Garland, Robert. "Murder and Melody Strange Stage Pals." *New York World-Telegram* 13 Sept. 1933.
54   Abel. "Plays on Broadway." *Variety* 19 Sept. 1933.
55   "The New Plays on Broadway." *Billboard* 23 Sept. 1933.
56   Herold, Don, Harry Evans, and Kyle Crichton. "Stop and Go Service: A Symposium of Criticism." *Life* Nov. 1933.
57   De Casseres, Benjamin. "Plays That Hit The Picture Idea." *Motion Picture Herald* 14 Oct. 1933.
58   "Music and Murder." *New Yorker* 23 Sept. 1933.
59   "With Music." *New Yorker* 30 Sept. 1933. [This is a capsule review, as opposed to the *New Yorker*'s full review published on 23 Sept. 1933.]
60   Hammond, Percy. "The Theatres." *New York Herald-Tribune* 13 Sept. 1933.
61   Anderson, John. "Half Musical, Half Mystery Comedy Presented with Earl Carroll Trimmings." *New York Evening Journal* 13 Sept. 1933.
62   Gabriel, Gilbert W. "*Murder at the Vanities*." *New York American* 13 Sept. 1933.
63   Atkinson, Brooks. "The Play." *New York Times* 13 Sept. 1933.
64   Mantle, Burns. "*Murder at Vanities* Mystery Revue." *New York Daily News* 13 Sept. 1933.
65   Gabriel, Gilbert W. "Murder and Music Will Never Mix." *Syracuse American* 24 Sep. 1933.
66   Mantle, Burns. "Plays and Players." *Springfield Union and Republican* (Springfield, MA) 24 Sep. 1933.
67   Garrits' name was spelled differently in different reviews. We have chosen to use the spelling most commonly printed in the *Murder at the Vanities* playbill, even though it features both "Garrits" and "Garritts." The spelling "Garrits" also appeared most commonly in the entertainment industry press, though "Garritts" and "Garritz" also appear.
68   Brown, John Mason. "The Play." *New York Evening Post* 13 Sept. 1933.
69   Pollock, Arthur. "The Theatres." *Brooklyn Eagle* 13 Sept. 1933.
70   Lockridge, Richard. "The New Play." *New York Sun* 13 Sept. 1933.

71   Bowen. "The Theatre." *Wall Street Journal* 14 Sept. 1933.

72   "Broadway in Review." *Theatre Arts Monthly* Nov. 1933.

73   "Feed Pepper to Your Little Boy." *Stage* Nov. 1933.

74   "Levine Continues Anti-Nudity War as Burly Houses Duck Dirt." *Billboard* 28 Oct. 1933.

75   "A Broadway Success." *New York Sun* 29 Sep. 1933; "*Murder* with Surprise $23,000 Take, First Money Show to Reach B'Way." *Variety* 19 Sept. 1933; "Two New Musicals in B'Way List Give Blah Season First Front." *Variety* 26 Sept. 1933.

76   The performance monitored was 31 Oct. 1933. See: "*Billboard* Laugh Survey Gives Title to Joe Cook." *Billboard* 11 Nov. 1933.

77   "Public Wants Cake." *Billboard* 30 Sept. 1933.

78   "*Murder at the Vanities*." *Stage* Mar. 1934.

79   "10 Fly 565 Miles to Attend Theatre." *Washington Post* 23 Sept. 1933.

80   Morehouse, Ward. "Broadway After Dark." *New York Sun* 25 Sept. 1933; "Elevator Man Has Ups and Downs: Jack Wherry, at the New Amsterdam, Has Been Hauling Chorus Girls for Twenty Years." *New York Evening Post* 29 Sept. 1933.

81   Lugosi was mentioned in the text of a few reviews that did not critique his performance, specifically those published in the *New York Daily News*, *New York Evening Journal*, the *Wall Street Journal*, and *Stage* magazine (in its November 1933 review). He was also mentioned in Burns Mantle's review for the *Chicago Tribune* (24 Sept. 1933). By contrast, outside of his name in cast listings, he was not mentioned in reviews published in the *New York American*, the *New York Herald-Tribune*, the *New York Times*, the *New York World-Telegram*, *Billboard*, or *Theatre Arts Monthly*.

82   Lockridge, Richard. "The New Play." *New York Sun* 13 Sept. 1933.

83   Brown, John Mason. "The Play." *New York Post* 13 Sept. 1933.

84   Pollock, Arthur. "The Theatres." *Brooklyn Eagle* 13 Sept. 1933.

85   Bowen, "The Theatre."

86   Abel. "Plays on Broadway." *Variety* 19 Sept. 1933.

87   "Music and Murder." *New Yorker* 23 Sept. 1933.

88   "Cummings' Crime Talk Shares Radio Honors With 'Buy Now.'" *Herald Statesman* (Yonkers, NY) 12 Oct. 1933.

89   "Tower Floor Shows To Mirror Broadway." *Brooklyn Eagle* 25 Oct. 1933.

90   Ibid.

91   "Radio Frolic Enlists Many Stage Favorites." *New York Times* 12 Nov. 1933; "Broadcasting." *The Evening Recorder* (Amsterdam, NY) 16 Nov. 1933; "Tonight's Radio Programs." *New York Sun* 17 Nov. 1933.

92   Radio Key Stations." *Olean Times-Herald* (Olean, NY) 17 Nov. 1933.

93   "Legit Grosses on New High with Quarter Million Total." *Billboard* 18 Nov. 1933; "Three New Probable Clicks on B'way Fatten Legit's New Season Percentage." *Variety* 24 Oct. 1933.

94   "B'way Smashes Maintain Top Pace; Trailers Off, New Clicks Needed." *Billboard* 14 Nov. 1933.

95   Mank, "The Hollywood Adventures of Pauline Moore."

96   "Theatrical Notes." *New York Times* 26 Sept. 1933.

97   "Eunice Coleman's Chance." *Variety* 19 Dec. 1933.

98   "Rennie Marooned." *Variety* 14 Nov. 1933.

99   "Theatrical Notes." *New York Times* 15 Nov. 1933.

100   "Earl Carroll Acts Role of Policeman." *New York Times* 27 Sept. 1933.

101   Aswell, James. "My New York." *Massillon Evening Independent* (Massillon, OH) 21 Oct. 1933.

102   Daly, Phil M. "Along the Rialto." *Film Daily* 29 Sept. 1933.

103   Aswell, James. "My New York." *Oshkosh Daily Northwestern* (Oshkosh, WI) 14 Oct. 1933.

104   Untitled article. *Newtown Register* (Elmhurst, NY) 16 Sept. 1933.

105   "Unionists Held for Trial in Carroll Case." *Variety* 19 Dec. 1933.

106   "*Vanities* Girls Off for Coast." *Film Daily* 23 Jan. 1934.

107   Wilk, Ralph. "A Little from 'Lots.'" *Film Daily* 2 Apr. 1934.

108   Alicoate, Charles. "Short Shots from Eastern Studios." *Film Daily* 31 Jan. 1934.

109   Abel, "Plays on Broadway."

110   "Theatrical Notes." *New York Times* 13 Nov. 1933.

111   "Newcomer to *Murder at the Vanities*." *New York Sun* 5 Dec. 1933.

112   Soanes, Wood. "Curtain Calls." *Oakland Tribune* 6 Dec. 1933.

Lugosi in the early 1930s. *(Courtesy of Bill Chase)*

Chapter 4

Belian Productions

Some people hear the term "revisionist history" and as a result believe that there are only two types: the original version, and that which has been revised. Others even look upon the term "revisionism" with disdain, as if its goal is to insidiously rewrite The Way It Really Was for ideological reasons. Some Great Man was great, for example, but now someone tries to argue he wasn't.

While historians and readers have many motives and biases that guide them, the reality is that the very writing of history is by its nature revisionist, even if usually in small respects. To the eyes of one historian, available evidence forms a different constellation than it might for another. Changes to the telling of a particular event thus unfold incrementally, and sometimes due to primary sources that resurface.

For example, many persons might believe Bela Lugosi's reluctance to play the Frankenstein Monster in what became James Whale's 1931 film represents a major gaffe. Here one could point not only to historians, but also to Lugosi's fourth wife, Lillian, who said:

[He should have stayed with it], even though Bela said he was going to cry sick that he can't do it, he couldn't go through it five hours every morning [for the makeup] and then I don't know how many hours it takes to take it off again. And then they made a special seat because you couldn't really sit down because each boot weighed twenty-five pounds and they were built up.

[His agent] should have knocked some sense into him and said, 'Look, you moan and groan and grunt, but then you'll be by yourself up there [in the horror film genre] and not have someone else [competing with you].'[1]

Perhaps she was correct, though of course the story of why Lugosi did not play the Monster is complicated and contradictory. It involves various people and various versions of events.[2] The one thing Whale and Lugosi and the others at Universal Pictures had in common was that none of them could have accurately predicted the film's box-office success, as well as the emergent stardom of its unknown actor Boris Karloff.

At any rate, even if Lugosi made a professional mistake as regards *Frankenstein* (or in some other cases, for that matter), there is no reason as a result to believe that he *always* made bad business decisions. Some writers have expressed that opinion, but it is much too hasty a generalization.

In the heyday of the old Hollywood, a small number of forward-thinking actors took it upon themselves to control their own careers as much as possible, rather than casting their fates to the prevailing winds of studio moguls. These range from Charlie Chaplin's formation of his own studio to Katharine Hepburn's acquisition of the rights to the play *The Philadelphia Story* so that she could herself control its film adaptation.

Bela Lugosi deserves a consideration for that select list of actors-turned-producers, an honor for which he has scarcely received credit. Whatever errors he did or did not make at given junctures of his career, the impression that he had poor judgment needs to be altered and revised. Specifically, he was somewhat ahead of his time in starting his own film production company, which he did on two separate occasions during the 1930s. Admittedly, Lugosi was not finally successful in these aims, but his vision was shrewd and forward-thinking.

Historical revisionism need not rewrite major aspects of history as we know it. In fact, it much more commonly augments what we know in very minor ways. For example, period newspapers – which could be just as (occasionally) inaccurate in the past as they can today – claimed that Lugosi would depart the cast of Earl Carroll's *Murder at the Vanities* in November 1933. His next job was a vaudeville show that opened in December of that same year. One definitely followed the other, and as a result it is easy for historians to draw a line between the two, as if the first *caused* the second.

But two primary sources have recently surfaced that suggest something different happened, something more complicated, and something that would involve Lugosi's own attempts at becoming a producer, at becoming the man in charge of his own acting engagements. One of these primary sources is a trade announcement:

[Lugosi, the] stage and screen diabolist, has just removed himself from *Murder at the Vanities* to *Pagan Fury*, a sweet little cut-throat tome by that peaceful citizen Sam J. Warshawsky, who learned playwriting in the RKO publicity department. Sam's play opens in Chicago soon.[3]

If accurate, this clipping provides a logical reason as to why the *New York Times* announced that Lugosi's departure from *Vanities* would occur in November.[4] It was not to go from a successful Broadway revue (with a film adaptation of the same in the offing) to headlining a brief vaudeville tour. Rather, it was to move from a Broadway show in which Lugosi had a

Lugosi and his wife Lillian. The dog is likely Lugosi's German shepherd Bodri.

relatively small role to a three-act play bound for Broadway with him as the star.

Granted, Warshawsky was largely unknown, even at the time, and certainly as compared to the infamous Earl Carroll. Who was he? Born in 1888, playwright Samuel Jesse Warshawsky, also known as Sam or S. J., had at least one silent film to his credit, *Gambling in Souls* (1919); Denison Clift – who later directed Lugosi in *The Mystery of the Mary Celeste* (1935) – had written its scenario.

Warshawsky had also authored at least two operettas, *Radical Lilly* and *Radical Rose*, as well as the 1932 play *Woman of Destiny*, the latter gaining him a degree of notoriety given its storyline of a woman who gets elected President of the United States.[5] And then there was his *Pagan Fury*; he licensed the rights to that play in 1932.[6]

The production of *Pagan Fury* starring Lugosi in 1933 was delayed, as were rehearsals for it. What this suggests is the real answer as to why Lugosi formed his vaudeville act; it would be a short-term, well-paying gig until *Pagan Fury* was underway. And it also explains why he did not leave *Murder at the Vanities* in November, as first announced. The second primary source that has surfaced notes that he actually remained in the *Vanities* cast until December 3, only two days before his vaudeville act premiered.[7] Having first planned to leave sooner to star in *Pagan Fury*, its delay seems to have prompted him to stay with Carroll as long as he could.

When Lugosi finished his brief vaudeville tour in December 1933, he and his wife Lillian

Lugosi and his wife Lillian (left), with unidentified friends.

returned not to the West Coast, but instead to New York City. He may well have been considering a second leg of the vaudeville tour, but he also had larger plans, plans that would allow him to assume command over his career.

In February 1934, Lugosi and his wife Lillian formed their own company, "Belian Productions." Incorporated in Manhattan by the couple and Hungarian-American journalist John Biro, Belian's purpose was to produce stage plays, musical productions, and vaudeville acts. [8] These plans speak less of an actor planning an immediate return to Hollywood filmmaking than to one who wanted to select and then produce his own live appearances. And *Pagan Fury* seems to have been first on the agenda.

After all, at roughly the same time, *Film Daily* reported that *Pagan Fury* starring Lugosi was finally bound for Chicago, a try-out run prior to a Broadway premiere.[9] The play was set to open in the Windy City in April of 1934.

That said, Belian Productions likely kept an eye on other possible ventures. In January 1934, for example, New York producers Wee and Leventhal – once described as "shoestring producers [who] managed to make a small profit each week on several revivals of plays of previous years" – were involved in a search for other plays that could star Lugosi.[10]

As for *Pagan Fury*, Lugosi himself seems to have secured the rights in mid-January 1934, if not earlier, shortly before (but perhaps in anticipation of) Belian's incorporation.[11] Robert Cremer's excellent and authorized biography of Lugosi quotes from a 1934 interview with Lugosi that appeared in the Hungarian-American newspaper *Az Ember*:

Lugosi and Lillian at a soccer practice (or game, perhaps).

It was such a sensational play that I couldn't remember ever having read anything better. It also had a part tailor-made for me. I finally signed a contract with the writer to bring the play to Broadway in the fall, because I was planning another vaudeville tour through the summer months.[12]

George Bancroft learned of the play and offered to produce it as early as March if he were given the lead role. Sam Warshawsky believed, as I did, that I was the man for the part and declined the offer. But Bancroft wanted the part so badly that he came to me with an offer of $2,000 if I would give it up. I refused, because seldom does a part in such a monumental and symbolic drama come to an actor.[13]

What about this role so captured Lugosi's imagination that he would forego continuing in *Murder at the Vanities* and also decline George Bancroft's offer? Though no copy of the script seems to survive, it is evident that *Pagan Fury*'s lead role was that of an artist, a painter of modern styles. In short, it was not a horror play.

Here was something absent from Lugosi's career since *Dracula* (1931), and largely absent since his arrival on American soil: the lead role in a non-horror production, particularly one that was not reliant on his persona of Lugosi the Foreigner.

True, there had already been efforts in that same direction. In 1933, for example, the *Hollywood Reporter* announced that Lugosi would play a featured role in *The Whipping Boss*, a story about the cruelties of southern chain gangs. It may well have been a reworking of the 1924 silent film of the same name. William Sistrom (who had earlier served as associate producer on the 1931 film *The Black Camel* with Lugosi) would produce and Howard Higgin (who would later write the original story that became *The Invisible Ray* in 1936 with Karloff and Lugosi) would direct.[14] But the project never got off the ground. It stalled and then died.

It would seem that Lugosi obtained the rights to *Pagan Fury* directly from Warshawksy (who seems to have regained them after the 1932 sale did not lead to a stage production). At any rate, *Pagan Fury* was stalled again in February 1934, with the Lugosis having to leave New York for Hollywood around the third week of that month.

Edgar G. Ulmer was to direct *The Black Cat* (1934) at Universal, uniting the team of Boris Karloff and Bela Lugosi for the very first time. It also marked Lugosi's return to the Universal lot for the first time in over two years.[15] Shooting on *The Black Cat* began on February 28, 1934, and, with retakes, wrapped about a month later on March 28.[16]

No more was heard of Belian Productions, at least in the trade press, but that does not mean *Pagan Fury* disappeared. Quite the contrary.

On March 22, 1934, even while *The Black Cat* was still in production, Lugosi wrote a letter to his old New York City friend, Dr. Edmond Pauker. The impetus was not a happy one. Lugosi had just received a telegram from the American Arbitration Association, requesting his presence at a hearing.

Warshawsky was attempting to regain the rights to *Pagan Fury* and/or be compensated for its delayed Chicago production. Lugosi told Pauker:

I have just finished my three-week job and have an offer for a next one with an early start which prevents me to be present personally at the hearing. You can understand that I cannot afford to throw away a rare opportunity of earning some money.

So I beg you to help me out of my cornered situation and ask Mr. Abramson that he shall accept my representation. In case Mr. Abramson could not be persuaded at all please try somebody else whom you judge fit, either another producer or Mr. Osso. I rely on your judgment entirely – Whom ever [sic] you choose please hand them all the enclosed documents. It is certainly understood that the American Arbitration Association should not know that you, one of the Arbitrators, are helping me to get my representor [sic] and it should be handled in a discreet way.

After I finish my next film I intend to return to New York to discuss my future with you which will be much easier not being worried for existence.

If I can do anything for you here in Hollywood before I leave for New York I would like to be at your service. Thanking you for your friendly feelings and for your so valuable advices [sic] and help...

Denison Clift, who directed Lugosi in *The Mystery of the Mary Celeste* (aka, *Phantom Ship*, 1935 GB/1937 USA), had written a scenario for *Gambling in Souls* (1919). Sam Warshawsky had written the story on which the scenario was based. *(Courtesy of Randy Nesseler)*

PS. Abramson would be the most qualified man to represent me but I know he is dicussted [*sic*] of Mr. Warshawsky's attitude and advised me the time I spoke to him about it to drop the whole matter, so I really don't know whether he would represent my spirit which still believes profoundly in *Pagan Fury* you will see and know.[17]

Lugosi apparently remained eager to produce *Pagan Fury*, but hoped to make another film before returning to New York and/or Chicago. Given that he was more interested in the play than he was in yet another horror film, his motives were probably financial.

Lugosi Back to Stage

Bela Lugosi will assume the star role in Sam Warshawsky's play, "Pagan Fury," which is slated for spring production.

From *Motion Picture Daily* of January 15, 1934.

● ● ● ACTING UNDER the green spot . . . . must be gloating glee for that mysterious gent Bela Lugosi . . . . This ʀtage and screen diabolist . . . . has just removed himself from "Murder at the Vanities" . . . . . . to . . . . . . "Pagan Fury" . . . . . a sweet little cut-throat tome . . . . . . by that peaceful citizen Sam J. Warshawsky . . . . . . who learned playwriting in the RKO publicity department . . . . . . Sam's play opens in Chicago soon . . . . . . and as we ʜad his first dittie "The Woman of Destiny" . . . . we predⁱⁿt that much will be left on the cutting room floor . . . . aftⁱ the screen adaptations are made . . . . . .

Published in *Film Daily* on January 16, 1934.

And yet he was certainly not eager to attend the arbitration hearing. After all, he didn't work on his next two productions in Hollywood – the serial *The Return of Chandu* (1934) and the feature *Gift of Gab* (1934) – until July 1934. Perhaps he was in negotiations for some unknown film project that failed to happen (or proceeded without his participation), hence his inability to travel to New York. But that is merely speculation, and one could just as easily speculate that he concocted an excuse so as not to have to face Warshawsky at the hearing and/or that he wanted the hearing to be delayed until he had enough cash to move the play into production.

On April 4, 1934, Dr. Pauker responded to Lugosi, bringing him up to date on the hearing's status:

I tried to persuade Mr. Abramson to represent you in the arbitration procedure but he explained that the Warshawskys being his friends he could not very well accept the appointment. As to your suggestion to have Mr. Osso representing you, this is also impossible since I would not be considered as impartial if a person of my office would represent you in this matter. I think Mr. Abramson's suggestion is the best. He suggests that you appoint a lawyer to represent you before the Arbitration Association. He believes that a lawyer would accept doing it for a fee of about $25 to $50. The papers you have sent me are untouched in the envelope. If you appoint a lawyer I would hand them over to him as they are.[18]

Pauker added that, despite his reservations, he would have attended the March 21 hearing on Lugosi's behalf, but it was postponed because "the other parties could not be gotten together."

Perhaps Pauker's letter took several days to reach Lugosi's hands. Perhaps not. But Lugosi did not write back until April 24, which might suggest that he considered the matter for a week or two before making up his mind as to how to respond:

Lugosi (second from right) on the set of *Gift of Gab* (1934); Boris Karloff is on the far left.

Since you are not sold 100% with the play I decided to call off the whole matter, voided my contract with Mr. Warshawsky, and I informed both the Arbitration Assoc., and Mr. Warshawsky accordingly. So you do not have to bother about the whole matter anymore. I thank you for your courtesy and friend ship [*sic*]. Please look over the documents I sent you and I leave it to your judgment which of them you would destroy or return to me.[19]

Unless it came via phone or in some missing correspondence, Pauker did not actually say that he wasn't "sold 100%" with the play. Here Lugosi may have merely concocted a polite excuse to extricate himself from the entire matter, perhaps because he could not raise enough money to produce the play.

But he was certainly not willing to give up on the idea of becoming his own producer. In the same letter to Pauker, Lugosi wrote:

Mr. Ernest Cortis has a most wonderful play [an apparent reference to Cortis' *Fiarri*]. He just sent me a copy and one to Mr. Abramson. To my estimation I am sure it would be a second *Dracula*, please find out from Mr. Abramson everything about it and act accordingly to your own best judgment.

The Lugosis in the mid-1930s.

Along with considering potential stories for live theatre, Lugosi also believed he could try to do what Hepburn would later do with *The Philadelphia Story*. His letter to Pauker continues:

> Universal is figuring on signing me up for several other pictures, so they are open and out to acquire proper vehicles for me. That is my tip for you to approach Universal with stories you handle. How about, Jokay's *Aranyember* [*Golden Man*], *Facia Negra* [*Black Face*], *Pater Peter* [*Father Peter*] and *Fejedelem* [*The Prince*] etc? I would suggest that we keep in constant contact with each other and work in our mutual interest.[20]

Whether Lugosi or Pauker actually discussed these ideas with anyone at Universal is unknown. None of the stories seem to have had in them the cinematic makings of *The Philadelphia Story*.

Pauker apparently contacted Cortis about *Fiarri*; at least, he promised Lugosi that he would.[21] But no movement occurred, not until April of 1936. That month, *Variety* announced Lugosi might star in a production of *Fiarri* at Hollywood's Music Box Theatre.[22] Once again the unproduced play vanished from the industry news, but it resurfaced again over a year later. In September 1937, *Film Daily* mentioned there was a "possibility" Lugosi might appear in a Broadway version of the show for producer Jack Linder.[23]

Though they never made it to the stage, *Pagan Fury* and *Fiarri* were not alone in their ability to capture Lugosi the Producer's imagination. Speaking about his plans in a Los Angeles newspaper, Lugosi explained, "Every time I get my thoughts centered on a role that I believe fits me, some other actors – and always great actors – get there first. So, what am I to do? I figured out that, so now I'll finance my own company and star in pictures that I want to play in."[24]

On September 16, 1935, *Daily Variety* told readers that *Cagliostro* would be the first film under the auspices of the new Lugosi company:

> Story, concerning life of Guiseppe [*sic*] Balsamo, Italian charlatan, is based on original by Andre de Soos and historical research of Lugosi. Al Kingston, who is negotiating the deal, flies east this week to arrange for release of product.[25]

The film never went before the cameras, nor did Lugosi's other efforts along similar lines.

In 1939, some two years before Universal produced *The Wolf Man* (1941), Lugosi purchased the rights to the Barkley Davis werewolf story *The Howling Death*. He told one journalist that it brimmed with "plenty of raw meat horror."[26] At roughly the same time, he also acquired the rights to *The Mysterious Abbe*, *The Witches of Sabbath*, *Torquemade* (a tale of terror set during the Spanish inquisition), and *The Emperor of Atlantis* (authored by Lugosi's friend Manly P. Hall). Those were all in addition to *The Sect of the Assassins*, coauthored by Barkley Davis and Lugosi himself.[27]

Like Belian, Lugosi's film companies and the literary rights he purchased came to naught. Nevertheless, revisionism is indeed necessary in the assessment of Lugosi's business acumen. Despite the fact his own projects did not get off the ground (and that he seems to have been poor at managing his personal funds), these were indeed his own projects. Whether trying to produce his own stage plays or his own movies, Lugosi was ahead of the curve in the early-to-mid 1930s, his efforts keenly prescient of what actors of the future would increasingly do, time and again.

(Endnotes)

1   D'Arc, James V. "Oral History Interview, Donlevy, Lillian Lugosi." L. Tom Perry Special Collections Library, Harold B. Lee Library, Brigham Young University, Provo, Utah. 20 May 1976.
2   For a lengthy discussion of the casting of the Frankenstein Monster, see: Rhodes, Gary D. *Bela Lugosi, Dreams and Nightmares* (Narberth, Pennsylvania: Collectables/Gotham, 2007).
3   Daly, Phil M. "Along the Rialto." *Film Daily* 16 Jan. 1934.
4   "Theatrical Notes." *New York Times* 13 Nov. 1933.
5   "Fox to Present Witty Picture." *Spokane Daily Chronicle* (Spokane, WA) 13 Aug. 1932. The catalog for the United States Copyright Office notes that Warshawsky copyrighted *Radical Lilly*, an operetta in three acts, on 26 Oct. 1916; he did the same with *Radical Rose*, also an operetta in three acts, on 16 Nov. 1916.
6   "Fox to Present Witty Picture."
7   "Newcomer to *Murder at the Vanities*." *New York Sun* 5 Dec. 1933.
8   "New Incorporations. New York." *Film Daily*. 5 Feb. 1934. Joseph P. Bicketon served as the attorney of record for the corporation. Like Lugosi, John Biro maintained a friendship with the Hungarian Count Michael (Mihály) Károlyi. Biro's brother Louis was a screenwriter for Alexander Korda's production company. For more information, see: Litván, György. *A Twentieth Century Prophet: Oskar Jászi, 1875 - 1957* (Budapest: Central European University Press, 2006).
9   "Coming and Going." *Film Daily* 7 Feb. 1934.
10   "News and Gossip of the Broadway Arena." *New York Times* 13 Jan. 1934.
11   "Bela Lugosi Acquires Play." *New York Times* 15 Jan. 1934.
12   Lugosi's statement here about a possible continuation of his vaudeville tour is supported by several period sources.
13   *Az Ember* (New York) 27 Jan. 1934, qtd. in Cremer, Robert. *Lugosi: The Man Behind the Cape* (Chicago: Henry Regnery, 1976).
14   "Sistrom To Make *The Whipping Boss*." *Hollywood Reporter* 16 Feb. 1933.
15   "Coming and Going." *The Film Daily* 7 Feb. 1934.
16   For more information on the production of *The Black Cat* (1934), see: Mank, Gregory William. *Bela Lugosi and Boris Karloff: The Expanded Story of a Haunting Collaboration, with a Complete Filmography of Their Films Together* (Jefferson, NC: McFarland, 2009).
17   Lugosi, Bela. Letter to Dr. Edmond Pauker. 22 Mar. 1934. [Available in the Edmond Pauker Papers, 1910-1957, Series I: Correspondence, 1915-1957, Box 42, Folder 11 at the New York Public Library/ Lincoln Center for the Performing Arts in New York.] Lugosi refers to *The Black Cat* (1934) as the first film, with the second likely being a follow up planned by Universal. As Universal delayed in finding a suitable property for Lugosi, *The Return of Chandu* (1934) by default became his next film assignment.
18   Pauker, Dr. Edmond. Letter to Bela Lugosi. 4 Apr. 1934. [Available in the Edmond Pauker Papers, 1910-1957, Series I: Correspondence, 1915-1957, Box 42, Folder 11 at the New York Public Library/ Lincoln Center for the Performing Arts.]
19   Lugosi, Bela. Letter to Dr. Edmond Pauker. 24 Apr. 1934. [Available in the Edmond Pauker Papers, 1910-1957, Series I: Correspondence, 1915-1957, Box 42, Folder 11 at the New York Public Library/ Lincoln Center for the Performing Arts.]
20   Ibid.
21   Pauker, Dr. Edmond. Letter to Bela Lugosi. 28 Apr. 1934. [Available in the Edmond Pauker Papers, 1910-1957, Series I: Correspondence, 1915-1957, Box 42, Folder 11 at the New York Public Library/ Lincoln Center for the Performing Arts.]

22   "Chinese Comedy for L.A." *Variety* 29 Apr. 1936.
23   "Lugosi for Broadway?" *Film Daily* 17 Sept. 1937.
24   Barnes, Eleanor. "Bela Lugosi to Produce Here." *Illustrated Daily News* (Los Angeles) 17 Sept. 1935.
25   "*Cagliostro* First Lugosi Indie." *Daily Variety* 16 Sept. 1935.
26   Mines, Harry. "Raves and Raps." *The Daily News* (Los Angeles) 18 June 1939.
27   Ibid.

Issue six of *Movie Comics*, dated September-October of 1939.

Chapter 5

Hollywood on Parade

After Tod Browning's film *Dracula* became a box-office success in 1931, American popular culture turned to Bela Lugosi for inspiration far more often than it did to Bram Stoker.

During Lugosi's lifetime, for example, other screen Draculas hued closely to his portrayal. However different they were physically and vocally, Lon Chaney, Jr. (in *Son of Dracula* in 1943) and John Carradine (in *House of Frankenstein* in 1944 and *House of Dracula* in 1945) are still infused with Lugosi's persona, certainly far more so than they are the bushy-haired and pointy-eared vampire in Stoker's novel.

Other Draculas came fast and furious after Lugosi's death in 1956; most of them evoked Lugosi to a greater or lesser degree. The clichéd, but still apt litany here would include everyone and everything from Christopher Lee and Frank Langella to Count Chocula and the Count von Count of *Sesame Street*. The continued dominance of the Lugosi Dracula over the Stoker description, or any other, for that matter, seems assured. Halloween decorations, greeting cards, video games: the list goes on and on.

Lugosi had scant opportunity to profit from such merchandise. In 1954, film director Ed Wood unsuccessfully tried to interest publishers in launching a Bela Lugosi comic book.[1] And the idea made sense. Horror comics flourished in the late forties and early fifties until Fredric Wertham's book *The Seduction of the Innocent* (1954) and Senator Estes Kefauver's subcommittee hearings on them forced the industry to develop a comic code that basically killed the genre.

There was no authorized Lugosi comic during his lifetime. The closest thing would be the sixth issue of *Movie Comics* in 1939, which featured an adaptation of the Lugosi serial *The Phantom Creeps*.

But there certainly were many other comics that appropriated Lugosi's persona. Even before the age of horror comics, a Lugosi-inspired vampire appeared on the cover of the

Weird Tales for June of 1936.

pulp magazine *Weird Tales* in June 1936, and – in a particularly notable example of his image trumping Stoker's vampire – artwork of Lugosi graced the cover of a 1947 edition of Stoker's novel. Then, once the horror comic craze got underway, Lugosi-inspired vampires appeared repeatedly, as on the covers of *The Beyond* (January 1951), *Eerie* (June 1952), and *Eerie* (August 1953).[2]

Horror comic: what a curious phrase, one that can be so easily stated and restated without any thought given to its fascinating contradiction. Strictly speaking, the word "comic" here refers not to humor, but instead to a particular medium, one with roots in humor, but one that expanded to include superheroes and scary monsters. Those who railed against horror comics saw little in them to laugh about, of course. Nevertheless, "horror comic" in its most literal sense implies a marriage of two opposite emotions.

Opposite, but not unrelated. Horror literature, plays, and films had long incorporated comic relief before comic books incorporated horror. One need only witness Charles Gerrard's performance as Martin in Browning's *Dracula*. There are terrifying moments in such movies, and so occasional humor allows for tension relief. That was, at any rate, what many writers and directors believed.

In other cases, the two categories merged into gallows humor, that wicked and uncomfortable style of black comedy that James Whale masterfully employed in *The Old Dark House* (1932) and *Bride of Frankenstein* (1935). Lugosi participated in the same tradition thanks to such films as *Invisible Ghost* (1941) and – quite memorably – *One Body Too Many* (1944), in which his butler character seemingly tries to poison just about everyone in the film.

And then there is a third category: the horror parody. As early as 1957, less than one year after Lugosi's death, Gabriel Dell appeared in Dracula attire on *The Steve Allen Show* to do his Lugosi imitation, all for the sake of comedy. At roughly the same time, Lenny Bruce began incorporating a Lugosi-Dracula impression into his stand-up routine. In 1958, television horror host Zacherley scored a top-ten hit with his novelty song *Dinner with Drac*. Even jazz drummer Philly Joe Jones joined in the fun with his 1958 album *Blues for Dracula*; directly inspired by Lenny Bruce, Jones supplied his own Lugosi-Dracula impression on the record.[3]

Lugosi-Dracula spoofs became so plentiful in popular culture from 1957 to the present that they would require an entire book to chronicle. But their roots predate the likes of Gabriel Dell and Lenny Bruce.

Beyond simply reneging on his vow to never play the vampire again after Browning's *Dracula*, Lugosi soon indulged in lampooning his own vampire image. Of course, one could argue that even he was not the first to do so. In the 1931 film, Mina (Helen Chandler) chides Lucy (Frances Dade) about her infatuation with the Transylvanian count; she imitates Dracula's accent in a manner not all that different than stand-up comedians would do over 25 years later, but she does so in the very same film that made that accent iconic.

In the wake of Browning's *Dracula*, others would attempt something similar. Disney's cartoon *Mickey's Gala Premiere* (1933) features animated caricatures of Hollywood's most famous stars, ranging from Clark Gable and Mae West to Jimmy Durante and the Marx Brothers. Lugosi's Dracula, Fredric March's Mr. Hyde, and Boris Karloff's Frankenstein

A publicity portrait of
Lugosi for *The Gorilla* (1939).
(Courtesy of Kristin Dewey)

Monster are among the cartoon celebrities in attendance at the premiere of Mickey Mouse's new film. In like fashion, an animated Lugosi-like Dracula appears in the cartoon *G-Man Jitters* (1939).

But these examples represent a distinct history apart from Lugosi spoofing himself. The first time he parodied his own image came in *Hollywood on Parade* No. A8, a short subject released in February 1933. As Chapter 2 noted, Lugosi arguably does not play Dracula in the short, but he does not quite play himself either. Rather, he plays a wax figure of "Bela Lugosi as Dracula," a fictionalized convergence of the two. Once the wax figure comes to life, he attempts to bite Betty Boop (Mae Questel) after intoning the comical line: "Betty... you have booped your last boop!" Cue audience laughter, even though the same basic action sent chills down moviegoers spines in 1931 and presumably did the same to at least a few Oregonians in Portland in 1932.

Lugosi would occasionally attempt to inspire horror comedy in the years that followed, whether in films like *The Gorilla* (1939) and *Mother Riley Meets the Vampire* (1952), or when he guest-starred on radio and television programs, and – more commonly still – at live appearances in theatres and nightclubs.

For Lugosi, the combination of horror and comedy accelerated in the 1940s, including in stage plays like *Arsenic and Old Lace*. But more than anywhere else, he honed the use of horror comedy, particularly the spoofing of Dracula, at a large number of vaudeville appearances. Vaudeville: that wonderfully American tradition in which theatres in large cities and small towns presented live acts of all kinds – drama, comedy, music, and more – usually on balanced programs that gave audiences a chance to see all of those genres during the space of a single afternoon or evening.

Here, then, we might reconsider whether the phrase "horror comic" really does constitute a contradiction of terms, at least in this context, when Hollywood star Bela Lugosi was himself on parade.

Vaudeville

By the time Lugosi left the cast of *Murder at the Vanities,* he was still in financial trouble, and the delays with *Pagan Fury* did not help. His bankruptcy was finalized on November 9, 1933, but at roughly the same time, the Internal Revenue Service filed a lien against him for $265 owed on his 1932 taxes.[4] Days later, *Film Daily* reported that Lugosi planned a vaudeville tour using *Dracula* as the basis for his sketch.[5] Quite likely, these events were related. In other words, here was an opportunity to generate money quickly. And so, Lugosi made his vaudeville debut in December 1933.

Lugosi had originally considered such a tour over one year earlier. Perhaps he sensed vaudeville could expand his public visibility, allowing him to reach out to his fans in person, as well as (crucially) to make extra money. In October 1932, *Variety* reported that Lugosi "is planning a picture house tour with a condensed version of *Dracula*, the play in which he would play the lead and produce it himself. Lugosi has opened negotiations with Louis Cline, theatrical rep for Horace Liveright, who produced the play."[6]

Lugosi and Frances Dade in *Dracula* (1931).

The negotiations were successful, as Lugosi was one of a group of Hollywood stars – the others being Lowell Sherman, Edward Everett Horton, H. B. Warner, and ZaSu Pitts – who were each offered a one-week engagement by the RKO theatre circuit.[7] Lugosi was serious enough that he considered investing $2,000 of his own money to develop an act.[8] But then he changed his mind. The RKO chain couldn't guarantee him enough bookings to ensure a return on the investment.[9] (This was a relatively common concern for stars considering vaudeville, as the necessary time and money upfront to develop an act were sometimes deemed too risky for brief bookings.)

While vaudeville thrived in America from the 1880s to the early 1930s, it also began a very slow but inexorable death at roughly the same time that Lugosi became interested in it. The reasons were many. In 1932, *Variety* noted three causes of the decline: comedy acts were beginning to lose the necessary connection with live audiences who were increasingly distracted by the films being projected on the same bills (as well as their newfound ability to move from seat to seat, instead of remaining in reserved seats); the drama on the screen itself became too much competition for the live dramatic acts; and free radio broadcasts were more enticing than paying to see similar fare on the stage.[10]

From the *Brooklyn Eagle* of December 5, 1933.

At time went on, though, Lugosi came to rely on vaudeville as an important component of his career, particularly in the late forties, when it was still dying, and yet still living as well. And he was often successful at it, appearing live onstage in brief sketches, rather than in three-act plays like *Murder at the Vanities*. Consider the following recollection from Pat Abernathy, a vaudeville veteran who worked with Lugosi around 1948:

New York City... so many theatres in the area and they all had a big stage and a place down below for the orchestra. We played those kind of theatres. And we would play with different acts. We had an agent who set up the things. And [Lugosi] just appeared with us.

... [In the act] he talked about where he was from and his background. He had a dark outfit on. The audience enjoyed him very much. He did some talking himself and then we got up there and talked with him. Did kind of a little act with him. It was improvised. But he really was impressive.

... We basically m.c.'d the Lugosi show. We had no problems with him. He had a good sense of humor.[11]

Abernathy's memories are important, attesting as they do to Lugosi's ability to improvise in live and sometimes unpredictable settings.

Lugosi's wife Lillian, who occasionally performed the role of the hypnotized maid in his vaudeville act in the forties, once told author Robert Cremer:

Vaudeville was much more difficult than the legitimate stage, because there was no invisible curtain separating you from the audience. You had to play to the audience, and timing was absolutely crucial. Bela had a wonderful sense of timing in building tension in the act. He was never out of character, even if the audience wasn't cooperative.[12]

Her snapshot memories – like Abernathy's – develop the picture of an actor capable of working successfully in the world of vaudeville.

The World Changes

Nearly a year and a half after initially considering vaudeville, Lugosi developed his *Dracula* act and signed for a four-theatre tour on the Loew's circuit, the booking long enough to merit his attention. The *New York Times* touted the chain's success in bringing Lugosi and (for a separate tour) Gregory Ratoff to its stages.[13] Live and onstage, Hollywood was to be on parade, numbering Lugosi among its vaudeville members for the first time.

Lugosi apparently used the latter part of November and early December 1933 to refine what became an 18-minute sketch. It began with an "explanatory trailer" that gave audiences narrative information about *Dracula–The Vampire Play*; whether the trailer was on film, spoken by a live narrator, or some combination of the two is unknown.

Then three live scenes were enacted: "First, the lover finds out his girl is a victim of a vampire; second, the boy ascertains who the vampire is; and last, the bloodsucker is done away with by means of a stake through his heart."[14] After that, Lugosi gave a curtain speech, breaking the fourth wall and talking directly to the audience.[15]

His act premiered at the Gates Theatre (2,868 seats) in Brooklyn, with advertisements promising, "Bela Lugosi (Dracula Himself) In Person."[16] The local press echoed the big news: "Brooklyn theatre audiences will have their first opportunity at seeing Dracula in the flesh when he begins a personal stage appearance today."[17]

Published in the *New York Evening Journal* on December 7, 1933.

Postcard depicting the Loew's State Theatre. (*Courtesy of Cezar Del Valle and Theatre Talks, LLC*)

The show played the Gates for three days, from December 5 through December 7, 1933.

Lugosi's act then moved to Loew's State Theatre (3,327 seats), a prestigious venue on Broadway in Manhattan, where it played from December 8 to 14. Also on the bill were Alex Hyde's all-girl orchestra (featuring Ruth Burns, Lois Sterner, and Lucille Kemp); Lew Parker's company (supported by Paul Murdock, George Townes, Marion Bailer and Bill Burdee, the group presenting Bob Hope's comedy act with the famous star's permission); singer Al Wohlman (who performed some old-fashioned pop songs with Harry Carroll); and – as the opening act – the Gay Boys, a team of five acrobats.[18] The entire vaudeville bill lasted 73 minutes.[19]

On the screen was Paul Muni in *The World Changes* (1933), a drama produced by First National. In the film, Muni played a man who becomes rich and notable, but handles his success poorly. Mary Astor portrayed his wife.

City newspaper notices were largely favorable to the bill and to Lugosi, even though they gave it brief coverage. The *New York Herald Tribune* claimed his act was "somewhat more novel than the ordinary headline piece"; the *Evening Journal* believed that, even in condensed form, the play was "just as gripping as ever."[20]

By contrast, trade publications spoke at length about Lugosi's act. *Billboard* published not one, but two reviews of it, the first of which was printed on December 16, 1933:

This current five-acter looks like a return to the old days when Martin Beck reigned supreme in vaude. It's strictly one of those bills where an acrobatic act opens, a singing act heavy on dramatics follows, then a sketch, then a comedy act and last a band flash.

State Features Bela Lugosi In 'Dracula'

Bela Lugosi, he-vampire of the famous mystery play "Dracula," is headlining at Loew's State Theatre this week. The star has condensed the play, enacting again the role of the weird and fiendish "Count." In its present form the

From the *New York Evening Journal* of December 11, 1933.

Published in the *Daily Mirror* (New York) on December 8, 1933.

From the *Baltimore Post* of December 14, 1933.

[The *Dracula* sketch is] very effective thruout [*sic*] and portrayed excellently by Lugosi and the unbilled mixed team assisting him.[21]

The trade's second review came one week later. Although written by the same critic, it is unknown as to whether he saw the act twice, or simply wrote a second time about the same performance:

For his personal appearance, Bela Lugosi steers clear of the conventional and brings to vaude the long-lost dramatic sketch.... Starts off slow because of the audience straining to catch on to the talk, but soon picks up to become thoroughly effective and interesting. Staged cleverly.[22]

In both reviews, the critic recorded that the audience seemed thoroughly interested in Lugosi's act, but nevertheless gave it only limited applause.[23]

Variety's critic Chic also caught the show at Loew's State, but was less kind than his *Billboard* counterpart. He told readers that Lugosi's act was:

evidently lifted from the [*Dracula*] stage play rather than the screen. Done in three scenes and prefaced by an explanatory trailer. Probably outstanding bits in the play, but rather bare and unformed when lifted out.

Sheet music from 1933 featuring Mary Small.

Bits are where Lugosi meets Minna [*sic*] and the final scene in which he is deprived of his ghoulish powers. Latter is the letdown, for the actor who plays the character is too light to carry the scene over, with Lugosi merely in the traveling coffin and unable to help. In view of the responsibility, this part should have been competently cast. As it is, a light reading deprives the ending of its punch. Such demonstration as is made is more for the memory of the star's work in the picture than appreciation of his present offering. The girl does better, but has less responsibility.

Better than the usual 'When I Was In Hollywood' style of personal appearance, but the excerpts show how much the screen was able to do for the play.[24]

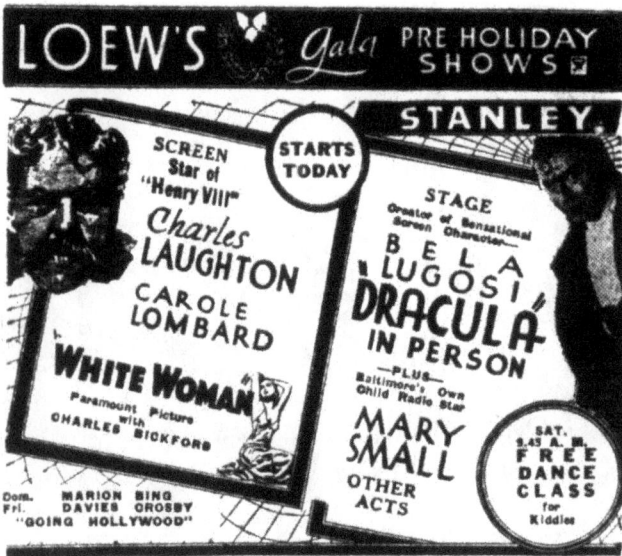

Published in the *Baltimore Post* on December 15, 1933.

On the same day, *Variety* published a second account of the State Theatre's show by the same critic, who added:

With Paul Muni on the screen and Bela Lugosi on the hoof, bill at the State has a decided picture tinge, which doesn't hurt any, though it doesn't seem to help much. House not better than usual Friday, though it's a better bill back of the foots than it looks in the newspapers.

Lugosi … does excerpts from *Dracula* and then, apparently by design, breaks down such effect as he may have created with a comedy curtain speech which he opens with a hope that the audiences will not suffer permanently from the chills. Helpful to the next act, but Lugosi would leave a stronger impression by sticking to character.[25]

In other words, Lugosi went beyond simply breaking the fourth wall. He introduced humor in his closing remarks. Here was a kind of horror comic.

During the early thirties, quite likely at the Loew's State, Violet Holler and her mother Rose set out to watch Lugosi's act. Violet's own daughter Barbara later recalled:

My mother and grandmother were also Hungarian nationals by birth, so when Lugosi came out on stage, mother, who, I guess was seated in one of the first few rows, called out to him in Hungarian. Happy to hear his native language, Lugosi had invited my mother and grandmother backstage, and together they shared cups of tea and some delicious Hungarian Apple Strudel...

Grandmother looked at him with sort of a jaundiced eye, since she wasn't sure if he was a real vampire or not, so convincing was his role. True also, was that grandmama was born a town or two away from Lugosi, which was quite near Transylvania and the Carpathian Mountains... so grandmother was not taking any chances, and the meeting came to a close almost immediately after the cups of tea and strudel were enjoyed! I guess she wanted to get out of there before there was a full moon, or whatever condition delights a true "vampire"![26]

[Lugosi also] offered them Tokay wine, which was his favorite, and they spent a lot of time toasting each other as well as toasting his success in the *Dracula* film.[27]

For many years thereafter, Violet corresponded with Lugosi, who had made a lasting impression on her.

The vaudeville show grossed $17,000 at the Loew's State, enough that the theatre had "no complaints."[28] From there, Lugosi immediately travelled to Baltimore, Maryland, playing one week at Loew's Stanley (3,287 seats), from December 15 to 21, 1933.

Though Lugosi does not seem to have changed his act, the rest of the Stanley bill was completely different. In support of Lugosi were Mary Small (a child contralto who had her own radio show); Grems,

From the *Washington Post* of December 22, 1933.

Fitz, and Murphy Brothers (comedians), the Jans and Lynton Review (music and tap dancing with Frankie Little, Joan Zappa, and Jimmy Smith), and Happy Harrison's Trained Animals.[29] On the screen was *White Woman* (1933), featuring Charles Laughton, with whom Lugosi had appeared in *Island of Lost Souls* (1932). Once again Lugosi was part of a traditional balanced program that evoked the vaudeville of earlier years.

Critical reviews of Lugosi in Baltimore were few in number, but certainly favorable:

With proper regard for his fans, and with the aid of two assistants, [Lugosi] offers a tabloid version of his thriller role, *Dracula*. It is a neat and novel attraction for the variety stage. In a curtain speech, Mr. Lugosi steps out of his character and assures us he is not a bad fellow after all – not nearly so bad as the big bad wolf![30]

Similarly, the *Baltimore American* claimed, "Reports have it that he often forgets that he is supposed to be the 'terror of the screen' long enough to chat with little children or pet some stray hound."[31]

The final stop for Lugosi's month-long tour was Washington D. C. at Loew's Fox Theatre (3,433 seats). The booking lasted from December 22 through December 28, 1933. On the screen were Jack Oakie and Ginger Rogers in *Sitting Pretty* (1933), as well as Disney's cartoon *The Night Before Christmas* (1933). On the stage were Al Gordon and His Canines (a dog act), the Three Sailors (slapstick comedians who had worked in *Earl Carroll's Sketch Book* in 1929), Nat Brusiloff and His Band (popular music), and Phil Lampkin's Fox concert orchestra, which performed a "Christmas version" of Rubinstein's *Kamennoi-Ostrow*.[32]

Published in the *Washington Post* on December 25, 1933.

The *Washington Daily News* was unimpressed, dismissing Lugosi's act as "mediocre" and complaining that Dracula was old news, that the "picture was made a long time ago."[33] Giving a brief description of the act, the city's *Evening Star* wrote that a "volley of drum music" acted as prelude to a "large bat which flies across the stage with an electric bulb stuck to its middle." From there, the "whittled down" version of the play unfolded, being cut to "such small proportions that most of the life has gone out of it."[34]

The key review appeared in the *Washington Post*. Its response was largely positive, even if it noted the inherent limitations that brief vaudeville acts faced:

On the stage, Bela Lugosi headlines the vaudeville goings-on in a condensed version of *Dracula*, which naturally loses much of the sustained suspense and... force of the longer play. Mr. Lugosi is still the ominous figure of the personified vampire bat, intent on bringing havoc into the lives of beautiful young women and it cannot be gainsaid that a considerable measure of horror still clings to the Bram Stoker drama.[35]

The *Post* also believed the overall bill represented an "excellent holiday program," one that was presented even on Christmas day.

On December 26, 1933, journalist Don Craig interviewed Lugosi backstage at the Fox Theatre in the "No. 1 dressing room." With the performances finished for the day, Lugosi removed his makeup while talking to Craig, who wanted to know if the actor was "still thrilled" to play Dracula. "No!" Lugosi exclaimed, "As a matter of fact, I'm sick of it!" Shifting into a more humorous tone, Lugosi laughed and asked Craig, "Suppose you were introduced as a vampire-bat every place you went? Well, that's the way it is with me. It's gotten so almost nobody but my wife calls me by my right name."[36]

Lugosi proceeded to explain that he liked the curtain speech in his vaudeville act better than the excerpts from *Dracula–The Vampire Play*. His reasoning: "I can show people that I really am not as bad as I look, you see." Craig soon left the dressing room and headed down a corridor for the elevator. Hearing a woman belting out *I Want to Be Happy* at the top of her lungs, he turned around. The singer was "Dracula's unhappy victim, Lucy, still dolled up in her white robe."[37] Horror and comedy met once again.

From the *Washington Post* of December 28, 1933.

Conclusion

To a large extent, Lugosi's 1933 *Dracula* sketch formed the foundation for all of his subsequent vaudeville, nightclub, and "spook show" appearances. An excerpt or two or even three from *Dracula–The Vampire Play*, and then direct an address to the audience that would often incorporate comedy, sometimes even with the assist of others in his act.

When corresponding in 1949 with a New York agent about obtaining new material for vaudeville and nightclub acts, Lugosi's request adhered to that same basic formula:

It just occurred to me that while Laszlo Bekeffy is in New York if you would try to get from him a couple dozen cabaret sketches which are suitable for vaudeville and night club. Keeping in mind what the general public expects from me. It is either mystery or horror, which may end in a comedy situation enabling the people to laugh off the horrible....[38]

During Lugosi's lifetime, he never had his own horror comic book. But in a world far from the pages of *Tales of the Crypt*, *The Vault of Horror*, and *Out of the Night*, Lugosi came to understand that at times the phrase "horror comic" was not quite as contradictory as it first seems.

(Endnotes)

1   For more information on Ed Wood's unrealized Lugosi projects, including the comic book, see: Rhodes, Gary D. *Bela Lugosi, Dreams and Nightmares* (Narberth, PA: Collectables, 2007).

2   While these comics featured Lugosi-like vampires, it is also true that many other horror comics of the era featured feral, animal-like vampires that appeared quite different than Lugosi.

3   "Reviews and Ratings of New Jazz Albums." *Billboard* 29 Dec. 1958.

4   "Times Square. News From the Dailies, Coast." *Variety* 14 Nov. 1933.

5   "Bela Lugosi in Vaude." *Film Daily* 22 Nov. 1933.

6   "Plan *Dracula* as TAB." *Variety* 11 Oct. 1932.

7   "Screen Names Leery of Accepting Vaude Dates with No Booking 'Time' Guarantee; Too Much of a Gamble." *Variety* 18 Oct. 1932.

8   Ibid.

9   Ibid.

10   "Vaude Coming Back – Beck." *Variety* 18 Oct. 1932.

11   Kaffenberger, Bill. Interview with Pat Abernathy. 24 Jan. 2013.

12   Cremer, Robert. *Lugosi: The Man Behind the Cape* (Chicago: Henry Regnery, 1976).

13   "Theatrical Notes." *New York Times* 25 Nov. 1933.

14   Harris, Sidney. "Bela Lugosi." *Billboard* 23 Dec. 1933.

15   Chic. "Variety House Reviews. State, N.Y." *Variety* 12 Dec. 1933.

16   "Loew's Leads in Brooklyn." *Brooklyn Eagle* 5 Dec. 1933.

17   "Lugosi at Gates." *Brooklyn Eagle* 5 Dec. 1933.

18   Information here compiled from various reviews, including: Harris, Sidney. "Lowe's State, New York." *Billboard* 16 Dec. 1933.

19   Harris, Sidney. "Lowe's State, New York." *Billboard* 16 Dec. 1933.

20   "Bela Lugosi, Film Villain, Playing at Loew's State." *New York Herald-Tribune* 9 Dec. 1933; "State Features Bela Lugosi in *Dracula*." *New York Evening Journal* 11 Dec. 1933.

21   Harris, Sidney. "Lowe's State, New York." *Billboard* 16 Dec. 1933.

22   Harris, Sidney. "Bela Lugosi." *Billboard* 23 Dec. 1933.

23   Harris uses the term "thoroughly" in his first review, though he spells it "thoroly" [*sic*].

24   Chic. "Vaudeville. New Acts. Bela Lugosi (3). *Dracula* 18 Mins. in Two and Three. State, N.Y." *Variety* 12 Dec. 1933.

25   Chic. "Variety House Reviews. State, N.Y." *Variety* 12 Dec. 1933.

26   Rothschild, Barbara. *New Jersey Memories*. http://www.virtualnetworknj.com/memories/ntheatre/rothschild01.htm. Accessed 13 May 2013. It is Mrs. Rothschild's view that this meeting between Lugosi and her mother and grandmother occurred after a screening of the film *Dracula* (1931) at a theatre in New Jersey while Lugosi was on a national in person tour to promote the film. This is problematic as there was no known live national stage tour by Lugosi at that time. It would seem far more likely that this incident occurred after one of the 1933 vaudeville performances. Perhaps the explanatory (and possibly cinematic) *Dracula* "trailer" that preceded Lugosi's live sketch act was mistaken for the actual feature film as the story was retold over the years.

27   Kaffenberger, Bill. Interview with Barbara Rothschild. 14 May 2013.

28   "Repeal Aids All Broadway B.O.'s, Even Holdovers; Music Hall With *Counselor* $96,000; Cap's $40,000 2d." *Variety* 12 Dec. 1933.

29   "Stanley Bill. Bela Lugosi and Mary Small on Stage." *Baltimore Post* (Baltimore, MD) 15 Dec. 1933; "Star of *Dracula* Tops Stage Bill At the Stanley." *Baltimore Sunday American* (Baltimore, MD) 17 Dec. 1933. Curiously, the short article in the *Baltimore Post* announced that Lugosi would "...present his own version of several mystery films, the scenes of which are included into a novelty vaudeville act." While this implied that the nature of the sketch had changed, the reviews of the later Washington, D. C. performances strongly suggest that the capsule version of *Dracula* had remained intact.

30   "Bela Lugosi Wins Fame Playing 'Horror' Parts." *Baltimore Sunday American* 17 Dec. 1933.

31   Ibid.

32   "Loew's Fox." *Washington Post* 23 Dec. 1933; "Next Week's Films." *The Evening Star* (Washington, D. C.) 21 Dec. 1933.

33   Craig, Don. "Man's Castle at Keith's; Fox Offers Sitting Pretty." *Washington Daily News* 23 Dec. 1933.

34   Melcher, E. de S. "Single Song Is Important to Fox Picture's Success." *The Evening Star* 23 Dec. 1933.

35   "Loew's Fox." *Washington Post* 23 Dec. 1933.

36   Craig, Don. *"Dracula* Proves Very Nice Person When He's Off-Stage." *Washington Daily News* 27 Dec. 1933.

37   Ibid.

38   Lugosi, Bela. Letter to Dr. Edmond Pauker. 16 Feb. 1949. [Available in the Edmond Pauker Papers, 1910-1957, Series I: Correspondence, 1915-1957, Box 42, Folder 11 at the New York Public Library/Lincoln Center for the Performing Arts in New York.]

A publicity portrait of Lugosi in *The Black Cat* (1934).
(Courtesy of Bill Chase)

Chapter 6

Expositions

Bela Lugosi's career changed in the years that followed *Dracula* (1931), but so did the horror film genre. As the years passed, critics usually gave less and less respect to genre films that were produced on lower and lower budgets. By the time of World War II, even the audience had changed, with youngsters making up a greater proportion of ticket-buyers than ever before.

Horror film characters – and the plots in which they appeared – evolved as well. Consider Universal's "monster rally" films of the forties. It would be reasonable to argue that the pairing of the title characters in *Frankenstein Meets the Wolf Man* (1943) led to the combined appearance of the Frankenstein Monster, the Wolf Man, and Dracula in *House of Frankenstein* (1944), *House of Dracula* (1945), and *Abbott and Costello Meet Frankenstein* (1948). Featuring just a single monster in one movie was no longer deemed sufficient. In fact, even three villains were not enough, as the aforementioned films also included a motley crew of mad doctors, hunchbacks, and/or villainous females.

All that said, such a historical narrative neatly skirts two important factors. Though the most famous Universal monsters did not meet one another inside horror movies of the thirties, that decade did see the rise of more than one monster featured in the running times of individual films. For example, *Dracula* (1931) and *Frankenstein* (1931) included vampire wives and a particularly cruel and disfigured lab assistant, respectively. *Daughter of the Dragon* (1931) and *The Mask of Fu Manchu* (1932) featured Fu Manchu and his depraved daughter. *White Zombie* (1932) sported zombies in the plural, just as *Island of Lost Souls* (1932) featured many a beast man. *Werewolf of London* (1935) actually gave viewers two werewolves, meaning Dr. Glendon and Dr. Yogami. Most famously of all, *Bride of Frankenstein* (1935) unleashed the Monster and his would-be mate on Depression-era moviegoers.

The other issue that should be considered is the fact that Hollywood's classic horror movies were founded not merely on what became recognizable monsters like Dracula and Frankenstein's Monster, but also on particular film stars and personalities. Unlike those American horror movies of the 1970s and 80s, in which a recognizable monster like Leatherface (in *The Texas Chain Saw Massacre* of 1974), Michael Myers (of *Halloween* in 1978), and Jason Voorhees (of *Friday the 13th* in 1980) could easily be portrayed by different actors in myriad sequels with their real-life names unknown to the general public, the earlier era relied as much or more on stars like Bela Lugosi, Boris Karloff, and Lon Chaney, Jr. as it did on monsters like Dracula, Frankenstein's Monster, and the Wolf Man.

Taken together, these factors suggest that the first really important pairing of Hollywood horror monsters was not *Frankenstein Meets the Wolf Man* (1943), but was instead *The Black Cat* (1934). No vampire or werewolf appears during its running time, but Bela Lugosi and Boris Karloff do. For the first time, two horror film stars were featured in the same movie. The rationale was much the same as would later guide a film like *House of Frankenstein*. Give audiences more monsters for the same money, and indeed the monsters in *The Black Cat* were larger than the narrative in which they appeared, meaning that Karloff and Lugosi's name value conjured memories of their earlier roles even while they themselves portrayed new characters.

That formula represents a key evolution in the 1930s horror film, one repeated on numerous occasions, as in the case of *The Raven* (1935), in which Lugosi's mad surgeon transforms Karloff's gangster into a hideous monster, a plotline that borrowed nearly as much from *Frankenstein* as it did from the Edgar Allan Poe poem on which it was ostensibly based. *The Raven* – which also incorporates sadistic torture and unbridled sexual desire – helped concretize the approach of pairing two horror movie stars in a single movie in order to heighten the terror content.

Here was an understandable marketing approach, even if its usage was also somewhat ironic. *The Raven* was released after the advent of the Production Code Administration. One of its many goals was to temper the use of violence and horror in a single film, rather than see it become heightened or amplified.

Bela Lugosi himself might have bemoaned the fact that he received second billing to Karloff in *The Black Cat* and *The Raven*, but his career nevertheless became increasingly dependent on the idea of teaming horror film stars. There were efforts that did not come to pass, such as an announcement in 1935 that Karloff and Lugosi would appear together in a film with Claude Rains and Colin Clive.[1]

And then there were the many movies that were produced, as in Lugosi's future work with Karloff in *The Invisible Ray* (1936), *Son of Frankenstein* (1939, which also included Basil Rathbone), *You'll Find Out* (1940, which also included Peter Lorre), and *The Body Snatcher* (1945), as well as in other films, such as those that featured him alongside Lon Chaney, Jr., Lionel Atwill, George Zucco, and/or John Carradine. And then there were efforts whereby Lugosi would be teamed with other monsters even if famous stars didn't portray them. In *The Ape Man* (1943), his mad scientist has a killer ape as a sidekick; in *The Return of the Vampire* (1944), his vampire has a werewolf lackey.

Similarly, we can return to 1935, the year of *The Raven*, and also consider Lugosi's (fake)

Lugosi, Karloff, and Lucille Lund in *The Black Cat* (1934).

Lugosi's zombies surround Beaumont (Robert Frazer, fourth from left) and grab Silver (Brandon Hurst, fourth from right) in *White Zombie* (1932). *(Courtesy of Kristin Dewey)*

vampire Count Mora being joined by the hauntingly memorable (and yet equally fake) vampire Luna in Tod Browning's *Mark of the Vampire* (1935). Two monsters in the same movie: its most striking publicity photographs depict both of them together, even though Luna was portrayed by the unknown actress Carroll Borland.

And so, the very approach that originated in earlier years – whether Lugosi teamed with Karloff in *The Black Cat* or, say, Lugosi's mad scientist accompanied by an ape in *Murders in the Rue Morgue* (1932), the latter being a recurrent monster in mystery stage plays and movies of the twenties – was by 1935 a cornerstone of Lugosi's Hollywood film career. Such would commonly be the case for more than two decades, including in Lugosi's final horror movie, *The Black Sleep* (1956); its cast also featured Basil Rathbone, Lon Chaney, Jr., John Carradine, and Tor Johnson.

By the mid-thirties, Lugosi's "in person" appearances often (though certainly not always) began to rely on a similar strategy, meaning that the actor was teamed either with other monsters (such as costumed "apes") or with other Hollywood stars, ranging from Boris Karloff to those made famous in non-horror movie roles.

Glad-Handing

In some cases, movie fans could only read about Lugosi's appearances with his fellow film stars, meaning those social events reported in the press that required personal invitations. It is true that Lugosi and his wife Lillian normally stayed at home or mingled with the Hungarian community in Los Angeles. As one newspaper account from 1935 claimed:

Carroll Borland and Bela Lugosi in a publicity portrait for *Mark of the Vampire* (1935).

Lugosi presenting a soccer trophy in the mid-1930s. *(Courtesy of Bill Chase)*

The present and fourth Mrs. Lugosi is a Hungarian girl who was Bela's secretary. Neither is acquainted with any Hollywood acting folk. Their friends are Hungarians, mostly all of long standing… 'Hollywood doesn't see much of me,' Lugosi commented, 'because I prefer the company of my wife, my dogs and my books. I suppose, because I don't go around much, that people have the impression I am a disagreeable guy. Oh, well, every man to his taste.'[2]

And yet, it would be incorrect to believe that the Lugosis were not acquainted with "any Hollywood acting folk." Lugosi did in fact appear at a variety of private Hollywood events and parties, even if he did so perhaps more for the sake of being friendly to the Right People in assist of his career than for pure pleasure.

For example, Lugosi attended the Western Association of Motion Picture Advertisers' (WAMPAS) meeting and show at the Writers Club in Hollywood on February 26, 1932. The event honored Carl Laemmle, Sr.'s 26th year in the motion picture business. Others present included Louella O. Parsons, Jean Hersholt, Anita Louise, Gloria Stuart, Onslow Stevens, Paul Kohner, and Lupita Tovar.[3]

During mid-February 1933, Lugosi made an impromptu appearance at Eugene Stark's Hollywood Cafe with his friend Willy Pogany; the two were entertained by actress Ferike Boros, who had appeared in *Svengali* in 1931.[4] Then, in the summer of that same year, Pogany hosted a tea party at his Hollywood hillside home for Lugosi and a number of other stars, among them Charlie Chaplin, Alice White, Claudette Colbert, and Adrienne Ames.[5]

However many of these parties he attended and whether or not he always enjoyed them is a matter apart from the various occasions when Lugosi did shake hands with everyday people, those movie fans who could only dream of attending parties with the likes of a Charlie Chaplin. As *Murder at the Vanities*, *Murdered Alive*, and the Portland version of *Dracula–The Vampire Play* illustrate, those who loved seeing Lugosi the star onscreen could thrill to him onstage, if they were fortunate enough to live near the venues and could afford the price of admission.

But then there were Lugosi's *other* appearances, personal appearances that found him attending various public ceremonies and events, ranging from soccer matches and political rallies to movie premieres. Not unexpectedly, many of Lugosi's personal appearances cast him in the role of the "horror man of the movies" or as "Dracula himself." His wife Lillian once recalled:

> This one time, it was a publicity stunt – I don't know where we were – someplace back east, the theatre thought it would be great publicity to have the reporters come to the hotel and have a casket in there. Well, the maids wouldn't come into the room....[6]

Directory of Places to Go at Exposition Today

Aerial image of the San Diego Exposition, published in the *San Diego Union* on May 29, 1935.

Frightening the staff may have been less the intent than frightening fans, but even then, Lugosi's personal appearances were tempered in their design, bearing a dual purpose. Goose pimples needed to number in high enough quantities as to preserve Lugosi's image, but not quite so many as to make fans too terrified to lay eyes on him in person, whether to ogle him from a distance or even to nervously approach him with pen and paper in hand.

And those fans sometimes approached not only Lugosi, but others that might be with him. For example, on March 14, 1934, Lugosi and Karloff famously appeared together at Universal Pictures to judge black cats in a contest used to publicize *The Black Cat*. No invitation was necessary for local kids to parade their ebony-colored pets in front of the two horror stars, but the studio did require that each of them leave with cats-in-hand.[7] The winning pet-owner received $15, but in a sense all of the attendees won, as they got to meet the two most famous horror movie stars in the world.

The California Pacific International Exposition

Of all of Lugosi's personal appearances during the 1930s, none remains more fascinating than his featured spot at the California Pacific International Exposition, held in San Diego during the spring of 1935. Expositions of this type had a long history, dating to at least 1791; such events regularly presented fairgoers with exhibits that ranged from science and

AMERICA'S EXPOSITION, SAN DIEGO, CALIFORNIA   5A-H1151

Postcard featuring the Hollywood Pavilion at the San Diego Exposition in 1935.

industry to the arts and world cultures. By the late nineteenth century, expositions featured the cinema as well, both as an emergent technology and as an entertainment medium.

Designed in part to promote and support the San Diego economy during the Great Depression, the Pacific International Exposition took place at the city's famous Balboa Park.[8]

Along with incorporating the already-standing Spanish Colonial Revival buildings, architect Richard Requa designed new halls inspired by Columbian structures and temples. Other buildings included a reproduction of London's Globe Theatre, the Ford Building (later home to the San Diego Air and Space Museum), and the Ford Bowl, an amphitheatre used for concerts.[9] Some 2,700 persons worked on the massive construction project.[10]

Hundreds of exhibits were assembled, including the Palace of Travel and Transportation, the Standard Oil Tower to the Sun, the House of Charm, Modeltown and Modernization Magic, the Palace of Better Housing, the Palace of Natural History, the Spanish Village, Zoological and Botanical Gardens, the Palace of Fine Arts, and the Palace of Photography. More exotic displays presented the Lost Continent of Mu, the One-Ton Mechanical Man, and the Zoro Garden Nudist Colony.[11]

To entice movie fans, another exhibit featured Gold Gulch, a "moviefied version" of a western town from the "riproaring '49 days." Famed art director Harry Oliver designed the Hollywood-style set, which became the Expo's largest concession.[12] Just prior to working on the project, Oliver designed the sets for *Mark of the Vampire*.

Even more evidence of Tinseltown's presence in San Diego came at the Hollywood Motion Picture Hall of Fame, held in what later became known as the Palisades Building. Created in the American Southwest Pueblo-style, the structure housed a museum sponsored by the Screen Actors Guild.[13] It included a functional sound stage, a variety of movie memorabilia from famous films, and other "movie oddities" to attract visitors on its opening day, Wednesday, May 29, 1935.[14]

Lugosi was but one of several actors who appeared at the exhibit in person when it was launched. On May 29, 1935, the *San Diego Union* reported:

A host of motion picture stars will perform on sets in the Hollywood Hall of Fame today as one of the Exposition's bright spots opens its doors.

Cameras will turn as the actors begin 'making pictures' in the spacious hall.

Among those who will greet visitors to the Hollywood of the Exposition are Francis Lederer, Lee Tracy, Binnie Barnes, Thelma Todd, Warren William, James Gleason, Robert Young, Ralph Morgan, Bela Lugosi, Edward Arnold and Lucille Gleason.

Officials of the motion picture guild [were] here preparing for the gala opening at the Hall of Fame yesterday and [said] other stars would make the building their headquarters.[15]

Others in attendance included Anita Louise, Estelle Taylor, and Katherine DeMille (daughter of Cecil B). Lillian Lugosi was also present, wearing what a local newspaper called a "smart white suit."[16]

The *Union* added that Warren William (who would later costar with Lugosi in *The Wolf Man* in 1941) and Thelma Todd (who had already appeared opposite Lugosi in *Broadminded* in 1931) were among the first to arrive at the Expo. Once the others appeared, the celebrities "traveled through the grounds,"

Crowds at the San Diego Exposition in 1935.

A film frame from the 1935 newsreel depicting the Exposition's "Hollywood Motion Picture Hall of Fame."

Frame from the 1935 newsreel depicting the interior of the Hollywood Motion Picture Hall of Fame.

Frame from the 1935 newsreel depicting Lugosi bowing just prior to kissing an actress's hand.

regularly being "stopped by visitors asking for autographs, photographs, and a lot of 'oh–are you so-and-so?'"[17]

However, despite the high expectations of its promoters, the Hall of Fame may not have become a major financial success. *Daily Variety* reported:

[The] Pacific International Exposition started with a bang, getting 101,000 first two days, most of the crowd coming from San Diego... First two days saw tight purses with everyone looking and few buying... Indicated as best money draw of the concessions is the Hollywood Hall of Fame, but with Actors' Guild, Dominos, fair and Fanchon and Marco all cutting in on take, it's doubtful if profit will be heavy. Opening day had Thelma Todd, Bela Lugosi, Walter McGrail, Richard Tucker, Jean Hersholt, Madge Evans and Victor Jory doing scenes from picture in set with all the studio apparatus.[18]

Not surprisingly, a similar view appeared only days later in the weekly edition of *Variety*:

Permanent act, the Grace Moore dressing room from *Sing Me a Love Song*, is the background for the acting. Stars and picture names are supposed to appear daily and work in scenes from pictures. Mob went for it opening day with Bela Lugosi, Thelma Todd, Walter McGrail, Kenneth Thompson and others of similar caliber appearing.

Lugosi in *The Raven* (1935).

However, for two bits, fans wanted to see Gable and Crawford. Though it looks like a strong moneymaker, concession will probably not show much of a net profit to any of the owners....[19]

In other words, along with its inherent challenges with turning a profit, it seems that at least some audience members believed that a 25-cent admission fee should have bought them the chance to see bigger names.

Unfortunately, it is difficult to determine whether Lugosi appeared at the Exposition for just a single day or – given inexact writing in two reviews – for perhaps as many as six days.[20] Either way, he quite likely enjoyed making this personal appearance, perhaps more than any other of his post-*Dracula* (1931) period. Here he was not wearing a cape and not scaring anyone.

Instead, as evidenced in surviving Universal newsreel footage, Lugosi appeared in a romantic role, portraying a man trying to impress a woman while at the same time attempting to shoo away his competition.[21] Ironically, then, Lugosi's appearance at the Expo gave audiences a demonstration of a type of film role that he had not played onscreen for some years.

And he was not assuming his pre-horror romantic roles with a cast of unknowns. Rather, he was part of a contingent of stars and featured players, none of them known for horror.

Beyond San Diego

Lugosi continued to appear at various events during the rest of 1935, including private parties. In September 1935, Lugosi, Karloff, and Peter Lorre were guests at a "gorgeous house party" given by actress and opera soprano Lily Pons; the press claimed that the horror trio tried to "scare the daylights out of each other" and that "straight-jackets" were provided for the guests who couldn't withstand the chills.[22] The following month, Carl Laemmle, Sr. invited Lugosi to a reception that Universal gave for opera singer Marta Eggerth. One publication told readers, "As she sang a group of Hungarian songs, Bela Lugosi (yes, the horror man) brushed a tear from his eyes...."[23]

On July 4, 1935, he appeared onstage at the Roxy in New York to promote *The Raven*.[24] Then, in November of the same year, Lugosi was named honorary president of the Los Angeles Soccer League.[25] In the mid-thirties, he regularly appeared at soccer games in the city and just as regularly signed autographs for fans attending the same.

In the years that followed, Lugosi's attendance at private Hollywood parties seems to have dwindled even as the number of his public personal appearances increased. To be sure, he would at times appear on his own or assisted by little-known actors. But in many cases – whether it would be with famous celebrities or with unknowns in monster costumes (such as the "apes" that accompanied him on occasion in the early fifties) – Lugosi often teamed with others when he was "In Person," following in the path of such films and events as *The Black Cat*, *The Raven*, and the California Pacific International Exposition.

(Endnotes)

1   Glass, Madeline. "Clive of England." *Picture Play Magazine* July 1935.
2   Keavy, Hubbard. "Hollywood Chatter." *The State Journal* (Springfield, IL) 14 Nov. 1935.
3   "WAMPAS Entertain at the Writers' Club." *Hollywood Filmograph* 27 Feb. 1932.
4   "Eugene Stark Is Making Popular Spot Out of Henry's." *Hollywood Filmograph* 11 Feb. 1933.
5   "Happy Days Are Here Again!" *The New Movie Magazine* Aug. 1933.
6   D'Arc, James V. "Oral History Interview. Donlevy, Lillian Lugosi." L. Tom Perry Special Collections Library, Harold B. Lee Library, Brigham Young University, Provo, Utah. 20 May 1976.
7   "Blackest Tabby to Win Prize." *Los Angeles Times* 13 Mar. 1934.
8   "Directory of Places to Go at Exposition Today." *San Diego Union* 29 May 1935; Booth, Larry and Jane Booth. "Do You Want an Exposition?" Available at: http://www.sandiegohistory.org/journal/85fall/wantexpo.htm. Accessed 25 July 2014.
9   Ibid.
10 Amero, Richard W. "Planning and Preparation." *California Pacific Exposition, San Diego, 1935-36.* San Diego Historical Center. Available at: http://www.sandiegohistory.org/calpac/35expo99.htm. Accessed 25 July 2014.
11 "Directory of Places to Go at Exposition Today."; "Do You Want an Exposition?"
12 Ibid.
13 Ibid.
14 "Directory of Places to Go at Exposition Today."
15 "Hollywood Ready To Show Picture Tricks at Expo." *San Diego Union* 29 May 1935.
16 "Movie Stars Don Informal Expo Clothes." *San Diego Union* 3 June 1935.
17 "Hollywood Moves in to Start Work on Sets at Expo." *San Diego Union* 30 May 1935.
18 McCall, George. "Expo Pulls 101,000 in Two Days But They Look, Don't Spend." *Daily Variety* 31 May 1935.
19 "Nudes Romp At S.D. Expo; Plenty Bare -- And Henry Ford; Without Fliv Chief Fair Would Be Sadly Lacking - Gold Gulch a Bonanza; Midway Tame." *Variety* 5 June 1935.
20 Reviews of the Exposition from the *San Diego Union* and *Variety* seem to place Lugosi in San Diego on 29 May as well as 4 June. As a result, it is possible that Lugosi participated daily for six days in the moviemaking exhibitions.
21 Narrated by Graham McNamee (a radio broadcaster who acted in the 1934 film *Gift of Gab*, in which Lugosi and Karloff also appeared), and with the segment title *San Diego Exposition Is Opened*, this *Universal Newspaper Newsreel* segment ran about one minute and forty-two seconds. The following images are depicted: an overhead view of the exposition grounds, a parade, various crowds going through the byways and entering the exhibit buildings, the official California state flag, a front view of the Hollywood Pavilion, a long shot of a movie set, a shot of Lee Tracy, a shot of a cameraman, a medium shot of Lugosi wooing an actress; a long shot of Lugosi shooing away a rival, another shot of a cameraman; some scenes of the thrill rides on the exposition midway; a large Masonic parade and meeting, a large Catholic parade and meeting, and the brief closing credits. The newsreel was released on 5 June 1935.
22 "Today in Hollywood." *Hollywood* Oct. 1935.
23 Zigmond, Helen. "Our Film Folk." *Wisconsin Jewish Chronicle* (Milwaukee, WI) 29 Nov. 1935.
24 "Purely Personal." *Motion Picture Daily* 3 July 1935.
25 "Chatter!" *Daily Variety* 13 Dec. 1935.

Lugosi in a publicity still for
The Invisible Ray (1936).

Chapter 7

Rivers of Blood

There is nothing permanent except change. Heraclitus supposedly said that approximately 2,500 years ago, but it could just as easily appear inside a modern fortune cookie. Brief, but insightful; smart, but obvious.

Too much focus on Bela Lugosi's Hollywood typecasting – a form of character repetition in genre films that were themselves founded on recycling narratives – risks distracting from the regular flux of his career, its ebbs and flows.

When asked about his Hollywood films from 1939 onward, Lugosi emphasized change, but not quite in the manner that Heraclitus did. Rather, for Lugosi, there was a single marker, a monolith representing rapid evolution, or – perhaps more clearly – devolution.

It was the "British ban" on horror movies that began in 1936, a moment in time that became one of the most important in the history of the genre. In this case, change resulted in the overall cessation of Hollywood horror film production. Lugosi's film career stalled, at least in large measure.

For him, the year 1936 began with the January release of *The Invisible Ray* (1936). Costar Boris Karloff had a larger role and received top billing in a font-size that sometimes dwarfed Lugosi's name. But the movie allowed Lugosi to play something of a "good guy," rather than a villain. And his work in it did not go without praise. The critic for *Film Curb* was emphatic:

> I am not a Karloff fan. He never permits me to forget he is an actor. He brings the stage with him to the screen. ... In sharp contrast with Karloff's performance is the smooth, human, and intelligent one of Bela Lugosi. He is an artist who conceals all evidence of his art, never for a moment suggesting the actor playing a part. I cannot understand why we do not see him on the screen more often.[1]

The critic concluded his point by arguing that, "no cast strong enough to submerge him as one of its members could be assembled in Hollywood."

Lugosi with Gloria Holden, the actress who portrayed the title role of *Dracula's Daughter* (1936). *(Courtesy of D'Arcy More)*

January 1936 also provided Lugosi with various film possibilities, including a role in *Dracula's Daughter*, Universal's sequel to the 1931 film. At the time, Lugosi had a three-picture contract with Universal that allowed him to make deals with other studios.[2] Republic signed him for an important role in *The House of a Thousand Candles*, the actor agreeing likely because Universal dropped him from its payroll around January 6, 1936. The studio did so because they temporarily considered cancelling *Dracula's Daughter*.

But once Universal decided to proceed with their vampire sequel, a trade press claimed on January 15, 1936 that its production would wait for the *Candles* shoot to be completed.[3] Carl Laemmle, Jr. (son of the studio's founder) initially seemed determined to find a way to include Lugosi in *Dracula's Daughter*, even though the vampire count had been destroyed at the conclusion of the earlier movie. In the end, Lugosi spent only one day on the *Candles* set, having to leave the cast due to illness.[4]

The major reason for Lugosi's eventual absence from *Dracula's Daughter* was not *The House of a Thousand Candles* or his illness. Instead, the reason was script-based and motivated by the overall sentiment at the Production Code Administration (PCA). On January 30, 1936, the *Hollywood Reporter* told readers that Dracula would stay dead in *Dracula's Daughter*. While Junior Laemmle thought of "flashing in Bela Lugosi in a prelude scene," he changed his mind as a result of "recent condemnations of undue horror stuff." And so Lugosi did not appear in the film, as his presence would have (apparently) heightened its horror content.

Nor did he appear in Universal's *Bluebeard*, though trades connected his name to it on

Mae Clarke and Irving Pichel in *The House of 1000 Candles* (1936).

more than one occasion during January and February of 1936. Also referred to as *Bluebeard's Eight Wives*, the tale was to be written by Bayard Veiller (of *The Thirteenth Chair* fame) and producer Dave Diamond. Set in France in 1870, its trick ending would reveal that a woman was the actual villain.[5] But Universal shelved the production for reasons similar to those that prevented Lugosi from appearing in *Dracula's Daughter*.

Lost roles hardly kept Lugosi out of the public eye. For example, he attended the Screen Actors Guild Ball at the Biltmore Hotel in February 1936. *Daily Variety* reported, "Mrs. Bela Lugosi, with her husband, rated plenty of attention in chartreuse chiffon, shirred at the bottom, with a green chiffon cape floating from her shoulders."[6] That they attracted eyes was impressive, as some 750 persons attended the event, including the likes of James Cagney, Joan Bennett, Errol Flynn, Barbara Stanwyck, Paul Muni, and Merle Oberon.[7]

That same month, on February 24, Lugosi appeared at a celebration honoring Carl Laemmle, Sr.'s thirtieth anniversary in the film business. Over one hundred film personalities attended, among them Al Jolson, James Whale, Cecil B. DeMille, Gloria Holden, Mervyn LeRoy, Gloria Stuart, Buster Crabbe, and others. Newsreel cameramen from Universal and Paramount shot the proceedings, though whether they captured Lugosi on film is unknown.[8]

Not long after, Mrs. Lugosi wore "chartreuse chiffon gathered in bands horizontally across the skirt" when accompanying her husband to the Ambassador Hotel on April 22, 1936. It was for yet another salute to Carl Laemmle, Sr., who decided to retire given the sale of his studio. Irene Dunne, D. W. Griffith, Mary Astor, Irving Thalberg, Lupita Tovar, and many others were also on hand.[9]

Theatre ballyhoo that promotes the Lugosi serial *Shadow of Chinatown* (1936).

The premiere and release of *Dracula's Daughter* came shortly before the salute to Laemmle, as well as press accounts covering the British ban on horror movies. On May 6, 1936, *Variety* told readers:

> Universal is ringing the curfew on horror picture production for at least a year, following release of *Dracula's Daughter*, just completed. … Reason attributed by U for abandonment of horror cycle is that European countries, especially England, are prejudiced against this type product. Despite heavy local consumption of its chillers, U is taking heed to warning from abroad. Universal for a long time had virtual monopoly on this type of production, with unusual success at box office. Studio's London rep has cautioned production execs to scrutinize carefully all so-called chiller productions, to avoid any possible conflict with British censorship.[10]

The report was accurate. However, it was not the old Universal of the Laemmles who rang the curfew bell; it was the corporatized "New U," its leadership having purchased the studio in the spring of 1936.

Why would a ban in Great Britain have necessarily dictated that Hollywood studios cease horror film production, when such movies could easily have been produced, even at low budgets, for domestic consumption? Prior histories have usually ignored this critical question or vaguely suggested that the fear of lost revenue abroad was enough to dictate Hollywood's production schedule. But that alone is not the answer.

After all, the combined total of theaters in Great Britain and Ireland in 1936 amounted to only 5,058.[11] In 1936, some 88,000,000 tickets were sold to American movie theatres *every* week, meaning approximately 4,500,000,000 for the year, which was in fact an increase of ten percent over 1935. The year 1936 also saw the opening of approximately 500 new American movie theatres.[12]

The reality is that the post-Laemmle Universal had been purchased parallel to the rise of the British ban, and one-third of the huge amount of money required to buy it came from England. In other words, some thirty-three percent of the studio most likely to produce horror movies was now owned in part by British interests.[13]

Since Lugosi was still under contract to Universal for another film, the studio cast him in *Postal Inspector* (1936), with "Lugosi the Foreigner/Lugosi the Criminal" playing a Mexican thief named Benez. The movie was shot during June of 1936. Then, in August and September, "Lugosi the Criminal" became a Eurasian scientist and murderer in *Shadow of Chinatown* (1936), a 15-chapter serial produced by Victory Pictures.[14]

Initially, Lugosi may have actually viewed the British ban as a positive, as he had little trouble finding work during the summer of 1936 once horror was no longer on Hollywood's

Lugosi and Michael Loring in *Postal Inspector* (1936). *(Courtesy of Kristin Dewey)*

Irene Nagy, guest of honor (along with Lugosi) at the La Honda Bowl on July 19, 1937

agenda. True, projects like *Bluebeard* disappeared from the horizon. So did a deal with British International Pictures. In May, Lugosi had agreed to appear in two of their films for $12,500 each; the productions were to be shot in London in September of 1936, but never got off the ground.[15]

In August 1936, *Motion Picture Daily* announced that Dr. Hugo Riesenfeld, famed conductor, composer, and sometimes producer-director, was negotiating a deal with Grand National for a series of four Lugosi films.[16] Like the British International projects, these went no further than the planning stages. But they would have given Lugosi the feeling activity was afoot, that additional new films would soon come his way.

After all, he did have more work that year than just *Postal Inspector* and *Shadow of Chinatown*. For example, he guest-starred on radio station WHN.[17] In June, at the *Night of 1000 Stars* in Los Angeles (staged by the Actors Fund of America), Lugosi and Rochelle Hudson enacted a scene from *Dracula* on a larger bill that included everyone from Bette Davis and Joan Crawford to Clark Gable and Victor McLaglen.[18]

Then, in September, *Billboard* announced that Lugosi had signed a deal with theatrical bookers Fanchon and Marco, who were just beginning to move into the field of radio; in October, perhaps as a direct outcome of that agreement, Lugosi appeared on WOR with Jackie Cooper.[19] And – though he had already been paid for them – films like *The Invisible Ray* (1936) continued to play major theatres in big cities into the autumn, keeping his name prominently displayed on at least some theatre marquees.[20]

Lugosi also kept up an active social life that was reported in the press. On June 6, Lugosi and Mayor Shaw opened the Hungarian National Day in Los Angeles; along with parade floats, the celebration featured Lugosi on a national radio hook-up.[21] Celebrity sponsors included Myrna Loy, Claudette Colbert, Joe E. Brown, Wallace Beery, and Paul Lukas.[22] That same month, two teams played soccer in LA for the "Bela Lugosi Trophy."[23]

In July, *Daily Variety* spotted Lugosi "beneath the stars listening to symphonies."[24] About a week later, he not only attended a concert, but also appeared onstage:

'Ladies and gentlemen – we had a very hot day today, didn't we?' Thus Bela Lugosi, noted film actor, began the short talk he made to the audience in the Redlands Bowl Tuesday night, being among the notables present to witness the performances of Waldeen, interpretive dancer, and Duci de Kerekjarto, violinist.

Eugenie Leontovich (second from left) in a touring roadshow version of *Tovarich* produced by Gilbert Miller.

As a fellow countryman of the Hungarian musician and a close friend, the actor spoke briefly but glowingly of Kerekjarto's genius....[25]

This performance – which occurred a week after the "beneath the stars" comment appeared in print, and thus was perhaps a separate event – was staged near San Bernardino.

On July 19, he became co-guest of honor (alongside beauty queen Irene Nagy) at yet another Hungarian celebration, this time held at the La Honda Bowl, in Oakland.[26] Mayor William J. McCracken presented him with the key to the city.[27] The event also featured "Bohemian music, sports and games, besides dancing."[28]

Trade publications and newspapers continued to report on Lugosi in the autumn of 1936 as well. In November, *Daily Variety* wrote that Lugosi had happily given Joe Penner an "eight-week-old police dog."[29] And Alice Hughes' column told readers that the actor had introduced her to "chicken paprika and other toothsome Hungarian tricks."[30] Such comments do not speak to a man who believed his film career was coming to an abrupt end.

Perhaps the clearest indication that Lugosi did not know that the British ban would prove so disastrous can be seen in his purchase of a colonial, ten-room home in Outpost Park in November 1936. Its cost was $31,000. Developers of the tract told the *Los Angeles Times* that Lugosi started "extensive additions on his two-acre wooded estate," and that he had also purchased an adjacent lot.[31]

At that time, he was still very much a well-known actor, one who was an Advisory Board member at the Screen Actors Guild, a role he would continue in 1937.[32] And he guest-starred

Lugosi and Lillian in a candid shot taken during the making of *The Mystery of the Mary Celeste* (1935), which would be released in America in 1937 as *Phantom Ship*.

on Mutual's *Lessons in Hollywood* on January 18, 1937; Betty Grable and Jackie Coogan were on the same program, which was hosted by Jackie Cooper.[33]

Lessons in Hollywood ... perhaps Lugosi was learning more of them by January of 1937, by which time film offers dwindled to none. "They had branded me with the stamp of an animal," he recalled later. "I was a horror actor, an animal, and they would not give me a chance."[34] In another interview, he added, "The mortgage company got my house. I sold one car and then the other. I borrowed where I could."[35]

Radio shows were few, and the stage did not beckon. Except once, in February of 1937.

Tovarich

Jacques Deval's *Tovaritch* (as it was originally spelled) premiered in France in 1933; in 1935, it was adapted into a French film of the same name. By 1937, it had been "translated into German, Italian, and Hungarian, with records established in twenty-four countries."[36] One of the major stage hits of the thirties, *Tovaritch* was not an ideological tract, as its

A portrait likely taken during the _Tovarich_ era. _(Courtesy of Bill Chase)_

EUGENIE LEONTOVICH

HOMER CURRAN
By Arrangement With
GILBERT MILLER

PRESENTS

TOVARICH

By JACQUES DEVAL
ENGLISH TEXT BY
ROBERT B. SHERWOOD

OSGOOD PERKINS
WITH
BELA LUGOSI

Cover to a souvenir program for *Tovarich* that was likely available at all performances in which Lugosi appeared. *(Courtesy of Bill Chase)*

title – which translates as "friend" or "comrade" – would occasionally imply to those unfamiliar with its narrative.

What was this wildly popular play that took country after country by storm? *Tovarich* comically tells the story of two Russian nobles, a Prince and Grand Duchess, who fled their homeland after the 1917 revolution. Poverty-stricken (save for an enormous amount of government money entrusted to the Prince by the Czar), the two become domestic servants for a banker in France.

Locating the once-exalted couple, Commissar Gorotchenko convinces the Prince to give the Czar's money to the Russian people on the grounds that it will prevent peasants from starving. In an odd twist of fate, even though he had once threatened to torture the Prince, Gorotchenko has become their *tovaritch*.

Algonquin Round Table member Robert E. Sherwood translated Deval's play for English speaking audiences. When it opened with the spelling *Tovarich* in London in April 1935, the recently knighted Sir Cedric Hardwicke – who later appeared opposite Lugosi in

The Ghost of Frankenstein (1942) – portrayed Prince Mikhail Alexandrovitch Ouratieff and Eugenie Leontovich became the Grand Duchess Tatiana Petrovna. The same production featured Francis L. Sullivan as Commissar Gorotchenko; he would later star opposite Lugosi in the ill-fated stage play *The Devil Also Dreams* (1950).[37] In London, *Tovarich* played some 550 performances.[38]

Gilbert Miller, who had produced the British version, also brought *Tovarich* to Broadway, where it opened at the Plymouth Theatre in October 1936. By the time it closed, *Tovarich* had been staged over 350 times. John Halliday played the Prince, Cecil Humphreys was Gorotchenko, and Marta Abba made her Broadway debut as the Grand Duchess.[39]

On February 10, 1937, *Daily Variety* reported that producer Homer Curran had finalized an agreement with Gilbert Miller to stage *Tovarich* in San Francisco and Los Angeles; five days later, the same publication announced that Curran had signed Eugenie Leontovich, Osgood Perkins, and Bela Lugosi for the three leading roles.[40] Lugosi may well have believed that

Tovarich would signal the end of what had simply been a temporary dry spell by allowing him to move into non-horror roles.

Only days later, Guaranteed Pictures released Lugosi's British film *The Mystery of the Mary Celeste* (1935) in America, having rechristened it as *Phantom Ship*. He was back in what was – at least to American eyes watching screens owned by the RKO Metropolitan circuit – a new film.[41] "All of the characters are realistically portrayed," *Film Daily* said.[42] Once again Lugosi's name was in lights, even if it brought him no money.

By contrast, *Tovarich* meant paychecks for all of its cast members. The play's star, Madame Leontovich (as she preferred to be called), was not only renowned for *Tovarich*, but also for her fascinating life, one not entirely different than Bela Lugosi's. Born in Czarist Russia in 1900, she studied acting at the Moscow Art Theatre, but then had to flee the country after the Red Revolution. While a refugee in Turkey, she met her future husband, actor Gregory Ratoff. In 1922, she arrived in America and attempted to master English. She became a naturalized citizen in 1927, and made a hit on Broadway in 1930 with *Grand Hotel*.[43]

Osgood Perkins, who had appeared in many Hollywood films and Broadway productions, assumed the role of Prince Ouratieff; he had most recently appeared in the play *End of Summer* in New York in 1936.[44] London cast member Bruce Campbell

Eugenie Leontovich as pictured inside the *Tovarich* souvenir program.

Osgood Perkins as pictured inside the *Tovarich* souvenir program.

BELA LUGOSI

Bela Lugosi, usually associated with the deep hued villainous portrayals such as his famous "Dracula," in "Tovarich" takes a radical departure from his former self and steps before the footlights in an entirely new characterization.

A distinguished actor of many notable successes in the legitimate theater and motion pictures, Bela Lugosi holds the distinguished reputation of having one of the largest fan followings of most actors today. He receives from four to eight and twelve dozen fan letters two and three times a day, requesting pictures, advice on theatrical career and any number of inquiries. And strange though it seems, he answers each and every letter, even though they are sometimes several months in arrears.

Lugosi as pictured inside the
Tovarich souvenir program.

reprised his role as Georges Dupont.[45] Meg Sheridan – who in reality was Lilian Fontaine, mother of Joan Fontaine and Olivia de Havilland – played Madame Chauffourier-Dubieff.[46] And Fay Helm, who later appeared with Lugosi in *The Wolf Man* (1941) and *Night Monster* (1942), was Olga.

As for Lugosi, Curran cast him as Commissar Gorotchenko. Exactly why Curran did what so many other producers refused to do – meaning cast Lugosi in plays and films that were not horror or crime stories – is unknown. Lugosi the Foreigner was certainly adept at portraying Russians, as in the case of *International House* (1933), a film that Curran might have seen and remembered.

While Gorotchenko does not show up until late in Act II, he is crucial in Act III and, as a result, to the play's title and its theme. *Tovarich* is a comedy, but Gorotchenko is a man with a checkered and sinister past. As a Soviet official, he was incredibly cruel to those he interrogated. At one point, he admits: "...the most horrible retribution you can think of will be no more than I deserve, because I was guilty of the most

Published in the *San Francisco Call-Bulletin* of March 19, 1937.

unpardonable of crimes."[47] Here is a character bearing a sadistic past, one that could almost fit into the world of Edgar G. Ulmer's film *The Black Cat* (1934).

The sub-Darwinian Gorotchenko adapts as needed. Above all else, he is a pragmatist. In his youth, he washed dishes in France to fund his degree in philosophy, though when returning to Russia he did not pack his idealism. "That was a bad time for idealists, you know," he says. "A few of them escaped into Finland, but the majority were submerged in rivers of blood."[48]

Pragmatism means that Gorotchenko's latest incarnation is that of a salesman. After one of his compliments, a female character confesses, "He's poisonous, isn't he? He'll make communists of us all." After successfully convincing the Prince and Grand Duchess to turn over the Czar's money, Gorotchenko departs with the remark, "Good-bye, Imperial Highness," a curious reference to deposed royalty, one that could have been – depending upon the actor's delivery – deferential, sarcastic, derisive, or some combination thereof.[49]

Several years later, Lugosi remembered his preparation for *Tovarich*, specifically recalling advice from Gregory Ratoff. During rehearsals, Ratoff got into the orchestra pit and "prompted Bela [on] how to recite his lines without the accent!"[50]

Prior to their big San Francisco opening, Curran and director Peter Mather staged tryouts on March 19 and 20, 1937 in Santa Barbara. The *Wall Street Journal* told readers, "Two companies will be playing *Tovarich* at opposite ends of the United States, beginning tonight … The Santa Barbara presentation is preparatory to engagements in San Francisco and Los Angeles."[51]

Artwork published in the *San Francisco Chronicle* of March 28, 1937. Lugosi is depicted on the far left.

The *Los Angeles Times* reported that *Tovarich* drew "capacity audiences" in Santa Barbara; among their numbers were a "large contingent of Hollywood actors, Los Angeles press representatives and Channel City society folk."[52] Reviewer John Scott noted Lugosi played his role "to good effect."[53] The *Morning Press* in Santa Barbara said as much, claiming a "large and festive" audience occupied every seat in the house to watch a "superb" cast at work."[54]

The Curran

Tovarich began its open-ended run in San Francisco on March 22, 1937. Capacity crowds packed the Curran Theatre, with the press drawing particular attention to the play's cast, its success in other cities, and its use of two revolving stages for rapid scene changes.[55] Director Peter Mather even boasted this version of *Tovarich* had a more perfect cast than the Broadway production.[56]

Fortunately for Lugosi and his colleagues, the San Francisco newspaper critics were largely impressed:

…San Francisco theatregoers have seldom witnessed high comedy of such brilliancy as that bestowed by the principals of this provocative piece….[57]

–*San Francisco Call-Bulletin*

…*Tovarich* is according to any standard ideal entertainment. No one would have objected if it had gone on and on and on. So delectable and sunshiny a piece of make-believe has not been seen here for ages. … *Tovarich* is really too good a play for anyone to miss.[58]

–*San Francisco Chronicle*

Photo of Lugosi, Leontovich, and Perkins as published in the _San Francisco Call-Bulletin_ of March 23, 1937.

> _Tovarich_ is one of those rare comedies that is exuberantly gay, subtle, in good taste, and pleasingly romantic. ... It is the exquisite acting and skilled craftsmanship of two dramatic artists [Leontovich and Perkins] that give it the sparkle and warmth and that delectable quality that makes you resent the Prince and Grand Duchess leaving you behind as they make their exit to the ball [at the end of the play].[59]
>
> –_San Francisco Examiner_

The _San Francisco News_ endorsed the play as well, but nevertheless argued that it was "not great."[60]

Ticket-buyers flocked to each performance, causing _Tovarich_ to gross $14,000, despite rain pummeling the city nearly every night of its first week.[61] Ticket sales remained high in week two, with the play grossing another $14,000.[62]

Madame Leontovich was the toast of the town. She was interviewed on the radio show _Behind the Footlights_. The _Call-Bulletin_ reported on her trip to Golden Gate Park.[63] And then the press announced that she had won 35 cents at "_Tovarich_ Day" at the nearby Tanforan racetrack.[64] In honor of the play, the Tanforan named races after each of _Tovarich_'s stars on April 1, 1937.[65]

Lugosi was apparently present at the Tanforan himself, and he too received a fair amount of press, including generally positive words about his performance:

In the role of the Soviet commissar appears that old horror film man, Bela Lugosi, sinister by playwright's command, but as often as possible with tongue in cheek. His continental bearing and actorial skill make the character sure-fire in his hands.[66]

–*San Francisco Call-Bulletin*

[Lugosi] is an excellent choice for the urbane and cultured commissar, and only needs to lift his voice more in some scenes to satisfy in the role.[67]

–*San Francisco News*

Bela Lugosi as the Soviet Commissar undoubtedly gave a capital performance. He appeared too late for this review.[68]

–*San Francisco Examiner*

Advertisements promoting *Tovarich* and the Tanforan racetrack appear side-by-side in the March 25, 1937 issue of the *San Francisco Call-Bulletin*.

Likewise, the *San Francisco Chronicle* told readers that a "discussion of Bela Lugosi's Commissar must be postponed until a later date."[69] Here is a bit of insight into the fact that newspaper deadlines sometimes meant critics reviewed plays without being able to see all of their final acts unfold.

The Lugosi name certainly attracted at least some audience members. On March 25, members of San Francisco's "Hungarian colony" paid tribute to Lugosi by crowding the theatre; among them were the Hungarian consul and members of his staff."[70] After the show, Lugosi entertained the group backstage.[71] Then, on approximately April 4, Lugosi was interviewed on the *Woman's Magazine of the Air*.[72]

Lugosi also gave two major interviews to the local press, the first to the *Call-Bulletin*. "It's about time the film producers were shown I can play roles like this *Tovarich*," he said, "or those I did for twenty years before coming to Hollywood."[73] At first, his comment seems to refer purely to the problem of typecasting. In the context of the British ban, it also speaks to his lack of film work.

He also talked with the *San Francisco News*, promising their reporter that his Gorotchenko whiskers were not stage makeup, but were in fact genuine. He also repeated his hopes of being post-typecasting, saying: "Horror pictures are definitely out, and I must do something else, and since Hollywood has typed me as a horror actor, I am pleased beyond measure to have the rich part of Gorotchenko in this play."[74]

When he was not performing or publicizing *Tovarich*, Lugosi could have spent time with

Two photos of Leontovich and Perkins as published in the *San Francisco Call-Bulletin* of March 23, 1937.

an old friend. His *Mark of the Vampire* (1935) costar Carroll Borland was in San Francisco; she opened in a Federal Theatre-produced play entitled *Help Yourself* on the very same night that *Tovarich* premiered at the Curran.[75] The stage farce played two weeks at the Columbia Theatre, with the *San Francisco Chronicle* calling Borland's performance merely "adequate."[76]

At any rate, *Tovarich*'s open-ended engagement became successful enough to lead to a third week at the Curran, and then a fourth (which grossed $12,000).[77] Its run finally ended on April 17.[78] By then, the *San Francisco News* claimed that *Tovarich* had "caused more talk than any other production of the past decade," adding that the show would have continued in the city had it not been for a scheduled opening in Los Angeles.

Near the end of the San Francisco engagement, the local press announced that Lugosi, perhaps on the strength of his successful performance as Gorotchenko, was "... thinking over a deal that would land him on the air in a mystery serial scripted by a San Franciscan, Dr. M. F. Clark."[79] Sadly for Lugosi, like so many other projects that were announced, further discussion of this one disappeared without a trace.

The Biltmore

Plans for *Tovarich* in Los Angeles were in the works for weeks, but its opening at the city's Biltmore Theatre was postponed due to the fourth week in San Francisco.[80] The Biltmore had been dark for some time, but was certainly well lit when *Tovarich* opened on April 19, 1937.

Leontovich with her husband, Gregory Ratoff, as pictured in the *San Francisco Call-Bulletin* of March 29, 1937.

Ticket prices topped at $5.50, with ads giving Lugosi third-billing under Leontovich and Perkins. Aside from some Federal Theatre Project shows, *Tovarich* was the only legitimate theatre production then being presented on the local stage.[81]

Mail-order ticket sales caused the premiere to sell out rapidly.[82] According to the *Los Angeles Times*, fans on opening night "neatly tied up downtown traffic."[83] A special police detail was on hand because of the sheer numbers of both ticket-holders and gawkers.[84] Radio station KMTR broadcast live from the theatre lobby that night.[85] According to the *New York Times*, the cast was:

[u]shered in by the searchlights and flash bulbs usually held in reserve for picture premieres, to say nothing of radio broadcasts and street crowds of unusual proportions. … The house was more than sold out for the opening performance.[86]

Total gross for the first night was an impressive $4,200.[87] Biltmore manager Peter Ermatinger declared that no prior Los Angeles stage premiere had ever caused such a "tumult."[88]

Madame Leontovich was ecstatic; her eyes "glowed" when she later recounted the evening:

Ah, but the most exciting opening I ever had. Sooch [*sic*] an audience. So intelligent listening; not missing a point! Faint I am still with the thrill of it. And to meet Charles Boyer and Claudette Colbert, who will play my *Tovarich* on the screen, was a privilege.[89]

She concluded by saying that "everyone [was] so sweet" to her in Los Angeles, particularly Norma Shearer.

Carroll Borland as Luna in *Mark of the Vampire* (1935).

Most reviewers in Los Angeles responded favorably, with the *Times* reporting that the show had much improved since its performances in Santa Barbara:[90]

Tovarich is a constant delight. It has the quality of joyousness.[91]

–*Los Angeles Daily News*

The agreeable, stimulating, witty comedy with its undertow of sharp drama of Russian patriotic concerns is ably staged and capitally played....[92]

–*Daily Variety*

Federal Theater Farce to Open Tonight at Columbia

TONIGHT the Columbia Theater presents "Help Yourself," a Viennese farce, for a two weeks' run. The play is the first in San Francisco of the Federal Theater's new road show policy. The original cast, which toured Southern California, will be seen here. Christopher Wyatt, the principal character of the play, is a wide-awake young American, who, desperate in his plight of unemployment, walks into the bank and helps himself to an executive position. Paul Reyner plays the part of Christopher Wyatt; Carroll Borland is the banker's daughter, who falls in love with Christopher.

Carroll Borland and Paul Reyner, appearing in "Help Yourself," new FTP production opening tonight at the Columbia.

From the *San Francisco Chronicle* of March 22, 1937.

...varied and pictorial settings and costumes intrigue the eye of the spectator throughout the brisk performance.[93]

–*Los Angeles Examiner*

The company is really achieving a great zest in the interpretation of an amusing and picturesque study of the aristocrats' efforts to overcome the effects of the revolution and ensuing poverty.[94]

–*Los Angeles Times*

There were exceptions, however. While generally impressed with the play's satirical mood, the *Hollywood Citizen-News* complained about its melodramatic scenes.[95]

But the Los Angeles press was unanimous when reporting that the audience on opening night was perhaps the most impressive assembled at any live theatre event during the past decade. Among the celebrities in attendance were Fredric March, Gloria Stuart, Douglas Fairbanks, Claudette Colbert, Mervyn LeRoy, Irene Dunne, Hedda Hopper, Sophie Tucker, Adolphe Menjou, Ann Sothern, Harold Lloyd, Charles Boyer, Irving Berlin, Otto Preminger, Dick Powell, Basil Rathbone, Chico Marx, and – creating some degree of comment because of the gum she smacked during the show – Simone Simon. Another notable audience member was Boris Karloff.[96]

What Karloff and his fellow audience members thought of Lugosi that night is unknown, but trade publications and local newspapers were impressed:

Bela Lugosi as the commissar, and Melville Cooper as the French banker, stand out.[97]

–*Daily Variety*

Two candid photos of Lugosi with an unknown person taken during the *Tovarich* run.
(Courtesy of Bill Chase)

Lugosi makes his Soviet official a forceful, slow-moving creature of logical arguments....[98]

–Los Angeles Examiner

He dominates his moments on the stage with natural and sustained acting.[99]

–Los Angeles Daily News

...Bela Lugosi [is] impressive as the commissar, in spite of occasional heaviness and difficult accent.[100]

–Los Angeles Herald and Express

Bela Lugosi, noted horror actor, is a unique choice for the role of the Soviet Commissar, but he turns in a clever performance and one that has improved mightily since the Santa Barbara engagement. He is sinister, but impressively dignified, and lends to his portrayal shadings of the shrewd schemer.[101]

–Hollywood Citizen-News

While not specifically blaming Lugosi, one reviewer did argue that his key scene should have been "spread along earlier scenes," rather than being played out as one extended exchange.[102]

During the rest of its run, *Tovarich* continued to make news. Leontovich and husband Gregory Ratoff guest-starred on Edwin Schallert's KFAC radio show *Tower of the Times* on

Walter Winchell SAYS: "Los Angeles sees something New York hasn't. La Leontovich in the role which swept London off its feet into her lap."

BILTMORE *THEATRE* MI. 3171 ★ BRILLIANT OPENING **MON. EVE. APR. 19**

Eugenie **LEONTOVICH** Osgood. **PERKINS** *in*

A GAY COMEDY OF PARIS

"**TOVARICH**"

Bela **LUGOSI** Melville **COOPER** MARY **FORBES**

OPENING NIGHT: ORCH. 5.50, BAL. 2.20, 1.65, 1.10, 55c
SEATS NOW ★ *Thereafter:* EVENINGS 2.75, 2.20, 1.65, 1.10, 55c
BOX OFFICE & AGENCIES MATINEES: WED. and SAT. 2.20, 1.65, 1.10, 55c, inc. tax

"Mme. Leontovich dazzles London." **—THE DAILY MAIL**
"Eugenie Leontovich is an artist of exquisite sensibility."
—LONDON EVENING STANDARD

Advertisement published in the *Hollywood Reporter* of April 14, 1937.

Lugosi, Perkins, and Leontovich in *Tovarich*.

April 25, 1937.[103] Actor Herbert Marshall saw the play three times during its run in Los Angeles; Fredric March saw it twice.[104]

And, once again, the Hungarian community heralded Lugosi's achievement. The performance of May 12, 1937 was dedicated to Lugosi, with more than 250 representatives from fourteen different Hungarian-American societies filling the seats. In something of a repeat of San Francisco, Lugosi entertained his guests backstage after taking his bows.[105]

Tovarich eventually closed on May 15, 1937. During its first three weeks, some 38,000 persons saw the play at the Biltmore, where it grossed $45,000; early reports suggested its fourth and final week was set to bring in another $10,000.[106]

Once the play closed, some of those involved onstage and backstage returned to San Francisco or New York. Remaining in Los Angeles was Melville Cooper; he had signed a contract with Twentieth Century Fox.[107]

Also staying in L.A. was Bela Lugosi.

Conclusion

After interviewing Lugosi about *Tovarich*, the *Los Angeles Times* told readers, "He likes it, and so do his audiences."[108] Talk of a Curran-produced version of the play in Chicago went nowhere, and – despite various subsequent productions in America – Lugosi never again appeared onstage in *Tovarich*.[109] Nor would he appear in Anatole Litvak's 1937 Hollywood film adaptation. Instead, Basil Rathbone played Gorotchenko, with Claudette Colbert playing the Grand Duchess and Charles Boyer the Prince.[110]

Nevertheless, given his good reviews and the enormous attention Hollywood paid to the Los Angeles production, it is extremely likely that Lugosi's Commissar Gorotchenko later won him the role of Commissar Razinin in Ernst Lubitsch's *Ninotchka* at MGM in 1939.[111]

But *Ninotchka* was two years in the future. In April 1937, Lugosi professed his aspiration that, "perhaps after *Tovarich*, they'll call me for something half-way civilized – no Draculas, White Zombies, Chandus, no 'Mysterious Mr. Wongs.'"[112]

His hopes were not fulfilled. Lugosi had to content himself with a single 1937 film role. In this case, it was as a criminal in Republic's serial *SOS Coast Guard* (1937), shot in June of that year.[113] Bearing the Russian name Boroff (which also sounds like a contraction of "Boris" and "Karloff"), Lugosi's character was not merely a bad guy, but – in a curious twist, given the British ban – a mad scientist who invents a disintegrating gas to sell to foreign powers. And so, for this serial he was Lugosi the Foreigner, Lugosi the Criminal, and Lugosi the Mad Scientist, all in one.

From the *Los Angeles Times* of April 19, 1937.

It may have helped temporarily, at least meaning a paycheck, but *SOS Coast Guard* did not lead to other film roles in the second half of 1937 or the first half of 1938. Adding insult to injury, despite the fact new horror films were verboten, some American theatres continued to screen *The Invisible Ray* in 1937.[114]

In fact, at least a few theatres in 1937 screened such old Lugosi movies as *White Zombie* (1932), *Murder By Television* (1935), and *Mysterious Mr. Wong* (1935).[115] Even his old 1933 serial *The Whispering Shadow* resurfaced that year. One theatre manager reported that it quickly built up a "strong following," so much so that he had "no regrets in playing it."[116] But such reissues did not bring Lugosi money.

Worse still was Columbia's first *Screen Snapshots* for its seventh series, released in October

Leontovich and Perkins in *Tovarich*, from the same version that starred Lugosi.

1937. It presented a history of film days gone by, ranging from Theda Bara, Mary Pickford, Clara Bow to the "horror age of Karloff and Lugosi."[117] Lugosi was onscreen again, not only without pay, but also as a historical character in the drama of Hollywood history. He was, at least in the eyes of some, Past Tense.

And so, turning once again to the stage, Lugosi attempted to secure a dramatic role in New York. In 1937 and 1938, he wrote to his old friend Dr. Edmond Pauker:

> I just read in the papers of the extension of your business. I would be very happy if you would try to do something for me on the usual 10% reimbursement.[118]

> Up until to date I have not heard from you and would like you to know that I am very eager to play a part on the stage either in New York or London. I understand that Gilbert Miller will produce the *Tragedy of Man* at the New York Fair. I played both leading parts in the original (in Hungarian)....[119]

Of Course It's Leontovich

HERE IS an intriguing caricature drawing of Eugenie Leontovich, the engaging star of "Tovarich," a gay comedy of exiled Russian nobility, now holding forth at the Biltmore Theater.

Artwork published in the *Daily News* (Los Angeles) on May 3, 1937.

Miller had, of course, produced *Tovarich* on Broadway in 1936. In a kind and diplomatically worded response to Lugosi's 1937 query, Pauker wrote:

I wish to assure you that I will do my best in order to interest the producers, who are planning to produce my plays, to consider your engagement. Of course you have to realize that not all of the plays contain such leading roles which would be suitable for you. If and when I will have a tangible proposition, I will of course write or wire you.[120]

Pauker's surviving papers do not include subsequent communications for 1937 or 1938. It would seem that he did not write; he did not wire. There was no need to do so. He had no work for Lugosi, no promising leads.

In September 1937, *Daily Variety* reported that Lugosi was "mulling an offer to do a horror play on the N. Y. stage," but nothing came of it.[121] As with *Pagan Fury* and *Fiarri*, the curtain never rose.

On December 1, the government filed a lien against Lugosi for unpaid taxes.[122] Then, on January 5, 1938, Lillian gave birth to Bela G. Lugosi, with Actors Relief helping to pay the medical bills.

(Endnotes)

1   "Some of the Latest: *Invisible Ray*." *Film Curb* 1 Feb. 1936.
2   "Lugosi for *Candles*." *Hollywood Reporter* 11 Jan. 1936.
3   "Hillyer Directs 'U' *Dracula's Daughter*." *Hollywood Reporter* 15 Jan. 1936.
4   "*1000 Candles* Finished." *Hollywood Reporter* 29 Jan. 1936.
5   "Woman Villain for *Bluebeard* at U." *Hollywood Reporter* 6 June 1935; "42 Universal Releases Announced." *Motion Picture Herald* 8 June 1935; "Production Analysis." *Film Curb* 25 Jan. 1936;

EUGENIE LEONTOVICH and Bela Lugosi in scene from "Tovarich," which will be seen at Biltmore.

From the *Los Angeles Examiner* of April 18, 1937.

Three "drama-minded" members of Westwood's Kappa Kappa Gamma plan a theatre party to see *Tovarich* with Lugosi. As published in the *Los Angeles Times* of May 2, 1937.

"Production Analysis." *Film Curb* 8 Feb. 1936. *Bluebeard* had in fact been mentioned as a Karloff project as early as 1932. See: "Parsons, Louella O. "*Bluebeard* Is Karloff's Next." *San Francisco Examiner* 19 Nov. 1932.

6   "Gals and Gab." *Daily Variety* 24 Feb. 1936.

7   "Actors Guild Fete Top in Class and Gay Jinks." *Daily Variety* 24 Feb. 1936.

8   "Laemmle Feted on 30th Anniversary." *Motion Picture Daily* 25 Feb. 1936.

9   "Gals & Gab!" *Daily Variety* 23 Apr. 1936.

10   International complaints about Hollywood horror films were not limited to the United Kingdom. By 1936, Nazi censors had closed the German marketplace to them. For more information, see: Peter A. Hagemann's "Eine fast erfolgreiche Unterdrückung der Affenliebe zum Filmwechselbalg" in Kraft Wetzel and Peter A. Hagemann. *Liebe, Tod und Technik: Kino des Phantastischen 1933 – 1945* (Berlin: Verlag Volker Spiess, 1977).

11   "33,220 Film Houses Running in Europe." *Hollywood Reporter* 22 Apr. 1936.

12   "U.S. Estimates 4,500,000,000 Attendance and Billion Gross." *Motion Picture Herald* 16 Jan. 1937.

13   Gary D. Rhodes describes the sale of Universal and the British funds used to purchase it at length in: "She Gives You That Weird Feeling": The Making of *Dracula's Daughter*, published in *Dracula's Daughter, The Original 1936 Shooting Script* (BearManor Media, 2015).

14   "Katzman Acquires Studio for His Enlarged Program." *Film Daily* 5 Aug. 1935; Schallert, Edwin. "Ziegfeld Banner Will Be Held Aloft by Talented Young Daughter Patricia." *Los Angeles Times* 5 Aug. 1936; "A 'Little' from Hollywood 'Lots.'" *Film Daily* 28 Aug. 1936; "Kiang Okays *Chinatown*." *Daily Variety* 29 Aug. 1936; "Katzman Starts Another." *Film Daily* 19 Sept. 1936. *Shadow of Chinatown*

was in production by August 28, though its exact start date is difficult to determine. Its fifteen-day shoot seems to have begun in late August and finished in September.

15 "Lugosi To Do Two for BIP at $12,500." *Hollywood Reporter* 23 May 1936.
16 "Dicker with Riesenfeld." *Motion Picture Daily* 24 Aug. 1936.
17 Sidney, Louis K. "A Theatre Showman in Radio." *Variety* 26 Aug. 1936.
18 "*Night of 1000 Stars* Huge Program Ready." *Los Angeles Times* 28 June 1936.
19 "F&M Branching Out Into Radio Talent Booking on Large Scale." *Billboard* 12 Sept. 1936.
20 See, for example: "Karloff Tops Again in Film." *Atlanta Daily World* 28 Sept. 1936.
21 "Hungarians to Parade in Celebration Sunday." *Los Angeles Times* 24 June 1936.
22 "Pix Aid Hungarian Fete." *Daily Variety* 27 June 1936.
23 "Victorians Cop Soccer Contest, 2-0." *Los Angeles Times* 8 June 1936.
24 "Gals & Gab!" *Daily Variety* 8 July 1936.
25 "Bowl Audience Sees Splendid Program; Bela Lugosi Talks." *San Bernardino Daily Sun* 15 July 1936.
26 "Lugosi at Oakland Fete." *Daily Variety* 10 July 1936.
27 "Welcome for Hungarians." *Oakland Tribune* 19 July 1936.
28 "Hungarian Societies Will Picnic July 19." *Oakland Tribune* 1 July 1936.
29 "Gals & Gab!" *Daily Variety* 6 Nov. 1936.
30 Hughes, Alice. "A Woman's New York." *Washington Post* 8 Nov. 1936.
31 "Bela Lugosi Buys Outpost Park Home." *Los Angeles Times* 8 Nov. 1936.
32 See, for example: "SAG, 13 Producers Sign 10-Yr. Peace Pact; Minor Opposition Loses Out." *Variety* 19 May 1937.
33 "More Guests for Cooper." *Motion Picture Daily* 18 Jan. 1937. Given the network and other guests, this is apparently a different program than Lugosi's radio show with Jackie Cooper in September 1936.
34 Sullivan, Ed. "Looking at Hollywood." *Chicago Tribune* 10 Jan. 1939.
35 Othman, Frederick C. "The Head Spook of Horrordom Pulls Himself Together Again." *Washington Post* 2 Sept. 1941.
36 "Curran Star's Acting Is Praised." *San Francisco Examiner* 29 Mar. 1937.
37 For more information on *The Devil Also Dreams*, see: Rhodes, Gary D. and Bill Kaffenberger. *No Traveler Returns: The Lost Years of Bela Lugosi* (BearManor Media, 2012).
38 "*Tovarich* Will Open Here April 19." *Los Angeles Times* 7 Apr. 1937.
39   Playbill for *Tovarich*. (New York: Plymouth Theatre, 1936).
40 "Curran Gets Rights for Frisco, LA *Tovarich*." *Daily Variety* 10 Feb. 1937; "Curran *Tovarich* in SF March 22, *Lady* March 1." *Daily Variety* 15 Feb. 1937.
41 "*Phantom Ship* to RKO Met." *Film Daily* 5 Feb. 1937.
42 "*Phantom Ship*." *Film Daily* 15 Feb. 1937.
43 See, for example: "Story of *Tovarich* Star." *San Francisco Examiner* 26 Mar. 1937; Hobart, John. "Leontovich Interprets Russian Soul." *San Francisco Chronicle* 28 Mar. 1937; "Leontovich, Starred in Comedy, Sits on Script to Ward Off Stage Jinx." *Hollywood Citizen-News* 9 Apr. 1937; Lawrence, Florence. "*Tovarich* Portrays Dreams of Its Star." *Los Angeles Examiner* 18 Apr. 1937.
44 For more information on Osgood Perkins and *Tovarich*, see: Hanifin, Ada. "Actor Needs Stage Sense." *San Francisco Examiner* 28 Mar. 1937; Hobart, James. "What Makes a Good Actor? Osgood Perkins Considers the Matter." *San Francisco Chronicle* 4 Apr. 1937.
45 "*Tovarich* for Curran." *San Francisco Call-Bulletin* 19 Mar. 1937. While he had played the role in London, Campbell was not the original Georges Dupont; that actor was John Buckmaster.
46 "Mother of 2 Film Players in *Tovarich*." *San Francisco Examiner* 8 Apr. 1937.
47 Deval, Jacques. *Tovarich: A Play in Three Acts*. Adapted by Robert E. Sherwood. (New York: Samuel French, 1937).
48 Ibid.
49 Ibid.
50 "Tragedy-Comedy Tradition Safe with Bela Lugosi." *Los Angeles Times* 6 Sept. 1943.
51 "*Tovarich* in California." *Wall Street Journal* 19 Mar. 1937.
52 Scott, John. "*The Women* Will Tour Next Fall." *Los Angeles Times* 23 Mar. 1937.
53 Ibid.
54 "Scintillating *Tovarich* Pleases Big Play Crowd." *The Morning Press* (Santa Barbara, CA) 20 Mar. 1937.
55 "*Tovarich* on Tonight at Curran." *San Francisco Examiner* 22 Mar. 1937; "Original Sets for *Tovarich*." *San Francisco Call-Bulletin* 7 Apr. 1937.

BILTMORE ★
Theatre MI. 3171

Eugenie
LEONTOVICH

Osgood
PERKINS
in

Last 2 weeks
Seats Now
Mat.—
Tomorrow

"TOVARICH"

INTERNATIONAL
COMEDY SUCCESS

Bela
LUGOSI

Melville
COOPER

Play by Jacques Deval

Evenings 2.75, 2.20, 1.65, 1.10, 55c

Mats.: Wed. & Sat. 2.20, 1.65, 1.10, 55c, Inc. tax

Published in the *Los Angeles Herald and Express* on May 7, 1937.

56 "S.F. *Tovarich* Is Held Best." *San Francisco News* 1 Apr. 1937.
57 "*Tovarich* in Curran Debut." *San Francisco Call-Bulletin* 23 Mar. 1937.
58 Hobart, John. "*Tovarich* Follows Exiled Russians to Paris." *San Francisco Chronicle* 23 Mar. 1937.
59 Hanifin, Ada. "*Tovarich* Opens at the Curran." *San Francisco Examiner* 23 Mar. 1937.
60 La Bella, Claude A. "Brilliant Audience Finds *Tovarich* Just to Its Liking." *San Francisco News* 23 Mar. 1937.
61 "*Tovarich* $14,000, Strong Start, S. F." *Variety* 31 Mar. 1937.
62 "*Tovarich* Healthy $14,000 in Frisco." *Variety* 7 Apr. 1937.
63 "Leontovich Joyous in 'Blossom Time' S. F." *San Francisco Call-Bulletin* 27 Mar. 1937.
64 "Gossip, Happenings on S. F. Rialto." *San Francisco Call-Bulletin* 3 Apr. 1937.
65 "*Tovarich* Day Today at Tanforan." *San Francisco Examiner* 1 Apr. 1937.
66 "*Tovarich* in Curran Debut." *San Francisco Call-Bulletin* 23 Mar. 1937.
67 La Belle, "Brilliant Audience Finds *Tovarich* Just to Its Liking."
68 Hanifin, "*Tovarich* Opens at the Curran."
69 Hobart, "*Tovarich* Follows Exiled Russians to Paris."
70 "Hungarians Will Honor Lugosi." *San Francisco Examiner* 25 Mar. 1937; "Lugosi Will Be Party Host." *San Francisco News* 25 Mar. 1937.

71 "Amenities at the Curran Tonight." *San Francisco Chronicle* 25 Mar. 1937.
72 "Frisco Chatter." *Daily Variety* 5 Apr. 1937.
73 First Nighter, The. "So Long, Dracula–Nice to Have Met You!" *San Francisco Call-Bulletin* 3 Apr. 1937.
74 La Belle, Claude A. "Those Gorotchenko Whiskers on Bela Lugosi Are Genuine." *San Francisco News* 5 Apr. 1937.
75 "Federal Theatre Farce to Open Tonight at Columbia." *San Francisco Chronicle* 22 Mar. 1937.
76 "*Help Yourself*–Fine Farce on Business." *San Francisco Chronicle* 24 Mar. 1937.
77 "*Tovarich* Third Week Will Start." *San Francisco Examiner* 30 Mar. 1937;
78 "*Tovarich* Will Continue Curran Run Until April 17." *San Francisco Chronicle* 9 Apr. 1937.
79 "Fan-About-Town." *San Francisco Chronicle* 12 Apr. 1937.
80 "Opening of *Tovarich* Here Postponed." *Los Angeles Times* 5 Apr. 1937.
81 *Tovarich* in LA Premiere at $5.50." *Variety* 21 Apr. 1937.
82 "Pry *Tovarich* Advance Debuts (19) at $5.50." *Daily Variety* 14 Apr. 1937.
83 Poff, Tip. "That Certain Party." *Los Angeles Times* 25 Apr. 1937.
84 "*Tovarich* in Premiere Tonight." *Los Angeles Daily News* 19 Apr. 1937.
85 "Homer Curran *Tovarich* Reopens Biltmore (19)." *Daily Variety* 16 Apr. 1937.
86 "That Sunshine Circuit." *New York Times* 25 Apr. 1937.
87 Oliver, W. E. "Leontovich, Perkins and Osgood Divide Honors." *Los Angeles Herald and Express* 20 Apr. 1937.
88 Lawrence, Florence. "*Tovarich* Big Hit on Biltmore Stage." *Los Angeles Examiner* 20 Apr. 1937.
89 Whitaker, Alma. "Stage Star Finds Film City Exciting." *Los Angeles Times* 25 Apr. 1937.
90 Schallert, Edwin. "*Tovarich* Well Played at Biltmore." *Los Angeles Times* 20 Apr. 1937.
91 Mines, Harry. "*Tovarich*, Smooth and Witty Comedy of Ex-Royalty." *Los Angeles Daily News* 20 Apr. 1937.
92 "Play Reviews: *Tovarich*." *Daily Variety* 20 Apr. 1937.
93 Lawrence, "*Tovarich* Big Hit on Biltmore Stage."
94 Schallert, "*Tovarich* Well Played at Biltmore."
95 Yeaman, Elizabeth. "Film Celebrities Pack Biltmore Theatre to See Opening of *Tovarich*." *Hollywood Citizen-News* 20 Apr. 1937.
96 "Gals and Gab." *Daily Variety* 20 Apr. 1937; "Around the Town with Chatterbox." *Los Angeles Times* 21 Apr. 1937; Parks, Aileen. "Film Folk Taste Real California Hospitality at Rancho House Party." *Los Angeles Times* 25 Apr. 1937. On April 17, 1937, the *Los Angeles Times* reported that Marlene Dietrich, Cary Grant, Billie Burke, Herbert Marshall, Olivia de Havilland, Stuart Erwin, and Ginger Rogers would also appear at the Biltmore premiere. Their names were not mentioned in *Daily Variety* after the opening; as a result, it is difficult to know whether all or part of that group actually attended or not.
97 "Play Reviews: *Tovarich*," *Daily Variety*.
98 Lawrence, "*Tovarich* Big Hit on Biltmore Stage."
99 Mines, "*Tovarich*, Smooth and Witty Comedy of Ex-Royalty."
100 Oliver, "Leontovich, Perkins and Osgood Divide Honors."
101 Yeaman, "Film Celebrities Pack Biltmore Theatre to See Opening of *Tovarich*."
102 Oliver, "Leontovich, Perkins and Osgood Divide Honors."
103 "Russian Actors in *Conversation*." *Los Angeles Times* 25 Apr. 1937.
104 Kendall, Read. "Around and About in Hollywood." *Los Angeles Times* 26 Apr. 1937.
105 "Hungarians Plan Honor for Lugosi." *Los Angeles Times* 10 May 1937. This article mentions that Francis Proiszl, Hungarian consular agent in Los Angeles, was invited to the May 12, 1937 performance. Whether he attended or not is unknown.
106 "Figures Attest Popularity of Play at Biltmore." *Los Angeles Times* 8 May 1937; "*Tovarich* Grabs $45,000 for 3 Biltmore Wks." *Daily Variety* 10 May 1937.
107 "*Tovarich* Ends Run Saturday." *Los Angeles Daily News* 11 May 1937.
108 "Film Villain Reforms on Biltmore Stage." *Los Angeles Times* 4 May 1937.
109 Mention of a possible Chicago production appears in: "*Tovarich* in Final Week." *San Francisco Call-Bulletin* 13 Apr. 1937.
110 Schallert, Edwin. "Rathbone Slated as Commissar in Screen Version of *Tovarich*." *Los Angeles Times* 27 Apr. 1937.
111 Here it is worth mentioning that, nine years later, critic Wood Soanes' recalled Lugosi's performance as Gorotchenko. See "Curtain Calls." *Oakland Tribune* 20 Feb. 1946.

Publicity still for *Tovarich* that depicts Lugosi, Leontovich, and Perkins.

A still for the film version of *Tovarich* (1937), which featured Basil Rathbone (left) as Gorotchenko.

112 First Nighter, The, "So Long, Dracula–Nice to Have Met You!"

113 "Lugosi in Serial." *Variety* 15 June 1937.

114 "What's On At Local Theatres." *New Journal and Guide* (Norfolk, VA) 25 Dec. 1937.

115 See, for example: Advertisement. *Joplin Globe* (Joplin, MO) 2 June 1937; Advertisement. *Lima News* (Lima, OH) 21 Aug. 1937; Advertisement. *Hammond Times* (Hammond, IN) 17 Dec. 1937.

116 "Serials." *Motion Picture Herald* 16 Oct. 1933.

117 "Relieves [*sic*] the Year." *Southtown Economist* (Chicago, IL) 21 Oct. 1937.

118 Lugosi, Bela. Letter to Dr. Edmond Pauker. 22 Sep. 1937. [Available in the Edmond Pauker Papers, 1910-1957, Series I: Correspondence, 1915-1957, Box 42, Folder 11 at the New York Public Library/ Lincoln Center for the Performing Arts in New York.]

119 Lugosi, Bela. Letter to Dr. Edmond Pauker. 26 July 1938. [Available in the Edmond Pauker Papers.]

120 Pauker, Dr. Edmond. Letter to Bela Lugosi. 6 Oct. 1937. [Available in the Edmond Pauker Papers.]

121 "Chatter." *Daily Variety* 15 Sept. 1937.

122 "Hollywood Inside." *Daily Variety* 2 Dec. 1937.

Lugosi in *Dracula* (1931), which was reissued to much success in 1938.

Chapter 8

The Tower of London

Searching for a cheap program to book at his movie theatre, Emil Umann scoured the list of possibilities at his local film exchange. Born in Russia, Umann had come to America as a young boy and later worked for William Fox and Rodney Pantages. In 1937, he opened his own 785-seat house on Wilshire Boulevard in Beverly Hills. It was named for his wife, Regina.[1]

In August 1938, Umann programmed *Dracula* (1931), *Frankenstein* (1931), and *The Son of Kong* (1933) as a triple feature, daring audiences to withstand so "much horror in one show."[2] The bill had much to commend it, including an admission price of only thirty cents. Lines on opening day unexpectedly stretched for two blocks, and the theatre played the films to capacity audiences over the course of several weeks, with ticket buyers coming from as far away as Fresno and San Diego.[3]

John Hamrick's Blue Mouse Theatre in Seattle then screened *Dracula* and *Frankenstein* as a double bill, refining the Regina's program into the form that most audiences would experience in the autumn of 1938. In a telegram that year, Hamrick described his success: "Unable to handle crowds opening day and second day yesterday equaled first day's business ... Combining these pictures [is a] showman's dream of good times here again."[4] As with the Regina, the Blue Mouse founded its advertising campaign on daring viewers to endure the horror.

Universal Pictures quickly ordered 500 new prints of both films and rapidly prepared a pressbook that described the two films as a double feature. Suggested ads challenged audiences to see the "double horror show of the century."

The studio heavily promoted the story of the 1938 horror revival. Industry trade publications and newspaper journalists followed in the same path, including a lengthy article in the *New York Times*.[5] Bela Lugosi would do much the same: "I owe it all to that little man at the Regina Theatre," he said in 1939. "I was dead and he brought me [back] to life."[6]

Here was a great story, one that no doubt appealed to many theatre managers at the time. While major chains existed, some of them even controlled by Hollywood studios, there were

Published in the *Los Angeles Times* on August 19, 1938.

also thousands of mom-and-pop cinemas. During the late twenties and early thirties, these small exhibitors faced myriad problems, not the least of which were the costly installation of audio equipment and then declining ticket sales due to the Great Depression.

These exhibitors also had regular battles with unions (particularly the projectionist unions), Hollywood studios (whose block-booking tactics tried to force them to book films they didn't want in order to schedule those they did), and each other (due to various forms of cutthroat competition, ranging from cheaper and cheaper ticket prices to instituting giveaway schemes like "Bank Night" and "Dish Night").

So the tale of the "little man" at the Regina Theatre igniting a major cinematic trend and thus reviving the genre was exciting and compelling. The small exhibitor's tail wagged the dog, and it did so in an era where the exhibitor's tail seemed otherwise bruised from regular kicks.

News of the Regina's success also had the added benefit of being true, a factor that wasn't always present in publicity stories originating in the Hollywood of the 1930s.

All that said, the story's legitimacy has prevented many film historians from asking what should have been rather obvious questions, arising from the knowledge that there is no text without context. In other words, what process allowed the Regina Theatre to book the films in question? After all, the Production Code Administration (PCA) had to approve all film

Artwork featured in Universal Pictures' pressbook for the reissue of *Dracula* (1931) and *Frankenstein* (1931) in 1938.

releases, including those made before the Code's adoption in 1934. Whether or not an old movie had provoked controversy in the past, it still had to be examined prior to its reissue.

In September 1936, *Motion Picture Herald* described a "marked trend towards reissues and repeats," given the increased need for product due to the popularity of double features, as well as to the perceived lack of new, high-caliber releases. Needless to say, studios saw many benefits in reissues, as they provided a chance to make more money off of films that were quite literally already in the can.[7]

And so the road to the Regina began even before the Regina opened for business. On June 9, 1937, the PCA informed Universal that a few changes would be necessary to *Frankenstein* in order to receive code approval, including the elimination of footage depicting a little girl being drowned. After being assured that the required deletions had been made, the PCA approved the film's reissue on October 15, 1937.[8]

Then, in early March 1938, Universal told the PCA that the studio wanted to reissue *Dracula*. After examining the old film, the PCA required a few changes, such as limiting the number of "groans and moans" heard during Dracula and Renfield's deaths, as well as the elimination of a curtain speech by Edward Van Sloan. Universal complied, and so the PCA granted Certificate of Approval No. 02021-R to *Dracula* in mid-March 1938.[9]

An ad mat for the double feature reissue as prepared by Universal.

The aforementioned changes to both films are widely known to fans of classic horror, and decades later led to restorations that have attempted (without complete success, unfortunately) to return the films to the way they were in 1931. However, the crucial point here is that these changes occurred months *prior* to the Regina Theatre screening, not as a result of it. Without these advance certifications, the Regina would never have been able to get prints of them from a film exchange.

And Universal did not undertake these changes in the vague hope that someday a small exhibitor in Beverly Hills would want to screen *Dracula* and/ or *Frankenstein*. In fact, various theatres screened *Dracula* and *Frankenstein* in 1938 *before* the Regina did. For example, New York's Rialto booked *Dracula* "on a revival" in April of 1938.[10]

Here then is the context behind the text of the Regina Theatre story. Or at least part of it, because the other logical question is why Universal – who had heeded the "British Ban" on horror in 1936 – chose to prepare *Frankenstein* for reissue in 1937 and then *Dracula* in the spring of 1938? Why did the studio experience a change of heart?

Answers to that question might be many, including the belief that horror for domestic release only could still prove profitable. Though they didn't produce the film, Warner Bros. certainly planned a version of *The Pit and the Pendulum* in 1937; the following year, *Dracula–The Vampire Play* returned to at least a few stages.[11]

The key reason for Universal's somewhat amended strategy was apparently financial. The studio reported a net loss of $588,285 for the 26-week period that ended April 30, 1938.[12] By contrast, the year 1937 saw the "first industry-wide profit making in seven years."[13] Horror, at least old horror, thus became an easy way for the post-Carl Laemmle "New U" to generate much-needed money.

And thus Emil Umann wielded the power to do what Lugosi on his own could not: put him back on the screen and, by extension, back on the stage as well.

The Comeback

For Bela Lugosi, the year 1938 proved even tougher financially than 1937. In January,

BELA LUGOSI IN PERSON

Theatre ballyhoo for the 1938 reissue. *(Courtesy of D'Arcy More)*

trades announced that he would appear "prominently" as the villain in the 15-chapter serial *The Secret of Treasure Island* (1938), but when it was released in April of that year, Lugosi was nowhere to be seen.[14]

In March 1938, he was a guest on Feg Murray's *Baker's Broadcast*. Boris Karloff appeared on the same show, with the two actors singing a song apparently written for the occasion: *We're Horrible, Horrible Men*.[15] But from that point until late summer of the same year, Lugosi seems to have had no work.

After Emil Umann made an amazing $3,000 gross for the first week of his horror triple bill in August 1938, he quickly hired Lugosi to make personal appearances at his theatre. Whether he contacted Lugosi's management or whether Lugosi contacted Umann is unknown, but Lugosi certainly appeared nightly on the Regina stage by the time of the triple bill's second and even more successful week.[16] Lugosi continued taking bows at the Regina for yet another week, with trades reporting that Universal might even send him on a national personal appearance tour.[17]

Instead, Lugosi signed a contract with Universal to appear in a new horror movie, one rushed into production to capitalize on what became something of a national craze. *Daily Variety* reported that *Son of Frankenstein* would feature Karloff, Lugosi, and – in the title role – Peter Lorre. In the end, Basil Rathbone replaced Lorre.[18] Not surprisingly, Karloff returned as the Monster, but Lugosi portrayed a new character, one that had not appeared in Mary Shelley's 1818 novel or any of its prior film or stage adaptations.

In a distinct departure from his generally dapper appearance, Lugosi was the broken-necked

From the *Boston Globe* of October 20, 1938.

and poverty-stricken Ygor, a murderous loner who forces the mad doctor's son to restore the Monster's strength. Lugosi later told Ed Sullivan that he would have turned down the role of Ygor had it not been for his money troubles, adding that "they only think I can scare children. It is very discouraging."[19]

But once he was playing Ygor, Lugosi found himself enjoying the role. And, as Chapter 2 noted, Ygor became the final addition to Lugosi's core battery of six Hollywood characters. Lugosi the Ygor (or Lugosi the Henchman, one might say) reappeared not only with that same name in *The Ghost of Frankenstein* (1942), but in similar roles in *The Black Cat* (1941), *The Body Snatcher* (1945), and *The Black Sleep* (1956). His work in *Son of Frankenstein* also nabbed him a five-year contract at Universal.[20]

Lugosi was in demand once again, for films, personal appearances, and interviews. For example, prior to departing by ship for England for the making of a movie called *The Dark Eyes of London* (1939), Lugosi hosted the press at the Waldorf-Astoria in Manhattan on March 23, 1939.[21] Among those he spoke to that day (or very soon thereafter) was Hy Gardner, whose syndicated *Broadway Newsreel* column ran in newspapers throughout America.

Being back in the public eye meant that fans new and old wanted to hear about Lugosi's life and his career. And so he talked about the following topics with Gardner:

On being afraid of the dark when a child

I never had a chance to be scared when I went to sleep because I came from a poor Hungarian family and there were too many of us in the house to be alone or to be frightened. But I found out that I was afraid to be alone when I first went to Hollywood. ... I moved into a very large house all by myself and though I had a couple working for me, they lived in a different wing of the home. And when I went to bed at night I never could fall asleep – It was so dreary and nerve-wracking. I'd read and read and read until the coming of the dawn. That seemed a little friendlier.

On marriage

... I got married the first time because I was lonesome and I needed companionship and I got it for two years. I was married to (my second wife) for 14 days, and before you go any further let me tell you that that was a long time compared to the duration of my third marriage. ... Exactly three days. ... I think that marriage is like everything else. It's a matter of a good break, and I finally found a woman six years ago who is a mother, a goddess, a watchdog, a secretary and a wife all combined. ... We're now on our seventh year together. ... I became a daddy 14 months ago and we've never been happier.

On his fans

Most people are very nice and I think that just as many of them that say 'hello' also say 'Come now, Bela, scare us.' Nevertheless, they look upon my parts of Dracula and Ygor just as characters and don't confuse it with my own personality.[22]

Rather than invoke any of his other horror characters, whether his mad scientists or otherwise, Lugosi placed Dracula and Ygor on prominent pedestals. At that stage, the name "Ygor" meant little to most Americans; in the days, weeks, years, and decades since *Son of Frankenstein*'s release, the name has become synonymous with Frankenstein and horror.

Soon after returning to America from the *Dark Eyes of London* shoot in England, Lugosi made an impromptu public appearance at Los Angeles Union Station:

> The 'glamour' boys do not get all the breaks. Bela Lugosi, just returned from a London picture assignment, took more than fifteen minutes to make his way from the train at the Los Angeles station to where Mrs. Lugosi and one-year-old Bela Jr. were waiting for him. A crowd of his picture fans swamped the famous character actor, now playing the star role in Universal's *The Phantom Creeps*.[23]

Published in June 1933. *(Courtesy of Dennis Phelps, as preserved in one of Bela Lugosi's personal scrapbooks)*

The Phantom Creeps would provide the cinema with one of its most bizarre robots; it also gave Lugosi an opportunity to play one of his most maniacal mad scientists. *Motion Picture Herald* called the 12-chapter serial "absorbing."[24] That was in September 1939, a year that was still fraught with possibilities.

The Warfield

In November 1939, *Motion Picture Herald* announced that the William Morris Agency was in talks with Lugosi to represent him for personal appearances.[25] He had already been asked

Basil Rathbone (left) as the title character in *Son of Frankenstein* (1939). Lugosi as Ygor and Karloff as the Monster are also present. *(Courtesy of Randy Nesseler)*

to do a vaudeville sketch at Chicago's State-Lake Theatre, but didn't proceed, perhaps because he was inundated with so many offers.[26] Soon thereafter, the same trade spoke of seeing Lugosi with a "boyish grin" in New York, the actor having travelled from California to New York to appear on a CBS radio show with Walter O'Keefe; he told the trade that he would play a werewolf with a "terrible case of rabies."[27]

Of all of his appearances in 1939, the most fascinating became one that he made with Boris Karloff in San Francisco. The occasion was a screening of *Tower of London* (1939) at the Warfield Theatre (which came just one week after Lugosi had been onscreen at the city's St. Francis in the 1939 film *Ninotchka*). A new horror movie, *Tower of London* starred Karloff, but not Lugosi. He had nothing to do with it, but Universal sent him to San Francisco all the same. Lugosi was a horror film star once again, and so that reason alone was enough to put him onstage in front of moviegoers.

Why San Francisco, in particular? Cliff Work, a former resident of the city, was at the time General Manager of Universal Pictures. *Boxoffice* informed readers that Work arranged the event, presumably due to the fact he had once lived there.[28]

The Warfield personal appearance was hardly Lugosi and Karloff's first together. As early as December 1932, the two actors were present at the dedication of the International Christmas Tree at the Hotel Christie in Hollywood. Also on hand were Anna May Wong, Claudette Colbert, Paul Lukas, and Olga Baclanova.[29]

Then, on March 14, 1934, Karloff and Lugosi appeared together at Universal City to publicize their film *The Black Cat* (1934). Dressed in their film costumes, the two dutifully judged a cat contest, the winning feline getting to appear in the film as the title character. First prize went to one Betty Firestone and her large black Persian.[30] Less than a month later, the two actors again joined forces for a personal appearance at Universal City Stage 4, which was dressed to look like an old fashioned "barn dance." The event was held in support of the Motion Picture Theatre Owners of America (MPTOA).[31]

Karloff as Mord in *Tower of London* (1939).

Some five years later, Lugosi and Karloff were in attendance at the American Legion Stadium for a massive Screen Actors Guild meeting. One account claimed the two did not sit together, but both were at ringside, the venue commonly being used for boxing and wrestling matches.[32] The meeting was not public, but at least one member of the press watched it unfold.

Most notably of all, perhaps, the duo was together at the Hollywood Pantages on May 3, 1934 for a screening of *The Black Cat* (1934).[33] Taking bows with them was costar Jacqueline Wells. Here was something of a precursor to the Warfield event, the very first time that Karloff and Lugosi had appeared together onstage.

For the *Tower of London* event, Karloff and Lugosi flew from Los Angeles to San Francisco on December 14, 1939.[34] With them was Mischa Auer, who would also appear at the Warfield. One newspaper account claimed that, after landing:

Mischa Auer, Bela Lugosi and Boris Karloff hopped nimbly out of the Mainliner at Mills Field Thursday night, ran briskly through the administration building, piled into a limousine, nodded 'Go ahead!' to their waiting police escort, and headed for San Francisco... Once on Bayshore highway, the long, low car moved slowly ahead behind the cop on the motorcycle... But they gained no speed: trucks, trailers, model T's passed them up....

The Messrs. Auer, Lugosi and Karloff muttered uncomplimentary mutters about San Francisco speed and service as boys on bicycles and even kids on skooters whizzed by them and hooted as they passed....

Finally, after what seemed hours, the limousine and the escort pulled up at the St. Francis [Hotel], and the three distinguished passengers got out... 'Say,' shouted Mr. Auer at the motorcycle copper, 'What was the trouble? Afraid of breaking the law?' ...

'Well,' confessed the officer, lowering his eyes and standing on one foot, then the other, 'to tell the truth – I couldn't get my siren to work!'[35]

That evening, the Karloff and Lugosi reunion continued at a local hotel, apparently in a very congenial manner. The two actors and their wives met as they arrived for the overnight stay prior to taking to the stage on Friday. The local press asked:

Newsreel film frame depicting Karloff and Lugosi examining black cats at Universal in 1934.

What happens when Frankenstein and Dracula meet? The answer is easy. They did it last night at Hotel St. Francis and to those who imagine them spending all their time thinking up rare forms of torture and the like, it would have been disappointing. Boris Karloff and Bela Lugosi approached each other with wide grins, said 'Hello. Meet the wife,' just like that. The wives went into a corner and started chatting about their respective children....[36]

As the two actors chatted, San Franciscans read about their forthcoming personal appearance, with newspapers reporting that Lugosi was not actually in the film. One added that the Warfield would mark the first time he had ever appeared onstage with Karloff, somewhat of an exaggeration given the aforementioned screening of *The Black Cat*.[37]

With regard to their December 15, 1939 appearance at the Warfield, city newspapers like the *San Francisco Chronicle* and the *San Francisco Examiner* did not review it, concentrating their efforts instead on the film.[38] The same was true of the *San Francisco News*, though its critic did mention that seeing Karloff and Lugosi in person allowed audiences to "satisfy" themselves that the duo were "just ordinary human beings like the rest of us."[39]

A letter to the editor of *Variety* – presumably written by someone working at the Warfield

– detailed the personal appearance at some length and with some harsh words:

The recent personal appearance of five Universal players in connection with the opening of *Tower of London* … stands as a glaring example of poor showmanship. Detailed at the opening by the m.c., Mischa Auer, as 'just a little something we knocked together on the phone on the way here–confidentially, it stinks,' the show lived up in every way to Auer's statement.

Equipped with poor material and in one case with none at all, it would seem that the picture might have had a better chance without their efforts. Auer offered two or three Hollywood jokes that the audience applauded out of politeness, and then [he] introduced John Sutton, a personable young man who stooged a minute or two and walked off holding his belly (we can understand that). Next, Boris Karloff came on. Got a big hand and proceeded to dish out a lot of 'up the year's from the Majestic to the Warfield,' and then said he'd overheard that there's better than even break [that the] Fair reopens in '40. Bela Lugosi tried hard for awhile and then presented Nan Grey, a great disappointment indeed. She is of the hand-kissing, arm-flinging, I-love-you-all-my-public variety.

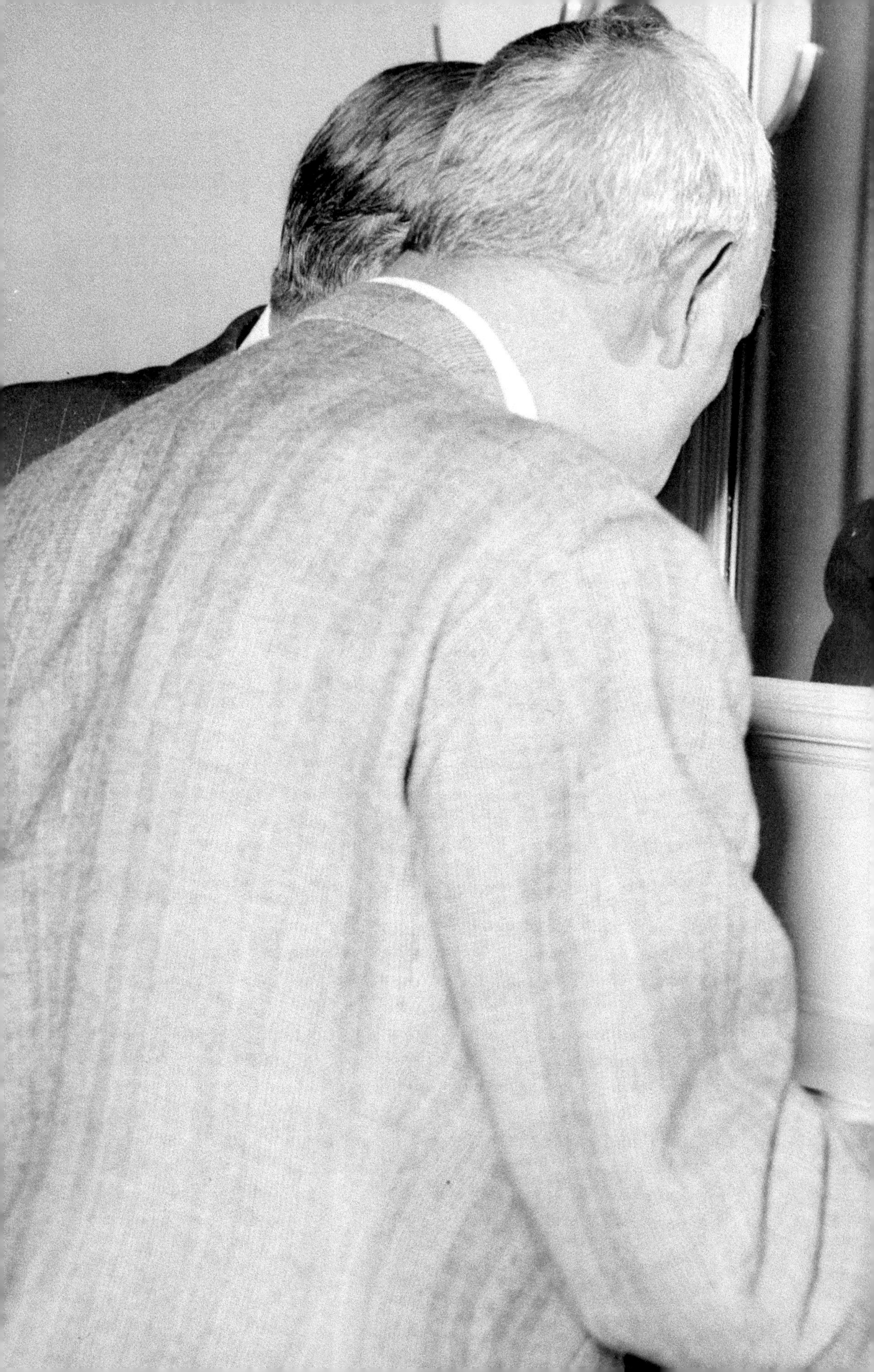

Lugosi and Karloff together in San Francisco for their Warfield appearance. *(Courtesy of the Bancroft Library, University of California, Berkeley)*

Lugosi and Karloff together in San Francisco in 1939 with John Sutton (left) and Mischa Auer (right). *(Courtesy of the Bancroft Library, University of California, Berkeley)*

All this might appear to be offset by the fact that the show was packed from noon 'til midnight by one pushover audience after another, mostly kids.[40]

Reporting elsewhere on the same subject, *Variety* confirmed the assessment about "packed" crowds, reporting that *Tower of London* would probably gross a "nice" $14,000 for its one-week stay at the Warfield, thus making it the "town's best bet."[41]

As for the belief that children were present in large numbers, the *San Francisco Call-Bulletin* broached the issue anecdotally when a journalist recounted:

When my Horace and the young O'Malleys heard that Karloff, their favorite scream star, was coming to Market Street, you couldn't have kept them out of the theatre with a portcullis.... I was outspoken in telling Horace that, history or no history, I didn't think all this bloody business was fit for for youngsters – particularly impressionable ones who will have nightmares about Mord [Karloff's character in *Tower of London*] instead of dreams about Santa Claus.[42]

"Don't be a censor!" young Horace responded, adding his prediction that "I bet every kid in town turns out to see it."

Conclusion

In November 1939, just before Lugosi appeared live in San Francisco, Emil Umann of the

Published in the *San Francisco Call-Bulletin* on December 16, 1939.

Trade advertisement from 1940 touting another Universal double feature.

Regina Theatre passed away at the young age of 37. The man who brought Lugosi back to life was himself dead, the cause being a "kidney ailment." [43]

Not long after his San Francisco appearance, Universal dispatched Lugosi to Chicago, alongside Vincent Price and Margaret Lindsay, to do a live promotion in support of *Black Friday* (1940) and *The House of the Seven Gables* (1940). The "double world premiere" was held February 29, 1940 at the RKO Palace (2,451 seats). [44] The event was perhaps better received than the *Tower of London* in San Francisco, with *Variety* claiming Lugosi and Price in person resulted in "bang-up exploitation" that grossed approximately $14,000, a "cheerful" result. [45]

Then, on January 21, 1942, Lugosi made a live appearance in support of yet another double feature. He appeared with Warren William, Lionel Atwill, Claire Dodd, Nat Pendleton, Maria Ouspenskaya and Evelyn Ankers, at Los Angeles' Vogue Theatre (897 seats) to ballyhoo a double feature of *The Wolf Man* (1941) and *The Mad Doctor of Market Street* (1942). [46]

Universal deployed its horror brigade again on March 26, 1942 in support of *The Ghost of Frankenstein* (1942). [47] Lugosi, Lionel Atwill, and Evelyn Ankers accompanied Lon Chaney Jr. to both the Pantages Theatre (2,812 seats) and the RKO Hillstreet Theatre (2,890 seats); the latter theatre presented Chaney with a plaque, dubbing him – rather than Karloff or Lugosi – the "new master character creator." [48]

Lugosi would also appear with Karloff at subsequent events. On March 14, 1940, for example, the two joined forces with a number of other famous names in skits featured at the *Gambol of the Stars* at the Ambassador Cocoanut Grove. [49] In front of an audience of around 700, the two horror stars acted as "bouncers" for Ernest Truex, chairman of the floor committee.[50]   Other celebrities in appearance (many of them dancing to the music of Guy Lombardo) included Mickey Rooney, Judy Garland, Eduardo Ciannelli, Bette Davis, and Edward G. Robinson.[51]

That Lugosi's career had been revived is without question. But the Lugosi of the *Tower of London* appearance was not the same as the Lugosi prior to the British ban. He and his persona changed, at least to a degree. Yes, he continued to appear at major studios, usually in supporting roles, just as he continued to star in B-movies. And his fame as Dracula continued onward, uninterrupted and unimpeded by his period of unemployment.

All that said, Lugosi's cinematic persona expanded thanks to Ygor, just as it changed to a small degree given his altered appearance. Whether it was his advancing age or the stress of his career problems or both, the Lugosi of 1939 and the World War II period looked markedly different than the Lugosi of 1936 and earlier. Aside from an occasional glimpse of wrinkles and graying hair was the weight gain in his face. Post-revival, Lugosi was noticeably older and paunchier. Gone was the svelte appearance of eternal youth that he carried during his fifties.

Lugosi's audience was in flux as well. No doubt movie fans flocked to see him and Karloff, whether live in San Francisco or onscreen at theatres throughout America. But the *San Francisco Chronicle* saw the vanguard of a new trend when it noted the *Tower of London* crowd consisted of "mostly kids."

Certainly some children enjoyed horror movies before the British ban, but they were part of a larger audience for what in some cases at least were relatively big-budget movies. Beginning in 1939 and continuing throughout the war and beyond, though, two things changed. One was the fact that the horror movie was an increasingly low-budget affair, whether at studios like Universal or at poverty-row enterprises like Monogram. And with those lower budgets came what many critics saw as increasingly improbable and juvenile storylines.

America's entry into World War II provided another key factor. Young and even middle-aged men found themselves out of America, with children, women, and the elderly becoming the majority of domestic ticket-buyers. And children like those who crowded the Warfield gravitated towards horror in large numbers, whether it was at the movie theatre, on the radio, or at live appearances by the likes of Bela Lugosi.

The *San Francisco Chronicle* was not alone in detecting the genre's growing dependence on a youthful audience. Consider the poem *Dracula, Frankenstein & Co.*, which was published in the *Los Angeles Times* in December 1938. As much as anything else, it offers insight into some of the very audience members who helped Emil Umann resurrect Lugosi's career:

Hush my baby; look and listen;
Through this double-feature show;
Watch the Karloff eyeballs glisten,
When he rolls them to and fro.
Nestle, baby, warm and cozy,

Lugosi as Bela the Gypsy in *The Wolf Man* (1941).

While the woodwind's eldritch moans;
Mark this time for B. Lugosi
Gnawing flesh from human bones.

Hark, the voodoo–drumbeat's rumble
Here the zombies whine and mew
'Mid the graveyard's weird ensemble –
Banshee, vampire, wraith, and ghoul.
These were old releases, honey,
Ere your dad became a man;
Gosh – and they were coining money
Long before your day began!

You were born too late, my pretty,
For this merry graveyard cult;
But the moguls bent in pity –
Here you have the chaste result.
In this new revival-issue
All my favorites grace the list!
Think – while I devoutly kiss you –
Think of what you might have missed![52]

(Endnotes)

1   "Obituary: Emil Umann." *Daily Variety* 22 Nov. 1939.
2   "Three Horror Pix for 30c Fills Local Theatre to Capacity 21 Hours a Day." *Hollywood Reporter* 6 Aug. 1938.
3   Ibid.
4   Qtd. in Advertisement. *Motion Picture Herald* 3 Sept. 1938.
5   "Revival of the Undead." *New York Times* 16 Oct. 1938.
6   Sullivan, Ed. "Looking at Hollywood." *Chicago Tribune* 10 Jan. 1939.
7   "Marked Trend Toward Reissues and Repeats." *Motion Picture Herald* 26 Sept. 1936.
8   Breen, Joseph I. Letter to Harry Zehner. 15 Oct. 1937. [Available in the file for *Frankenstein* in the Motion Picture Association of America, Production Code Administration collection at the Margaret Herrick Library in Beverly Hills, CA.]
9   Harmon, Francis S. Letter to J. D. Miller of Universal Pictures Co., Inc. 17 Mar. 1938. [Available in the file for *Dracula* in the Motion Picture Association of America, Production Code Administration collection at the Margaret Herrick Library.]
10   "*Marco Polo* with Strong $90,000 and *Old Chicago* 62G Stand Out on B'way; Allen Jones Ups *Tom*, 28G." *Variety* 13 Apr. 1938. Another example of a theatre screening *Dracula* in 1938 prior to the Regina was the Liberty in Lincoln, Nebraska. See "It's Mickey Rooney Week in Lincoln; Both Pix Okay." *Variety* 6 July 1938.
11   "Maguire Top Gal in 2." *Daily Variety* 8 May 1937; "Barrington Next FTP Show at Playhouse." *Daily Variety* 1 Feb. 1938; "Military Strawhatter." *Variety* 4 May 1938.
12   "Columbia Reports Net Profit of $438,268 for Nine Months." *Motion Picture Herald* 18 June 1938.
13   "First Industrywide [sic] Profit Making in Seven Years Is Highlight of '37." *Motion Picture Herald* 1 Jan. 1938.
14   "Don Terry Gets Top Spot in Columbia Serial." *Daily Variety* 20 Jan. 1938; "Marathon Heroing." *Variety* 26 Jan. 1938.

Sir Cedric Hardwicke as Ludwig Frankenstein and Lugosi as Ygor in *The Ghost of Frankenstein* (1942).

15 "Feg Murray's Guests." *Daily Variety* 8 Mar. 1938.
16 "Lugosi P.A.'s at Regina as House Sees 2d $3,000 Wkly. Take." *Daily Variety* 13 Aug. 1938.
17 "Horror Trio Booking for Frisco; Gets $3,110." *Daily Variety* 20 Aug. 1938.
18 "New U Horror Pic Ready; Lorre, Karloff, Lugosi Star." *Daily Variety* 13 Oct. 1938.
19 Sullivan, "Looking at Hollywood."
20 "Lugosi's Five Year Deal Proves Horror Films Rate Revival." *Hollywood Reporter* 14 Jan. 1939.
21 "Purely Personal." *Motion Picture Daily* 24 Mar. 1939.
22 Gardner, Hy. "Broadway Newsreel." *Brooklyn Eagle* 5 Apr. 1939.
23 "Studio Chatter." *Harrisburg Telegraph* (Harrisburg, PA) 27 May 1939.
24 "*The Phantom Creeps*." *Motion Picture Herald* 2 Sept. 1939.
25 "Constance Bennett Tour." *Motion Picture Herald* 11 Nov. 1939.
26 "Units Replace Vaude at Chicago State-Lake And Agents Burn Up." *Variety* 25 Oct. 1939.
27 Qtd. in Cunningham, James P. "Asides and Interludes." *Motion Picture Herald* 11 Nov. 1939.
28 "S'Francisco." *Boxoffice* 16 Dec. 1939.
29 "Alien Stars to Hail Tree." *Los Angeles Times* 16 Dec. 1932.
30 "Hollywood Inside." *Daily Variety* 15 Mar. 1934. The story also reported several cats fighting as well as escaping and apparently eluding all attempts to get them out from under a bungalow on the Universal lot. *Daily Variety* also referred to this event on 14 Mar. 1934, thus confirming the date on which it took place.
31 "Who Hoedown Gid'ap There Frankenstein." *Motion Picture Daily* 11 Apr. 1934.
32 Coons, Robbin. "Hollywood Sights and Sounds." *Columbus Enquirer* (Columbus, GA) 5 Sep. 1939. The writer of the article observed, "they're dressed for the most part like the congregation at your neighborhood church. Like them, they're just working people and some of them don't work too often at that... The talk goes on with 'justice' the theme, to cheers and applause. It's like a football rally with a grim undertone. Finally Lawrence Tibbett speaks, leads in the *Star-Spangled Banner* and the meeting's over. Plenty of people have been called names."
33 "Young Screen Player Will Bow Tonight." *Los Angeles Times* 3 May 1934.
34 "Chatter." *Daily Variety* 15 Dec. 1939.
35 Caen, Herb. "It's News to Me – Saturday Scrapbook." *San Francisco Chronicle* 16 Dec. 1939.
36 "Frankenstein and Dracula – They Meet! Nobody Hurt." *San Francisco Chronicle* 15 Dec. 1939.
37 Hanifin, Ada. "Highlights and Shadows." *San Francisco Examiner* 11 Dec. 1939.
38 See, for example: Hobart, John. "*Tower of London* Built on Historical Plot of Horror." *San Francisco Chronicle* 16 Dec. 1939; Hanifin, Ada. "Grim Drama of Royalty is at Warfield." *San Francisco Examiner* 16 Dec. 1939.
39 Schwartz, Katherine. "*Tower of London*, New Universal Film, Chills Movie-Goers." *San Francisco News* 16 Dec. 1939.
40 Smith, B.J. "Calls Show Properly Described." Letter to the Editor. *Variety* 10 Jan. 1940.
41 "Xmas Giving Frisco B.O. Honors; *Bright Boys*-Ams Mediocre $13,000." *Variety* 20 Dec. 1939.
42 Chestnutt, James G. "Four Kings Are Cut in on a New Deal." *San Francisco Call-Bulletin* 16 Dec. 1939.
43 "Obituary: Emil Umann," *Daily Variety*.
44 Rhodes, Gary D. *Bela Lugosi Dreams and Nightmares* (Narbeth, PA: Collectibles, 2007).
45 "*Grapes*-Vaude Pick Up Steam in Chi to $40,000; Whodunit Duo Cheerful $14,000, *Wife* Cold 5G." *Variety* 5 Mar. 1940.
46 "P.A.'s Boost Horror Pix." *Daily Variety* 22 Jan. 1942.
47 Durant, Alta. "Gab." *Daily Variety* 26 Mar. 1942.
48 Ibid.
49 "Actors Rehearsing Skits for Star Ball at Grove." *Daily Variety* 8 Mar. 1940.
50 "700 Attend Festive 4-A Ball at Grove." *Daily Variety* 15 Mar. 1940.
51 Wickersham, Ella. "Movie Stars Turn Out for Gala Gambol." *Los Angeles Examiner* 15 Mar. 1940.
52 B.W.W. "*Dracula, Frankenstein, & Co.*" *Los Angeles Times* 17 Dec. 1938.

A portrait of Lugosi from
Black Friday (1940).
(Courtesy of Randy Nesseler)

D.E. 43.

Chapter 9

Murder and Bela Lugosi

I n the early summer of 1950, a New York production company named Rao Video, Inc. offered TV stations a weekly, thirty-minute program called *Welcome to the Past*, featuring Bela Lugosi in an "unusual series of horror and suspense twisters, with that master of horror... weaving in and out of stories in a new and different way. For those who love the weird, the eerie and the supernatural, this is it."[1] The asking price was $4,000 per episode. Apparently not enough stations signed up, as the show was never produced.

But then, in what could have been a reworking of the same idea, New York station WPIX-TV actually did air one of the most fascinating and yet most unknown Lugosi projects ever made. It was a one-hour show called *Murder and Bela Lugosi* that premiered on September 18, 1950 in an 8:30PM EST time slot. Though the format was somewhat different than *Welcome to the Past*, the same title would have worked, because *Murder and Bela Lugosi* was: "the first film show on TV to also have the star of the film version in person ... Lugosi will offer bits of narration to complement showings of many of his old movies...."[2]

The idea was a logical one, given that many of Lugosi's B-movies were already appearing on TV broadcasts, and that the new show cost relatively little money to produce: Lugosi on what was presumably a simple set providing some commentary to the camera. Or – given that scant details have emerged – Lugosi's voice only, providing narration.

Either way, here Lugosi was not quite playing himself, but instead a public version of himself, the "horror man" of the movies. And that new narration was interwoven with Lugosi playing other, more clearly fictional characters in clips from his old films: it was meta-horror of the first order. The program also seems to have transformed Lugosi into the first horror film host on television.[3]

The choice of *Murder and Bela Lugosi* for a title was a good one. After all, horror radio shows of the late 1940s had been attacked for being a bad influence on children; that fact might have caused producers to latch onto the word "murder" instead. And then there is the fact that the show's clips likely came from the movies Lugosi made for Monogram, PRC, and/or other low-budget companies like Victory and Imperial-Cameo. Rather than being Dracula or other monsters in those poverty-row horrors, he was usually Lugosi the Criminal and/or Lugosi the Mad Scientist. And that meant he was out to murder someone, if not several people.

Consider the roles he played shortly after his comeback from the British ban on horror movies. He was a bomb-dropping scientist eager to destroy entire populations in *The Phantom Creeps* (1939); even his iconic role of Ygor in *Son of Frankenstein* (1939) was more murderer than monster, as the broken-necked character used Frankenstein's monster in order to take revenge on those who had hanged him. Lugosi onscreen was often murderous, and would continue to be even after 1939, including in *Black Friday* (1940), which paired him once again with Boris Karloff.

"Dracula" Cast

Bela Lugosi will be the only star on a forthcoming hour-long show over WPIX on Sept. 18th. Lugosi will offer bits of narration to complement showings of many of his old movies. Seen on Thursdays. 8:30-9:30 p.m. "Murder and Bela Lugosi" will be the first film show on TV to also have the star of the film version in person.

From *Radio Daily* of September 3, 1950.

By that time, Lugosi's career featured momentum of a type that he could only have dreamed about during the dark days of 1938. True, he was never again to have the kind of star power he did in the immediate period after *Dracula* (1931). But Lugosi was a presence onscreen, one that generated money and publicity for Lugosi offscreen. The year 1940 illustrates that very fact.

For example, there was his behind-the-scenes work on *Fantasia* (1940). *Modern Screen* informed readers about Lugosi's involvement in Walt Disney's classic animated feature:

When Bela Lugosi had a call from the Walt Disney studios the other day, he proceeded over there considerably perplexed about what kind of role the cartoonist had dreamed up for him. The actor was met by Disney and Leopold Stokowski. 'Mr. Stokowski will direct his orchestra in music symbolizing the eruption of a volcano,' Disney explained, 'and will you please interpret the volcano?' Lugosi admitted it was something of a shock to be called on for anything of this nature, but, being of the old school, he launched into the assignment.

So successful was his interpretation that moving pictures were taken of him. These will later be used as models by the Disney artists when drawing the erupting volcano for the animated cartoon. 'Guess I'm one actor,' said Lugosi, when it was all over, 'who doesn't have to worry about being typed.'[4]

A Los Angeles newspaper also reported that Lugosi's "histrionics" would be used as the "model for a baleful volcano."[5] By contrast, subsequent accounts claimed that Lugosi twirled his cape on camera so as to provide inspiration for how the devilish character Tchernabog should appear. In the end, animator Bill Tytla did not find the Lugosi footage particularly helpful, but that scarcely mattered in the context of 1940.

Lugosi received a paycheck and good publicity, just as he would in a touring show that same year, one that featured music, dance, comedy, and – in a prescient manner – film clips with narration not unlike *Murder and Bela Lugosi* would offer on television a decade later.

Stardust Cavalcade

Individual vaudeville acts presented by film stars fell out of favor to a degree during the 1930s, but by the end of the decade, the trend returned in a somewhat new form, with numerous celebrities packaged together by famous Hollywood columnists. In late January 1940, *Daily Variety* described these shows, giving Louella O. Parsons credit for coming up with the idea:

Personal appearance tour idea ... is putting additional gray hairs in heads of major studio chiefs. Fad has reached such proportions there are not enough players to go round, and situation has become generally embarrassing to lot execs. [Parsons'] jaunt, for which six major plants each contributed one personality, set a precedent, and now every chatterer who services a daily paper or radio outlet is on the scent.[6]

8:30 WCBS—Arthur Godfrey's Talent Scouts.
WPIX—"Murder and Bela Lugosi" (Premiere).
WNBT—Symphony Orchestra. Nadine Conner, Guest; Howard Barlow, Conductor.
WATV—Finals of "Miss Television 1950" Contest, Dick Jennings, M. C.
WABD—Al Morgan Show.
WJZ—Author Meets the Critics, Review of "Truman, Stalin and Peace," Irwin Ross and James F. Murray, Critics.

Published in the *Brooklyn Eagle* on September 18, 1950.

Among the chatterers listed were Jimmie Fidler, Jimmy Starr, Hedda Hopper, and Ed Sullivan. Despite the zeal with which these columnists tried to line them up, the shows rapidly became unpopular with some actors. Their key complaint: the tours generally lasted eight weeks, "during which they might lose out on a [film] role that would mean the break of a lifetime."[7]

When tapped by Ed Sullivan for one of these package shows in 1940, Bela Lugosi readily agreed. His contract with Universal was not exclusive and at that moment the studio had no immediate plans for him. And Lugosi was apparently not concerned that he would lose out on a major role at another studio; that, or Sullivan's paychecks appeared safer and more enticing than spending a few months waiting for a role in Hollywood that might not appear.

As for Lugosi's new employer, comedian Alan King once quipped, "Ed Sullivan can't sing, can't dance, and can't tell a joke, but he does it better than anyone else." While Sullivan's talent did not lie strictly in being an entertainer himself, he had an uncanny ability over the years to put together variety shows in such a way as to give the public what it wanted, most famously on his long-running CBS television program.

Artwork of Ed Sullivan used to promote *Stardust Cavalcade.*

Born in Harlem, New York in 1901, Sullivan started his career as a newspaper reporter. After writing a feature about Broadway for the *New York Daily News,* he was given the opportunity to pen a regular show biz column called *Little Ole New York.* Sullivan also hosted various entertainers on his radio show. Based on the success of both of these, he eventually began emceeing revues at theatres. Perhaps this was what led him to mount a star-studded vaudeville show for a national tour.[8] Its title: *Stardust Cavalcade,* which may itself have been inspired by Hoagy Carmichael's famous song *Stardust.*

Sullivan's initial plans were to launch a twelve-week tour in late February or March 1940, with Peter Lind Hayes being a featured actor.[9] *Stardust Cavalcade* would premiere at the Lyric in Indianapolis on March 22, with its cast including Lugosi, Jean Parker, Lon Chaney, Jr., Marjorie Weaver, Douglas McPhail, Phyllis Brooks, Carol Landis, and Gloria Blondell. Music Corporation represented the show, asking $8,500 a week plus a percentage of the gross for theatrical bookings.[10]

But for reasons unknown, the schedule and talent changed. As of March 15, 1940, *Daily Variety* announced a "seven and possibly nine week" tour that would feature Lugosi, Helen Parrish, Marjorie Weaver, Arthur Treacher, Douglas McPhail, Betty Jaynes, Vivien Fay, and one non-film star, the hoofer Peg Leg Bates.[11] That cast list became final, though the schedule remained in flux.

Plans included an opening in Dayton, Ohio on March 26, with a schedule that would move to Pittsburgh, Washington, D. C., New York, Baltimore, Cleveland, and Chicago; there were also "pending" deals for Buffalo and Cincinnati.[12] Though Dayton remained the premiere city, the rest of the schedule solidified as Pittsburgh, Steubenville, Hartford, New York, and Washington, D. C.

To make their first show, the cast travelled together on the historic Chief passenger train, which was then part of the Atchison, Topeka, and Santa Fe Railway. On the same train was Eddie Cantor, who watched the troupe rehearse and even dispensed advice to Helen Parrish and Marjorie Weaver.[13] All the while, Sullivan kept writing his newspaper column, telling readers:

This morning at 8:15 o'clock, our troupe of movie stars and starlets was waited upon at Albuquerque, N.M. by couriers from the Governor, dignitaries from Coronado Indians in full regalia, leather skinned cowboys and other deputations who met us at the

Helen Parrish, one of Lugosi's costars in *Stardust Cavalcade*.

Santa Fe station with whoops, hollers, bands and scrolls. The scrolls were elaborate parchments from the State of New Mexico inviting [our entire cast to] act as guests of honor at the Quarto-Centennial.

It was a pleasant demonstration of interest and good will but, believe me, it scares the bejeebers out of you to awake to an ear-splitting war cry and find a painted Indian staring beadily at you from the door of a Pullman drawing room. Eventually we scared the Indian chief: he rapped on one drawing room and Bela Lugosi opened the door. The Indian backed away hastily. He had seen *Dracula*.[14]

Sullivan also described the fans who crowded the station platform at Albuquerque, writing that the "older children scared the younger by pointing to Bela Lugosi and hissing: 'Dracula.'"[15] In another column, Sullivan drew attention to the burgeoning friendship between Lugosi and Treacher, who passed the time by discussing Hungarian cuisine.[16]

Dayton, Ohio

Stardust Cavalcade made its national premiere at Dayton's 1,800-seat Colonial Theatre on March 30, 1940 and gave performances through April 3. It was paired with *Congo Maisie* (1940), a feature film starring Ann Sothern. Lugosi took fifth billing after Sullivan, Weaver, Treacher, and Parrish, with ads touting him in much the same way as they would throughout the show's run: "*Dracula* himself ... The Famous 'Horror Man' of Many Screen Smashes!"[17]

Commenting on opening night jitters among the cast, Sullivan wrote in one of his columns of the time:

HOLLYWOOD VISITS YOUR [H]OME TOWN!

When a famous columnist brings screen stars in person to your local theatre he encounters headaches galore which he herewith frankly describes

By Ed Sullivan

I'M writing this piece on a train going from Dayton, Ohio, to Pittsburgh, Pa., where early tomorrow morning, on the stage of the Stanley Theatre, I'll send a group of Hollywood "names" through a rehearsal of the vaudeville show we will present there. This will be Hollywood's third personal invasion of Pittsburgh within a few months. Louella Parsons and Jimmy Fidler both have preceded us with vaudeville units composed of movie performers, because this will go down in movie-vaudeville history as the year in which Hollywood, after insisting for too long a time that it wanted to get back on the stage, actually did just that. Every time you turned your head, it seemed that another columnist was escorting a troupe of movie performers into the five-a-day circuits. On top of that, groups of Hollywood performers banded together without columnists at the helm and engaged in their own cross-country hops.

With me in this particular troupe are Universal's Helen Parrish; 20th Century-Fox's Marjorie Weaver; free-lance comedian Arthur Treacher; horror-man Bela Lugosi and the M.-G.-M.'s "Babes in Arms" duet of Douglas MacPhail and Betty Jaynes. From vaudeville, for good measure, I recruited Peg-Leg Bates, an amazing southern Negro boy who dances better on one leg than most dancing stars ever dance on both legs, and Vivian Fay, the toe-dancer you saw in "A Day at the Races" and "The Great Waltz."

The reason I have outlined the entire company for you is to give you a complete picture of the problems that must be encountered when such a Hollywood company is organized for a six-week invasion of the vaudeville stages of the country. The signing of each one of these players presented a problem that was completely individual, and the solution of each problem resulted in a volume of red tape that is staggering in retrospect. Because Louella Parsons and Jimmy Fidler must have encountered these same difficulties, I think that an exposition of them will be of interest to you movie fans, because this is a phase of Hollywood with which you are not familiar, although it concerns you in your theatres.

Here is what actually happens when Hollywood tries to go to the rescue of vaudeville.

My idea was to assemble a show that the bigger presentation houses could buy for $7,500 a week. For that sum of money, I wanted to offer the theatres performers from the movies who had definite box-office names. Yet obviously within the framework of a $7,500 weekly budget, it would be impossible to sign a Marlene Dietrich, who would want not less than $6,000 a week, or even a Lupe Velez who would want $7,500 a week. Railroad transportation from the West Coast and back would average about $500 a week on a four-week jaunt. There were other expenses that had to be provided for out of that $7,500, plus performers' salaries.

Having played quite a lot of vaudeville, I wanted above all things movie performers who actually could DO SOMETHING on a stage. I didn't propose to throw them all into a series of dramatic sketches and let the devil take the hindmost. I wanted youth and charm. I wanted comedy. I wanted novelty. Bela Lugosi certainly offered novelty; Lugosi working with Arthur [*Continued on page 67*]

Accompanying Ed Sullivan on his tour of the country are above: Universal's Helen Parrish; center: horror-man Bela Lugosi; upper right: free-lance comedian Arthur Treacher; right: 20th Century-Fox's Marjorie Weaver; below: M-G-M's "Babes in Arms" duet of Betty Jaynes and Douglas MacPhail, who are Mr. and Mrs. in private life. Vivian Fay and Peg Leg Bates, of vaudeville, are also featured in the troupe.

From *Silver Screen* of June 1940.

Your reporter turned actor here Saturday on the stage of the RKO Colonial Theatre, and although he has played quite a lot of vaudeville, he confesses that his stomach was tied up in agitated knots... once you get in action, the nervousness disappears, outside of knees that have a tendency to give off a castanet effect, but waiting for that 'go' signal is concentrated nervous tension. It communicates itself to the best of them. Bela Lugosi, Arthur Treacher... all were a bit jittery before the first show, but relaxed immediately they walked into the spotlight and heard the theatre applauding them....[18]

And the applause was plentiful. One newspaper suggested the Dayton crowd might have been the "most receptive audience" of 1940.[19]

Local criticism was also positive, at least in large measure. The *Dayton Daily Journal* claimed that the troupe gave a "bang up performance."[20] The *Dayton Daily News* was even more thorough:

Marjorie Weaver and Helen Parrish, the glamour girls of the unit, join with Betty Jaynes to sing the humorous ditty, *Boris* (Karloff), *Bela* (Lugosi) and *Charles* (Laughton).

Bela Lugosi appears wearing his *Dracula* cape, in white makeup, a green light playing over his features, and looking like death warmed over. He joins in the song with Treacher and dances off the stage with him, quite a change from his usual role. When Sullivan introduces the entire cast in the finale, [Lugosi] explained he always played romantic parts before he was cast as Dracula....[21]

Not only was the song about horror actors a kind of humorous historical survey, but so too was a film reel that Sullivan projected and narrated as part of the live show. The *Daily News* told readers it featured old footage of everyone from Sarah Bernhardt and Jack Dempsey to Rudolph Valentino and Lon Chaney. Commentary and clips, even if not focused on murder and Bela Lugosi.

The most lengthy and most important review of the Dayton show appeared in *Variety*:

Ed Sullivan's seven-week vaude tour with a group of Hollywood players is breaking in currently at the Colonial and is marked by dandy crew putting on a fast-moving, highly entertaining show. There wasn't a slip at the first show and few signs of nervousness.

The columnist emcees the show and does a neat job of it, wielding a firm hold over the proceedings but not forgetting a little humor now and then to spice the remarks.

The unit tees off. Treacher comes running down the aisle and suddenly finds that he has landed on a theatre stage... Helen Parrish plays Charlie [McCarthy] to [Treacher's] Edgar Bergen singing of *If I Could Be a Dummy on Your Knees*.

Bela Lugosi's sepulchral voice is heard offstage with its gruesome haw-haw-haw, to the accompaniment of flickering lights, and later he sneaks up behind Treacher, who, turning around and facing him suddenly extends his hand and cracks 'Dr. Lugosi,

Published in the *Dayton Daily News* of March 29, 1940.

I presume' ... Sullivan, Treacher and Lugosi combine for a short song session with *Ragtime Cowboy Joe*, adding a few dance steps. A little more of this act and something in the way of a skit for Lugosi would improve the setup.

For a finale, the m.c. has each one telling what he or she would like to be and then, assuming the masks of such personalities, they bring on the final curtain with a song....[22]

From the *Dayton Daily Journal* of March 29, 1940.

From the *Pittsburgh Post-Gazette* of April 5, 1940.

On at least one occasion, if not the entire tour, Lugosi's mask was, curiously enough, that of the Frankenstein monster, a role that – as of 1940 – only Boris Karloff had played in Hollywood.[23]

Highlighting the successful run at the Colonial, Ed Sullivan waxed enthusiastic in reporting the financial and audience reactions: "Our Hollywood gang is busting records in its first week at the RKO Colonial Theatre, playing to standees five and six deep. Arthur Treacher, Bela Lugosi ... won notices in the local papers that will make their coast studios sit up and take notice."[24] So did future theatres booking *Stardust*, as Lugosi's billing in subsequent appearances rose to as high as third place.

Billboard agreed that Lugosi and the others had made a hit, informing readers that the Colonial's weekly gross was "skyrocketing" thanks to the show.[25] In the end, *Stardust Cavalcade* generated $11,977 at a theatre whose average weekly take was only $5,000.[26]

Pittsburgh

Greeted by cool temperatures as the troupe arrived by rail, the *Stardust Cavalcade* show opened at Pittsburgh's 3,719-seat Stanley Theatre on April 4, 1940. On the screen was *It All Came True* (1940), which costarred Ann Sheridan and Humphrey Bogart. Until they finished a week later on April 11, the troupe staged their show four times daily, starting at 12:55PM and ending at 9:30PM. At least, that was the schedule for all days except April 7, when the troupe performed *Stardust Cavalcade* for "one day only" at Steubenville, Ohio's 2,000-seat Capitol Theatre.[27]

Once again, a critic was on hand to watch the show for *Variety*, but he was not quite as positive as his predecessor:

Of all the columnists to come out of Hollywood this season with stardust in their wake, Ed Sullivan is by far the best of the lot. That's not so surprising, however, inasmuch as he's an old hand at the vaude game, a thoroughly schooled showman and salesman who has the assurance of a veteran at this personal stuff. But it isn't just Sullivan either, it's the way he's shaped the available talent into a neat whole, with little that smacks of the usual personals....

Arthur Treacher comes in from the audience, ostensibly late, for some crossfire with Sullivan that's okay. At same time, he plants the fact that he doesn't believe in bogey men which keeps up as a slick running gag all the way to Bela Lugosi's eventual meeting with him.

Published in the *Pittsburgh Press* on April 5, 1940.

... Long planted meeting of Lugosi and Treacher follows, with former supposedly scaring Treacher only to ask for his autograph, and then the two of them joining Sullivan for a comically corny song and dance to *Ragtime Cowboy*....

... For the finale, Sullivan discovers through question and answers, which work up a lot of laughs, that all of his charges would rather be someone else, whereupon the lights go down and come up again to reveal the boys and girls wearing masks of their faves. Something wrong somewhere with this climax, however, since it doesn't come off properly. May be bit too sudden. Either that or some of the masks aren't very good duplicates and by the time the talent dons 'em, some of the mob may have forgotten who they're supposed to represent. Would be better to have 'em do it while the lights are up, with Sullivan repeating the names.[28]

Despite his minor reservations, this critic added that *Stardust* had "practically a full house" on its opening day.

Local critics were also pleased with the show. The *Pittsburgh Press* detailed its cast as follows:

... Bela Lugosi keeps his famous horror characterizations in a comedy vein and wins his share of the laughs.

... With four gals... who can actually do something, Doug McPhail to sing, Bela Lugosi to burlesque his hair-raising screen roles and Arthur Treacher to juggle gags in sure-fire fashion, Columnist Sullivan can't miss. His show ranks 'tops' among those presented by the Hollywood scribblers-turned-vaudevillians who have stopped in town.[29]

In like fashion, the city's *Sun-Telegraph* reported that Lugosi was a "slick asset" to the group, at least when he was healthy enough to appear.[30] Apparently he missed two days of performances due to illness.

A local journalist noticed Lugosi seemed under the weather while conducting an interview with him for the *Pittsburgh Press*:

Bela Lugosi was not feeling well Saturday afternoon and it wasn't just makeup which gave him a ghastly greenish pallor. Four others were in the dressing room or I wouldn't have stayed there. Any minute I expected to see bats flying about. He had a demoniac stare in his eyes – that murderous gleam of old Count Dracula himself. But the horror man who has made millions shiver declares the current world deals out more horrors than ever dreamed of on the screen. 'Unemployment,' he says in sepulchral tone, 'is the greatest of all horrors; war the second.'[31]

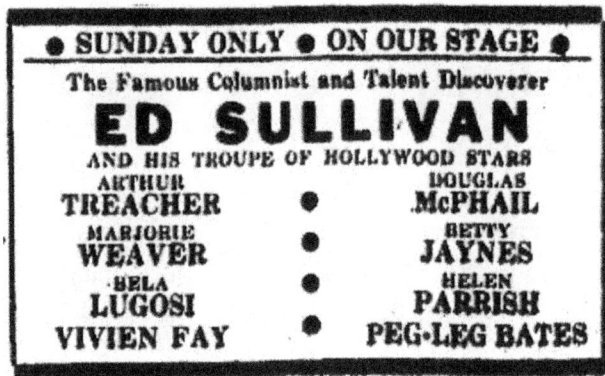

● SUNDAY ONLY ● ON OUR STAGE ●
The Famous Columnist and Talent Discoverer
ED SULLIVAN
AND HIS TROUPE OF HOLLYWOOD STARS

ARTHUR TREACHER	●	DOUGLAS McPHAIL
MARJORIE WEAVER	●	BETTY JAYNES
BELA LUGOSI	●	HELEN PARRISH
VIVIEN FAY	●	PEG-LEG BATES

From the *Steubenville Herald-Star* of April 5, 1940.

At roughly the same time, Lugosi met with Dr. Martin I. J. Griffin, the Dean of Duquesne University's College of Arts and Sciences and a self-declared expert in horror. The two men discussed their belief that "women are the horror-film customers," with Lugosi admitting that "women frequently write him offers of their blood, believing he needs it to live."[32]

In his own newspaper column, Sullivan described the Pittsburgh run as a success, telling readers that the troupe "not only got rave notices in Pittsburgh dailies but also busted week-end records … The Stanley Theatre alley is so jammed with autograph fans after every show that we have to have our meals served backstage most of the time."[33]

Thanks to numerous advertisements in the press and on local radio, the Stanley's overall gross was approximately $17,500.[34] That was a little above average for the theatre, a happy result given that the Stanley paid $7,500 for the troupe's appearance.[35]

Hartford, Connecticut

Having left Pittsburgh's cloudy skies and occasional rain, the *Stardust Cavalcade* cast drew attention from fans while travelling northeast to Hartford via New York's Grand Central Station:

> The thing that staggers you on such a cross-country hop as this is the magnitude of the publicity that the movies rate 24 hours in every day. ... Just how this works out was best proved when our crowd, en route from Pittsburgh, paused long enough to get a fresh train at Grand Central Station. Within a minute, Arthur Treacher, Helen Parrish, Bela Lugosi, Marjorie Weaver and the rest of them were completely hemmed in by a circle of hundreds of people. Some of them just stood and stared; others asked for autographs, and as the word spread through the terminal, the police had to form a cordon to wedge a passage to the train gate....[36]

Sullivan Unit 17G, Best of Columnist Shows at Stanley

PITTSBURGH. — Ed Sullivan's unit fared best of the three troupes brought to the Stanley by Hollywood columnists the past few months. His $17,000 gross was slightly above average, despite little accredited help from the film, *It All*

Published in *Billboard* on April 20, 1940.

Despite greeting admirers, the troupe arrived in Hartford in time for the April 12 to April 15, 1940 run at the city's 3,064-seat State Theatre.

The *Hartford Courant* interviewed Lugosi shortly before the show opened. He shared numerous stories with readers, including his standard tales of his pre-Dracula romantic roles and his career woes during the British ban. "Don't let him get started on the subject of his son if you have things to do and places to go," the journalist said of the proud father. "And don't let him talk to you in Hungarian proverbs because he makes the 'Confucius says' line look weak by comparison."[37]

The most thorough review of the Hartford show also appeared in the *Courant*, which reported:

> The entire spirit of [Sullivan's] 'little review' is a relaxed, informal one, with no extravagant claims being made by him for any one player, with the result the audience is not built up to a dreadful let-down as happened recently when another such Hollywood parade was offered... they each come on, do their turns, each turn, by the way, tied to the other by the patter and showmanship of Arthur Treacher. And the audience smiles, laughs and makes merry both at, and with, the company.

> ... Bela Lugosi plays along with Arthur Treacher whose dead-pan expression, quick-on-the-trigger mind, and general, eager awkwardness, keeps the act tied together with stitches of laughter.[38]

The review concluded by assuring locals that the show represented "A-1 Hollywood entertainment for your money."

The *Hartford Times* offered kind words as well, drawing particular attention to Lugosi and Treacher. "From the moment [Arthur Treacher] rushes down the aisle and joins Ed Sullivan on the stage, he has the audience in gales of laughter. A playful feud between him and Bela Lugosi adds to the fun."[39]

New York, New York

Stardust Cavalcade next moved to the 3,327-seat Loew's State Theatre in New York from April 18 to April 24, 1940, during which time Lugosi stayed at the Hotel Astor at Times Square. On the same bill was the Jean Arthur-Fred MacMurray comedy film *Too Many Husbands* (1940).

Unlike prior stops on the tour, the troupe now faced varied competition from major celebrities appearing at other venues, ranging from Lupe Velez in person on the same bill with *Dr. Cyclops* (1940) at the famous Paramount Theatre to the Capitol's live show of Eddie Cantor and George Jessel.[40] But the competition was professional rather than personal. Ed Sullivan – who was still writing his newspaper column – implied that both Velez and Cantor appeared in the audience of *Stardust Cavalcade* while it was in Manhattan.[41]

Opening night found Lugosi and his colleagues being "honored" at Loew's State in a "testimonial" featuring such persons as Abbott and Costello, Ray Milland, Simone Simon, Edward Albert, Sophie Tucker, Eddie Cantor, and George Jessel.[42] Though it was reported in

From the *Hartford Courant* of April 12, 1940.

more than one newspaper, details on this "testimonial" are few; what the contingent of stars actually said or did is unknown.[43]

For the third occasion, a *Variety* critic was on hand to view *Stardust*, his review making clear that the show underwent at least minor changes:

Sullivan's unit is compact, the tendency to hold the routines down to their meatiest. Only Peg Leg Bates, unipedic colored [sic] dancer, sticks around a little too long, his final number being dragged out quite far. He is a hit of the first water, however, and gives the show a strong start.

... Then, after latter's routine, he has a socky session with Treacher relating to film butlers, etc. Latter also does a poem gag. Here and elsewhere Sullivan takes some good-natured ribbing.

Betty Jaynes and Douglas MacPhail ... follow. They open with the duet, *Where or When*, from *Babes [in Arms]*, doing it nicely. *Student Prince* is a little tougher for Miss Jaynes, but clicks, while *Indian Love Call* serves as a surefire encore.

... Following some clowning which sets pretty well, [Betty Jaynes, Marjorie Weaver, and Helen Parrish do] a special *Wives of the Horror Men*, this in turn bringing on Lugosi as Dracula in a bit with Treacher. Latter then has his chance to sing a few bars of *Ragtime Cowboy*, mostly as a gag.

Sullivan has dug up a lot of old motion-picture clips and copyrighted the compilation. Film is thrown on the screen, with the columnist at the side in serious vein and also gagging, getting quite a lot of chuckles.

... Another Metro featured player in the troupe is Vivian Fay, who does a toe dance in swing tempo [featuring] pirouettes that are very good.

Photo montage published in the *Hartford Courant* on April 12, 1940. Top L to R: Weaver, Fay and Parrish. Sullivan is the center. Bottom L to R: Lugosi, Jaynes, MacPhail, and Treacher.

Calling out the whole company, Sullivan carries forth with talk, gags, clowning for an effective finish built principally around the angle of what each artist would like to be outside of what he or she is.[44]

Variety concluded by affirming, "aside from its b.o. value, [*Stardust Cavalcade*] is a thoroughly enjoyable hour's entertainment."

Billboard fleshed out details of the New York show even further, claiming that the talent had:

... little to offer individually, but as a group, and under Sullivan's cool and collected guidance, kill an hour entertainingly.

Particular credit should go to Sullivan for his novel way of using Arthur Treacher, the very English butler, and Bela Lugosi, the boogey man, who have no vaude acts of their own. Several bits engaging the trio and running throughout the show are really funny.

... Marjorie Weaver and Helen Parrish [and Betty Jaynes] pitch in the vocal strength for something they call *Wives of the Horror Men*, cooed to the *Oh Johnny* tune.

Sullivan revives his *Famous Firsts* screen flashes in which silent and loud screen notables are seen in their early appearances. It is short and different.

... All return to the finale to engage in seemingly rehearsed 'ad lib' bits with Sullivan, winding up with the Hooray for Hollywood ditty and using masks of their own screen favorites.[45]

Further details regarding Lugosi appeared in the *New York Herald-Tribune*, which reported that he entered the stage wearing his Dracula cape after the conclusion of *Wives of the Horror Men*, initially scaring the vocal trio, but then "meekly asking for Treacher's autograph."[46]

Published in the *Hartford Times* on April 13, 1940.

Overall, the *Herald-Tribune* believed the show was "fast moving, lively, and honestly entertaining." What the rest of the New York press thought is hard to determine. Most of them did not review the show, even though they publicized it and even kept readers abreast of the troupe's social activities.

For example, on the afternoon of April 17, 1940, Lugosi and his fellow cast members were guests of honor at a cocktail reception at the Hurricane Club, a new cabaret that took over the space of the old Paradise Restaurant.[47] It featured faux palm trees, female dancers in grass skirts, and shifting special effects that simulated rain, wind, and blue skies. Lugosi and some of the others returned later that same night to help with the official opening; also present were Betty Grable, Harry Richman, Eddie Bracken, Ethel Merman, Franchot Tone, and Burgess Meredith.[48]

Stardust Cavalcade. **From left to right are Arthur Treacher, Lugosi, and Ed Sullivan.**

Towards the end of the New York run, Lugosi spent an evening at the Versailles Club; Gladys George, John Garfield, Bert Lahr, and Bramwell Fletcher were present that same night.[49] He also stopped by the Beachcomber, where the bartender offered him a Zombie cocktail; Lugosi's tongue-in-cheek response was, "No, make mine a small bier," something of a riff on a line used in *Stardust Cavalcade*.[50] Then, in yet another high profile social appearance, Lugosi dined with Arthur Treacher at Sardi's restaurant.[51]

In his quest to maintain friendly ties to the press, Lugosi also appeared at the American Newspaper Publishers Convention. One account claimed:

Most star-studded bill in years was the line-up of talent for the King Features Kingtown Karnival at the American Newspaper Publishers Convention, with Lucy Monroe leading a cast which included, among many others, Victor Moore, Olsen and Johnson, Johnny Green, Kay Kyser, Arthur Treacher, Erin O'Brien-Moore, Frank Luther and Bela Lugosi.[52]

Months later, Lugosi would reunite with Kay Kyser, the two appearing in RKO's *You'll Find Out* (1940), which also featured Boris Karloff, Peter Lorre, and *Stardust Cavalcade*'s own Helen Parrish.

But perhaps Lugosi's most fascinating appearance during the Manhattan run came at the

"Four A's Ball" held on April 21 in the grand ballroom of the Waldorf-Astoria. The name resulted from a group of unions collectively known as the Associated Actors and Artists of America. "Virtually every star in New York will entertain," wrote the *New York Daily News* in a fairly accurate prediction.[53]

Lucy Monroe opened the event by singing *The Star-Spangled Banner,* and then John Barrymore performed a "couple of scenes" from *Hamlet.* Others on hand (and apparently doing quick bits) included Abbott and Costello, Jack Benny, Bill Robinson, Red Skelton, Tyrone Power, and Ed Sullivan.[54] Lugosi's name was mentioned in advance, and so presumably he attended the event.[55]

Mingling with other stars and the kinds of wealthy New Yorkers who attended such gatherings took up a fair amount of Lugosi's schedule. But then, even in the Big Apple, he also made time to meet individually with fans. For example, Lugosi feted 20-year-old admirer Jack A. Miller in his Loew's State dressing room, after having sent the fan a signed letter to use as a stage door pass.[56] Miller later recalled:

> My girlfriend was with me that day ... she was actually too timid to meet [Lugosi] and she stayed at the stage door. ... I was told the number of Lugosi's dressing room and I knocked a bit forbiddingly at the door. His wife, Lillian Arch, invited me in and Bela came over from his makeup table. It was between the first and second shows, and he extended his hand.

From the *New York World* of April 17, 1940.

> ... Before I left the small dressing room, with its large open trunks, a bottle of what looked like vodka on the table, and the costume and dresses hanging on the door, Bela signed eight different photos for me, including one to my girlfriend, Vivian, who he expressed disappointment in not meeting.[57]

Miller concluded his tale – which he shared decades later with film historian Gordon R. Guy – by proudly saying, "It was a meeting I will always treasure."

Lugosi also met with another big fan that week, aspiring novelist and screenwriter John Frank Mauro. The *New York PM Daily* reported:

6 Film Stars To Be Honored At Loew State

A gala "welcome to Broadway" celebration will be staged at Loew's State Theatre tomorrow in honor of the six movie stars who are appearing in person in the vaudeville show.

The testimonial will be offered during the 10 p. m. stage show and among the personalities expected to participate are Sid Silvers, Raye and Davis, Eddie Davis, Abbott and Costello, Ray Milland, Simone Simon, Bert Frohman, Lyle Talbot, Edward Arnold, Eddie Cantor, George Jessel, Sophie Tucker and Col. Jay C. Flippen.

The group of film personalities who will be on the stage are Arthur Treacher, skyscraper tall comedian; Bela "Dracula" Lugosi; Marjorie Weaver, 20th Century-Fox's starlet; Helen Parrish, Douglas MacPhail, Betty Jaynes and Vivian Fay. Ed Sullivan, Hollywood columnist who has brought the troupe East for personal appearances, will act as master of ceremonies.

Published in the *New York Journal and American* on April 17, 1940.

For most of his 29 years John Frank Mauro, a midge-sized shoe clerk with a Joe. E. Brown grin, has been a palpitating lover of fiendish films in general and Bela Lugosi's fiendishness in particular. Whenever his neighborhood playhouse, which is in Flatbush, offered a double-dose of screaming-meemies like *The Raven* and *The Black Cat*, he would... sit, quivering joyously, through two or three showings.

Since his boyhood ... John has hankered to write. His formal education ended in Brooklyn's Public School 45. He has managed, however, to sweat out several full-length bogey tales ... 'I do not believe in the short story. I once studied art and learned that a good picture must be complete.'

First time John beheld Mr. Lugosi, gorging himself, as Dracula, on human blood, he knew that he sat face to face with his destiny. Mr. Lugosi, he concluded at once, was a great artist who needed ever more horrendous vehicles. So John scurried home ... and began pouring his soul into nightmare literature.

... It was tough going because he had never written much except public school compositions. But after 13 months he had some 40,000 words. They added up to a woolly-wild phantasmagoria called *Rhapsody in Death*... [featuring] a scientist with an inferiority complex... [who] lures victims to be tortured and murdered by ingenious devices.

When Mr. Bela Lugosi read about [it], he was fit to be tied. 'It's wonderful,' he wrote back. 'I couldn't sleep until I had finished it, and even then I couldn't sleep.' And he promised to write a preface, if ever John's masterwork should be published...

But John's super big moment came when Mr. Lugosi appeared in person at Loew's State Theatre and permitted John to visit him backstage....

A rare image of Lugosi on the set of *You'll Find Out* (1940). Peter Lorre is on the far right.

So memorable was Mauro's in-person meeting with Lugosi that, the newspaper claimed, the eventual publication of his novel was "anticlimactic" by comparison.[58]

Even though most fans didn't get to meet Lugosi, quite a few bought tickets to see *Stardust Cavalcade*. Its opening day generated "very big" business.[59] *Daily Variety* reported that the Loew's State "had more customers at one monitored matinee screening than did Eddie Cantor at the Capitol.[60] By the end of the run, the State's box-office took in approximately $29,000, which was above its normal weekly gross.[61]

Washington, D. C.

The Sullivan unit arrived by train at Washington, D. C.'s Union Station early on April 25, 1940. That same day, just prior to opening at the 3,432-seat Capitol Theatre, the stars of *Stardust Cavalcade* hosted a press gathering at the Hotel Carlton's North Lounge.[62] A columnist for the *Washington Daily News* commented:

> If Loew's Capitol continues to hold Thursday afternoon meet the press cocktail parties for its visiting Hollywood troupes, it'll have to find a bigger hall than the Carlton's North Lounge. Counting the two dozen youngsters camped in the lobby, armed with open autograph books, yesterday's reception for Columnist Ed Sullivan's crew of star and starlets took on the proportions of a convention.

So long as Loew's is willing to foot the refreshment bill and the Carlton doesn't mind its sofas being walked on by photographers after angle shots and the guests of honor continue to arrive a day ahead of their local opening, however, they will constitute events worth anybody's time to crash.

Of the three columnist-toted outfits the Capitol has corralled so far this season, Mr. Sullivan's is not only the most varied but, at least in preview, the most interesting. It's also the most tickled because the boys and girls have topped Louella Parsons' and Jimmie Fidler's groups in almost every stop.[63]

MEET & GREET THE STARS

AT THE

1st Annual Entertainment & Ball

OF THE ASSOCIATED ACTORS AND ARTISTES OF AMERICA

JOHN ★ JANE
BARRYMORE ★ PICKENS
JACK ★ MOLLY
BENNY ★ PICON
CROSS ★ BILL
& DUNN ★ ROBINSON
PAUL ★ RED
HAAKON ★ SKELTON
HAL ★ ED
LEROY ★ SULLIVAN

And Other Stars of Stage, Screen & Radio

Dancing to Johnny Green's Orch.

APPROVED BY THEATRE AUTHORITY

4 A

Waldorf-Astoria
49th ST. ENTRANCE

Grand Ballroom

SUN. APR. 21 - 9 P.M.

Tickets per person, Including Supper—$7.50 plus tax

ON SALE AT

Committee Headquarters, 46 W. 47th St., BRy. 9-3558

From the *New York Post* of April 18, 1940.

Members of the press interviewed the cast members that afternoon, one of them being Lugosi. He denied the existence of "human vampire bats" even while admitting he believed in them when playing Dracula in an effort to conjure the sincerity the role required.[64]

During the same event, a reporter from the city's *Evening Star* tried to elicit information about the real Lugosi, the man offscreen:

Even the corny idea of asking Mrs. Lugosi, who was boss in the Lugosi ménage, proved futile. The Dracula man, as harmless looking as the Potomac in June, turns out to be a fellow who lives in a home which has no boss –unless perhaps it is the Lugosi baby, who is now 2 1/2 years old. Mr. Lugosi's vocation may be horrifying people who go to movies, but his avocation is collecting objets d'art and listening to good music.[65]

Somewhat jaded about the entire event, the reporter added quite matter-of-factly, "[Lugosi] didn't frighten us a bit."

His use of the plural "us" may not have been accurate, certainly insofar as the young fans standing outside of the hotel door hoping to meet the stars and get autographs. Lugosi seems to have been the only member of *Stardust Cavalcade* who bothered to meet them and sign his name into their autograph books.[66]

Those young fans weren't the only happy Washingtonians that week. After *Stardust Cavalcade* opened on April 26, the often hard-to-please *Washington Post* critic gave it an excellent review: "Every member of the troupe is a competent performer and their ensemble

Mr. Mauro has spun an admirable fantasy in his "Rhapsody in Death." I could not sleep until I had finished reading it-- and then I could not sleep. Such is the hypnotic grasp it exerts on the imagination.

In one sense it is quite understandable that I should find it a fascinating story: I have a natural and inborn affinity for the slightly weird and morbid. As a small boy in Transylvania, I heard many tales of vampires, werewolves and other strange animals and monsters of the dark. I listened, not frightened, but enthralled and spell bound.

This peculiar allergy to things super-natural has its origin in that strange race of people of whom I am a part -- the Magyars. We accept it as neither fortune nor misfortune, but merely as fact, that there are no others in Europe like us. When we are happy, we are always a little sad. And we love the mysterious because we understand it and feel its influence in our lives. To us, it is very real and tangible. It is a part of the psychology of all Transylvanians.

Yet, for all of my natural sympathies, it has become second nature with me to view weird brama with the calculating eye of an expert. Starting with the stage and screen versions of "Dracula," I frequently have played strange and mysterious characters, vested with super-natural and incredible powers. Thus, for some years past such stories have been the mainstay of my livelihood, and, perforce, I have read them by the score.

So, both as an expert and as a lover of these exciting tales, I pay tribute to "Rhapsody in Death" as an outstanding work, constructed with good craftmanship and adequate suspense. It should succeed admirably as a book, a play or a motion picture.

It is not often that an actor writes prefaces for books. Therefore, I plead indulgence, for I must express myself in a language not my own. I sincerely hope that Mr. Mauro's book will have the success that it merits, and that the fine and horrible characters that he has conceived will come to be known by all who appreciate a good yarn gruesomely told.

B. L.

finale is a wow ... Arthur Treacher, Bela Lugosi and Master of Ceremonies Sullivan keep a steady stream of comedy flowing ... The act moves smoothly with a genuine professional polish."[67]

The *Evening Star* was equally positive, assuring readers that the show had been "written" rather than "tossed together," resulting in "amusing and enjoyable entertainment." The reviewer particularly praised the reel of film clips that Sullivan narrated, calling the footage a "treat for your memory."[68] Welcome to the past, in other words.

Appearing on the same bill with *Stardust Cavalcade* was the Tyrone Power feature film *Johnny Apollo* (1940). The troupe gave four performances per day until closing on May 2, 1940.[69] *Billboard* estimated the show would gross $18,000, thus making it the biggest success in what was otherwise a rather lackluster week for the city's theatres.[70]

Then, from May 3 to May 6, 1940, the *Stardust* troupe played three shows a day at the Palace Theatre in Akron, Ohio. On the screen was *French Without Tears* (1939) starring Ray Milland. In a May 4 review, the *Akron Beacon Journal* responded favorably to Lugosi's "burlesque" of his horror image. The same newspaper also reported on a tea party held by the sorority Kappa Kappa Gamma in honor of Marjorie Weaver,

Published in the *Evening Star* (Washington, D.C.) on April 26, 1940.

who had been a member during her college days.

From there, the cast journeyed to Youngstown, Ohio for two final play dates: May 7 and 8, 1940 at the city's Palace Theatre. Raymond Massey in *Abe Lincoln in Illinois* (1940) was on the screen. Along with performing onstage, Lugosi and the others guest-starred on radio station WFMJ on May 7. Reviewing the stage show the next day, the *Youngstown Vindicator* declared that Lugosi was "very friendly and certainly not fearsome." As for Sullivan, he would write in his column that the troupe had performed together some 200 times.

With the tour over, the cast returned to the West Coast via Chicago on the Santa Fe Chief; Sullivan was with them, as he went on vacation in the Pacific Northwest before returning to New York.[71]

Plans for a Chicago date were cancelled because the "players were tired out," particularly Marjorie Weaver, who was "suffering from a wrenched back sustained in a backstage fall."[72]

Lock Up Your Daughters

Lugosi arrived in Hollywood on May 11, 1940. At roughly the same time, trades announced he would costar with Boris Karloff once again, this time in *The Monster of Zombor*.[73] Regrettably, the film was never produced. Announcements suggesting Lugosi would play in summer stock that year did not materialize either.[74] And so he instead moved on to such projects as *You'll Find Out* and *The Devil Bat* (1940). While trading on his Dracula persona to a degree, the latter B-movie cast Lugosi as a murderous scientist: it was exactly the kind of low-budget movie that *Murder and Bela Lugosi* likely used for clips in 1950.

Even though the tour was over, *Stardust Cavalcade* did not disappear from Lugosi's life. In August 1940, the Hays Office expressed anger at a Rheingold beer ad published in the June 22 issue of the *New Yorker*.

Yessir, It Was Quite a Party:

It's still a toss-up whether the working press or the guests of honor had a better time at the Capitol's reception yesterday for its Hollywood stars and starlets. (1) Marjorie Weaver and Helen Parrish strike an unrehearsed pose with normally shy News-Acme Photographer Johnny Thompson; (2) Vivien Faye smiles her prettiest; (3) Douglas McPhail and Betty Jaynes (Mrs. McPhail) pause to admit their little daughter is the most wonderful baby in the world; (4) Marjorie scares heck out of Bela (Dracula) Lugosi; (5) Helen greets a flash-bulb with a "Hey, wait a minute!;" (6) Arthur Treacher in a gay moment; (7) Marjorie again, this time meeting News-Acme Photographer Frank Cancellare on his own ground.

Published in the *Washington Daily News* on April 26, 1940.

It featured Ed Sullivan uttering the phrase "My beer is a dry beer," a line from the show. Arthur Treacher, Marjorie Weaver, Betty Jaynes, and Lugosi endorsed it as well, a poor choice given that Will H. Hays frowned on film stars promoting alcohol. "Ordinarily this scoff-law attitude would have incurred a spanking," *Variety* wrote, but given the four's involvement with Sullivan in the tour, they "were let off lightly" with "harsh looks."[75]

Despite the beer kerfuffle, Sullivan continued to mention Lugosi favorably many times over the years in his newspaper columns. And then he booked Lugosi for an appearance on the television version of *Little Ole New York* on WPIX-TV on June 1, 1950, just a few months

From the *New Yorker* of June 22, 1940.

　BELA LUGOSI IN PERSON

before the start of Lugosi's *Horror and Magic Stage Show.*[76]

But perhaps the most lingering effect of *Stardust Cavalcade* would be the idea of projecting and interacting with old film footage, a la Sullivan's *Famous Film Firsts.* In 1947, *Variety* reported that Lugosi was appearing live with *Dracula* (1931) onscreen. "Midway in picture, Lugosi inserted an eight-minute act, in which he used a girl partner and re-enacted a chill sequence from the footage."[77] At least that was what the trade claimed; it is difficult to determine if the act was ever staged.

The following year, the Beegle Brothers proposed a two-hour "monster show" that would tour various movie theatres. Karloff, Lugosi, and Lorre would appear with a "program of excerpts from their old horror films."[78] Here again was a variation on what Sullivan had done with *Famous Film Firsts*, and yet here again was a project that never got off the ground.

But *Murder and Bela Lugosi* did happen. It is difficult to determine how many episodes were filmed; one was definitely broadcast, and perhaps a second as well.[79] Audiences watching WPIX-TV in 1950 got to see Lugosi do much the same with his old films as Sullivan had in *Stardust Cavalcade.* He took

For full details of the Nation-wide contest with over **£5,000** in prize money to be won

Please apply to:—

QUEENS HOUSE,
LEICESTER SQUARE,
LONDON, W.C.2

"Lock up your Daughters"

THE FIRST EVER QUIZ FILM

Specially produced for the horror, suspense-seeking fans, "LOCK UP YOUR DAUGHTERS" has an added attraction . . . . it is the first "Quiz" film.

Bela Lugosi, as Doctor Marlow, specialises in vampirism through hypnosis. For his experiments, he uses brides, or beautiful women in the prime of their lives. Among these is Betty Mansfield.

Whilst travelling with her fiancee, in search of her missing cousin, Zena, they stop at a wayside Cafe. Her fiancee goes to a telephone box; whilst he is away, Betty is lured to the Laboratory. Doctor Marlow is waiting for her to commence his experiment; it appears that for years he has been trying to bring back to life, his lovely young wife, but has never found a suitable girl . . . . Betty, he declares, is so like her, that this time it must work. Fortunately for Betty, her fiancee, with the aid of the local Police, arrives at the Doctor's laboratory in time to stop the completion of his experiment.

| 4590 feet. | Reg: No. F24364 | Cert 'X' |

NEW REALM PICTURES LIMITED
QUEENS HOUSE,
LEICESTER SQUARE,
W.C.2.
Tel.: GERrard 6302 (5 lines)

A press sheet for *Lock Up Your Daughters* (1959). *(Courtesy of Jean-Claude Michel)*

stunt offering..
   Production:—The picture, compered by Bela Lugosi, has a slight story about a vampire doctor who experiments on young women in order to bring back to life his lovely young wife and this provides legitimate excuses for the extracts from Lugosi thrillers. Its players range from The

Published in *Kinematograph Weekly* on 26 Mar. 1959.

Saw an interesting old horror film last week called LOCK UP YOUR DAUGHTERS which had Bela Lugosi introducing a series of blended excerpts from several of his old horror films –none of which I'd seen before. Sam Katzman was the man concerned. There was supposed to be a prize for guessing the answer to this "The first filmic quiz" but as they never gave you any method of answering the quiz like forms to fill in there was nothing I could do about it. Not that I knew them anyway.

Excerpt from Alan Dodd's letter for Forrest J Ackerman, dated 1 Feb. 1960.

NEW REALM PICTURES *presents* *Bela Lugosi* *in* "**LOCK UP YOUR DAUGHTERS**"

Lobby card for *Lock Up Your Daughters*. *(Courtesy of Dr. Robert J. Kiss)*

viewers on a journey through old footage, acting as host in what should have been an unforgettable televised event.

Except that it was forgotten. *Murder and Bela Lugosi* has remained unknown until now.

That is, unless it has been known under another name and as part of an even later project. In 1959, New Realm Pictures, Limited of Great Britain released a compilation of Lugosi clips entitled *Lock Up Your Daughters*. A review in *Kinematograph Weekly* on March 26, 1959 claimed Lugosi "compered" (meaning "hosted") the old movie footage.

Similarly, Lugosi fan Alan Dodd wrote to Forrest J Ackerman shortly after seeing the film in 1960, when the screening was fresh in his mind.[80] His claim, made long before there would have been any value in fabricating a tale of unseen Lugosi footage: "[*Lock Up Your Daughters*] had Bela Lugosi introducing a series of blended clips from several of his old horror movies."[81] To another correspondent, Dodd claimed that the film dated to "about 1951," placing it close to the time in which *Murder and Bela Lugosi* was created.[82]

Unfortunately, no print of the film has surfaced in the modern period. In the 21st century, the notion of unseen Lugosi footage in such a compilation has struck many as improbable, if not impossible. What is the logic used to decry these *two* primary sources that both claim otherwise? Questions have been raised about where such Lugosi narration could have originated; when was it recorded (or even filmed), and for what original purpose, given that Lugosi died three years prior to the release of *Lock Up Your Daughters*, a film released in Great Britain?[83]

Murder and Bela Lugosi quite likely provides the answer, with the little-known TV show being released with or without amendments in the United Kingdom in 1959 under a different title. Even the running time of *Lock Up Your Daughters* – which England's *Monthly Film Bulletin* gave as 50 minutes in a 1959 notice – speaks to this possibility, as *Murder and Bela Lugosi* featured a similar duration.[84] Its time slot was sixty minutes but, with commercials and station breaks, the actual running time would have been shorter. That, or those behind *Lock Up Your Daughters* could have re-edited Lugosi's voice from *Murder and Bela Lugosi*, even from raw footage or recordings.

Much about Lugosi's career has been forgotten, that is certain. And when little-known facts are remembered, they are fascinating and sometimes surprising, perhaps even more so than *Murder and Bela Lugosi*. After all, who would have ever believed that Lugosi would have worn a Frankenstein mask in a live show? Or that, most bizarre of all, that he sang *Ragtime Cowboy Joe* with Arthur Treacher before dancing offstage?

(Endnotes)

1   *"Welcome to the Past." Radio Daily Program Special* Summer 1950.
2   "'Dracula' Cast." *Radio Daily–Television Daily* 18 Sep. 1950.
3   It is true that, beginning on 19 Apr. 1950, producer Wyllis Cooper appeared on a spooky soundstage to introduce episodes of WCBS-TV's program *Stage 13*. The show repeatedly featured James Monks, who later appeared as a horror-style host (along with his black cat Thanatopsis) on the WCBS show *Tales of the Black Cat*, which was first broadcast on 8 Nov. 1950. Likewise, from 8 Sept. 1950, John Carradine acted as host of *Trapped* on WOR-TV; the program began as a mystery before turning to horror on 20 Oct. 1950, its name in TV listings changing at that time to *Trapped: Tales of the Supernatural*. However, what distinguished *Murder and Bela Lugosi* from these early efforts was that the Lugosi show had Lugosi hosting old clips in a manner similar to what Vampira and Zacherley would later do with old feature films, hence our argument that Lugosi was likely the first horror film host on television. By contrast, programs like *Stage 13* and *Trapped* broadcast entirely new content shot for television.
4   "Versatile Bela." *Modern Screen* Feb. 1940.
5   Carroll, Harrison. *Los Angeles Evening Herald Express* 15 Nov. 1939.
6   "Chatterers Swamp Studios with the P.A. Demands." *Daily Variety* 25 Jan. 1940.
7   Ibid.
8   "Ed Sullivan (1902 [*sic*] - 1974), Master of Variety." Available at: http://www.edsullivan.com/about-ed-sullivan/. Accessed 16 Aug. 2013.
9   "Hayes and Sullivan to do 12-Wks. P.A.'s." *Daily Variety* 25 Jan. 1940.
10 "Ed Sullivan Troupe Opens Tour Mar. 22." *Daily Variety* 24 Feb. 1940.
11 "Sullivan Troupe Opens March 26 in Dayton, O." *Daily Variety* 15 Mar. 1940. In his column "Looking at Hollywood" (as published in the *Chicago Tribune* on 15 Mar. 1940), Sullivan also noted that the tour's cast included film and stage actress Astrid Allwyn.
12 Ibid.
13 Sullivan, Ed. "Ed Sullivan On Tour; Vaudeville Safari Aboard the Chief, Eastbound." *Pittsburgh Press* 27 Mar. 1940.
14 Ibid.
15 Sullivan, Ed. "Ed Sullivan On Tour." *Pittsburgh Press* 29 Mar. 1940.
16 Sullivan, Ed. "Looking at Hollywood." *Chicago Tribune* 13 Mar. 1940.

17   Advertisement. *Dayton Daily News* 29 Mar. 1940.
18   Sullivan, Ed. "Ed Sullivan On Tour." *Pittsburgh Press* 1 Apr. 1940.
19   Gay, Chuck. "Down the Aisle." *Dayton Daily News* 30 Mar. 1940.
20   "Film Troupe at Colonial." *Dayton Daily Journal* 30 Mar. 1940.
21   Gay, Chuck. "Down the Aisle." *Dayton Daily News* 30 Mar. 1940.
22   "New Acts Unit Review Ed Sullivan Unit (Colonial, Dayton)." *Variety* 3 Apr. 1940.
23   Frankenstein films made prior to the 1931 version with Karloff were not filmed in Hollywood.
24   Sullivan, Ed. "Ed Sullivan On Tour; Bagdad-On-The-Pacific." *Pittsburgh Press* 2 Apr. 1940.
25   "Ed Sullivan Big 10G in Dayton, O." *Billboard* 13 Apr. 1940.
26   "Ed Sullivan's Troupe Scores on Eastern Tour." *Film Daily* 12 Apr. 1940.
27   Advertisement. *The Herald-Star* (Steubenville, OH) 6 Apr. 1940.
28   Cohen. "Stanley, Pitt." *Variety* 10 Apr. 1940.
29   Fortune, Dick. "Ed Sullivan's Troupe Is Packed With Talent – Columnist Gets Strong Support From Screen Stars On Stanley Stage; One-Legged Dancer Stops Show; Screen Feature Stars 'Oomph Girl.'" *Pittsburgh Press* 6 Apr. 1940.
30   Krug, Karl. "Musical Comedy and Drama On Screen With Variety On Stage." *Pittsburgh Sun-Telegraph* 6 Apr. 1940.
31   Monahan, Kaspar. "Show Shops Notes on Some Celebrities. Including Cohan, Ed Sullivan and Lugosi." *Pittsburgh Press* 8 Apr. 1940.
32   "Bela Lugosi, Dr. Griffin Swap Chills." *Pittsburgh Sun-Telegraph* 7 Apr. 1940.
33   Sullivan, Ed. "Ed Sullivan In Pittsburgh." *Pittsburgh Press* 9 Apr. 1940.
34   "*True* – Sullivan OK $17,500, Pitt." *Variety* 10 Apr. 1940.
35   "Sullivan Unit 17G, Best of Columnist Shows at Stanley." *Billboard* 20 Apr. 1940.
36   Sullivan, Ed. "Ed Sullivan On Tour U.S. Index." *Pittsburgh Press* 16 Apr. 1940.
37   Christoph, M. Oakley. "For Your Information." *Hartford Courant* 11 Apr. 1940.
38   "Film Columnist Brings Gay Show To State Stage; Ed Sullivan and Arthur Treacher Vie for Laugh Honors." *Hartford Courant* 13 Apr. 1940.
39   "Movie Comic Just as Funny on the Stage." *Hartford Times* 13 Apr. 1940.
40   Advertisements. *New York Sun* 16 Apr. 1940.
41   Sullivan, Ed. "Hollywood on Broadway." *New York Daily News* 22 Apr. 1940.
42   "6 Film Stars to be Honored at Loew [sic] State." *New York Journal and American* 17 Apr. 1940.
43   "Celebs to Fete Movie Vaudevillians Tonight." *New York Post* 18 Apr. 1940.
44   "State, N.Y." *Variety* 24 Apr. 1940.
45   Honigsberg, Sam. "Vaudeville Reviews." *Billboard* 27 Apr. 1940.
46   "Ed Sullivan Leads Show of Film Stars at State." *New York Herald Tribune* 19 Apr. 1940.
47   Johnson, Malcolm. "Cafe Life in New York." *New York Sun* 17 Apr. 1940.
48   Johnson, Malcolm. "Cafe Life in New York." *New York Sun* 20 Apr. 1940.
49   Johnson, Malcolm. "Cafe Life in New York." *New York Sun* 23 Apr. 1940.
50   Kilgallen, Dorothy. "The Voice of Broadway." *Mansfield News-Journal* (Mansfield, OH) 3 May 1940.
51   Eaton, Hal. "Going To Town." *Long Island Daily Press* 25 Apr. 1940.
52   Burke, Andy and Small, Frank. "On the Square." *Livingston Republican* (Genesco, New York) 16 May 1940.
53   "AAAA Ball." *New York Daily News* 20 Apr. 1940.
54   Advertisement. *New York Post* 18 Apr. 1940; "Four A's Ball." *New York Post* 20 Apr. 1940; Advertisement. *New York Herald Tribune* 21 Apr. 1940; "A.A.A.A. Gives Benefit Ball." *New York Herald Tribune* 22 Apr. 1940.
55   "Stars to Appear in Four A's Show." *New York Journal and American* 17 Apr. 1940.
56   Lugosi, Bela. Letter to Jack Miller. 17 Apr. 1940.
57   Miller, Jack A. "Bela Lugosi: A Meeting Remembered." *Castle Dracula Quarterly* Vol. 1, No. 1 (1977).
58   Kobler, John. "Some Like It Phantasmagory." *New York PM Daily* 25 Oct. 1940.
59   Honigsberg, "Vaudeville Reviews."
60   "Cantor, Jessel Nab $7,500." *Daily Variety* 19 Apr. 1940.
61   "*Mothers* – Cantor-Jessel N.G. $35,000, Ed Sullivan Unit – *Husbands* Big 29G, *Meet* – Wayne King OK 35G in N.Y." *Variety* 24 Apr. 40.
62   Craig, Don. "Seven Hollywood Folks – Loew's Tosses a Party for Movie Stars and Starlets Bowing at Capitol Today." *Washington Daily News* 26 Apr. 1940.
63   Ibid.
64   Ibid.

65   Carmody, Jay. "Something Must Be Done About Press Parties – This One Produces No News At All, Just Some Amiable People With Whom One Chats." *The Evening Star* (Washington, D. C.) 26 Apr. 1940.

66   "Being on a Personal Appearance Tour Is Good for the Ego, Hollywood's Best Gentleman's Gentleman Tells the Press." *Washington Post* 26 April 1940.

67   "Rich Man-Gangster Film Play Costars Power and Lamour; Sullivan Revue Clicks." *Washington Post* 27 Apr. 1940.

68   MacArthur, Harry. "Tyrone Power Gets Rough in New Film at Capitol." *The Evening Star* 27 Apr. 1940.

69   "Where and When – Current Theatre Attractions and Time of Showing." *The Evening Star* 26 Apr. 1940.

70   "D.C. Houses Off; 18Gs for Sullivan." *Billboard* 4 May 1940.

71   "Sullivan Resumes in N.Y. Aug. 1." *Variety* 24 Apr. 1940.

72   "Sullivan Troupe In." *Daily Variety* 11 May 1940.

73   "Pic Sales Sharpshooting Decried by U's Scully." *Daily Variety* 13 May 1940.

74   Eaton, Hal. "Going To Town." *Long Island Daily Press* 24 Apr. 1940.

75   "Screen Players Bally a Brewery; Hays Froths, Ed Sullivan 'So-Whats?'" *Variety* 14 Aug. 1940. Given that Sullivan was not a film star, the PCA had no oversight of his activities. In the 6 Dec. 1941 issue of the *New Yorker*, he (and he alone) appeared in another advertisement for Rheingold Beer.

76   Sullivan, Ed. "Little Old New York." *The Morning Herald* (Uniontown, Pennsylvania) 7 June 1950.

77   "Hollywood Inside." *Daily Variety* 10 Dec. 1947.

78   Monagan, Kaspar. "Show Shops." *Pittsburgh Press* 9 Aug. 1948.

79   It is certain that *Murder and Bela Lugosi* aired on September 18, 1950. It is also possible that it aired a second and even third time on September 25, 1950 and October 2, 1950. Available TV listings for the same day of the week and time slot on WPIX list their plans for those two weeks as "To Be Announced."

80   "*Lock Up Your Daughters*." *Kinematograph Weekly* 26 Mar. 1959.

81   Dodd, Alan. Letter to Forrest J Ackerman. 1 Feb. 1960.

82   Qtd. in Michel, Jean-Claude. Letter to Gary D. Rhodes. 15 May 1994.

83   It is true that a film buff named Patrick McCann wrote to historian Tom Weaver on 5 Dec, 2001, noting that he had seen *Lock Up Your Daughters* in Ireland. He said, "The film had voice over [*sic*] narration. By whom? I don't know." He does not claim that the film did not have voiceover (though he claims it did not include new footage of Lugosi), but rather that he says he does not know who spoke the voiceover. Here the following must be taken into account: McCann was writing about a film that he had seen decades earlier, as opposed to Alan Dodd, who as an adult Lugosi fan saw the film and wrote to Forrest J Ackerman only one week after viewing it. Secondly, McCann told Weaver the film had a running time of 61 minutes. This is dramatically at odds with the *Monthly Film Bulletin*, which noted the film was only fifty minutes long. Thirdly, McCann states that *Lock Up Your Daughters* – which he likens to a "documentary" – included clips of the MGM film *Mark of the Vampire* (1935), a claim for which there is no other evidence whatsoever. This point seems unlikely, given that *Mark of the Vampire* was (and remains) under copyright. Fourthly, McCann also described another New Realm/E. J. Fancy film for Weaver. Entitled *Lock Your Doors*, the film was – according to McCann – "another Lugosi compilation with clips from all Monogram Lugosi films including *The Ape Man* and *Return of the Ape Man*, as well as clips from *White Zombie*. However, McCann is very much incorrect here. Gary D. Rhodes owns a print of *Lock Your Doors*, which is nothing more than a retitled version of *The Ape Man* (1943) with New Realm's name appended to it. In short, McCann's memories of these two films seem at odds with known facts, thus making his overall description of *Lock Up Your Daughters* not necessarily reliable.

84   The listing for *Lock Up Your Daughters* was published in *Monthly Film Bulletin* in April 1959.

Bela Lugosi as the
title character in
The Ape Man (1943).
(Courtesy of Bill Chase)

Chapter 10

The Vampire Returns

"**A**n army marches on its stomach." So claimed Napoleon Bonaparte. Or Frederick the Great. The quotation has been credited to both men, even though it's possible that neither of them actually said it.

At any rate, the armies of the twentieth century depended on far more than food. Military success required energy beyond human strength and resilience. The Allied and Axis Powers in World War II had to rely heavily on home front production, including of gasoline and coal.

In early March 1943, the United Mine Workers of America adopted a resolution seeking an increase of $2 per day for each member in advance of their upcoming contract renewals.[1] The War Labor Board viewed these demands with much trepidation, in part because they were still grappling with unhappy aircraft workers on the West Coast.[2] Negotiations were deadlocked, with President Franklin Roosevelt ordering the mines to be kept open while talks continued.[3] In return, union leader John L. Lewis asserted that "profiteering" corporations treated his members unfairly.[4]

Some 2,000 union miners went on strike in early April 1943, a fraction of the 530,000 in America; they quickly returned to work.[5] Talks between all parties forged ahead, but then an increasing number of workers went on strike in late April.[6] On April 28, Lewis announced that the industry would be "paralyzed in the absence of new agreements" once existing union contracts expired at the end of the month.[7] The situation was growing worse, not better.

Armies in the Second World War also depended heavily on fuel, as much as any soldier depended on food. One of Rommel's major problems in Africa in 1942 was a lack of gasoline.[8] He was not alone. Allied generals like George Patton regularly clamored for more gas to advance their armies. "My men can eat their belts," Patton once carped, "but my tanks gotta have gas."[9]

But it wasn't just troops who relied on gasoline. As Will Rogers quipped during the Great

Depression, "America was the only nation in the history of the world to go to the poorhouse in an automobile."[10] The people of the United States relied on their cars and the fuel to run them, including the vast number who drove to work at factories that built the very machinery on which the military relied.

Along with so many other products (including tires), the federal government rationed the amount of gasoline that each American vehicle could use. In January 1942, the *New York Times* reported that the "American motorist, long the envy of the entire world, is about to learn how the other half live."[11] Rationing occurred incrementally, with Roosevelt declaring a nationwide curb in September of 1942.[12] Before the end of that year, the Office of Price Administration set mileage restrictions for the whole of the United States.[13]

Hollywood experienced these restrictions in more ways than one. Film critics working for the Office of War Information scrutinized movies for dialogue that not only referred specifically to the war abroad, but also for domestic issues like "Transportation Conservation" and "Rationing." Among the myriad extant records are those for the Bela Lugosi movie *The Ape Man*, released in March 1943.

One critic informed the OWI that, in *The Ape Man*'s plot, a "certain newspaper photographer joins the Army Signal Corps and is replaced by a girl. This is the only reference made to the present world conflict." But the critic also noted two aspects of the plot relevant to the home front:

Reduction of private car driving. The newspaper man and girl travel back and forth to the old mansion in his roadster, almost without reference to gas or rubber.

Gasoline rationing: 'Let's go,' says Billie, as they get into his car, 'If you've got any gas.' This remark does not seem to allude particularly to the rationing of gasoline, but it could.

Such was the seriousness of these concerns that government documents examined a Bela Lugosi horror film, one released shortly before he himself began travelling.

There is no text without context, and World War II, including its effect on the home front, was vividly real when Lugosi agreed to appear in a revival tour of Hamilton Deane and John L. Balderston's 1927 *Dracula–The Vampire Play*. It was Lugosi's first chance to act in the three-act play since 1932, and it was his very first actual tour in the same.

But the 1943 tour was certainly not the first attempt to revive the play. In March 1938, one press account claimed that producer Ben Lundy (who had revived both *The Cat and the Canary* and *The Bat* in 1937) intended to stage *Dracula* with Lugosi.[14] Then, on the heels of his Hollywood comeback in late 1938, the Chicago Repertory Theatre announced that it had booked several plays: "other prospects, some of them conditional, [were] *Death Takes a Holiday* [and] *Dracula*, in the hope that Bela Lugosi could be borrowed from the films...."[15] Nothing came of these plans.

Almost two years later, in late spring of 1941, Lugosi's friend and New York theatrical agent

The cover of a souvenir program for the 1943 version of *Dracula–The Vampire Play.* *(Courtesy of Fritz Frising)*

Chamberlain Brown attempted to interest the actor in touring the "summer playhouses" in a stage production of *Dracula*.[16] While definitely interested "in a good Broadway play," Lugosi informed his friend that "… my established film salary is $2,500 a week so you can appreciate that I couldn't be interested in playing summer stock…."[17] Then, in September 1941, Jimmie Fidler wrote that Lugosi had "been inked for a two-year tour of 124 cities" in the play.[18]

In the late summer of 1942, *Variety* told readers: "Bela Lugosi leaves Wednesday for Chicago following final scenes of Monogram's *Bowery at Midnight* [1942] to begin rehearsals for stage presentation, *Dracula*, at the Cohan Grand Opera House."[19] Shortly thereafter, it was reported that Lugosi:

… trains for Chicago Sunday, opening Sept. 4 in *Dracula* at the Cohan Grand Opera House. While doing the four-week run in the stage piece, Lugosi will also make personals in film houses there playing Monogram features in which he appears. … After the Chicago engagement play goes on the road with a New York opening scheduled for early winter.[20]

One paper even claimed Lugosi actually had arrived in Chicago on August 26, 1942 for the four-week engagement and that "… his contract is arranged so that he can make personal appearances on afternoons not taken up with *Dracula* matinees."[21]

O. D. Woodward.

While Lugosi's arrival in Chicago may well have occurred, that version of *Dracula* did not.

Several months later, in April 1943, the press announced that "Bela Lugosi, himself, in person, will be along before many moons in a revival of *Dracula*, in which he created the title part 16 years ago before succumbing to the lure of Hollywood…."[22] In mid-April, the *New York Times* added that the cast would also include Lowell Gilmore and Murray Bennett. Neither actor (who would have portrayed Harker and Renfield, respectively) appeared.[23]

What failed to materialize on these earlier occasions finally came to fruition in the spring of 1943 when Harry H. Oshrin, a well-known theatrical attorney, engaged Lugosi for a stage tour of *Dracula*. Chosen to direct *Dracula* was theatrical veteran O. D. Woodward, who had directed Lugosi in a 1928 production of the same play.[24]

Woodward's career reached back as far as 1897, during "the years of the active American stock theatre renaissance," and he subsequently managed "successful permanent stock organizations" in Kansas City, Omaha, Denver, Seattle, and Spokane.[25] In an interesting turn of events, Dwight Frye – later to work with Lugosi in the 1931 film *Dracula* – joined

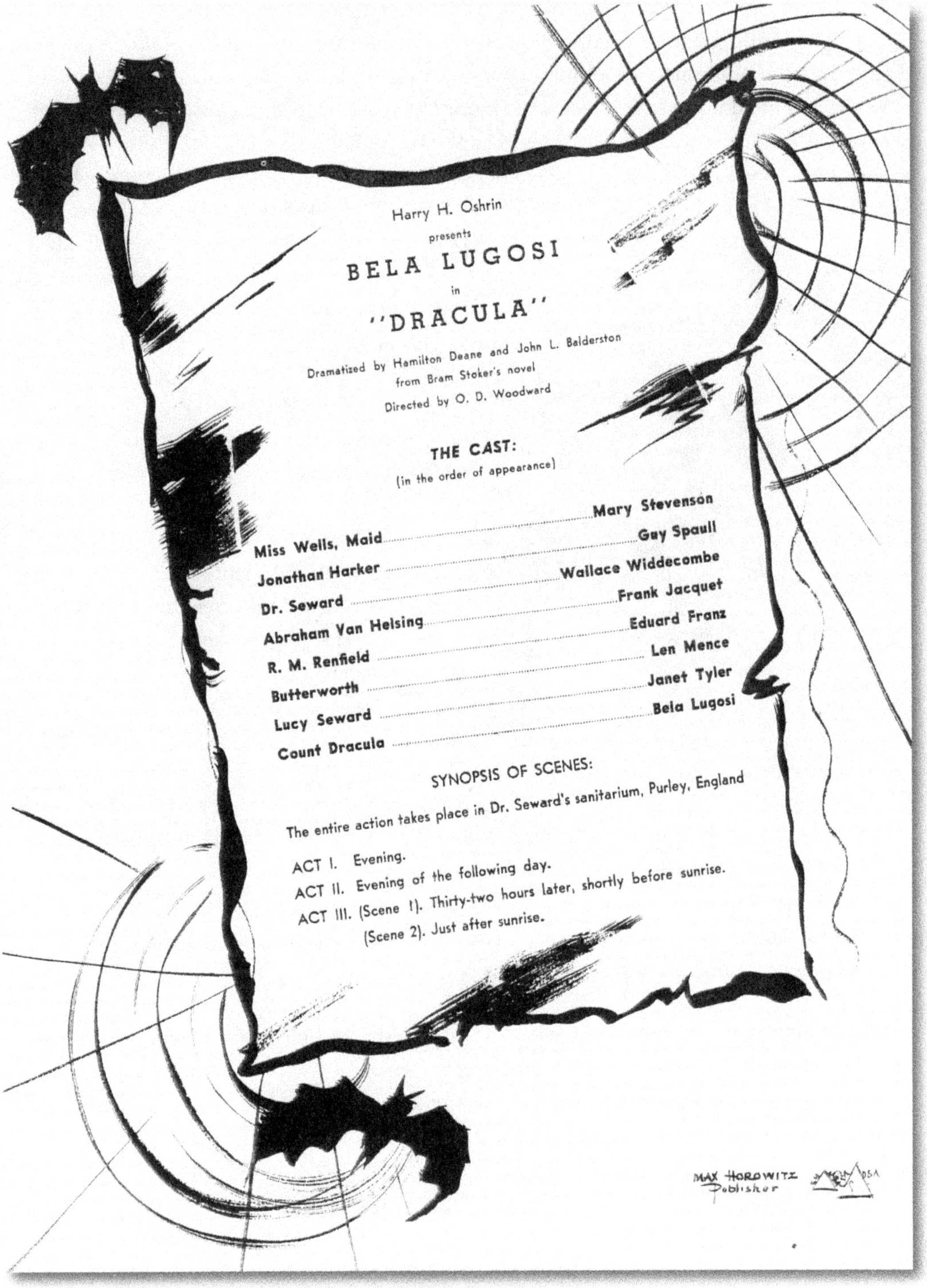

Harry H. Oshrin

presents

BELA LUGOSI

in

"DRACULA"

Dramatized by Hamilton Deane and John L. Balderston
from Bram Stoker's novel
Directed by O. D. Woodward

THE CAST:

(in the order of appearance)

Miss Wells, Maid .... Mary Stevenson
Jonathan Harker .... Guy Spaull
Dr. Seward .... Wallace Widdecombe
Abraham Van Helsing .... Frank Jacquet
R. M. Renfield .... Eduard Franz
Butterworth .... Len Mence
Lucy Seward .... Janet Tyler
Count Dracula .... Bela Lugosi

SYNOPSIS OF SCENES:

The entire action takes place in Dr. Seward's sanitarium, Purley, England

ACT I.   Evening.
ACT II. Evening of the following day.
ACT III. (Scene 1). Thirty-two hours later, shortly before sunrise.
         (Scene 2). Just after sunrise.

MAX HOROWITZ
Publisher

The 1943 revival cast list as published in the play's souvenir program. *(Courtesy of Lynn Naron)*

Woodward's stock company (The Woodward Players) in Spokane in 1918.[26]

Horror continued to preoccupy Woodward in 1929 when he staged *Dracula* on the West Coast. John L. Balderston sued him for $10,000 as a result, the play's coauthor alleging that Woodward did not currently possess the rights to the show. Nevertheless, Woodward forged ahead with *Dracula* again in 1931, staging a version without Lugosi in St. Louis.[27] A decade later, he directed *Death Takes a Holiday* in Los Angeles, casting Frederick Pymm (who had earlier toured as the lead in a roadshow version of *Dracula*) as Prince Sirki.

Eduard Franz, who played Renfield.

When a journalist once asked Woodward about *Dracula*, he replied, "[It] is a symbolic play and unless the audience accepts the power of the supernatural the play's premise is lost. Its strength, naturally, lies in the fact that people refuse to believe such things."[28]

Armies march on their stomachs, but vampires hover in the shadows.

Cast and Crew

At some point in early 1943, Bela Lugosi allegedly attended a film screening, dropping in at a neighborhood theatre specifically to see an unnamed competitor:

'He was doing a mighty fine job, too,' commented Lugosi, 'for suddenly in a particularly savage and horrifying scene, the young lady on my left, a perfect stranger, gave a terrific gasp and the next thing I knew she had thrown her head around and against my shoulder.'

So Bela Lugosi, the big bad Bogey Man found himself consoling a fair damsel in distress, something he has not done since the early days of his career.

When the picture ended, Lugosi gallantly asked if she would care for an ice cream soda.

'The more I thought about it, the more amusing it became,' he continued, 'for the young lady, so profuse in her thanks for my ministrations, had no idea that her mysterious knight was another Bogey Man. I debated whether or not to tell her and finally decided it was worth another spell of hysterics.'

'At first, she refused to believe it but after I had emptied the contents of my wallet and shown her a driver's license and visiting cards, she admitted I was not telling her a fib. She laughed heartily at her strange adventure, then suddenly her face clouded.'

Lugosi in the 1943 revival of _Dracula–The Vampire Play_. Location unknown.

'But darn it,' she fumed, 'it's really happened but when I tell the crowd in the office tomorrow, nobody will believe a word of it!'[29]

Whether or not this was a true story (the mention of the driver's license immediately makes one suspicious since Lugosi did not drive), it certainly reflects the positive nature of Lugosi's relationship with his fans.

Just before leaving Hollywood for the East Coast, during the week of March 25, Lugosi made a personal appearance in support of _The Ape Man_, then in its initial release:

Monogram's _The Ape Man_ and _Kid Dynamite_ [1943] open first runs at the Colony, Hollywood Boulevard house tomorrow, with special campaign being launched to plug estimated three week stay at the house. Scale has been upped to 55 cents to carry first run bill and theatre and studio are sharing in expense of campaign, which includes radio plugs. Bela Lugosi, star of _The Ape Man_, will do appearance second week of run....[30]

One month earlier, Lugosi had signed with Monogram for yet another trio of films, part of a group that would collectively become known as the "Monogram Nine."[31]

Part of Lugosi's contract for *Frankenstein Meets the Wolf Man* (1943). *(Courtesy of David Wentink)*

Shortly before the *Dracula* tour began, Lugosi was in New York City for rehearsals, having arrived there by April 13.[32] Lugosi – and perhaps others in the troupe as well – stayed at the Essex House, a luxury Central Park 44-story high hotel known for its six-story high name sign located on the roof.[33] As one newspaper anecdotally reported: "Riding in an Essex House elevator Frank Crumit turns to Julia Sanderson and remarks: 'I've got the funniest creepy feeling all of a sudden.' What Frank and Julia didn't know is that the man next to them was Bela ('Dracula') Lugosi."[34] While in New York, Bela Lugosi met with fellow actor Oscar Homolka at the famous Sardi's Restaurant, where the two chatted "amiably over afternoon beverages."[35]

Then, on Easter Sunday, April 25, Lugosi guest-starred on radio's popular *Texaco Star Theatre*, which featured Fred Allen. He publicized the *Dracula* revival and added that his most recent film was *Frankenstein Meets the Wolf Man* (1943), in which he played the Monster. The Universal horror movie had opened on March 5, the very same day as *The Ape Man*.

After exchanging banter with Allen, the two enacted a comedic skit in which Allen proposed renting Lugosi's home, which – with the assist of the show's cast and some wonderful sound effects – was made to seem bizarre. In a humorous allusion to wartime rationing, Lugosi announced that he "used to burn oil, but I converted to people." Later, when he attempts to infuse Allen's "nerve" into his new monster in mad doctor-style, Lugosi becomes frightened by a man knocking at his front door: the chairman of his draft board.

As for Lugosi's costars in *Dracula–The Vampire Play*, presumably Harry H. Oshrin and/or O. D. Woodward cast the fascinating group in New York City, though no data seem to exist regarding that process, or, for that matter, exactly when they were cast, although it seems probable that they signed contracts in either March or April 1943.

Born in Wisconsin in 1885 (which made him roughly the same age as Lugosi), Frank Jacquet (whose name was also commonly spelled "Jaquet") assumed the role of Abraham Van Helsing.[36] The portly actor had regularly appeared onstage since the late nineteenth century, and seems to have even worked as a magician for a period of time.[37] He made his film debut in 1934, and from there usually played small parts; his credits include *The Man They Could Not Hang* (1939) and *Black Friday* (1940), the latter featuring Lugosi. Jacquet had one of his better wartime roles in *Corregidor* (1943), which opened during the *Dracula* tour.[38]

Eduard Franz joined the cast as R. M. Renfield. Born as Eddie Schmidt in Wisconsin in 1902, he first worked on stage in Greenwich Village in 1924. He subsequently acted in such plays as *The Emperor Jones* with Paul Robeson and *Desire Under the Elms* with Walter Huston.[39] At the end of 1942, he appeared on Broadway in *The Russian People*, and then in *We Will Never Die* at Madison Square Garden in March 1943, a mass memorial for the Jewish victims of the Nazi regime.[40] Immediately before beginning rehearsals for *Dracula*, Franz worked in a Cleveland production of *Harem Scarem*.[41]

Taking the role of Dr. Seward was the esteemed Wallace Widdecombe, who had costarred

Response to *Frankenstein Meets the Wolf Man* as published in *Motion Picture Herald*.

Published in the *Bridgeport Post* on April 25, 1943.

in a number of British productions in the late nineteenth century with Sir Henry Irving, the man for whom novelist Bram Stoker not only worked, but also on whom he partially based the character Dracula. Widdecombe made his way to New York in a 1901 version of *A Message from Mars* and then toured America in the same production. Though he returned to England to enlist in World War I, Widdecombe subsequently resumed his American career.[42] Less than a year before the *Dracula* revival, he acted in *Othello* with Paul Robeson and Jose Ferrer.[43]

Guy Spaull, who became Jonathan Harker, had made his Broadway debut in 1938.[44] Months prior to *Dracula*, he had appeared in the mystery *I Killed the Count* in New York. By the spring of 1943, Spaull's name had been mentioned in conjunction with at least two Broadway plays, though he did not finally appear in either.[45] Janet Tyler, whose career was still at a very early stage, portrayed Harker's beloved Lucy.

As for the rest of the cast, Mary Stevenson played Miss Wells, the maid, and Len Mence appeared as Butterworth. Stevenson had been understudy to Gertrude Beach in *Janie* on Broadway in 1942; she had also worked in radio.[46] The English-born Mence had been a professional actor since at least the 1920s.[47] He was also an accomplished painter, his work having been exhibited in New York City in 1936.[48]

On one occasion, Lugosi discussed his costars, none of whom had ever worked with him save Jacquet. He was intrigued to:

...see that the thriller is now being approached in a very different manner by a new cast of people, some who have never even seen the play. Unlike me, they have no

BELA LUGOSI IN PERSON

preconceived notions of how the dramas should be projected, and they are all eager to contribute something of their own ideas, which is not bad and at times very interesting, I think.[49]

Rehearsals with this cast began in April and continued until as late as the 28th of that month.[50] The *New York Times* reported that the play would travel to Bridgeport, Hartford, Boston, Philadelphia, and Washington, D. C. That limited list suggests that other cities on the pending tour were booked at a later date.[51]

Lugosi and Janet Tyler, printed in the *Bridgeport Post* on April 29, 1943.

Back from the Grave

"I really believe this is a propitious time for a revival of *Dracula*," Lugosi told the press, adding:

I think audiences need the emotional release and a certain stimulus which this kind of escapist entertainment provides. ... after a session of pure, undiluted stage horror, like this, the public is better equipped to cope with the realities of the day.[52]

KLEIN MEMORIAL

TOMORROW EVENING at 8:15

HARRY OSHRIN

presents

THE EMINENT STAR OF STAGE & SCREEN

BELA LUGOSI

(on stage in person)

In the strangest, most terrifying thriller of all time —

DRACULA

Prices 1.10 - 1.65 - 2.20 - 2.75

SEATS NOW AT BOX OFFICE

Open Daily 10 a. m. to 9 p. m.

Tel. 3-6166

From the *Bridgeport Telegram* of April 29, 1943.

While Lugosi may well have believed these words, he also participated in what became more than just a revival: it was, even if to a limited extent, a variation on the 1927 Hamilton Deane-John L. Balderston play.

It is difficult to determine the degree of those changes, but they were apparently made prior to *Dracula*'s opening night. More than one columnist in 1943 referred to the revival as a "streamlined" version of the Deane-Balderston original.[53] "There have been some changes made," one of them wrote.[54]

But the alterations may have gone beyond the mere excising of given dialogue or entire scenes. Another newspaper article argued that Lugosi himself brought the play "up to date."[55] Whoever was responsible, Lugosi likely agreed with the approach, which at minimum included altering two lines of dialogue:

...the efforts to 'streamline' it ... are pretty crude pieces of remodeling it, one of which seemed to involve a reference to Mr. Renfield as a 'flying jitterbug' (wow!), and another a reference to atom smashing.[56]

At least one "change" was not really a change, however. A newspaper critic in Cleveland mistakenly believed that Dracula's choice of airplane as a mode of travel to England was one of the amendments, when in fact an airplane is mentioned in the original 1927 play; here the critic was perhaps recalling the use of a ship in Stoker's novel and/or the 1931 film version.[57]

Other changes would have to do with the exhibition of the play. The *Washington Post* noticed the lack of nurses in attendance to assist fainting audience members, a common component of *Dracula* productions in the late twenties.[58] Secondly, while it must be stated with caution, some (and only some) advertisements and playbills for the 1943 version did

Lugosi and Janet Tyler in a photograph autographed in Bridgeport, Connecticut. *(Courtesy of the Bridgeport History Center at the Bridgeport Public Library)*

not use the explanatory phrase *The Vampire Play* (as had usually been the case in earlier versions), perhaps because the character Dracula was so well known by World War II.

To help generate additional revenue and offset the apparent anticipation of rather austere playbills at some venues, Harry H. Oshrin compiled and published a souvenir booklet entitled *Bela Lugosi in Dracula*. It includes some of the usual playbill information, such as a cast listing, while also offering a combination of aged fan magazine articles about Lugosi with photographs from some of his then-recent films, including *Invisible Ghost* (1941), *The Corpse Vanishes* (1942), *The Ape Man* (1943), and *Frankenstein Meets the Wolf Man* (1943).[59]

The key question was how *Dracula* would resonate with 1940s audiences. While Lugosi was correct that it provided escapist entertainment, the issue was more intrinsic to the play itself. "It's a nice gruesome play, and I know you'll like it," a young woman told her companion as the two entered a performance of the 1943 revival.[60] But would it still scare audiences? Could it still hold them enthralled, regardless of whatever other problems they faced during the war? Would they "like" it, as the woman predicted her friend would?

What transpired during the space of approximately eight weeks in 1943 hardly presented simple or singular answers to these questions.

Artwork published inside the play's souvenir program.

Bridgeport, Connecticut, April 30, 1943

The troupe assembled in Bridgeport on April 29. Given gas rationing, one would be inclined to think they travelled by train, though the troupe and their sets might well have been able to use cars and trucks because they were involved in what was termed "in-course-of-work driving."[61] If so, each automobile would have likely needed to transport three or more passengers.

At any rate, the company held a rehearsal on its first evening in the city. During the same night and the next morning, electricians installed the "intricate lighting system" that the play required.[62] All of this hard work anticipated the revival's first performance, which unfolded while the energy industry was still enmeshed in problems.

Just before opening night, six New England governors demanded the "equalization of gas rationing throughout the country, believing the one and a half gallons per week allotted to their citizens was too low."[63] On April 28, the War Labor Board – which had tried in vain to get coal miners to resume work – turned the situation over to President Roosevelt. By that time, 67,000 miners had already gone on strike. Such news headlined papers all over America on April 29, including in Bridgeport.[64]

The next day, on April 30, 1943, *Dracula* premiered at the Klein Memorial Auditorium, a 1,400-seat Art Deco proscenium theatre that first opened its doors in 1940. The city built the theatre with funds willed to it by an attorney named Jacob Klein. Designed by a local architect, the Klein featured bronze doors and a marble lobby, along with inlaid wood and geometric motifs.[65]

Dracula drew a "near-capacity" audience, generating a "swell" $2,682.[66] One local critic believed Lugosi deserved "most of the acting honors." He added:

...good support also came from Frank Jacquet as Abraham Van Helsing, a Dutch scientist, and Eduard Franz as R. M. Renfield, a madman. Other company members, including Mary Stevenson, Guy Spaull, Wallace Widdecombe, and Len Mence were adequate. Janet Tyler made a pretty victim for Dracula's evil attacks.[67]

The overall verdict was relatively positive: "The play ran fairly smooth for an opening."[68]

And yet, the inaugural public performance was hardly perfect. Despite a strong notice, Jacquet found "more or less difficulty remembering his lines at times and Spaull made a wrong entrance."[69] By the time these words appeared in print, however, the troupe had likely left town, with Lugosi and the others presumably aware that the coal strike continued unabated, despite President Roosevelt's order that miners return to work. In fact, the conflict seemed to be growing more problematic.

Playbill SEASON 1942 • 1943

HORACE BUSHNELL MEMORIAL HALL, HARTFORD, CONN.

Saturday • MAY 1

Matinee at 2:30 • Evening at 8:15

HARRY H. OSHRIN

presents

BELA LUGOSI

in

"DRACULA"

Dramatized by HAMILTON DEANE and JOHN L. BALDERSTON from BRAM STOKER'S Novel • Directed by O. D. WOODWARD

From the playbill in Hartford, Connecticut.

Hartford, Connecticut, May 1, 1943

From Bridgeport, the *Dracula* company travelled some sixty miles to stage two performances on Saturday, May 1, a matinee at 2:30PM and an evening performance at 8:15PM. The venue was Hartford's best theatre, the Bushnell Memorial Hall.

Built in 1930 as a "living memorial" to Hartford minister Dr. Horace Bushnell, the

The Bushnell Memorial Hall. *(Courtesy of the Hartford Public Library)*

Georgian Revival-style theatre seated 2,800. Its Art Deco interior featured a suspended ceiling that sported the largest hand-painted mural of its kind in the country. By 1943, the Bushnell hosted far more than just the "best Broadway plays." It was also home to a symphony series, a "Light Opera" ballet series, and the "most distinguished motion pictures."[70] Lectures were given on its stage as well, including one the very night prior to Lugosi's appearance. The topic: *Our Axis Enemies*.[71]

It is probable that – given advertisements on the cover of the playbill – Lugosi and the others stayed at the Hotel Bond. They may have enjoyed the "savory flavor of hickory-broiled food" at the Heartstone restaurant on Maple Avenue; it also advertised on the playbill cover.[72]

While in Hartford, Lugosi very likely read the headlines. By April 30, the coal miners' contract expired, causing the numbers of strikers to balloon to approximately 450,000.[73] The following day, FDR ordered the government to take over the coal mines and appealed to John L. Lewis to encourage members of the United Mine Workers to return to work.[74] With indications of higher pay in the offing, mining operations restarted on May 3.[75]

In the local newspapers, advertisements for *Dracula* featured the obligatory vampire bats, but other coverage took a different approach. For example, the *Hartford Courant* used a photograph of Lugosi from *Murders in the Rue Morgue* (1932) to promote the play, and told readers that Lugosi owned Hollywood's "strangest" house.[76] The *Hartford Times* published a short biography of Lugosi that focused on his pre-Hollywood years, including his life in Hungary. The same paper also made the quite bizarre and certainly false claim that Lugosi's favorite hobby was big game hunting, alleging that he had even travelled to Africa with Frank "Bring 'Em Back Alive" Buck.[77]

The power of Lugosi's performance seemed to win over the *Hartford Courant*, who wrote:

As a withered old gaffer who went all through this bat-out-of-hell business when Hamilton Deane and John Balderston first connived to put Bram Stoker's novel on the stage years ago, I confess I found my thoughts wandering and speculating on the possibility of replacing Scarpia with 'Count Dracula' in *Tosca*, which had been given in the same hall two nights previously. But apparently a whole new generation has grown up since the original *Dracula* days, because the audience seemed to thoroughly enjoy this opus made up of vampirism and a dash of green gelatin.

From the *Hartford Times* of May 1, 1943.

As a matter of fact, and to give Stoker's devil his due, *Dracula* remains a reasonably entertaining thriller despite all the years it has been around. Parts of it will make even the most naïve and youthful theatergoer giggle, but by and large it stacks up pretty well with today's shockers, and, to open old wounds, I would rather sit through it again than through *Angel Street*.[78]

Part of the success of this revival, of course, is due to the presence of Bela Lugosi, who by means of some capably sinister acting, an appropriate profile, an out-size opera cape and an unusually high-waisted pair of trousers, creates a lively idea of what a vampire might look and act like, if there were such things as vampires. ... In the present situation, Mr. Lugosi is being aided very well by Frank Jacquet as the professor who knows all about demonology... The other members of the cast carry along through the horror as best they can, which ranges from competently to so-so....[79]

Here is an early sign of the revival's key concern: would *Dracula* inspire laughs or thrills or both?

Immediately after *Dracula* left the city, the Bushnell forged ahead with its arts and entertainment series. The Ballet Russe de Monte Carlo appeared onstage the very next evening.[80] As for Lugosi, he remained in Hartford, at least in a sense. On May 2, the Astor Theatre screened *The Ape Man*.[81]

Boston, Massachusetts, May 3-15, 1943

Touring actors and musicians often appreciate longer bookings, which allow a temporary respite from the grind of the road. For the *Dracula* troupe, Boston became their longest tenure, as they stayed approximately two weeks in the city. Despite their brief appearances in Bridgeport and Hartford, the revival company likely saw Boston as their official premiere. Lugosi had himself called Boston the opening city on Fred Allen's radio show.

The film *Frankenstein Meets the Wolf Man* paved the way for Lugosi's appearance. In March 1943, it scored a three-week holdover at Boston's Trans-Lux Theatre. Newspaper advertisements – which gave Lugosi second billing after Lon Chaney, Jr. – warned all comers that the theatre would not be responsible for "any person or persons under [a] doctor's care who cannot withstand shock or terror."[82]

Photos published inside the play's souvenir program.

Thanks to a booking from J. J. Leventhal, who operated a "well-known Subway Circuit" group of theatres, *Dracula* premiered on May 3 at the Plymouth Theatre.[83] The 1,500-seat showplace had a long life in Boston, opening on September 23, 1911.[84] The Plymouth soon became a leading venue for legitimate roadshows and pre-Broadway try-outs. Audiences watched such shows in a theatre designed to have an intimate setting. As one article claimed, "gentle and effective lighting with methods other than central chandelier, less stairs to travel up to reach the two balconies and plenty of lavatories were some of the noted features."[85]

The same persons who saw such ads also read about the ongoing struggles of World War II. On May 3, the Boston papers announced that the Allies had captured 600 enemy soldiers in North Africa.[86] In the days that followed, American troops advanced on Bizerte and Tunis, thus driving the Nazis to the sea.[87] Just before the play's first week came to an end, the Allies captured 50,000 more soldiers.[88]

On the home front, hundreds of thousands of drivers faced a "reappraisal" of their gas rations as a direct result of the "heavy overseas military" needs.[89] Such news ended hopes that a possible lift of a pleasure-driving ban would bolster the number of live shows in Boston.[90]

Movement in the coal industry was underway as well. On May 2, President Roosevelt spoke over the airwaves, denouncing the coal strike, with John L. Lewis calling a 15-day truce the same day. As a result, 530,000 miners went back to work on May 4, some even sooner.[91] That week, the government refused to negotiate with the union and insisted their actions were harming the war effort.[92]

Union members were hardly alone in their discontent; many other American workers agreed with the miners' right to increased pay.[93] Eleanor Roosevelt echoed the same, telling an interviewer that the workers' conditions were deplorable. While she refused to discuss John L. Lewis, the First Lady

Published in the *Boston Herald* on April 25, 1943.

From the *Boston Globe* of March 24, 1943.

did state: "I believe that the settlement of the strike should be brought about in the light of what the miners and their families have lived through for the past ten years. I think they are entitled to concessions."[94] Put another way, these workers could hardly have afforded to purchase tickets to see Lugosi in person.

To help publicize *Dracula*, the *Boston Herald* published an article purportedly written by Lugosi himself:

I have sort of an affection for this role and since to this day people refer to me as 'Dracula' Lugosi, I feel a paternalism towards the character very much akin to that which Frankenstein must certainly have felt for the monster he created.

Bela Lugosi, celebrated portrayer of horror roles on the screen, who opens tomorrow evening at the Plymouth Theater in the title role of the famous vampire play, "Dracula."

Published in the *Boston Herald* on May 2, 1943.

Ordinarily I am a very pleasant soft-spoken gentleman, I think, affably observing the world from my six-feet-two-inches. I love gypsy music, dogs, and Hungarian food, which is natural, I think you will agree.

However, I am an avowed Roosevelt disciple and I think without a doubt the President is the greatest outstanding personality of the day. I am a firm believer in his ideas and ideals and you can put that down in spades.[95]

Such comments may have been prepared in advance of the Boston visit, as similar quotations appeared in other newspapers during the tour.

By contrast, the *Boston Globe* seems to have undertaken an original interview with Lugosi and his wife. The couple spoke of their home, which they likened to a Swiss chateau, and their son, who imitated "every role his father plays, and he can writhe and distort his face and go through each sinister motion that his famous father has done on the screen."[96]

The same newspaper's critic was generally positive about *Dracula*'s opening performance, despite a belief that its effect was not what it once was:

Dear, dear, how fashions change in the theatre. Once women shrieked and fainted when they saw *Dracula*, and strong men trembled in the dark. As a matter of fact, some still do, because there were gasps and delighted little cries of fright last evening. Supernatural somehow is a perishable commodity in the theatre, and *Dracula* is, I am afraid, not the shocker it once was.[97]

Echoing those same sentiments was Helen Eager in the *Boston Evening Traveler*:

In the years that have passed since the cloak wearing, green-lighted vampire first made audiences shudder and shriek, the movies have given the public a thorough education in horror – many of the films with the same Mr. Lugosi. This intensive course has taken the edge off anything projected in the three walls of a theatre, especially such plays as *Dracula*. But it's still a lot of fun watching the players grimly and seriously going through the hammy business of keeping Dracula in his place.[98]

The *Boston Post*, which took the opportunity to record negative audience response, was even less kind:

It is meant to shock and startle its audiences. It does both in this current version ... it does even more. It nauseates. The fact that its actors have not yet learned all their lines is no help. ... There are some scenes which for sheer marrow-chilling shock are unmatched. There are some others which reduced last night's audience to derisive laughter. [99]

But it was left for the *Boston Herald* to level the greatest criticism against the play:

...Bram Stoker's chiller-diller about the un-dead and their cute little tricks seems definitely old-fashioned and when performed as it is in the present case with

From the *Boston Herald* of May 2, 1943.

all the solemnity that should attend an important state funeral, it becomes [a] matter for giggles rather than anything more serious. The acting has a portentous and hollow ring that almost drowns out some of the more stunningly uninspired speeches, and every entrance and exit of Bela Lugosi in a green spotlight and opera cloak is a masterly example of Jekyll Out-Hyding Frankenstein. Ham may be rationed in the meat markets, but you can still buy it in the theatre for the price of a ticket, and audiences today appear to enjoy it as much as ever.[100]

Overall, it was as if the critics were unimpressed – save for Lugosi's performance, which they generally praised – and as if they had disdain for those theatregoers who enjoyed the play, even if the audience response seems to have been a mixture of genuine fright and skeptical laughter.

Variances in critical and audience reactions can be seen in two other publications that reviewed the show. For example, a reviewer from the *Christian Science Monitor* wrote:

... this is the first time that Bela Lugosi, whose name is so closely associated with the title role, has played it [in Boston]. And it must be admitted that he does a sepulchrally excellent job, with the aid of a swirling opera cloak, green lights, and other appurtenances of the stage vampire. Despite the rather wordy style of the play, *Dracula* succeeded in giving the audience the measure of thrills that most of those present expected.[101]

Variety was far less enthused, feeling that *Dracula* was "as corny a show as has been seen here in years." Nevertheless, the trade admitted the play was "... a powerhouse... drawing a nifty $9,000 on first week."[102] A subsequent report in *Billboard* amended that figure, citing instead a "neat" box-office take of $9,500.[103]

Mary Stevenson, as she appeared in the *Boston Globe* on May 9, 1943.

During his two-week stay in Boston, Lugosi fans received an extra treat when, on the evening of May 6, he graced the radio waves on a locally-produced program called *The Drama Shop*. He took the lead in a horror drama written especially for him:

After having died twice on the stage of the Plymouth Theatre today – matinee and evening – Lugosi, the fiendish vampire... will again come to life for a 'guest star appearance' on *The Devil's Henchman* radio program over WMEX at midnight tonight. Mr. Lugosi will be heard in an original play entitled *From Spirit to Flesh*, especially written for him by Milton Yakus, director of the WMEX Drama Shop. *From Spirit to Flesh* is a weird horror-drama concerning the activities of an inhuman creature who escapes from an old clock for a period of 10 minutes.[104]

Milton Yakus later became a famous songwriter, penning such tunes as *Old Cape Cod*. Yakus also continued his relationship with Lugosi. In a subsequent letter to the budding writer, Lugosi announced:

I have just returned from my four months tour with *Dracula*. I got in touch with the William Morris Agency here in Hollywood and asked them to inquire from their New York office about your stories. As yet, I have not heard from them; but as soon as I get their reply I will let you know.[105]

Nothing seems to have come from Lugosi's efforts on behalf of Yakus, which were not dissimilar to numerous other occasions in which Lugosi attempted to promote given writers to Hollywood studios.[106]

That same week, the Africa campaign ended successfully for the Allies, with Winston Churchill visiting Washington, D. C. to confer with FDR on plans for the pending invasion of Europe.[107] Allied triumphs in Italy led Hermann Göring to take "command" of the country.[108] All the while, the coal mining disputes burned in the background as an ongoing problem.

Dracula's box-office gross dropped to $7,000 for the second week, though *Billboard* interpreted that amount to "still be in the chips."[109] In fact, the same publication subsequently revised that figure, claiming its final week made $7,400, a "very good showing."[110] Such numbers were at odds with *Variety*'s report that the play's second week generated as much as $8,400.[111]

Only three days after *Dracula*'s final performance on May 15, noted horror film actor and occasional Lugosi costar Lionel Atwill appeared at the same venue in *The Play's The Thing*.[112]

During Lugosi's stay in Boston, he continued his long-standing tradition of visiting nightspots and reuniting with old friends while on the road. In this case, Lugosi spent time in Boston's "film district" chatting with Bill Erb (a radio broadcaster), Maurice Wolf (a local MGM executive) and Bert MacKenzie (the local manager for MGM).[113]

Troops training at Camp Framingham during World War II.

Camp Framingham, Massachusetts, May 14, 1943

Thanks to the efforts of Private Richard Brennan, the *Dracula* troupe – while still based in Boston – agreed to perform a matinee for soldiers at Camp Framingham. Though originally scheduled for May 9, Lugosi and his colleagues instead delayed their single appearance until Friday, May 14, at 3:30PM EST. Brennan also hoped to "secure" the services of a "well known musical unit … from a Boston theatre or night club."[114] But the soldiers did not hear such music, and they certainly did not view the full three-act play.

Military installations at Framingham date to at least the Civil War. As early as 1873, the camp existed for training and assembling the "Massachusetts volunteer militia."[115] In 1898, the Ninth Regiment mustered out of camp for the Spanish-American War; the Eighth Regiment assembled there prior to being sent to Cuba following the same conflict.[116]

From May 1942 to December 1943, the camp became home to the 181st infantry. On the day that Lugosi took to the stage at the camp in 1943, newspapers described various Allied advances. British and American pilots over Germany had just completed the "mightiest aerial offensive of the war."[117] In Tunisia, the Allies triumphed over the enemy, capturing some 175,000 German and Italian soldiers, an achievement that provoked riots in Berlin.[118]

The *Dracula* troupe originally intended to stage their entire play, even though according to one press account they "feared before making this first appearance at a military camp that soldier audiences would go only for variety show types of entertainment." Another hesitation may have been the inability to transport their full stage equipment. Lugosi even apologized to the soldiers for being unable to use "all the apparatus which helps to make the play the thriller that it is...."[119]

That was perhaps the reason that the troupe performed only the second act of *Dracula*. A review of the performance noted "some of the cast wished that they had done the whole play, so well received were their efforts." The group did augment their show with two curtain speeches, one by Eduard Franz, in which he "frighten[ed] the timid members of the audience into watching for vampires in the shadows on their way from the theatre." Here was a variation on the speech that concludes the Deane-Balderston play.

Lugosi gave the other talk, "in which he thanked the boys for being a fine audience and expressed his desire to do all he can for morale."[120] Shortly thereafter, the cast toured the camp and then ate in the mess hall. Mary Stevenson reported that the kitchen was the "cleanest she [had ever] seen."[121]

Advertisement promoting the play's appearance in Philadelphia. *(Courtesy of Ted Okuda)*

Philadelphia, Pennsylvania, May 19-29, 1943

After the Boston leg of the tour ended on May 15, Lugosi and company had three free days and apparently stopped briefly in New York City before heading on to Philadelphia. In his column, Walter Winchell said he spotted Lugosi on Central Park South at around the same time. The actor was buying a fresh ice cream cone for a little girl who had accidentally dropped her own.[122]

From there, the group appeared for eleven days at the Locust Street Theatre in Philadelphia, the second lengthiest stay they had on the tour. Built originally as part of a multi-story office building, the 1,580-seat venue screened films and staged live productions.[123] The theatre – which had opened in 1927 with a screening of *What Price Glory* (1926) – featured a Gothic interior and exterior.[124]

"An incident as strange as any that transpires on

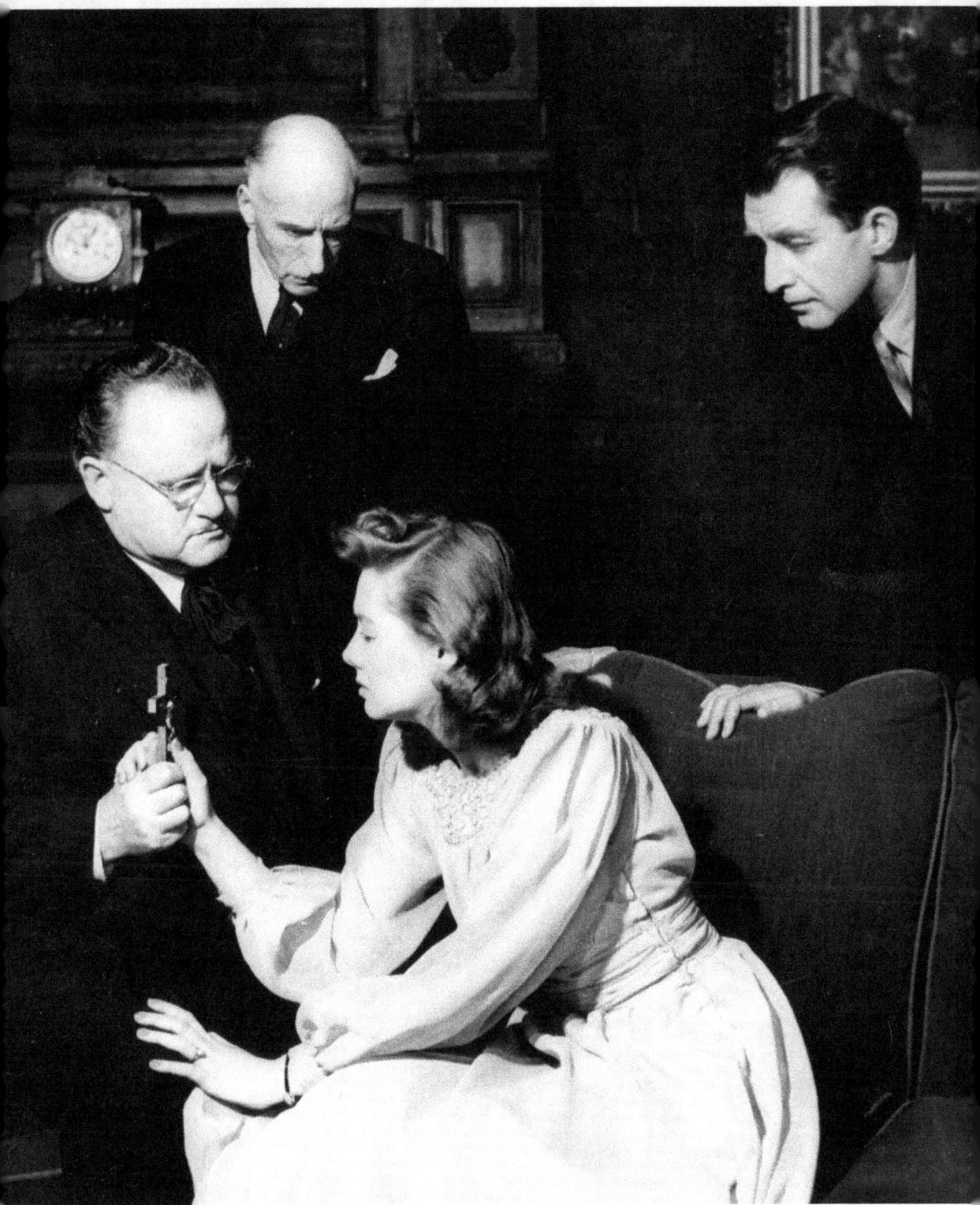

A tense scene in the 1943 version of *Dracula–The Vampire Play*. This image was likely photographed in Philadelphia. *(Courtesy of the Free Library of Philadelphia, Theatre Collection)*

Lugosi's Dracula and Franz's Renfield, perhaps photographed in Philadelphia in 1943. *(Courtesy of the Free Library of Philadelphia, Theatre Collection)*

Lugosi with actor Joseph Schildkraut in Philadelphia in May 1943.

stage in *Dracula* took place the other afternoon at rehearsal in the Locust," the *Philadelphia Daily News* said on May 19, 1943. "Barney Abrams, the box office man, saw the woman first, an attractive brunet in her early thirties, who paced up and down the lobby."

The newspaper quoted her as saying, "My husband is an army lieutenant away on duty. I've seen Mr. Lugosi in the movies several times and have terrible dreams about him. I thought that if I had the chance to see him in person, I might get rid of the dreams." Hearing her story, Abrams sent her backstage to Sam Schwartz, the company manager, who told her to take a seat. Wearing a short sleeve shirt, Lugosi soon appeared before the woman, who reportedly "fled screaming" out of the theatre.[125]

Not surprisingly, the European theatre received far more press in 1943 than the Locust Street. Newspapers covered the bombing of Berlin, as well as continued air assaults on

Italy.[126] While Churchill encouraged Italians to oust Mussolini, FDR told Americans that the US government had increased war aid to Russia.[127]

During *Dracula*'s stay in Philadelphia, the government clarified the "pleasure-driving" ban, which forbade "driving for amusement or recreation purposes."[128] Newspaper journalists also anticipated cuts in gasoline rations for the Eastern states.[129] One industry trade noted that "such warm weather attractions as ... theatres" would be particularly hit hard by increased rationing.[130]

Publicist George "Lefty" Miller did his part to divert journalists from such stories to *Dracula*, distributing all manner of handouts to the press and regaling them with stories of Bram Stoker and Edgar Allan Poe. He even managed to get himself mentioned in the *Philadelphia Daily News*, speaking about his son, who had "seen plenty of action in the Pacific."[131] Miller also facilitated an article in the *Philadelphia Record* that described Lugosi's passion for stamp collecting.[132]

Reviewing *Dracula*, the city's *Evening Bulletin* praised Lugosi, Eduard Franz, and Frank Jacquet. The paper announced that the play "still has the power to challenge the credulity and emotions of an audience," adding that Lugosi and Franz received loud applause.[133]

The *Philadelphia Daily News* responded favorably as well, reassuring readers that "time has neither mellowed the frightening power of Dracula nor blunted the superstition of vampires. ... [Bela Lugosi] is convincing enough to frighten even himself under the green spot where his makeup turns a ghastly gray."[134] Likewise, the *Philadelphia Evening Star* described a "large and enthusiastic audience, from which screeches and screams were heard at many high points of the play."[135]

The *Philadelphia Inquirer* noted its own response and tried to gauge the audience as well:

The audience gave some anticipatory shudders as the house lights went out before the performance of *Dracula* last night at the Locust St. and there were wolf howls, squeals and one honest to goodness 'Look out, he'll kill her!', intermittently thereafter to complement the eerie sounds from across the footlights. Perhaps the revival of the vampire play didn't really chill anyone, but without doubt it did get an audience reaction.[136]

The *Inquirer* praised Lugosi's performance, but the *Philadelphia Record* found nothing positive to report, arguing, "There are too many strange and terrifying things going on in the world today for the mock-horrific doings of *Dracula* to seem very important or convincing."[137]

Dracula's first week grossed an "okay" $8,000; the second week made an "okay" $7,500.[138] Its moderate success became the Locust Street Theatre's final attraction of the season.[139]

On May 20, the second day of his stay in Philadelphia, Lugosi visited the Globe Hoist Company, attending a dinner and rally. Here was an important opportunity to assist in the war effort. Asked to give a speech, Lugosi scribbled some words on the inside of an instruction manual for Globe military trucks. He told the assembled crowd:

Lugosi giving a speech at the Globe Hoist Company in Philadelphia on May 20, 1943.

...as you know, This [*sic*] war of ours is not an ordinary war, where soldiers of opposing countries clash in battle and where the war is won by the country wich [*sic*] has the more heroic soldiers. This war of ours is a total war, in wich [*sic*] our enemies emploi [*sic*] all there [*sic*] men and women, making use of every bodies [*sic*] skill and ability to the fullest degrie [*sic*].

If we want to, not only to withstand, but to conquer the efforts of our enemies we have to do the same thing. Otherwise, we are going to loose [*sic*] this war, wich [*sic*] would mean the lose [*sic*] of our freedom and lieberty [*sic*]. There is [no] dout [*sic*] in my mind that we do not want to loose [*sic*] all of this, and that we all ar [*sic*] giving to give over talent and ~~effort~~ our effort in a super human way.[140]

Lugosi's words helped launch the Globe Hoist Company into a record-breaking streak of wartime equipment production.

Fort George G. Meade, Maryland, May 23, 1943

Even prior to the declaration of war, troops at Fort Meade saw a "flesh-and-blood girl show" in April 1941 and "yelled their heads off in high-glee."[141] Views on what soldiers might want to see changed after the war began, however. For example, Eva Le Gallienne appeared in *Uncle Harry* at Fort Meade in October 1942. She insisted that soldiers appreciated legitimate theatre plays over "burlesque."[142]

Only a few months later, the *Baltimore Sun* wrote: "Originally doubtful whether soldier audiences wanted anything much more serious than leg shows, New York theatrical people are convinced now that any good play will draw as large and appreciative audience at any army camp as anywhere."[143]

The Post Special Service Office presented *Dracula* at Fort Meade thanks to "contact man" Sergeant Sam Pearce, who had journeyed to Philadelphia to arrange the appearance. Such late scheduling might have necessitated tickets priced at a quarter each, noticeably higher than some of the shows they staged in 1942.[144] That said, the troupe did not transport their usual sets, relying instead on original sets created by soldier Milton Howarth and constructed by the Engineers Camouflage Battalion.[145] After spending time as a prisoner of war, Howarth became a professional artist.[146]

The cast gave their single performance of the complete play at the War Department Theatre No. 4 on Sunday, May 23, at 2:30PM, with Lugosi and the others donating their services.[147] The *Fort Meade Post* detailed the event:

A little fearful of how a modern, sophisticated army audience would receive this drama of vampires and werewolves, the cast showed its tenseness at first. But thundering applause as the curtain fell on the first scene brought forth one of the suavely horrifying performances for which Bela Lugosi has been noted since creating the role in 1927.

Postcard showing Fort George G. Meade in Maryland in 1943.

A 1943 machine gun drill at Fort George G. Meade during World War II.

Refusing to be horror-stricken, the audience was quite willing to be entertained. Some soldiers laughed at the idea of 'wolves howling in the streets of London,' but all laughter hushed when Dracula swooped on the limp form of Lucy Seward to drink her blood ... the eerie green stage lighting for each appearance of Dracula, and the shrieking exit of one girl.[148]

The *Post* proceeded to acclaim the work of Eduard Franz, Len Mence, Guy Spaull, Mary Stevenson, and Janet Tyler, whose "flimsy gowns" caused "frank and vociferous admiration" from the assembled audience.

Prior to leaving Fort Meade, Lugosi said that he preferred the work of Hollywood to the "steady grind" of the legitimate stage.[149] Perhaps at the age of sixty he was feeling the effects of being on the road. And perhaps he was unhappy that audience responses to the play included laughter.

Buffalo, New York, May 31-June 5, 1943

Lugosi was a man of two minds about the character Dracula, sometimes embracing the role, at least for financial reasons, and at other times eschewing it with disdain. After arriving in Buffalo, which he did by roughly May 28, if not earlier, Lugosi spoke about the vampire

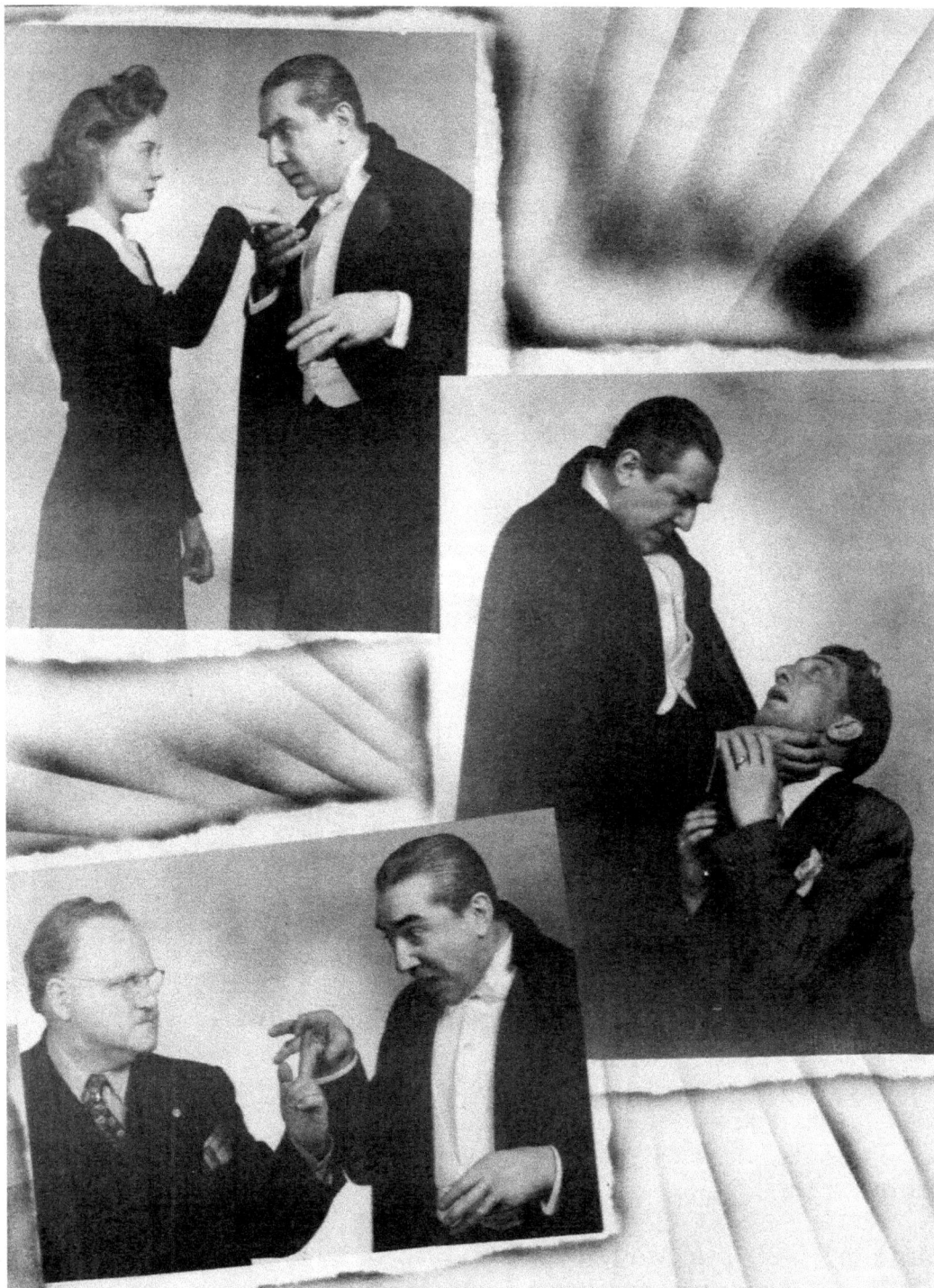

Photos published inside the play's souvenir program.

and horror in general, recounting yet again Hollywood's veto on horror films in 1936 following the British ban:

> I had been so long associated with horror parts by then ... that I rapidly started on the downward skid ... I was facing a personal horror called bankruptcy. Ultimately, however, Hollywood relented and resumed making horror pictures. Now I am solvent again.[150]

The Buffalo press outlined Lugosi's strong association with horror, claiming that his role of Dracula had led him to play everything from "Georgian monsters to baying werewolves." Another article published a Lugosi filmography that included *Frankenstein Meets the Wolf Man*, as well as movies he never made, including *The Ghost Creeps*.[151]

In addition to reading coverage about himself, Lugosi likely kept abreast of the second national strike of coal workers since the tour began. The walkout of some 530,000 workers started on June 1, with the union demanding more pay.[152] By June 5, John L. Lewis agreed that workers would return to work, but both sides of the dispute decried their opponent's tactics.[153]

Gas rationing continued to cause troubles as well. In his May 20 article "How to Crank a Horse," Groucho Marx joked: "Who said the automobile is here to stay?"[154] In the days that followed, a frustrated drive-in theatre in New Jersey shut down due to the "pleasure-driving ban."[155] In Newark, police confiscated 635,000 stolen and counterfeit gasoline stamps.[156] In Rochester, coupons worth over ten million gallons of gas were stolen from a rationing headquarters.[157] And in Pittsburgh, where the *Dracula* company would soon appear, a local rationing board discovered that the city mayor had violated the rules.[158]

Even *Dracula* was not immune from troubles. The period between the Fort Meade show and opening night in Buffalo involved a shake-up of three cast members. The reason is unknown, but it would seem that at least two of the changes occurred at nearly the last minute, as surviving Buffalo playbills do not reflect the names of new actors who – according to newspaper coverage – did appear onstage in the city.

Buffalo audiences saw Esther Snowden portray Miss Wells, taking over the role from Mary Stevenson, and Charles Francis as Dr. Seward, replacing Wallace Widdecombe.[159] That said, they probably paid more attention to the blonde-haired and green-eyed Mary Heath, an actress with limited experience who filled the part vacated by Janet Tyler. At least one critic

Appears in First Lead Role at the Erlanger

MARY HEATH

TWIN CITY NATIVE HAS FIRST MAJOR ROLE IN DRACULA

Mary Heath, Niece of Rev. William T. Heath, Co-stars With Bela Lugosi

From the *Buffalo Evening News* of June 2, 1943.

drew comparisons between Heath and Madeleine Carroll.[160]

Why Janet Tyler left is unknown, though Heath may well have been nearby when the need for a replacement arose. She had longstanding ties to Buffalo, having been born in nearby North Tonawanda. Her father was Paul Silas Heath, a Presbyterian minister who had published a well-distributed religious pamphlet in 1942.[161] And Heath had portrayed Lucy in a small production of *Dracula–The Vampire Play* sponsored by the Westchester (New York) Woman's Club in 1942.[162]

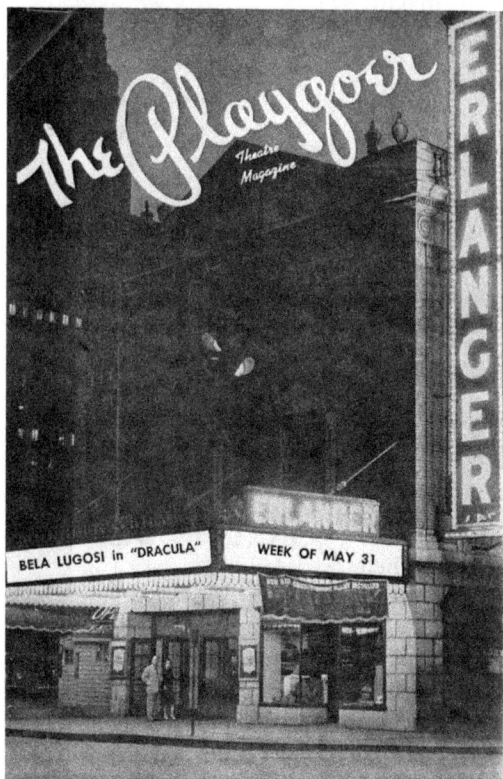

The playbill cover for the Buffalo performances.

The local *Buffalo Evening News* gave Heath as much publicity as they had Lugosi. In an interview, she described her nascent acting career:

My parents never for a moment opposed my wanting to go on the stage. If I wanted to be an actress, they told me, I should try to be a good one. I think they were a little doubtful as to my first starring vehicle, but they haven't expressed their doubts to me.

But her mother did gently express some doubts to a journalist, who quoted her as saying, "We were a little upset at first – it's such a horrible play, all green lights and shadows – but if Mary doesn't mind playing with vampires, I guess we can stand it."[163]

Buffalo audiences and Heath's friends and relatives had numerous occasions to see *Dracula*, which was staged at the city's Erlanger Theatre each evening from May 31 to June 5, as well as two matinees. Advertisements heralded it as a "sensational mystery story that has amazed three continents."[164]

The grand opening of the Erlanger Theatre was on September 4, 1927. The nearby Statler Hotel had constructed the theatre specifically as a place where its guests could go for an evening's entertainment. With 1,500 seats, the Erlanger was never intended for films but only for stage presentations. Mahogany doors opened onto an "Alabama cream marble" lobby with a light green ceiling.[165]

After referring to *Dracula* as the "crustacean of chillers," the *Buffalo Evening News* told readers:

Mr. Lugosi had little difficulty in terrorizing audiences and his fellow players. His slit-

Lugosi during an unidentified performance as Dracula.

eyed leer seemed even more fiendish in the pale green light on the stage than on celluloid. … Frank Jacquet and Charles Francis are fine … [and] Eduard Franz gives a sustained performance as the count's demented victim, who thrives on flies and spiders and who is on the verge of being promoted to humans by the devilish Dracula.[166]

In conclusion, the newspaper admitted that, "for a push-cart, *Dracula* seems fairly-well stocked."

And yet those opinions were quite at odds with *Variety*, which also critiqued the Buffalo performance:

Ultra chiller picts in double feature lineup have dulled the edge of horror plays, unless they are of unique or superlative quality like *Arsenic and Old Lace*, which this one definitely is not.

Youngsters who constitute the bulk of audiences for these shows are emotionally calloused and appear to be teetering continually on whether to laugh or just mind their manners.

And, as a topper in the ineffectiveness of this mechanical and cumbersome opus, Bela Lugosi's portrayal of the ghoulish werewolf just doesn't add up to contemporary

Published in *Szabadság* on June 1, 1943.

conceptions of the epitome in fiendishness. His delineation is slack and blurred and lacks the sharp edges of characterization essential to credence, while his accent and bearing add almost a paternal note to the supposedly gory and goose-pimply role.[167]

The critic concluded with the damning insight, "For the worst acted and directed performance of the season, this one takes the palm...."

Dracula failed to do as well in Buffalo as it had in some of the other cities on the tour, taking in "less than a mild $6,000."[168] Perhaps its success was hampered to a degree by major transportation issues that week in Buffalo; cutbacks in gas coupon values led to wildly overcrowded trolleys and buses.[169]

Cleveland, Ohio, June 7-13, 1943

"I always wanted to see ghosts," Bela Lugosi told his fellow countryman, a journalist from Cleveland's Hungarian newspaper, *Szabadság*. "I'm very thankful to this nice Transylvanian vampire, who has been taking care of me for sixteen years now. I've done many films that have scared the world from America to Africa, but *Dracula* is the most memorable of all."[170] The actor spoke those words shortly after arriving in Cleveland on June 6.[171] Beginning on June 7, *Dracula* played seven evening performances at the Hanna Theatre, as well as three matinees.

As for the English-speaking press's publicity for the vampire play, the *Cleveland Plain Dealer* published an article on Lugosi and his wife in its *Women's Magazine and Amusement Section*. It featured Lugosi's previously mentioned remarks about the British Ban on horror films.

The local press described Lillian Lugosi as the actor's "buffer and advisor."[172] Another

Artwork published in the *Cleveland Plain Dealer* on June 8, 1943.

article called her "Mrs. Dracula," reporting that she wore a "diamond-studded gold bat pinned on her dress when she arrived yesterday. It's a good luck piece of jewelry, she explained, given to her when her actor-husband flew into Broadway's limelight 18 years ago as the vampire of *Dracula*."[173] Likely the journalist story got it wrong; Lugosi probably gave the pin to Lillian in the early thirties.

When the classically designed Hanna Theatre opened in 1921, Dan R. Hanna dedicated it to his late father, one-time owner of the Euclid Avenue Opera House.[174] A unique feature of the 1,535-seat theatre was its curtain: "It was common practice for traveling companies to leave their mark backstage on theatre curtains; it might be a shirt or poster stitched into the lining; an original drawing by the scene designer; signatures of the cast; anything which proclaimed 'We were here!'"[175]

As for current events, the *Cleveland Press* informed readers that the Allies were ready to move one million troops from Africa and bombard southern Europe with their "mightiest war machine" yet. During the rest of *Dracula*'s run, Allied planes "blasted" Sicily and took control of the cities of Pantelleria and Lampedusa.[176]

Gas rationing was certainly underway in Ohio at the time, with newspapers reporting that further cuts in allotments would likely come later in the summer.[177] Fears also mounted over a possible tire shortage in the Cleveland area.[178]

From the *Cleveland Press* of June 8, 1943.

Parallel to those efforts were ongoing disputes between the War Labor Board and America's coal miners. On June 10, Secretary of the Interior Harold Ickes announced that some 530,000 miners would be fined one dollar per day for their recent five-day strike. Enormous pressure caused him to rescind that plan in less than 48 hours.[179] Nevertheless, the US Congress passed a "drastic anti-strike bill" on June 12, which required thirty days' notice in advance of any walkout.[180] President Roosevelt quickly vetoed the would-be law.[181]

Despite such global and domestic troubles, Milton Krantz remained optimistic. Having become manager of the Hanna Theatre in 1941, the young Krantz made numerous changes, including increasing the number of seats.[182] Just after *Dracula* opened in Cleveland, he told Omar Ranney of the *Cleveland Press* that his current and upcoming seasons would stage great shows. He had recently visited New York, returning home with the belief that roadshows would soon get better than at any previous time during the war.[183]

Whether Krantz included *Dracula* in that category is unknown. Writing in the *Cleveland Press*, Ranney praised the production:

...*Dracula* can still scare 'em. There were screams at the Hanna Theatre last night, both on the stage and in the audience.... Mr. Lugosi, who is an expert at that sort of thing, was in fine form.

...And you couldn't help but feel sorry for his victim, Mary Heath. She was an attractive blonde, and she had such a SCREAM!

Just to gain an extra-positive proof that this play was scary, we gave ourselves a double dose at last night's opener, standing in the wings backstage during the third act. A young lady who introduced herself as the stage manager warned us that the lights would be going on and off, and that if we thought it might be a mite too scary, well ... we could help ourselves to a slug of wolfbane.

... Just our luck, then, to be standing where the vampire made his entrance when all the lights went out. He brushed right past us. Yow! And at that moment, the dogs got to howling. Not real dogs, but an awful good imitation.[184]

Ranney concluded with praise for Lugosi, Franz, and Mence. His only reservation about the entire production was Jacquet's performance, which Ranney claimed was "lacking in authority."

But critic Peter Bellamy of the *Cleveland News* reported a quite different version of events:

Published in the *Cleveland Plain Dealer* of June 13, 1943.

...alas, the ghastly old ghoul is suffering the ravages of time like the rest of us. Theatrically speaking, he just hasn't got that old drive anymore. That this is not an auspicious time for a reappearance of this time-honored old melodrama was aptly demonstrated at the Hanna last night. ...Personally, we feel almost sad to see what the years have done to *Dracula*.

...The audience last night seemed to have many juveniles among it. They appeared to look upon this respected old melodrama more as an amusing comedy. Indeed, after the second act curtain when Dracula had attacked the jugular vein of the girl, an irreverent spectator was heard to say, 'He dood it!'[185]

All that said, Bellamy commended Frank Jacquet for imbuing his role with "considerable authenticity."

William F. McDermott of the *Cleveland Plain Dealer* situated himself somewhere between his two colleagues:

From time to time you wonder if the actors can possibly mean what they say to be taken seriously. The real danger often appears to be not that the vampire will suck the life's blood from poor Lucy, but that the whole cast will expire from laughter at what they have to say and do.

... Yet the old shocker has a curious power. The members of last night's audience were obviously held by it. They didn't believe it, but they were willing to suspend disbelief. They laughed, but they laughed nervously. They engaged themselves in a spontaneous conspiracy to take it seriously and they begged to be frightened.[186]

The reviewer praised Lugosi, Franz, Jacquet, and Joy Nicholson, and ended with the remark, "The play is terribly old-fashioned and ridiculously melodramatic but few people will leave the theatre before it is finished."

Given the publication dates of their respective reviews, all three critics had to have attended the opening performance. Their contradictory reactions to *Dracula* were perhaps not unusual, as critics often disagree. However, their views about audience reactions seem clearly at odds with one another, an important reminder of how limited and problematic primary sources can be.

Perhaps not surprisingly, Lugosi's greatest cheers came from *Szabadság*, which told readers the "excellent Hungarian actor" brought Dracula to life as a "soul-shaking" and "scary" character, one that represented an "artistic" kind of "dignity," as opposed to Boris Karloff's characters, which were merely "frightening on the outside." Readers learned that Lugosi's local performance provoked screams from the audience, "especially from women."[187]

Pittsburgh, Pennsylvania, June 14-19, 1943

Much of the publicity for *Dracula*'s appearance in Pittsburgh concentrated on Lugosi. The *Pittsburgh Post-Gazette* described him at length:

Bela Lugosi, the vampire who eats like a man, opened his cavernous mouth and sank his fangs into a succulent forkful of 'toltot kaposta' – which, in the jargon of the blue plate special, is known as stuffed cabbage. Lugosi was... the dinner guest of Emma Hall, proprietress of [Emma's Café] at 109 Grant Street. Minus his ghoulish, grey-green makeup and dressed in sports clothes, the actor had brought his wife and the entire cast of *Dracula* to Emma's... for a post-performance repast.

Emma, as she prefers to be known, like Lugosi a native of Hungary, had met the actor backstage and invited him and his wife to partake of his favorite dish, stuffed cabbage. Elated over his acceptance, Emma subsequently invited several friends to attend the dinner. Lugosi complicated matters slightly, however, by bringing along the cast, eight in number – all of them wan from the rigors of the stage and direly in need of nourishment. While the Hall ménage sat disconsolately in a corner and looked hungrily at the heavily-laden table, Lugosi and his associates proceeded to demolish the platter of 'toltot kaposta.'

With the dish, they had salad, French fried potatoes, meat loaf and 'retes' – strudel. Lugosi made the Saturnalia complete by regaling himself with claret. 'This has my big okeh,' he said, chomping a huge bit of cabbage. Lugosi's 'big okeh,' he explained parenthetically,

The playbill cover for the Pittsburgh performances.

Artwork published inside the play's souvenir program.

is expressive of sincerity. His 'little okeh' is just courtesy. Beside him sat his wife, Lillian, a vivacious brunette wearing a white, diaphanous blouse with flowing sleeves. It was held together at the throat by a silver clasp shaped like a miniature vampire bat.

Mrs. Lugosi reached for the French fries and her sleeve swished over the salad. She drew her arm back hurriedly, but not before the sleeve had become tinged with salad dressing at the elbow. Mrs. Lugosi looked annoyed. After he had devoured four helpings of stuffed cabbage, Emma asked Lugosi solicitously if he would have some more. 'I'm playing ghost,' remonstrated the actor. 'Imagine anyone playing ghost with a stomach.' At the table sat two of Dracula's victims in the play, Mary Heath, who plays Lucy, and Joy Nicholson, who plays Miss Wells. 'They need plenty of vitamins,' mused Lugosi. 'They must build up their blood for me.'

Lugosi took time out from his masticating to proudly display a picture of his five-year-old son, Bela Jr. 'He wants to become a fireman or an airplane pilot,' the father confided. After the meal, Lugosi put aside the claret and called for a sturdier liquor. 'I drink beer with a Scotch chaser,' he said. 'No you don't,' contradicted Mrs. Lugosi. 'You drink Scotch with a beer chaser.' Lugosi shrugged. 'She is Dracula's boss,' he said. Emma put a nickel in the jukebox and played a native Hungarian dance. Mrs. Lugosi suggested that her husband and Emma should dance a 'czardas.' 'I'm sorry, I'm too full,' declared Lugosi, patting a taut waistline. As he walked out the door, Blackie, Emma's pet cat, arched its back, stiffened its tail, and meowed fearfully.[188]

The *Post-Gazette* concluded its tale with appropriate flourish: "Dracula disappeared into the night."

Built by Samuel F. Nixon in 1903, Pittsburgh's Nixon Theatre was located on the corner of Sixth Avenue and William Penn Place. Crowned by a large dome, it was "arguably the most opulent theatre in city history. The ornate interior was designed in the Louis XVth style, with acoustically treated walls. Inside the theatre were massive imitation marble columns capped with solid gold. The walls were paneled to look like damask silk, framed in a molding and styling of green, gold and red. Velvet and silk draperies added to the decorum."[189]

In between giving performances, Lugosi and his colleagues probably kept abreast of the war. As the play opened, the Allied forces bombed Sicily and warned Italy to be prepared for

Lugosi at Emma's Café in Pittsburgh.

invasion.[190] News from the Pacific Theatre included the downing of 77 Japanese planes and twelve Japanese ships.[191]

Reports on the home front were not necessarily as positive. *Billboard* believed that numerous venues for live music would have to close in the Midwest due to gas rationing.[192] And in Pittsburgh, two motorists had their ration books suspended after breaking the ban on non-essential driving by visiting the South Hills Country Club.[193] That verdict came immediately after the federal government had told citizens, "If you are in doubt as to the necessity and importance of that trip you've been thinking about, don't take it."[194]

The coal dispute raged as an even greater problem. Demanding travel pay, the United Mine Workers threatened a third strike.[195] In return, the War Labor Board ordered the miners to sign an agreement outlawing strikes for the rest of the war.[196] As the week continued, the two parties edged closer and closer to the end of their temporary truce, with some 20,000 miners already refusing to work.[197]

By contrast, numerous actors certainly worked at the Nixon. The week prior to *Dracula*'s opening, the theatre hosted a revival of *The Bat* with ZaSu Pitts. In an interesting advertisement *faux pas*, *Variety* reported:

Press agents for both *Bat* and *Dracula* revivals in Pittsburgh last week got a start when they looked at big weekly ads in the dailies for the thrillers, which follow each other at Nixon in Pitt. Layouts appeared side by side and at the top of each of them was a big black bat hovering across the body of the copy. By the time they realized the coincidence, it was too late to change the mats, but they were corrected [the] following week, of course. Over-all impression was that ZaSu Pitts was going to play *The Bat* one week and Bela Lugosi the next.[198]

Despite his long history in the theatre, Lugosi had never appeared onstage in *The Bat* or any of the other popular old dark house plays that thrilled Broadway in the teens and twenties.

After viewing *Dracula*, the *Pittsburgh Press* critiqued the play for its readership:

Headed by Bela Lugosi, an experienced practitioner of the black arts these many years in the movies, it's an uncommonly good crew of actors engaged in the outlandish clap-trap that is *Dracula*.

To the accompaniment of backstage noises – the howling of dogs, the maniacal laughter of our crazy man, whistlings of bats (I suppose bats whistle), Dracula goes about his hellish business.[199]

In the final analysis, the critic believed, "*Dracula* is better than *The Bat*, last week's entry." The *Pittsburgh Sun-Telegraph* agreed that *Dracula* had bested *The Bat*, adding that its:

...original weird appeal still holds to a great extent, and the way it is being staged leaves little to quibble about.

Mr. Lugosi carries an extremely difficult role, especially in this sophisticated style, with surprising ease, and in the strict *Dracula* tradition which he created.

Mr. Frank Jacquet is an eminent successor to Mr. Edward Van Sloan as Van Helsing, just as Mr. Eduard Franz is a worthy follower of Mr. Bernard Jukes and Mr. Dwight Frye in the exacting and different characterization of Renfield ... Miss Heath, a capable young actress, brings a realistic pathos to the role of Lucy....[200]

The review concluded by noting that *Dracula* was not the "super-charged spine-freezer it used to be. But it was worth the present revival, and last night's audience gave every indication of believing so."

The city's *Post-Gazette* was less kind in its outlook than other papers had been:

Last week *The Bat* came back to the Nixon and there was the heavy smell of ancient limburger all over the place. This week it's *Dracula* and the corn's just as old but a lot greener. For age hasn't laid such a withered hand on this ancient tale of the one-man blood bank and B pictures haven't completely staled its honorable hokum.

It's a right good cast that Mr. Oshrin has assembled, by the way, for this *Dracula*, although what the doggone package of graveyard and gruesome is without Mr. Lugosi is another thing. Somehow he injects just the right touch of boo, which isn't surprising since he's been creeping up and down spines in one form or another for a considerable number of years, and then this Miss Heath gives some substance to his werewolf. As a matter of fact, this Miss Heath would not only bring out the werewolves in packs, but also any and all other kinds of wolves, up to and including the 1943 kind.[201]

Despite reservations, the critic adjudged "this *Dracula*" to be not "bad at all."

By the end of the six-day run the box office take at the Nixon was fairly weak. *Variety* noted:

Curtain came down on legit season at Nixon rather perfunctorily last week with Bela Lugosi in revival of *Dracula* barely pulling in $5,300... Show didn't receive such bad notices either, profiting by the fact that crix compared it to *Bat* week before and gave the old horror drama all the best of it, but too many things were against it, mostly the heat.[202]

From the *Washington Post* of June 17, 1943.

Published in the *Washington Post* on June 20, 1943.

A subsequent article in the same publication added that Dracula had made just a "few hundred" more than *The Bat*.[203]

Washington, D. C., June 21-26, 1943

By January 21, President Roosevelt was preparing "imminent action" because half of Pittsburgh's steel plants had closed due to striking workers.[204] Pennsylvania miners went on strike that week as well, ignoring John L. Lewis' order to return to their jobs.[205] At roughly the same time, the US Congress overrode Roosevelt's veto of their anti-strike bill.[206]

In Chicago, a gasoline dealer was arrested for illegal possession of gas coupons; in New York, another man was barred from selling gasoline for the duration of the war after peddling

NATIONAL

"America's First Theatre"

BELA LUGOSI

The playbill to the show's appearance in Washington, D.C.

counterfeit coupons.[207] "The road to North Africa is strewn with the bodies of dead American soldiers and sailors," a commissioner for the Office of Price Administration admonished violators, adding, "Your acts have contributed to the breakdown of the whole program."[208]

It was into this milieu that Lugosi and company arrived in Washington, D. C. to stage *Dracula* for one week at the National Theatre, which had no air-conditioning. Once known as the "Theatre of Presidents," the National Theatre is situated on a prime and prestigious location on Pennsylvania Avenue just a few blocks from the White House. Its original building opened on December 7, 1835.[209] After a terrible fire necessitated major repairs, the National reopened in 1850.[210]

The theatre had first planned to stage *The Bat* with ZaSu Pitts the week prior to *Dracula*.[211] However, for reasons unknown, Pitts and her producer cancelled, thus leaving the National Theatre dark for several days prior to Lugosi's arrival.[212] The same would be the case after *Dracula* ended, as the play closed its 1942-43 season.[213]

The day before the first performance, Lugosi indicated that, "he was rather relieved to find himself back in the role of a relatively innocuous bloodsucking vampire." Lugosi also said that he was happy to be back onstage in a legitimate theatre play. "It will be a real thrill to hear an audience gasp in terror. The more horrified they are, the better I like it."[214]

Though brief on details, the *Washington Daily News* gave *Dracula* a positive notice, as did the *Washington Times Herald*, whose critic wrote: "It seemed to me that Mr. Lugosi has lost none of his fine talent for the macabre ... he should be seen in this if only for the pleasure of witnessing a weird tour de force. ... I don't see why you shouldn't see it."[215]

The *Washington Post*'s critic was also pleased what with she saw, informing readers that *Dracula* was:

...ghoulish enough for grandpa and ghoulish enough for grandma, [and] goes right on its gruesome way with similar effects on the present generation.

... Mary Heath plays Lucy Seward with the sweetness and submissive charm the role needs. The force of the play depends largely upon whether we like Lucy enough to care whether the Count gets her or not, and Mary Heath's Lucy is sympathetic.

Eduard Franz gives a harrowing performance as the young fly-and-spider eating madman whom Dr. Seward keeps in the sanatorium. His big mobile face reflects the complicated, irrational logic of the feverishly active pathological mind. Frank Jacquet as Van Helsing is briskly authoritative; he has a bedside manner that is most convincing, and he can even wave a cross at the vampire with dignity.

As for Bela Lugosi, there's only one thing to say. Lugosi is to the business of scaring hell out of the customers as Petty is to the production of pin-up girls, as Count Fleet is to racing. Just tops.[216]

Program of the Play

(Program continued from page 13)

CAST

(In order of their appearance)

MISS WELLS, Maid....................JOY NICHOLSON

JONATHAN HARKER....................GUY SPAULL

DR. SEWARD.....................CHARLES FRANCIS

ABRAHAM VAN HELSING............FRANK JAQUET

R. M. RENFIELD....................EDUARD FRANZ

BUTTERWORTH ....MARY HEATH

LUCY SEWARD........................JANET TYLER

COUNT DRACULA.....................BELA LUGOSI

(Program continued on page 17)

From the interior of the playbill in Washington, D.C.

The unit set is cleverly planned to lend itself to the representation of three scenes with only minor changes; and it is an effective one, somber and with an effect of great age and dignity.[217]

Overall, the *Post*'s positive review claimed that, "everybody has a good creepy evening of it."

The city's *Evening Star* had a very different reaction, bemoaning the revival as a "weak and senile echo" of its earlier self:

In a wan way, Mr. Lugosi and his collaborators do struggle to strike terror in the hearts of the customers. The customers, however, either laugh or remain politely aloof, a reaction strangely calculated to give Dracula chills, if he should happen to be listening.

…Bram Stoker's old chiller is a boring old fogey of a play, unworthy of the attention of an uninspired summer stock company. Its creaks are those in the joints of age, more productive of sympathy than terror.

… Mr. Lugosi looks and talks not unlike a kindly old grandfather playing games with the kiddies who, in turn, get the impression gramps is a silly old fool.[218]

The same newspaper gave limited praise to Joy Nicholson as the maid, but qualified it by adding "that can only mean there was something terribly wrong with the rest of the lines for Miss Nicholson definitely is no Katharine Cornell."

In a more light-hearted vein, the author of a political gossip column managed to get backstage to see Lugosi during the run of the show:

In an attempt to forget Congressional disturbances, I dashed down to the National Theatre to get a little cheer from their last play of this season. It turned out that they were doing that gay little play, *Dracula*, with Bela Lugosi furnishing the major thrills. Actually, after being on the hill and seeing some of the stuff that goes on up there, *Dracula* wasn't half as frightening as it might have been. Afterwards, desiring a closer look at the horror man, I went backstage where he complacently sat, with a cigar in his mouth, and a smile on his face.[219]

The columnist told Lugosi that he was "perfectly horrible" in the play. That brought a laugh from Lugosi, who was busy signing autographs.

Dracula took in $2,500 from advance sale tickets for its opening night.[220] This final leg of the tour became quite successful. *Variety* wrote:

In the face of blistering heat and housed in a non-air-conditioned theatre, Bela Lugosi in *Dracula* … grossed $8,000 last week, considered exceptional in the face of

Lugosi and Mary Heath, published in the *Washington Post* on June 22, 1943.

atmospheric opposition. Three of the four notices from critics were friendly, but one Monday night scribe, applying the conventional Broadway yardstick, gave the mystery thriller a thorough toasting.[221]

Lugosi likely departed from Washington, D. C. pleased with his local reception. But he not only left the nation's capitol, he left the revival.

Conclusion

According to the *New York Times*, Harry H. Oshrin's *Dracula* terminated in Washington D. C. because of "Lugosi's movie commitments," adding that "later in the fall, the movie actor plans to resume the road tour."[222] The actual extent to which Oshrin considered a second tour is hard to determine. Certainly it is true that, at a much earlier stage, Chicago had been mentioned as another possible destination.[223] But that booking did not finally occur. Nor did any others.

What continued to rage were the European and Pacific Theatres of World War II, as well as problems on the home front. Gas rationing proceeded, though an increasing number of persons attacked the pleasure-driving ban.[224] Coal miners went on strike for two weeks just after the *Dracula* tour ended, leading President Roosevelt to sharpen the "teeth" of the War Labor Board.[225] And yet more strikes occurred in October and November 1943.[226]

Neither of the two actresses who played Lucy had particularly notable careers, though Janet Tyler did appear in the Broadway version of *Harvey* in 1944.[227] By contrast, Len Mence found consistent work, reaching a pinnacle with *The King and I* on Broadway from 1950 to 1954.

Until Wallace Widdecombe died in 1969 at age 100, he was the oldest living member of Actors Equity.[228] Guy Spaull, who died in 1980, later worked in such Broadway productions as *Witness for the Prosecution* and *My Fair Lady*.[229]

After *Dracula*, Frank Jacquet forged ahead, playing small parts in a vast number of films and television programs, including *Black Magic* (1944), *D.O.A.* (1950), *Ace in the Hole* (1951), and *Rancho Notorious* (1952). Horror film viewers likely remember him best for portraying the doctor in *The Vampire's Ghost* (1945). He died in 1958 at the age of 73.

Certainly the greatest success of any *Dracula* costar came to Eduard Franz, who appeared in Broadway plays with some regularity until 1969. His film career began in 1947, and from there he went on to act in *Wake of the Red Witch* (1948), *The Thing from Another World* (1951), *The Ten Commandments* (1956), and *The Four Skulls of Jonathan Drake* (1959), the latter being a horror movie in which Franz portrayed the title character. He died in 1983, his last role being a small part in *Twilight Zone: The Movie* (1983).[230]

As for the venerable director O. D. Woodward, the 1943 revival became something of a culmination. The man who staged *Dracula–The Vampire Play* with Lugosi on the West Coast ended his career with the same vampire tale. He fell ill soon after the tour ended and then died in 1946.[231]

Lugosi made a rapid departure from Washington D. C. and, either via overnight train or an all-night trip by car with Lillian at the wheel, arrived in Chicago on June 27, the day following the final tour performance of *Dracula*. The brief stopover on the way back to California allowed Lugosi to attend an important organizational meeting for the Hungarian-American Council for Democracy (HACD).

Were Lugosi's film commitments the real reason that the *Dracula* tour ended? That is difficult to say, but Hollywood had beckoned. Lugosi quickly found himself back on the screen, and back on the stage as well, even if in a different production than *Dracula*.

(Endnotes)

1   "Coal Miners Adopt $2 Pay Rise Demand." *New York Times* 6 Mar. 1943.
2   "WLB Faces a Showdown with Unions on Wages." *New York Times* 7 Mar. 1943.
3   "President Orders Mines Kept Open, Parleys Continued." *New York Times* 23 Mar. 1943.

4   "Lewis Challenges No Strike Pledge." *New York Times* 27 Mar. 1943.

5   "2,000 Coal Miners End Strike." *New York Times* 5 Apr. 1943.

6   "3,000 Miners Vote Defiance to WLB." *New York Times* 26 Apr. 1943; "15,000 Miners Out, WLB Wires Lewis to End Stoppages." *New York Times* 27 Apr. 1943; "50 Mines Closed by Coal Strikes." *New York Times* 28 Apr. 1943.

7   "Lewis Stands Pat in Coal Impasse." *New York Times* 29 Apr. 1943.

8   Mitcham, Samuel W., Jr. *Rommel's Desert War: The Life and Death of the Afrika Korps* (Mechanicsburg, PA: Stackpole, 2007).

9   Irzyk, Albin F. *Gasoline to Patton* (Oakland, OR: Edlerberry, 2004).

10   Robinson, Ray. *American Original: A Life of Will Rogers* (New York: Oxford University Press, 1996).

11   "War Days for the Motorist." *New York Times* 4 Jan. 1942.

12   "Nation-Wide Curb Pledged Soon by Roosevelt after Baruch Asks Action." *New York Times* 11 Sept. 1942.

13   "Rationing of Gas Goes into Effect on National Scale." *New York Times* 1 Dec. 1942.

14   Lyons, Leonard. "The Post's New Yorker." *Washington Post* 12 Mar. 1938.

15   "Summer Plays for Chicago." *Christian Science Monitor* 16 May 1939.

16   Brown, Chamberlain. Letter to Bela Lugosi. 17 May 1941. [Available in the Chamberlain and Lyman Brown Papers, and Undated, Series II: Correspondence, Box 64, Folder F.9 at the New York Public Library/Lincoln Center for the Performing Arts in New York.]

17   Lugosi, Bela. Letter to Chamberlain Brown. 24 May 1941. [Available in the Chamberlain and Lyman Brown Papers, and Undated, Series II: Correspondence, Box 64, Folder F.9.]

18   Fidler, Jimmie. "In Hollywood." *Long Island Journal* 24 Sept. 1941.

19   Durant, Alta. "Gab." *Daily Variety* 11 August 1942.

20   "Lugosi Heads For Chi To Play *Dracula*." *Daily Variety* 20 Aug. 1942.

21   "Dracula Lives Again." *Dallas Morning News* 27 Aug. 1942.

22   Oakley, Annie. "The Theatre and Its People." *Windsor Daily Star* (Windsor, Ontario, Canada) 24 Apr. 1943.

23   "Holy Week Lay-Off for Touring Shows." *New York Times* 19 Apr. 1943.

24   "Obituaries – O. D. Woodward." *Daily Variety* 10 Jan. 1946.

25   Ehlers, D. Lane. "American stock company management as reflected in the career of O. D. Woodward, 1897 – 1922." Available at: http://digitalcommons.unl.edu/dissertations/AA19700081. Accessed 30 May 2013; "O.D. Woodward." *Billboard* 24 July 1920. "O.D. Woodward." *Billboard* 18 Feb. 1922.

26   "Laura (Bullivant) Frye." Available at: http://www.zoominfo.com/p/Laura-Frye/9476020. Accessed 30 May 2013.

27   "St. Louis Stocks Flourish." *Billboard* 24 Oct. 1931.

28   "Appeal to Audiences Held Vital." *Los Angeles Times* 15 July 1928.

29   "Bogey Man Lugosi Comforts Damsel." *Brooklyn Eagle* 31 Jan. 1943.

30   "*Ape, Dynamite* In Colony First Run." *Daily Variety* 17 Mar. 1943.

31   "Studio Contracts." *Variety* 17 Feb. 1943.

32   "Coming and Going." *Film Daily* 13 Apr. 1943.

33   Untitled Article. *New York Post* 21 Apr. 1943.

34   Eaton, Hal. "Going To Town." *Long Island Press* (Long Island, NY) 24 Apr. 1943.

35   Kilgallen, Dorothy. "Miss Midnight's Notebook." *Lowell Sun* (Lowell, MA) 29 Apr. 1943.

36   Jaquet was also the spelling of his legal name. However, in this chapter we opt instead for the spelling "Jacquet" given that it was the spelling used on most of the publicity materials and, as a result, in most of the critical reviews for *Dracula–The Vampire Play* in 1943.

37   "Tampa, Fla." *Billboard* 26 July 1908; "Stock Notes." *Variety* 29 Sept. 1926; "St. Louis Ring, 1. I. B. M., Stages Show for Tornado Sufferers." *Billboard* 29 Oct. 1927.

38   "*Corregidor*." *Variety* 2 June 1943.

39   "Character Actor Eduard Franz Dies at 80." *Los Angeles Times* 15 Feb. 1983.

40   "New Plays on Broadway." *Billboard* 9 Jan. 1943; "Muni, Robinson in Pageant." *New York Times* 4 Mar. 1943.

41   "Plays Out of Town." *Variety* 31 Mar. 1943.

42   "Wallace Widdecombe." *Variety* 23 July 1969.

43   "Robeson's *Othello*." *Variety* 12 Aug. 1942.

44   "Guy Spaull." *New York Times* 8 Jan. 1980.

45   "*I Killed the Count*." *Variety* 9 Sept. 1943; "Six Shows to Open Here Next Month." *New York Times*

24 Feb. 1943.

46 "News of the Stage." *New York Times* 28 Dec. 1942; "Names, Novelty on St. L Op's Sked; Heavy Scale." *Billboard* 29 May 1943.

47 "*Wild Rose* Has Good Music, but Theme and Book Are Weak." *Billboard* 2 Oct. 1926; "Suave Heroes Turn Rough and Ready in New Films." *Los Angeles Times* 14 May 1935.

48 "New City Art Show Ready." *New York Times* 30 Nov. 1936.

49 Lugosi, Bela. "Bela Lugosi, Star of *Dracula*, in Person." *Boston Herald* 2 May 1943.

50 "Shows in Rehearsal." *Variety* 28 Apr. 1943.

51 See, for example: "Holy Week Lay-Off for Touring Shows." *New York Times* 12 Apr. 1943.

52 Lugosi, Bela. "Bela Lugosi, Star of *Dracula*, in Person."

53 "*Dracula*, with Bela Lugosi, Opens for Week at National." *Washington Daily News* 22 June 1943.

54 Maynard, John. "*Dracula*, in Its Old Form, Opens at the National." *Washington Times Herald* 22 June 1943. [For the other review mentioned in this sentence, see: "*Dracula*, with Bela Lugosi Opens for Week at National." *Washington Daily News* 22 June 1943.]

55 *Philadelphia Bulletin* 15 May 1943.

56 Carmody, Jay. "Lugosi Revives *Dracula* in a Manner of Speaking." *The Evening Star* (Washington, D. C.) 22 June 1943.

57 Bellamy, Peter. "The Play." *Cleveland News* 8 June 1943.

58 See, for example: "*Dracula* Still Chills at National, with Lugosi in Original Role." *Washington Post* 22 June 1943.

59 This booklet also eschewed the phrase *The Vampire Play*.

60 C.D.W. "The Stage." *Boston Globe* 4 May 1943.

61 "Additional Mileage Granted by OPA to All Using Gas for Biz; Applies to Non-Shortage Areas." *Billboard* 8 May 1943.

62 "*Dracula* Catches a Pretty Victim." *Bridgeport Post* 29 Apr. 1943.

63 "New England Asks Equal 'Gas' Ration." *New York Times* 24 Apr. 1943.

64 "WLB Sends Coal Wage Fight to Roosevelt." *Bridgeport Telegram* 29 Apr. 1943.

65 "History." Available at: http://theklein.org/about-the-klein/. Accessed 26 May 2013.

66 "*Dracula* Swell $2,682, Bridgeport, 1." *Billboard* 15 May 1943.

67 Russell, Fred H. "*Dracula* Brings Chills to Klein." *Bridgeport Post* 1 May 1943.

68 Ibid.

69 Ibid.

70 Qtd. in the 1943 Bushnell playbill for *Dracula*.

71 Advertisement. *Hartford Times* 30 Apr. 1943.

72 The 1943 *Bushnell Playbill* for *Dracula*.

73 "Miners Idle, FDR's Action Waited." *Bridgeport Post* 1 May 1943.

74 "U.S. Seizes Coal Mines." *Hartford Times* 1 May 1943.

75 "Accord Seen on Substantial Mine Pay Boost." *Hartford Times* 3 May 1943.

76 "In Terrifying Play Here Today." *Hartford Courant* 1 May 1943; "Lugosi Occupies Strangest House in Film Capital." *Hartford Courant* 25 Apr. 1943.

77 "Bela Lugosi, Son of Hungarian Banker, Preferred Acting Career." *Hartford Times* 30 Apr. 1943.

78 Here the reviewer makes reference to Patrick Hamilton's 1938 stage play, which was originally titled *Gas Light* when staged in England in 1938 and then adapted for the screen in 1940 (with the spelling changed to *Gaslight*). It opened on Broadway as *Angel Street* in 1941. George Cukor's 1944 film version with Charles Boyer restored the title to *Gaslight*.

79 "*Dracula* Is Seen Again at Bushnell." *Hartford Courant* 2 May 1943.

80 Advertisement. *Hartford Times* 1 May 1943.

81 Advertisement. *Hartford Times* 1 May 1943.

82 Advertisement. *Boston Globe* 24 Mar. 1943.

83 "Shubert Majestic Kayoed in Boston." *Billboard* 15 May 1943.

84 "Charles Presents... The USA Retro Times – Once Upon A Time In Boston's Theatre District: The Story of the Plymouth Theatre... aka... The Gary." Available at: http://usaretrotimes.blogspot.com/2011/02/once-upon-time-in-bostons-theatre.html. Updated 28 Feb. 2011. Accessed 25 May 2013.

85 "Charles Presents... The USA Retro Times – Once Upon A Time In Boston's Theatre District: The Story of the Plymouth Theatre... aka... The Gary."

86 "600 Fall Prisoner to Yanks, French." *Boston Herald* 3 May 1943

87 See, for example: "Yanks Slap Pincers on Bizerte." *Boston Herald* 4 May 1943; "Yanks Driving Nazis

to Sea." *Boston Post* 4 May 1943; "Yanks Now Ready to Shell Bizerte." *Boston Post* 5 May 1943; "3 Allied Columns Near Bizerte." *Boston Herald* 6 May 1943; "Entire Nazi Front Reels Back." *Boston Herald* 7 May 1943;

88 "Allies Capture 50,000; 400 Planes Hit Sicily." *Boston Herald* 10 May 1943.
89 "Order New Check on Gas Rations." *Boston Post* 4 May 1943.
90 "Drive Ban Lift Boosts Biz and Talent Demands." *Billboard* 1 May 1943.
91 "Lewis Halts Strike; Lashed by Roosevelt." *Boston Herald* 3 May 1943.
92 "U.S. Not to Negotiate Mine Pact." *Boston Herald* 4 May 1943.
93 "Mark Starr Doubts Miners Will Work." *New York Times* 2 May 1943.
94 "First Lady Pleads for Coal Miners." *New York Times* 9 May 1943.
95 Lugosi, Bela. "Bela Lugosi, Star of *Dracula*, in Person."
96 "*Dracula* a Relief from Real Horror." *Boston Globe* 9 May 1943.
97 C.D.W. "The Stage." *Boston Globe* 4 May 1943.
98 Eager, Helen. "Bela Lugosi in *Dracula* Revived at Plymouth." *Boston Evening Traveler* 4 May 1943.
99 "*Dracula* Opens at Plymouth." *Boston Post* 4 May 1943.
100 Hughes, Elinor. "*Dracula*, with Bela Lugosi, Opens at the Plymouth Theatre." *Boston Herald* 4 May 1943.
101 D. M. "*Dracula* Revived." *Christian Science Monitor* 4 May 1943.
102 "*Showtime* Wow 26G in 12 Hub Showings." *Variety* 12 May 1943.
103 "*Drac* Neat 17G, *Show Time* Fat $50,000, 2 Hub Wks.; *Claudia* 6th Wk. 9G; *Candida* $3,5000, *Door* 5G." *Billboard* 29 May 1943.
104 "Lugosi on Horror Radio Play Tonight." *Boston Herald* 6 May 1943.
105 Lugosi, Bela. Letter to Milton Yakus. 22 July 1943.
106 For more information on other authors who Lugosi promoted to Hollywood studios, see Rhodes, Gary D. *Bela Lugosi, Dreams and Nightmares* (Narberth, Pennsylvania: Collectables/Gotham, 2007).
107 "Africa Campaign Ends; Von Arnim Is Captured." *Boston Herald* 13 May 1943; "Churchill in U.S. to Map Invasion Plan." *Boston Post* 12 May 1943.
108 "Goering Takes Over Command of Italy." *Boston Post* 11 May 1943.
109 "*Drac* Neat 17G, *Show Time* Fat $50,000, 2 Hub Wks.; *Claudia* 6th Wk. 9G; *Candida* $3,5000, *Door* 5G."
110 "Hub Season Stretches as 3 New Ones Open; *Jr. Miss* Holds Up as Inclemency Crabs Other Takes." *Billboard* 29 May 1943.
111 "Boston Looks to Good Summer Biz, *Claudia* 6th–Final Neat 8G in 3d Visit." *Variety* 19 May 1943.
112 Advertisement. *Boston Post* 15 May 1943.
113 "Regional News – Boston." *Showmen's Trade Review* 8 May 1943.
114 "Camp Framingham News." *Framingham News* Undated 1943 clipping, courtesy of the Framingham Public Library of Framingham, Massachusetts.
115 "Five Days Satisfy The Soldiers." *New York Times* 24 July 1887.
116 "Mustering Out Troops." *New York Times* 30 Aug. 1898.
117 "Greatest Bombings of War Rock Europe; U.S. Forces Attack Japs on Attu Island." *Boston Herald* 14 May 1943.
118 "Wild Riots Break Out in Streets of Berlin." *Boston Post* 14 May 1943.
119 "Camp Framingham News." *Framingham News* 17 May 1943.
120 Ibid.
121 Ibid.
122 Winchell, Walter. "On Broadway." *Augusta Chronicle* (Augusta, GA) 14 May 1943.
123 Haas, Howard B. "Locust Street Theatre." Available at: http://cinematreasures.org/theaters/22730. Accessed on 25 May 2013.
124 Ibid.
125 Gaghan, Jerry. "Cross Town." *Philadelphia Daily News* 19 May 1943.
126 "Air Assaults Crack Italy's War Defenses." *Philadelphia Inquirer* 26 May 1943.
127 "Churchill Bids Italy to Oust Duce, Quit War." *Philadelphia Inquirer* 26 May 1943; "U.S. Increasing War Aid to Russia, Roosevelt Reveals." *Philadelphia Inquirer* 26 May 1943.
128 "Thousands Halted in Move to End Pleasure Driving." *Philadelphia Inquirer* 21 May 1943.
129 "10-12% Reduction in B, C Books Is Due." *New York Times* 19 May 1943.
130 "Drive Ban Keeps Listeners Home." *Broadcast Advertising* 24 May 1943.
131 Gaghan, Jerry. "Cross Town." *Philadelphia Daily News* 12 May 1943.
132 Finn, Elsie. "Menace with Cold Feet – That's Bela Lugosi." *Philadelphia Record* 19 May 1943.
133 D. W. B. "Bela Lugosi Stars in Vampire Thriller." *The Evening Bulletin* (Philadelphia, PA) 18 May 1943.
134 Bushman, Leonore. "Bela Lugosi as Dracula Starred on Locust Stage." *Philadelphia Daily News* 18

May 1943.

135 *"Dracula* Drawing Crowds to Locust." *Philadelphia Evening Star* 18 May 1943.

136 Singer, Samuel L. "Lugosi Stars in Revival of *Dracula." Philadelphia Inquirer* 18 May 1943.

137 Bronson, Arthur. *"Dracula* Revival Opens at Locust." *Philadelphia Record* 18 May 1943.

138 *"St. Mark* Neat $14,200 in Philly." *Variety* 26 May 1943; *"Blossom Time* $19000 Philly." *Variety* 2 June 1943.

139 *"Student* $22,800 in Phila; 4 Wks. Carded; Eve Due." *Billboard* 15 May 1943.

140 Though listeners obviously would not have known about Lugosi's various spelling errors, they are represented herein exactly as he wrote them.

141 "Fort Meade's First Girl Show Gets Enthusiastic Reception." *Baltimore Sun* 6 Apr. 1941.

142 "Soldiers Would Enjoy Best Plays, Eva Le Gallienne Says." *Baltimore Sun* 12 Oct. 1942.

143 "Drama Slated at Fort Meade." *Baltimore Sun* 13 Dec. 1942.

144 Amrine, Private Mike. "Bela Lugosi Here with *Dracula* Sunday." 21 May 1943.

145 "Bela Lugosi Is Seen in Play at Fort Meade." *Baltimore Sun* 24 May 1943.

146 Playbill for *Dracula*. Fort Meade, MA. 1943.

147 "Bela Lugosi Here with *Dracula* Sunday." *Fort Meade Post* 21 May 1943.

148 "Lugosi and Troupe Make Hit with Full House." *Fort Meade Post* 28 May 1943.

149 Ibid.

150 "Bela Lugosi Heads Cast of *Dracula." Buffalo Evening News* 29 May 1943.

151 Martin, W. E. J. "Lugosi Back in First Hit." *Buffalo Courier-Express* 30 May 1943.

152 "Lewis Cuts Pay Demands to $1.50; Operators Offer $1; Pits Unopened." *Buffalo Courier-Express* 2 June 1943.

153 "Roosevelt Confers with Aids on Plan to Reopen Coal Mines." *Buffalo Courier-Express* 3 June 1943; "Miners Return to Work Monday; Lewis OK's Move, Assails WLB." *Buffalo Courier-Express* 5 June 1943.

154 Marx, Groucho. "How to Crank a Horse." *Los Angeles Times* 30 May 1943.

155 "Union, N.J. Drive-In Folds After Two Weeks." *Variety* 2 June 1943.

156 "Seize Huge Cache of Ration Stamps." *New York Times* 4 June 1943.

157 "Gas Ration Books Stolen." *New York Times* 9 June 1943.

158 "Denied Gasoline, Gets New Car." *New York Times* 5 June 1943.

159 Snowden's name appears in the Erlanger playbill. By contrast, Francis' name appears only in a review published in the *Buffalo Evening News*.

160 Cohen, Harold V. "Bela Lugosi at the Nixon in *Dracula." Pittsburgh Post-Gazette* 15 June 1943.

161 Heath, Paul Silas. *Christians Face the Postwar World (Social Progress Pamphlets)*. Department of Social Education and Action, Board of Education, Presbyterian Church, 1942.

162 "Imperial Players to Give Thriller." *The Daily Argus* (Mount Vernon, NY) 27 Oct. 1942.

163 "Twin City Native Has First Major Role in *Dracula." Buffalo Evening News* 2 June 1943.

164 Advertisement. *Buffalo Evening News* 29 May 1943.

165 "The Erlanger Theater, 1927 – 1956." Available at http://wnyheritagepress.org/photos_week__2006/erlanger/erlanger.htm. Accessed 26 May 2013.

166 Kowalewski, Ed. "Green Spotlights Help Lugosi Scare as Stage *Dracula." Buffalo Evening News* 1 June 1943.

167 Burton. *"Dracula." Variety* 9 June 1943.

168 *"Dracula* Brr 6G." *Variety* 9 June 1943.

169 "Buffalo War Council Protests ODT Order Cutting Bus Service." *Buffalo Evening News* 2 June 1943; "Mayor Asks Boost in Gas Rations as Crowds Jam Street Cars, Buses." *Buffalo Courier-Express* 4 June 1943.

170 "Drakula Maszk Nélkül." *Szabadság* (Cleveland, OH) 10 June 1943.

171 "Influence of Thrillers." *Cleveland Plain Dealer* 7 June 1943.

172 "Dracula Is Stamp Fiend Off the Stage." *Cleveland Plain Dealer (Women's Magazine and Amusement Section)* 6 June 1943.

173 "Influence of Thrillers." *Cleveland Plain Dealer*.

174 "Hanna Theatre – The Encyclopedia of Cleveland History." Available at: http://ech.cwru.edu/ech-cgi/article.pl?id=HT. Updated 22 October 2012. Accessed 26 May 2013.

175 "The Hanna Theatre Curtain." Available at http://www.clevelandmemory.org/hanna/. Accessed 26 May 2013.

176 "Zero Hour Near in Allied Drive." *Cleveland Press* 7 June 1943; "Planes Blast Sicily, Pantelleria." *Cleveland Press* 10 June 1943; "Air Power Wins Pantelleria Isle." *Cleveland Press* 11 June 1943; "Lampedusa Yields to Allied Air Might." *Cleveland Press* 12 June 1943.

177 "Ohio Gasoline Cuts Unlikely Before Aug. 1." *Cleveland Press* 10 June 1943.

178 "Tire Replacement Problem May Curtail Driving Here." *Cleveland Press* 9 June 1943.

179 "Ickes Backs Down on Miner's Fine; Strikes Feared." *Cleveland Press* 12 June 1943.

180 "Drastic Anti-Strike Bill Passed, Goes to President." *Pittsburgh Sun-Telegraph* 13 June 1943.

181 "Congress Rebels." *New York Times* 26 June 1943.

182 Simonson, Robert. "Milton Krantz, Longtime Manager of Cleveland's Hanna Theatre, Is Dead at 94." 23 Oct. 2006. Accessed 2 Mar. 2014. Available at: http://www.playbill.com/news/ article/102904-Milton-Krantz-Longtime-Manager-of-Clevelands-Hanna-Theater-Is-Dead-at-94.

183 Ranney, Omar Ranney. "Hanna Chief Sees Road Show Boom." *Cleveland Press* 10 June 1943.

184 Ranney, Omar. "Lugosi Still Frightens as Vampire Dracula." *Cleveland Press* 8 June 1943.

185 Bellamy, Peter. "The Play." *Cleveland News* 8 June 1943.

186 McDermott, William F. "Bela Lugosi Revives an Old-Time Melodrama of Life Among the Vampires." *Cleveland Plain Dealer* 8 June 1943.

187 "Dracula — Lugosi Bélával." *Szabadság* 10 June 1943.

188 Johnson, Vincent. "Green Vampire Dines Voraciously On Stuffed Cabbage in Grant Street – Sheds 11-Foot Bat Wings, Swoops Down on Emma's Café." *Pittsburgh Post-Gazette* 19 June 1943. While this article's content is preserved precisely, it is worth noting that the following spellings would be more accurate than those that appear in it: rétes, czárdás, and töltött káposzta.

189 "The Nixon Theatre." Available at http://www.brooklineconnection.com/history/Facts/ NixonTheatre.html. Accessed 25 May 2013.

190 "Italy Warned: Stand by for Allied Invasion." *Pittsburgh Sun-Telegraph* 15 June 1933.

191 "US Sub Raids Sink 12 More Japanese Ships; Allies Step Up Aerial Blasting of Sicily." *Pittsburgh Post-Gazette* 15 June 1943; "Turks Recall Vichy Envoy in Protest on Gestapo." *Pittsburgh Sun-Telegraph* 17 June 1943.

192 "Midwest Gas Cut Will Close Many Band Locations." *Billboard* 19 June 1943.

193 "2 Drivers Lose Gas Rations." *Pittsburgh Sun-Telegraph* 17 June 1943.

194 "Planning Vacation Trip? If in Doubt, Don't Go, ODT Says." *Pittsburgh Press* 16 June 1943.

195 "WLB May Cut Mine Pay Raise." *Pittsburgh Sun-Telegraph* 16 June 1943; "Court Action is UMW Card in Coal Game." *Pittsburgh Press* 17 June 1943;

196 "Labor Board Denies Pay Raise to Miners." *Pittsburgh Sun-Telegraph* 18 June 1943.

197 "Lewis, Operators to Confer Again." *Pittsburgh Sun-Telegraph* 19 June 1943.

198 "Inside Stuff – Legit." *Variety* 9 June 1943.

199 Monahan, Kaspar. "Show Shops: Lugosi Stars in *Dracula* at the Nixon." *Pittsburgh Press* 15 June 1943.

200 "*Dracula* Given Good Revival in Nixon with Lugosi in Title Role." *Pittsburgh Sun-Telegraph* 15 June 1943.

201 Cohen, Harold V., "Bela Lugosi at the Nixon in *Dracula*."

202 "*Dracula* Helps Scare Pitt Nixon Into Fold." *Variety* 23 June 1943.

203 "Nixon, Pitt, Grossed 485G in 35-Week Season." *Variety* 30 June 1943.

204 "Federal Action Imminent as 530,000 Strike." *Washington Daily News* 21 June 1943; "Strike Closing 19 Steel Plants." *Washington Daily News* 22 June 1943.

205 "Miners in Revolt on '20-Cent Truce.'" *Washington Daily News* 23 June 1943; "Only Sixth of Men Return to Mines in Pennsylvania." *Washington Daily News* 24 June 1943.

206 "Congress Rebels." *New York Times* 26 June 1943.

207 Gasoline Dealer Barred for Fraud." *New York Times* 25 June 1943.

208 "Gas Cut's Success Put Up to Dealers." *New York Times* 26 June 1943.

209 "A Narrative History of the National Theatre." Available at: http://www.nationaltheatre.org/ location/narrative.htm. Accessed 26 May 2013.

210 Ibid.

211 "*Doughgirls* Big 15G D. C. Advance." *Variety* 2 June 1943.

212 "Duffy-Pitts *Bat* Shelved in D. C.; Nat'l on Fence." *Billboard* 12 June 1943.

213 "*Doughgirls* Western Co. Neat 16G in D. C. Break-In." *Variety* 9 June 1943.

214 "He's Happy, Really – *Dracula* Lugosi Glad to Be Back Where He Can Actually Hear the Audience Shriek." *Washington Post* 20 June 1943.

215 Maynard, John. "*Dracula*, in Its Old Form, Opens at the National." *Washington Times Herald* 22 June 1943.

216 The references here are to pin-up artist George Petty, whose work regularly appeared in the magazines *Esquire* and *True*, as well as to Count Fleet, a thoroughbred racehorse who became a Triple Crown champion in 1943.

217 Kelly, Marjorie. "*Dracula* Still Chills at National, with Lugosi in Original Role." *Washington Post* 22 June 1943.

218 Carmody, Jay. "Lugosi Revives *Dracula* in a Manner of Speaking." *The Evening Star* (Washington, D. C.) 22 June 1943.

219 Chatmas, Penny. "Government Girl in Washington." *Hearne Democrat* (Hearne, TX) 2 July 1943.

220 *"Eyre* for D.C., Cowl Maybe in *X*, July." *Variety* 23 June 1943.

221 "Lugosi – *Dracula* $8,000 in Washington." *Variety* 30 June 1943.

222 "All-Negro Opera Kollmar Project." *New York Times* 26 June 1943.

223 "Notes of the Theatre." *Chicago Tribune* 25 Apr. 1943.

224 "Gas Restrictions Widely Protested." *New York Times* 30 June 1943.

225 "War Appeal Made to Hard Coal Men." *New York Times* 30 June 1943; "Coal Miners Rush to Resume Digging." *New York Times* 6 July 1943; "WLB Gets New Powers to Solve Labor Puzzle." *New York Times* 22 Aug. 1943.

226 "WLB, Lewis Unite in Plea to Miners for End of Strikes." *New York Times* 17 Oct. 1943; "President Pledges 'Decisive Action' to Get Coal Mined." *New York Times* 30 Oct. 1943; "Coal Strike Cuts Output of Steel." *New York Times* 8 Nov. 1943.

227 Nichols, Lewis. "The Play." *New York Times* 2 Nov. 1944.

228 "Wallace Widdecombe Is Dead; Oldest Member of Equity, 100." *New York Times* 16 July 1969.

229 "Guy Spaull." *New York Times* 8 Jan. 1980.

230 "Character Actor Eduard Franz Dies at 83." *Los Angeles Times* 15 Feb. 1983.

231 "Obituaries – O. D. Woodward." *Daily Variety* 10 Jan. 1946.

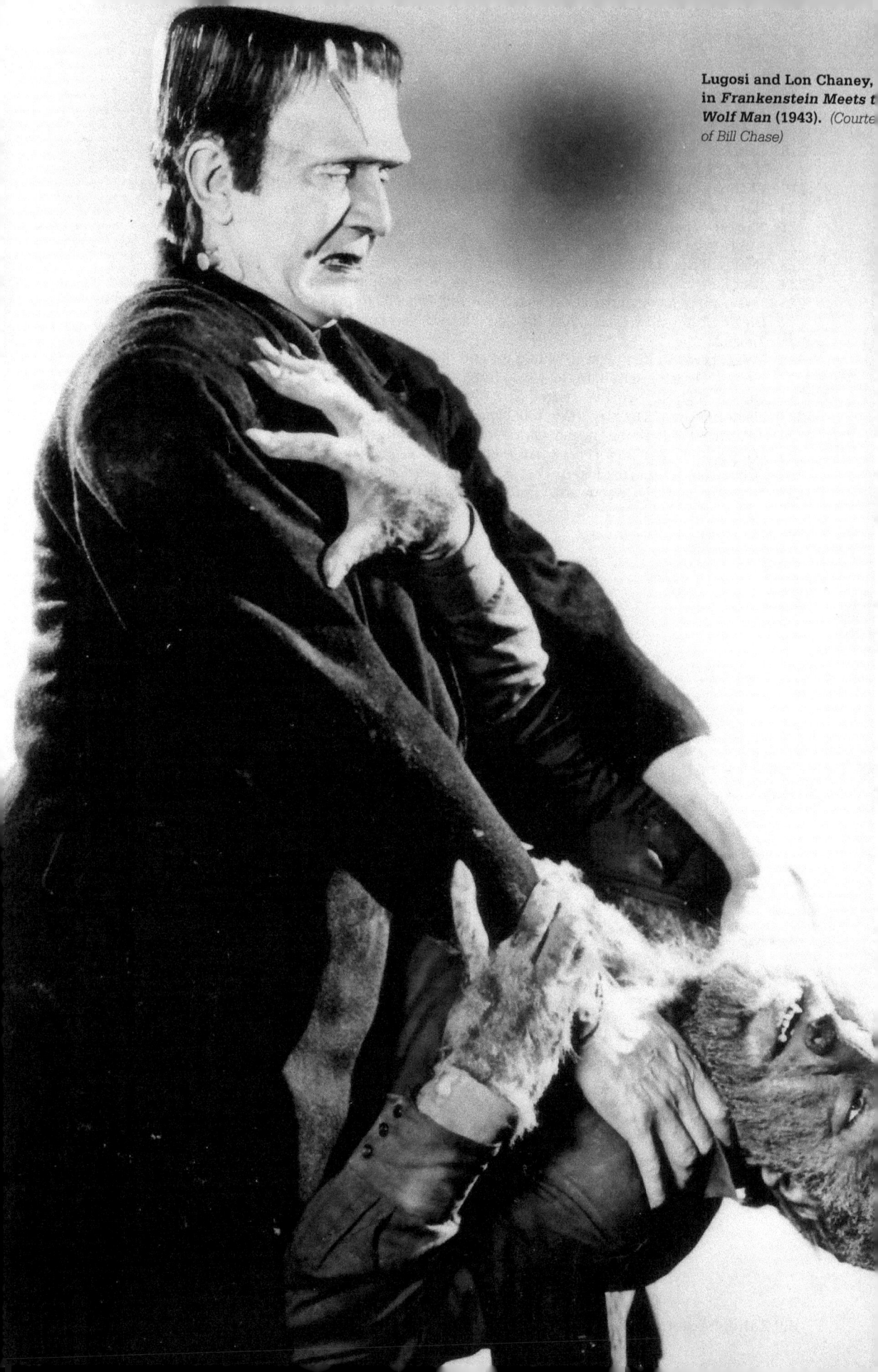

Lugosi and Lon Chaney, in *Frankenstein Meets the Wolf Man* (1943). *(Courtesy of Bill Chase)*

Chapter 11

All the Colors of the Rainbow

R ather than perceiving history as easily identifiable links in a chain, it is possible to use another metaphor, that of a multi-faceted jewel. Though it may be a one gemstone, it has no single surface. In other words, many legitimate perspectives can be brought to bear on the same story.

Consider Bela Lugosi's career in 1943. It would be quite valid to argue that twice that year he played roles already made famous by Boris Karloff. The first was when he became the Monster in *Frankenstein Meets the Wolf Man* (1943); the second was when he played the murderous Jonathan Brewster in a stage version of *Arsenic and Old Lace*. Karloff rose to fame as the Monster in the James Whale-directed 1931 film, and Karloff had also created the Brewster role on Broadway in 1941.

One could go even further and suggest that not only was Lugosi taking on roles that Karloff had already played, but he was also doing it in lesser productions. Universal horror movies of the forties were somewhat more meager affairs than those of the early thirties. And the Broadway stage was certainly not where Lugosi trod the boards as Jonathan Brewster.

Such a narrative is none-too-different than oft-told tales of Karloff and Lugosi, or – to invoke the billing and publicity sometimes preferred by Universal – "Karloff and Bela Lugosi," the former heralded first in a larger font size and by surname only. Put another way, Lugosi fared worse than Karloff in Hollywood, whether in the horror genre or otherwise.

That story has had much traction, spawning myriad articles, books, and documentary films about the duo. And it is very definitely worthy of extended consideration. It is not inaccurate; quite the contrary. But it is only one facet of history. There are others.

Returning to the notion that Lugosi twice assumed Karloff roles in 1943, it is equally possible to argue that such instances are not a clear example of anything, other than perhaps the fact that horror film actors – and actors in general – play roles, and sometimes

Lugosi and Karloff together in a publicity still for *Black Friday* (1940). *(Courtesy of D'Arcy More)*

those that have been performed by others.

When it comes to the Frankenstein Monster, tales of Universal casting that part in the summer of 1931 are rife with troubling contradictions, but the reality is –whatever else happened – Bela Lugosi was indeed considered for the role before Boris Karloff.

Then, in 1932, Boris Karloff played the title role in *The Mummy*. Reviewing the film, Wood Soanes at the *Oakland Tribune* insightfully wrote:

> The wheel of cinema horror that began to move with *Dracula* completed its revolution at the Orpheum yesterday with the presentation of *The Mummy*. The two pictures have much in common, and, curiously enough, little in common with the multitude of shriek and giggle contraptions that have come in the interim.[1]

The similarities include the return of key cast members from *Dracula* (like Edward Van Sloan and David Manners) and crew members (like Karl Freund) and even props (like a bedroom lamp), as well as an analogous supernatural storyline that – as scholar Paul Jensen noted decades after Wood Soanes – even features similar scenes, notably the reworking of Van Helsing's use of a mirror into Muller's use of a photograph. In both cases, the supernatural villain loses his composure when confronted with the given props. Likewise, both villains

Lugosi as a Nazi fifth columnist in *Ghosts on the Loose* (1943). *(Courtesy of Jack Dowler)*

shrink at the site of a given talisman, whether the crucifix or the image of Isis.[2]

Another facet thus shines. Lugosi played the Frankenstein Monster prior to Karloff, even if just in a 1931 screen test. He played the Mummy before Karloff, even if in that character's earlier incarnation as Dracula. And – to continue the argument – Lugosi also portrayed a mad scientist on screen (in *Murders in the Rue Morgue* in 1932) prior to Karloff doing the same in – depending on one's definition of what constitutes such a character – *The Mask of Fu Manchu* (1932) or *The Invisible Ray* (1936).

Returning to 1943, it is undeniable that Lugosi played the Frankenstein Monster, though he did so not only after Karloff, but also after Lon Chaney, Jr. in *The Ghost of Frankenstein* (1942). And despite *Frankenstein Meets the Wolf Man*'s narrative in the released film, it is also worth considering that Lugosi was as much reprising his role of Ygor from *Son of Frankenstein* (1939) and *The Ghost of Frankenstein* as he was playing the Monster. That was certainly the shooting script's original conception, meaning Ygor's transplanted brain in the Monster's body.

All that said, these examples reveal perhaps little of value, other than collectively serving as a reminder that Lugosi and Karloff frequently inhabited shared roles. The overriding reason was financial, given that producers redeployed successful stories (and variations of them) for financial gain. Hence Lugosi in *Arsenic and Old Lace*, a stage play that let him portray a particular character in his own particular style.

Lugosi would not star in _Arsenic and Old Lace_ in 1942, despite an offer to do so. *(Courtesy of the New York Public Library, Billy Rose Theatre Division)*

Given facets of a jewel shine more brightly than others, but only when light from a particular direction is shed on them. Horror film historians have spent an incredible amount of time (and word count) on the joint subject of Karloff and Lugosi, but it is also possible to speculate that Karloff played a very minor role in Lugosi's life, and that he was but one of many persons – onscreen (like Lon Chaney, Jr., who starred in so many of Universal's horror movies in the 1940s) and off-screen (meaning a range of decision-making studio executives and film producers and directors) – who affected Lugosi's film career.

Was Lugosi obsessed with Karloff, as some writers have implied, or did he bear a hatred of the actor, as Tim Burton's fictional film _Ed Wood_ (1994) suggests? Such facets might sparkle thanks to crafty storytelling, but are supported by precious little trustworthy evidence. Lugosi may not have been particularly fond of Karloff and may well have been resentful of his success, but that hardly means that Karloff dominated his thoughts on a regular basis. Seeing inside a gemstone is hard to do, if possible at all.

Likewise, Karloff seems not to have been particularly obsessed with Lugosi. In 1940, having appeared with Lugosi and Peter Lorre in _You'll Find Out_ (1940). Karloff remarked that "Peter and Bela are both good fellows."[3] For the rest of his life, Karloff said little of Lugosi beyond noting that he was a great technician who did not learn English well enough.

More than anything else, including anything to do with Karloff, Lugosi's 1943 performance in *Arsenic and Old Lace* signified his first real opportunity to explore comedy onstage in front of live American audiences, a process that – at least from his perspective – did not involve Boris Karloff. And Brewster's famous dialogue that he murdered a man who said he "looked like Boris Karloff" was of course changed to "looked like Bela Lugosi."

Summer 1943

Though *Arsenic and Old Lace* became Lugosi's key career move in mid-1943, the trade press very clearly spoke of other roles, other possibilities.

In early June, for example, Universal Pictures was "whipping up a million-dollar rendezvous of all horror-picture principals under the title *Chamber of Horrors*." The announced cast was staggering: Lon Chaney, Jr., Boris Karloff, Bela Lugosi, Peter Lorre, Claude Rains, Henry Hull, George Zucco, and Lionel Atwill.[4] Later that same month, Lugosi was touted for a role in the horror-comedy *They Creep by Night*, an RKO project set to costar him with Boris Karloff and Peter Lorre.[5]

At roughly the same time, Lugosi's latest film premiered, *Ghosts on the Loose* (1943) – which Monogram had filmed in February 1943 – featured the East Side Kids comically stumbling into a group of fifth columnists who were secretly printing Nazi publications.[6] "Bela Lugosi [gives] an extra touch for the trade," *Daily Variety* said, "even though the bogey man doesn't figure too prominently in the proceedings."[7]

Published in the *San Francisco Chronicle* on August 1, 1943.

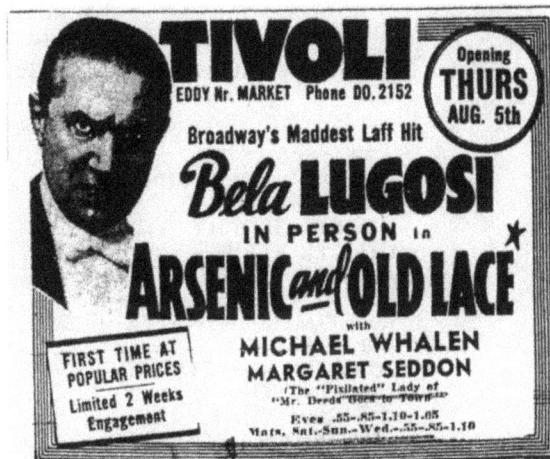

Published in the *San Francisco Chronicle* on August 2, 1943.

And so talent agents Richard Kline and Sam Howard, who represented Lugosi in 1943, decided to take matters into their own hands and spotlight the actor in an important role on the stage. Though they had little experience with producing plays, Kline and Howard found backing for a live production of *Arsenic and Old Lace* on the West Coast, specifically in San Francisco and Los Angeles. They would draw upon talent they already represented, Lugosi foremost among them.[8] And they hired Harold Winston – a Hollywood dialogue director who had previously worked on the film version of *Arsenic and Old Lace* (released in 1944, but filmed in 1941) – to direct the production.[9]

TIVOLI THEATRE

EDDY STREET NEAR MARKET   Telephone DOuglas 2152

UNDER THE DIRECTION OF THE BLUMENFELD THEATRES

BEGINNING THURSDAY NIGHT, AUGUST 5, 1943
Matinees Wednesday, Saturday and Sunday

JOE BLUMENFELD

and

ROBERT GOODHUE

of

KLINE-HOWARD INC.

Present

BELA LUGOSI

in

"Arsenic and Old Lace"

A Comedy of Murders

by

Joseph Kesselring

with

Michael WHALEN • Margaret SEDDON • Minna PHILLIPS

CAST
(In the order in which they speak)

ABBY BREWSTER	MINNA PHILLIPS
THE REV. DR. HARPER	P. J. KELLY
TEDDY BREWSTER	HERBERT CORTHELL
OFFICER BROPHY	JAMES METCALFE
OFFICER KLEIN	HAROLD H. BERMAN
MARTHA BREWSTER	MARGARET SEDDON
ELAINE HARPER	LOUISE ARTHUR
MORTIMER BREWSTER	MICHAEL WHALEN
MR. GIBBS	EDWARD COLEBROOK
JONATHAN BREWSTER	BELA LUGOSI
DR. EINSTEIN	HENRY SHARPE
OFFICER O'HARA	CHARLES JORDAN
LIEUTENANT ROONEY	FRANK SHANNON
MR. WITHERSPOON	HOUSLEY STEVENS

SYNOPSIS OF SCENES
The entire action of the play takes place in the living-room
of the Brewster home in Brooklyn. Time: the present.

ACT I
An afternoon in September

ACT II
That same night

ACT III
Scene 1. Later that night
Scene 2. Early the next morning

Staged and Directed by
HAROLD WINSTON

CREDITS:
Stage Manager...Edward Colebrook
Assistant Stage Manager .... Harold H. Berman

Advance publicity for the play in San Francisco. *(Courtesy of the Free Library of Philadelphia, Theatre Collection)*

Film actor Michael Whalen made his San Francisco stage debut as Mortimer Brewster in this version of *Arsenic* and received second billing after Lugosi.[10] Third-billed was Margaret Seddon as Martha Brewster; she had earlier played small roles in such films as *The Hunchback of Notre Dame* (1939) and *Sherlock Holmes in Washington* (1943). Ads for *Arsenic* drew attention to her appearance as the "pixilated" lady of *Mr. Deeds Goes to Town* (1936).

Also in Kline-Howard's cast were Louise Arthur as Elaine Harper, Henry Sharpe as Dr. Einstein, and Minna Phillips (who had played over 500 roles during her 37-year career) as Abby Brewster.[11] More than one press account claimed that Alison Skipworth would appear in the play as well (presumably as either Abby or Martha Brewster), but that was not to be.[12]

The Tivoli

In 1913, San Francisco's new Tivoli Theatre was constructed on the site of what had been the Tivoli Opera House. The luxurious building sported 1,385 seats.[13] Originally the Tivoli featured only stage productions, but later it screened movies. In the early forties, the theatre was closed until the Blumenthal theatre chain reopened it in 1943 for legitimate stage productions.[14] And for its first attraction, the "completely refurbished" Tivoli hosted *Arsenic and Old Lace* with Lugosi.[15]

Opening night was August 5, 1943, a delay from the original announcement of July 29.[16] Marshall scheduled Wednesday and Saturday matinees at 2:30PM; evening shows began at 8:30PM. Though *Arsenic* had already appeared in San Francisco on four prior occasions (including as recently as May 1943), two factors made the Kline-Howard production unique. To begin, it marked Lugosi's

BELA LUGOSI

Published in the *San Francisco Examiner* on August 5, 1943.

inaugural appearance in the lead role.[17] The other is that it marked the first time on the West Coast that *Arsenic* had been presented at "popular prices"; tickets for the evening performances ranged from only fifty cents to $1.50.[18]

Capitalizing on Lugosi's live appearance were two local movie theatres. The Embassy booked *Frankenstein Meets the Wolf Man* (1943) for two days to coincide with the play's premiere.[19] The Esquire did the same with *Ghosts on the Loose* (1943), which it screened on a double bill with *Rhythm of the Islands* (1943).[20]

"He eats omeletes and uses a napkin"

BELA LUGOSI

By Dwight Whitney

I AM HERE to report something which may prove startling at first. Don't be too disillusioned, but Bela Lugosi had parsley omelette for lunch last Wednesday. And he used a napkin, too. Contrary to any fly-by-night reports which may be circulating around, Mr. Lugosi does not exist solely off herbs and potions, nor does he have a mobile laboratory in which he practices alchemy before breakfast, as, I believe, was once a story given some credence by an overzealous press agent.

As a matter of fact, the occult, the pseudo-occult, and all the horrific Hollywood ramifications thereof, bore Mr. Lugosi considerably. That is, they bore him only insomuch as he has been forced, by a theatrical happenstance, to overindulge himself in what Hollywood euphemistically calls horror. He is the actor whose very name will strike terror into the heart of all but the most unsusceptible, and there is hardly a month goes by when he does not transplant the brain of at least one anthropoid into the body of a man, or hold a nocturnal tryst with a zombie.

NOT that Mr. Lugosi doesn't look the part. He has the long thin fingers of an artist, the gaunt face with small, searching eyes and black eyebrows which curl sinisterly around his eye-sockets until they almost touch the cheekbones, and the loose, rambling frame which lends him an air of the unworldly such as one might find in Edgar Allan Poe. In truth it is not difficult to imagine him among his beakers and test tubes carrying on nefarious experiments in a subterranean crypt.

But Lugosi is not a professional ghoul, he is an actor. In Hungary where he was born on October 3, 1883, he trained at Budapest's Academy of Theatrical Art, and by 1913 was the leading actor in that city's famous Royal National Theater where he played everything from Hamlet to Cyrano to Lilliom. His professional marriage to the horrors was consummated in 1927 when Horace Liverwright, then a producer, was looking around for somebody to play Count Dracula in the American production of the fabulously successful English adaptation of Bram Stoker's minor classic.

From that day to this he has been playing Dracula in all the imitations and bastardizations of which the scriptwriters are capable. "Dracula," Lugosi says, is the only horror play ever written. He originally played it because it "added a new color to the rainbow of my character parts." Then the rainbow became permanent.

LUGOSI'S interest ended there. From then on it was a marriage of convenience. He has never read any more of the world's occult literature than might be expected of the normally alert reader. He has read and admired A. Conan Doyle but has never particularly appreciated the mystic in Doyle's make-up which make the Sherlock Holmes series among the finest detective stories ever written.

Instead, he pours all his energy into what he calls "dry reading." The library of his Hollywood retreat is packed with weighty tomes on economy, history, politics, and social evolution. He is an active anti-fascist, a self-styled "extreme liberal democrat." He reads twenty newspapers a day. "You must learn to read a newspaper the way you learn a profession. An amateur cannot read a modern newspaper and get anything out of it."

His favorite newspaper on the Coast (with which he acquainted) is Los Angeles Liberal Daily News. He has definite ideas about newspaper publishers and editorial policy. He subscribes to The Reader's Digest, Time (which he took for ten years and just recently gave up), The Nation, The New Republic, The New Masses. In fact, and Forum as well as a dozen Hungarian magazines.

He has recently been active in forming a Hungarian anti-Fascist committee among Hungarians in America and was later elected president. Into this project he packs all the power of his political convictions. He knows his own people well enough to realize that "they cannot deal with the Nazi feudalism." This man who goes around frightening little children at night is one of the most conscientious workers for what he calls "one hundred per cent ideal democracy" during the daytime.

In Hollywood, he has a wife and five and a half year old son whom he installed in a house of his own design in North Hollywood. He makes on the average of five or six pictures a year, all of them bad. The average Hollywood horror costs upwards of $75,000 which is cheap by Hollywood standards. If a producer would spend money and employ topnotch writers, Lugosi thinks the movies could do something to equal the stature of Dracula. There is a place for a good horror picture; it supplies a need which is best explained in the Greek theory of tragedy, a catharsis.

THE trouble with the movies, Lugosi agrees, is that there are very few people who understand that what you can see, no matter how horrible, is not half as frightening as what you CAN'T see. It is the imminency and not the actuality. Only the great macabre writers like Poe understand that.

As it is Hollywood has a peculiar tendency. Lugosi says to turn a shocker into a third degree entertainment, with a bludgeon instead of a rapier.

Strangely enough, Lugosi's house would seem to bear out in certain respects the popular notion of what the private life of the demonologist should consist. His estate is surrounded by a wall four feet thick, with a large iron gate covered with elaborate grillwork and on which sets a sign reading, "Beware of the Dog." To enter one must first knock (I think three times is the correct number) on a heavy oak door, whereupon, if his papers are correct, he is admitted through a tiny door to one side. Once inside he will find a spacious lawn with Lugosi's Swiss chateau sitting in the middle of it. Inside the house he will find high paneled ceilings, heavy leather furniture, windows set in lead, a large fireplace and a spittoon.

There is no reliable information as to whether or not the Lugosis have a pet vulture sitting over the mantlepiece. I once met a man who claimed he saw it, but this no doubt was an hallucination.

Besides the humanities, Lugosi's interests lie in sculping and hunting. He also has a mania for stamp collecting, a relatively pedestrian pastime in which he finds a curious fascination.

SINCE 1927, he has only appeared on the stage twice, "Murder at the Vanities," for Earl Carroll in 1933 and a recent revival of "Dracula" (which he says was in every way up to the original company) in which he has just toured the East. He is here to do a play of which he is particularly fond—for two reasons. First, it is a magnificent comedy to him, and most important, it partially emancipates him, temporarily, from the limitations of the type of role he has always had to play.

He has never seen Boris Karloff play Jonathon Brewster in "Arsenic and Old Lace." This he deems fortunate because an actor will automatically pick up certain mannerisms from watching another actor play the part, no matter how hard he may try to keep his interpretation absolutely

(Continued on page 16)

But the spotlight of attention was on Lugosi in Person, both from audiences and from critics:

It's a pity that a certain school of producers on the Coast is under the impression you can put on a show without bothering to rehearse it first. ... I am afraid the haphazard approach is not ideally suited to a play like *Arsenic and Old Lace*....[21]

–*San Francisco Chronicle*

...the cast was not ready for the public. Lines were fumbled. Lights went off and on when they shouldn't. Sometimes a scene would go thoroughly well. Then another would half fall to pieces.[22]

–*San Francisco Examiner*

Once the play gets smoothed down and the lines come a little more freely to the mouths of the players, it will be seen that this is, in general, a very well chosen cast. ... And since one must be just in all things ... let us mention that the trained critical ear perhaps caught more slips than did the audience for the laughs were many and frequent and uproarious.[23]

–*San Francisco News*

In other words, the critics were harsher than the audiences that crowded the theatre on opening night.

Lugosi found himself at the center of local publicity. More than one newspaper drew attention to the uniqueness of his appearance in *Arsenic*, reporting that it was his very first comedic performance on the American stage.[24] Yes, he had appeared in vaudeville, but here he was in his first comical three-act play. Here was a humorous role, even if the storyline also included horrific elements. When speaking with Alexander Fried of the *San Francisco Examiner*, Lugosi claimed he enjoyed acting in horror movies, but underscored his wish that they "be only one shade, as it were, in a rainbow of varied roles."[25]

San Francisco Chronicle journalist Douglas Whitney interviewed Lugosi two days before the show had opened. He told readers that Lugosi possessed an "air of the unworldly such as one might find in Edgar Allan Poe," but also excitedly shared the revelation that "he eats omelets and uses a napkin," a nod to the fact that Lugosi off screen was very different from his screen persona.[26]

Intrigued more by his personal life than his career, Whitney also wrote that Lugosi was an "extremely liberal democrat" whose favorite West Coast newspaper was the *Daily News* of Los Angeles. The actor also subscribed to:

The Reader's Digest, Time (which he took for ten years and just recently gave up), *The Nation, The New Republic, The New Masses, In Fact,* and *Forum,* as well as a dozen Hungarian magazines.

...Besides the humanities, Lugosi's interests lie in sculpting and hunting. He has a mania for stamp collecting, a relatively pedestrian pastime in which he finds a curious fascination.[27]

As for Dracula, it had – in a variation on the phrase he spoke to the *Examiner*, one that must have captured his imagination – "added a new color to the rainbow of my character parts," but of course that color had since outshone all others.

But now there was Jonathan Brewster, and Lugosi's performance fared better in local reviews than the overall play:

Lugosi really manages to make vagrant shivers use one's spine for a runway.[28]

–San Francisco News

Published in the *Los Angeles Times* on August 20, 1943.

Lugosi's talent for bogeyman grimaces and sinister action serve him admirably in the role of Jonathan Brewster.[29]

–San Francisco Call-Bulletin

Bela Lugosi – big, intense, and mean – was the murderous Jonathan. His impersonation was different from the already familiar one of Boris Karloff, but – barring occasional uncertainty – about equally effective.[30]

–San Francisco Exami130ner

I think, undoubtedly, Bela Lugosi has in him the makings of a Jonathan Brewster which is the equal, or perhaps superior, of Boris Karloff's masterful reading.... Let's trust that within the week the Tivoli's electricians will have learned their light cues well enough to give him half a chance.[31]

–San Francisco Chronicle

While critics naturally drew comparisons between Lugosi and Karloff, the local press did make clear the fact that Lugosi had never himself seen Karloff in the role.[32]

During the play's run in San Francisco, Lugosi found time to mix with both the press and the public. On August 4, from 5 to 7 PM, he hosted a cocktail party for the press at the Hotel St. Francis.[33] Then, to entertain the troops in the area, Lugosi made a guest appearance at the local Stage Door Canteen:

Bela Lugosi, the actor, was standing on the Stage Door Canteen stage, entertaining a

Newspaper photograph promoting *Arsenic*. From left to right are Michael Whalen, Louise Arthur, and Lugosi.

MUSIC BOX Theatre
6126 HOLLYWOOD Blvd
— HI. 7111 —
Tonite 8:30
EVES. 50¢ 75¢ $1, $1.50
MATS. SAT.-SUN.
50¢ 75¢ $1.00

First Time at Popular Prices!
Box Office Now Open
BELA LUGOSI in !
"**ARSENIC** *and* **OLD LACE**"
with **MICHAEL WHALEN • MINNA PHILLIPS • IDA MOORE**

by JOSEPH KEYSELRING

Published in the *Daily News* (Los Angeles) on August 25, 1943.

house packed to the doors with servicemen. 'As you know,' he said in a haunting voice, 'I have a reputation for horror roles. So, perhaps, when I appear before you, there should be no light, except a green spotlight, playing eerily upon me from somewhere in the wings… there should be fog, and the sharp cry of a beautiful woman in distress… there should be the howl of hungry wolves…' At the mention of wolves, his audience, to a man, turned their faces ceiling-ward [and] gave vent to an ear-splitting 'Wa-hoo-oo!'[34]

Arsenic ended its San Francisco run on August 18, 1943, grossing a "neat" $17,000 for two weeks.[35] Taking its place at the Tivoli was Edward Everett Horton in *Springtime for Henry*, which was also backed by Kline-Howard.[36]

Published in the *Daily News* (Los Angeles) on October 2, 1943.

The Music Box Theatre

Only two days after closing in San Francisco, *Arsenic and Old Lace* opened at the Music Box Theatre in Los Angeles. Originally known as the Carter DeHaven Music Box, the venue had opened in 1926. By 1943, it had become a 980-seat home for the legitimate stage.[37]

Harold Winston continued as director, with the cast unchanged, save for Ida Moore replacing Margaret Seddon. Similar to San Francisco, publicity heralded the play's first appearance in Los Angeles at "popular prices."[38] Evening tickets ranged from only fifty cents to $1.50. Matinees – held on Saturdays and Sundays, but not Wednesdays – ranged from fifty cents to $1.00.[39]

Arsenic's run was open-ended, staying at the Music Box "for as long as the milking holds out."[40] The local press reported that advance ticket sales were "big," and that "scores of film celebrities" had reserved tickets for its opening performance.[41]

Local critics had in fact seen three prior versions of *Arsenic* in Los Angeles, but that didn't prejudice them against the Kline-Howard production, which was more polished than it had been on opening night in San Francisco:

Story is too well known to local playgoers to touch on, but one difference first nighters commented on was the freshness of the cast.[42]

–*Los Angeles Evening Herald and Express*

...in some ways the current cast lends a fresher and livelier spirit to the unfoldment of the play than did the well-routined one from New York.[43]

–*Los Angeles Times*

At the Music Box, the play is given a considerably more animated performance than heretofore.[44]

–*Los Angeles Daily News*

An excellent cast sets the comedy to a swift pace.... Last night's house gave consistent applause to all the actors.[45]

–*Los Angeles Examiner*

Lugosi with wife Lillian and son Bela at Christmastime, perhaps of 1943.

Audiences seem to have applauded loudly night after night. *Arsenic* grossed a healthy $8,500 during its first week and was on track to do just as well or "slightly better" its second week.[46] Even during its third week, it grossed an "excellent" $8,300, and was set to make another $8,000 for its fourth.[47]

Once again, the press noted that *Arsenic* marked Lugosi's first comedic stage work in the United States.[48] During its run, Lugosi would even happily admit that, "If the producers had known how eager I was to play comedy, they could have got me without salary."[49]

The Los Angeles critics were also impressed with Lugosi onstage, perhaps even more than their San Francisco counterparts had been:

Lugosi gets praise for his sinister portrait of the murdering thug....[50]

–Los Angeles Evening Herald and Express

Bela Lugosi, as Jonathan, is perfect as the menace.[51]

–Hollywood Citizen-News

...plenty of praise may be bestowed on Lugosi for his sinister, brilliant, and satirical portrait.[52]

–Los Angeles Times

The *Daily News* went even further, declaring that Lugosi endowed his characterization with a "vitality that was lacking in Boris Karloff's portrayal. The result is a faster, more acceptable pace."[53]

Such vitality was impressive, particularly because Lugosi soon found himself extremely busy. Columbia Studios cast him as the lead in its horror film *The Return of the Vampire*

(1944). Shooting began on August 20, 1943, with Nina Foch, Frieda Inescort, and Matt Willis playing opposite Lugosi.[54]

Catching him for a quick interview, the *Los Angeles Times* claimed, "Lugosi was supping on salad, not crunching bones as might have been expected. For he has no time for dinner between working on the film *Return of the Vampire* during the day and *Arsenic* at night, so he eats after the show."[55]

Earl Bellamy, Columbia's assistant director for *The Return of the Vampire*, later recalled:

> A very funny thing happened: Bela gave out tickets to everybody to come up and see him in *Arsenic and Old Lace* [at the Music Box Theatre]. We all went, and the funny thing was that he gave us all seats right down front – we had the first and second row of seats 'cause it involved all the crew. And if you moved, why he would look down and see you, and watch what you were doing, whether you were leaving the theatre or *what*. When the intermission time came, we all wanted to go, it was so terrible [*laughs*], but we *couldn't*. He'd stiffed us by putting us in the first two rows. We had to sit through the whole play – he really *got* us with those first and second row seats. He kept us under lock and key![56]

Bellamy further described *Arsenic* by mentioning his belief that Lugosi was "so bad" in it.

The dual schedule of film and theatre was strenuous, no doubt. And yet, Lugosi did have an afternoon to himself in either late August or early September, at which time Hedda Hopper claimed that he "hurried down to the Red Cross blood bank ... to have his veins opened – and found out that he [was] anemic!"[57]

Then, in late August, Lugosi received an offer to appear in a forthcoming Broadway play called *Horror Show*.[58] Though that play did not go forward, other films did. In fact, due to his commitments with Monogram for two more movies, Lugosi had to leave the *Arsenic* cast on September 22. Frank Conroy took his place as Jonathan Brewster for the rest the run, which forged ahead for another month until closing on October 24, 1943.[59]

Originally, the "wiseacres" of Los Angeles had bet that Kline and Howard would be lucky to get a two-week run out of *Arsenic*, given its prior appearances in the city. Audiences had proven them wrong.

Conclusion

Thanks to *Arsenic and Old Lace*, Michael Whalen's Hollywood career – which had been going "downhill" – experienced a "sudden upswing." Likewise, Minna Phillips nabbed a three-picture deal with MGM as well as an offer from Universal. And Kline and Howard confidently proceeded with the creation of their own "motion picture company," one designed to draw upon the actors they represented.[60]

Completing his work on *The Return of the Vampire*, Lugosi awaited the start dates of two Monogram films, *Voodoo Man* (1944) and *Return of the Ape Man* (1944); thanks to *Arsenic*, *Voodoo Man*'s planned August shoot had already been delayed.[61] On September 20, 1943,

Daily Variety reported that Monogram had also signed John Carradine, George Zucco, and Frieda Inescort to appear in those same two films.[62] In the end, Zucco appeared only in *Voodoo Man*, and Inescort – whom Monogram presumably considered as a direct result of her role in *The Return of the Vampire* – appeared in neither.

Lugosi starred in both films, which remain charming examples of poverty-row horrors. And then he would return to Jonathan Brewster once again, mere months after his inaugural performance in the role.

In a filmed interview in 1951, Lugosi famously said that Dracula "never ends."[63] Neither would his version of Jonathan Brewster, certainly not during his own lifetime.[64] Real gemstones withstand the test of time.

(Endnotes)

1   Soanes, Wood. "The *Mummy* Is New Type of Cinema Horror." *Oakland Tribune* 11 Feb. 1933. The title of Soanes' article is a reference to the fact *The Mummy* was different than other recent, post-*Dracula* horror films; he strongly argued that *The Mummy* is quite similar to *Dracula*, as his quotation suggests.
2   Jensen, Paul M. "*The Mummy* (1932)," *Boris Karloff*. Ed. by Gary J. and Susan Svehla. (Baltimore, MD: Midnight Marquee, 1996).
3   "Cinnamon and Old Toast." *New Yorker* 1 Feb. 1941.
4   "U Masses Top Scarers for Horrific Epic." *Daily Variety* 7 June 1943.
5   "*An American Story* to be Auer's Initial RKO Picture." *Daily Variety* 21 June 1943.
6   "Mono *Ghosts* Rolls." *Daily Variety* 9 Feb. 1943.
7   "*Ghosts on the Loose*." *Daily Variety* 9 June 1943.
8   Wright, Virginia. Untitled. *The Daily News* (Los Angeles) 15 Oct. 1943.
9   "*Arsenic and Lace* Has Bela Lugosi as Killer-Chiller." *Daily Variety* 23 Aug. 1943.
10 First Nighter, The. "*Arsenic* Returns with Bela Lugosi." *San Francisco Call-Bulletin* 6 Aug. 1943. In 1944, Whalen would appear on Broadway in *Ten Little Indians*.
11 Whitney, Dwight. "*Arsenic* Revived at the Tivoli." *San Francisco Chronicle* 7 Aug. 1943.
12 "*Arsenic* Reopens Tivoli." *Billboard* 31 July 1943; *Dark Eyes* Ending Its Run Tonight." *New York Times* 31 July 1943; "Frisco Tivoli Reopens with Dick Marshall." *Daily Variety* 27 July 1943; *Arsenic and Old Lace* Cast Are Stage Veterans." *San Francisco Chronicle* 10 Aug. 1943.
13 Kelley, Tim, Harvey, Caitlin Paige and Fortuna, Kara. *Historical Context Statement, Mid Market Historical Survey (Draft)* (San Francisco, CA: San Francisco Redevelopment Agency, 2011).
14 "Frisco Tivoli Reopens With Dick Marshall." *Daily Variety* 27 July 1943.
15 "Lugosi Stars at Tivoli Thursday." *San Francisco Call-Bulletin* 3 Aug. 1943.
16 "*Arsenic* Reopens Tivoli." *Billboard* 31 July 1943.
17 "*Porgy* Boffo $27,000, *Arsenic* 17G, Frisco." *Variety* 12 May 1943.
18 Advertisement. *San Francisco Chronicle* 1 Aug. 1943.
19 "*Frankenstein Meets Wolf Man* at Embassy." *San Francisco News* 2 Aug. 1943.
20 Advertisement. *San Francisco Chronicle* 6 Aug. 1943.
21 Whitney, "*Arsenic* Revived at the Tivoli."
22 Fried, Alexander. "Renovated Tivoli Opens Season of Stage Plays with *Arsenic*." *San Francisco Examiner* 7 Aug. 1943.
23 La Belle, Claude A. "*Arsenic and Old Lace* Uproariously." *San Francisco News* 6 Aug. 1943.
24 "*Arsenic* at Tivoli Tonight." *San Francisco Call-Bulletin* 5 Aug. 1943; "Lugosi's Comedy Role Is His First in 20 Years." *San Francisco Chronicle* 14 Aug. 1943.
25 Fried, Alexander. "Those Chilling Horror Roles! Bela Lugosi Loves 'Em." *San Francisco Examiner* 15 Aug. 1943.
26 Whitney, Douglas. "The World of Drama." *San Francisco Chronicle* 8 Aug. 1943.
27 Ibid.
28 La Belle, "*Arsenic and Old Lace* Uproariously."
29 First Nighter, The, "*Arsenic* Returns with Bela Lugosi."
30 Fried, "Renovated Tivoli Opens Season of Stage Plays with *Arsenic*."

31   Whitney, "*Arsenic* Revived at the Tivoli."

32   Whitney, Douglas, "The World of Drama."; "San Francisco Theatregoers' Guide." *San Francisco Chronicle* 8 Aug. 1943.

33   O'Brien, Robert. "San Francisco." *San Francisco Chronicle* 5 Aug. 1943.

34   O'Brien, Robert. "San Francisco – Call of the Wild." *San Francisco Chronicle* 23 Aug. 1943.

35   "S.F. *Arsenic* Neat $17,000." *Billboard* 28 Aug. 1943.

36   Ibid.

37   Gabel, William and Erickson, B. "Music Box Theatre." Available at http://cinematreasures.org/theaters/493/. Accessed 22 Feb 2014.

38   "*Arsenic* in First 'Pop' Run." *Los Angeles Evening Herald and Express* 19 Aug. 1943.

39   Advertisement. *Los Angeles Times* 20 Aug. 1943.

40   "*Arsenic and Lace* Has Bela Lugosi as Killer-Chiller." *Daily Variety*. 23 Aug. 1943.

41   Lawrence, Florence. "High Hilarity in *Arsenic and Old Lace*." *Los Angeles Examiner* 21 Aug. 1943.

42   Rialtan, The. "*Arsenic* Gets Fresh Treatment." *Los Angeles Evening Herald and Express* 21 Aug. 1943.

43   Schallert, Edwin. "*Arsenic* Again Affords Diabolical Enjoyment." *Los Angeles Times* 21 Aug. 1943.

44   Hanna, David. "Stage Review." *The Daily News* (Los Angeles) 21 Aug. 1943.

45   Lawrence, "High Hilarity in *Arsenic and Old Lace*."

46   "*Blackouts* 14G, LA; *Lace* 8 ½ G, *People* 4 1/2 G." *Variety* 1 Sept. 1943.

47   "*Arsenic* Neat $8,300, *People* $4,700 in L.A." *Variety* 15 Sept. 1943.

48   "Bela Lugosi Makes Comedy Debut at Music Box." *Los Angeles Examiner* 17 Sept. 1943.

49   "Tragedy-Comedy Tradition Safe with Bela Lugosi." *Los Angeles Times* 6 Sept. 1943.

50   Rialtan, The, "*Arsenic* Gets Fresh Treatment."

51   Redelings, Lowell F. "*Arsenic and Old Lace* Scores at Music Box." *Hollywood Citizen-News* 21 Aug. 1943.

52   Schallert, "*Arsenic* Again Affords Diabolical Enjoyment."

53   Hanna, "Stage Review."

54   "*Daily Variety* Production Chart." *Daily Variety* 27 Aug. 1943.

55   "Tragedy-Comedy Tradition Safe with Bela Lugosi."

56   Qtd. in Weaver, Tom. *A Sci-Fi Swarm and Horror Horde: Interviews with 62 Filmmakers* (Jefferson, NC: McFarland, 2010).

57   Hopper, Hedda. "Looking at Hollywood." *Chicago Tribune* 4 Sept. 1943.

58   Durant, Alta. "Gab." *Daily Variety* 1 Sept. 1943.

59   Wright, Virginia. Untitled. *The Daily News* (Los Angeles) 15 Oct. 1943.

60   Ibid.

61   "Katzman Sets Lugosi." *Daily Variety* 8 Sept. 1943; "Lugosi's Hocus-Pocus." *Variety* 30 June 1943.

62   "Mono Nails Horror Trio." *Daily Variety* 20 Sept. 1943. Inescort's name appeared again in "Monogram Marching On." *Daily Variety* 29 Oct. 1943.

63   Lugosi said these words to interviewer Jack Mangan on the television program *Ship's Reporter* in December 1951.

64   To offer evidence of this claim, Chapter 12 of this book will examine Lugosi's 1944 tour in *Arsenic and Old Lace*. With regard to Lugosi's numerous summer stock appearances in the same play after World War II, see: Rhodes, Gary D. and Bill Kaffenberger, *No Traveler Returns: The Lost Years of Bela Lugosi* (BearManor Media, 2012). For information on Lugosi's 1954 appearance in the play in St. Louis (staged just over two years prior to his death), see: Rhodes, Gary D, *Bela Lugosi, Dreams and Nightmares* (Narberth, Pennsylvania: Collectables/Gotham, 2007).

Lugosi in *One Body Too Many*
(1944). *(Courtesy of Kristin Dewey)*

Chapter 12

Horror Noir

Neon lights flash down upon wet streets, but there is never enough rain to wash away the sins of the city. Long, dark shadows conceal many of life's secrets. No matter how intelligent or wise, the male lead lacks key information to decode the puzzles that vex him. And if he ever does learn the whole truth, it's too late to make a difference. He is an alienated man, one whose psychological and geographical journeys are thorny.

Film noir conjures such images. Screenwriter and critic Paul Schrader has described these movies as a "a darkening stain," the result of a "new mood of cynicism, pessimism, and darkness which had crept into the American cinema."[1] Along with German Expressionism, noir's important precursors included horror films like *Dracula* (1931) and *Murders in the Rue Morgue* (1932), both starring Bela Lugosi.

In 1944, while noir was beginning to flourish in Hollywood, Lugosi starred in the most lengthy and grueling acting tour of his entire American career. He returned to the role of Jonathan Brewster in *Arsenic and Old Lace*, replacing Boris Karloff in the middle of a tour that would take him first through the American South and then north into New England.[2]

Having played Brewster onstage in 1943, Lugosi was quite familiar with the play. Its setting, dialogue, and deliciously dark sense of humor were well known to him. And while he had not previously acted in many of the cities on the 1944 tour, they hardly represented obstacles. Though tiring and sometimes uncomfortable, the tour allowed Lugosi and his fellow troupers to travel by rail with few difficulties.

For ticket-buyers, the new *Arsenic* tour had much to commend it, ranging from the opportunity to enjoy one of Broadway's biggest hits on their local stages to the chance to see Bela "Dracula" Lugosi live and in-person. Eyes fixed excitedly on him in the darkness of

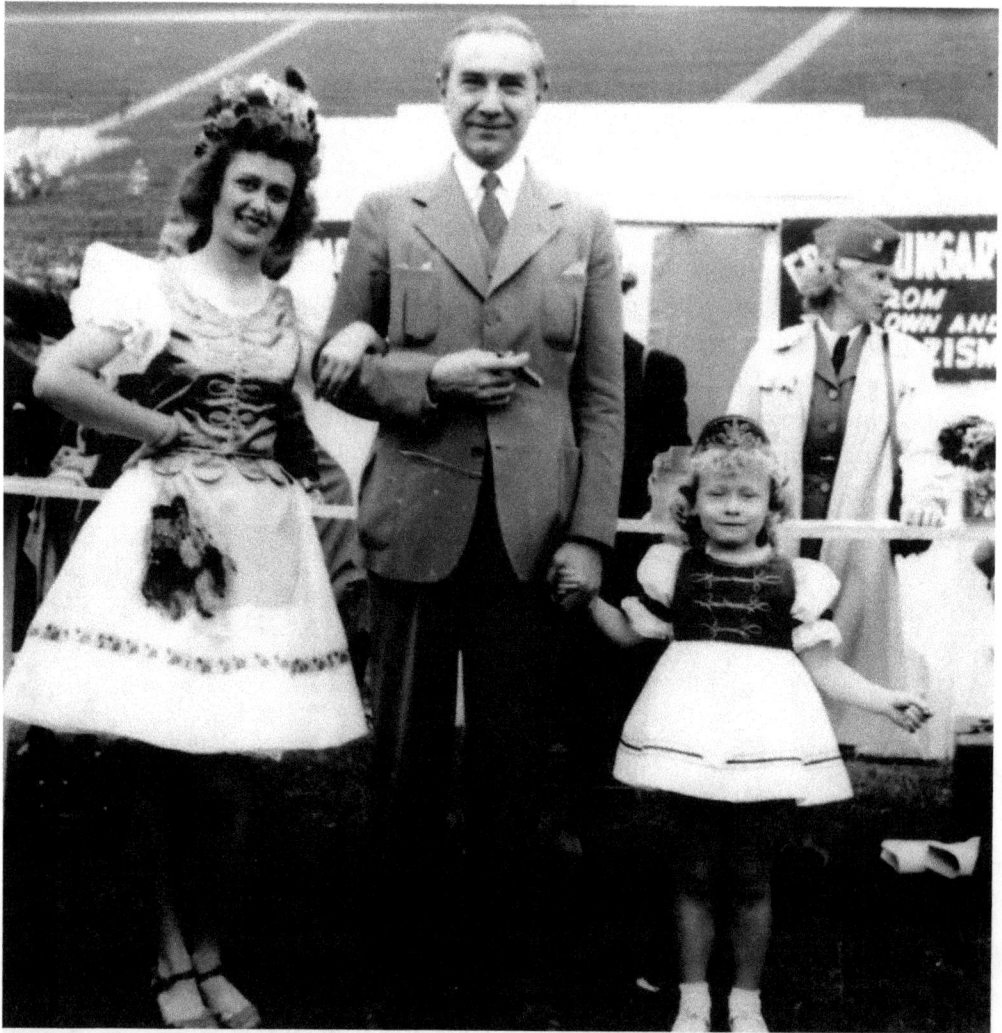

Lugosi at an unidentified event held in support of Hungarian liberation from the Nazis.

EASY COME—HARD GO—Bela (Dracula) Lugosi, famed for years for his movie and stage portrayals of a human vampire preying upon the blood of fair ladies, looks horrified as Red Cross Nurse
Henrietta Roger tests his hemoglobin at the New York Donor Center of the R. C. Blood Program.

With the assist of nurse Henrietta Roger, Lugosi gives blood during the war to the Red Cross in New York City.

many a theatre, but audiences were hardly the only people observing Lugosi in 1944.

Not unexpectedly, the show's backers eyeballed Lugosi from a distance, especially the box-office receipts that he helped generate. And this time, those persons included actor Boris Karloff, who had invested in *Arsenic and Old Lace* and as a result was set to collect "fat dividends" from the tour.[3] Each dollar paid to see Lugosi generated a coin for Karloff.[4]

Universal Pictures watched Lugosi as well, particularly in terms of his movie *The Return of the Vampire* (1944), which was released shortly before he joined the *Arsenic* cast; theatres continued to screen it even after the tour ended. Columbia Pictures had produced the film, which not only starred Lugosi in a variation on Dracula, a character to which Universal owned the film rights, but which also featured a werewolf, the meeting of two monsters being not unlike Universal's *Frankenstein Meets the Wolf Man* (1943).

Hungarian activist Oscar Jászi.

But there were others monitoring Lugosi as well, some without his knowledge, such as the Federal Bureau of Investigation. And then there were those in the US government that he knew about, notably the Office of Strategic Services. However, he was bereft of key information about their objectives, about their interviews with his detractors, and about the sheer amount of space given to him in their voluminous files.

Amid dark shadows, unfavorable rumors about Lugosi and his political life festered during 1944 due to a bizarre cast of real-life characters who did not always have Lugosi's welfare in mind. Here was a story of wartime suspicions and intrigue. Here was a story about who was standing in the shadow of whom. Here was a story exhibiting – to rewrite the closing line in John Huston's noir classic *The Maltese Falcon* (1941) – the stuff that nightmares are made of.

The Politics of War

In 1936, the Portland *Oregonian* quoted Lugosi's concern about the gathering storm on the other side of the Atlantic:

A loyal American now, he is praying daily that Europe does not plunge into another war. 'The world has had too much war, and so have I,' he said. 'I was twice wounded in the last one, the first time fighting the Russians in the Carpathian Mountains and next on the Italian front. I went into the war a lieutenant and I came out a badly wounded captain of infantry.'[5]

In the public sphere, Lugosi had usually been quiet on the subject of politics since the time of his arrival in America in December 1920. But when war once again broke out in Europe, all of that changed.

In November 1940, over a year before the bombing of Pearl Harbor, Lugosi – who was at the time honorary president of the Magyar House of Southern California — telegraphed the US Secretary of State to assure him of the loyalty of "10,000 Hungarian born residents of Los Angeles County."[6] The fact that Hungary's dictator Miklós Horthy had – at least to a degree – aligned himself with the Axis Powers prompted Lugosi's actions.

America's declaration of war meant Lugosi became outspoken in his support of President Franklin D. Roosevelt, as well as in his desire to see Hungary's liberation. By 1942, he

Office of Strategic Services (declassified) document HU-480. *(Courtesy of the National Archives and Records Administration, College Park, Maryland)*

had become a much-sought-after speaker at events targeted at Hungarian-Americans. For example, in March of that year, Lugosi performed at the first Red Cross benefit sponsored by the United Hungarian-American Defense Federation. Also present were Ilona Massey, Michael Curtiz, and Victor Varconi.[7]

Then, in February 1943, he donated a "carved ivory figure" from his personal collection to help raise money for the British War Relief Society. Andrea Cheever Cowdin was in charge of the "celebrities corner" where Lugosi's item appeared for sale.[8] Her husband, J. Cheever Cowdin, had masterminded the financial side of the buyout of Universal Pictures from Carl Laemmle, Sr. in 1936, a move that helped give teeth in America to the British ban on horror films.

The Office of Strategic Services

Given his concerns about the limitations of US intelligence, President Roosevelt established the Office of Strategic Services (OSS) in June 1942. Based somewhat on MI6 in the United Kingdom, the OSS carried out all manner of objectives during the rest of the war. Spying on the Axis Powers, infiltrating the Nazi government, training foreign troops sympathetic to the Allies: these were among the many accomplishments of a group that was a direct forerunner to the Central Intelligence Agency (CIA).

From 1942 to 1945, some of the OSS's 13,000-odd employees also formed a branch to investigate foreign nationalities in America. The loyalties of Hungarian-Americans were of real concern: that led them directly to Bela Lugosi.

Over 180 surviving pages of declassified government files chronicle the OSS research on Lugosi and Hungarian-American political organizations involved in wartime activities. Exactly when they first began to monitor Lugosi is difficult to determine, as no surviving documents for 1942 or early 1943 mention him.

But Lugosi appeared on the OSS radar by June 22, 1943; a report dated that day details an interview that an agent conducted with him. The fact Lugosi was in Washington, D. C. for *Dracula–The Vampire Play* might have provided a convenient geographical excuse for the meeting, one that might have been planned so as not to alarm him. During the interview, the agent learned that Lugosi had written articles for Hungarian-American newspapers representing the far left and the far right, and that he consistently championed the post-war leadership of Count Michael (Mihály) Károlyi, who had led a left-wing Hungarian government for a few months after the end of World War I.

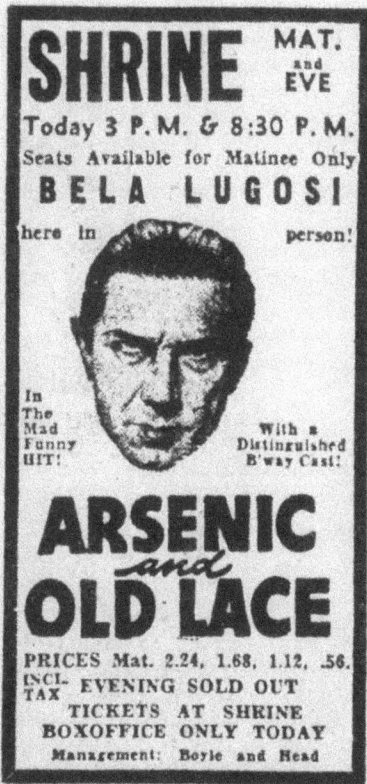

From the *Oklahoma City Times* of January 29, 1944.

To the OSS, Lugosi lost no time in describing others in the Hungarian-American political community, as well as his hostility to those whom he disliked or disagreed with. "In conclusion," the report noted, "Mr. Lugosi asserted that he would gladly give up a lucrative movie career if he could be of help in advising the United Nations' administrative authorities in Hungary after the conclusion of hostilities."[9] Perhaps Lugosi – tired of battling the Hollywood system in order to make money – envisioned a post-war Károlyi Hungarian government and some scenario in which he could represent it in America.

During the interview, Lugosi received a phone call from Tibor Kerekes, Executive Secretary of the conservative American Hungarian Federation (AHF), the largest and most influential group of its kind. The two men agreed to meet, something that was not lost on the OSS

Lugosi and Betty Zane Richardson, as published in the *Daily Oklahoman* on January 29, 1944.

agent. "The man is a pirate," Lugosi complained, "but I am anxious to see what he wants, and not to seem unapproachable to any faction." He promised to let the OSS "know the results" of the Kerekes meeting.[10]

But unbeknownst to Lugosi, the OSS immediately spoke to Kerekes. Upon request, Kerekes confidentially gave his own report of the meeting, at which he lobbied Lugosi to drop his affiliation with the left-wing Hungarian-American Council for Democracy (HACD) and align himself with the AHF. Lugosi suggested the same in reverse to Kerekes, who informed the OSS that their discussion had "ended politely, but coolly."[11]

What was the HACD? It was a group that developed in 1942 out of two previous organizations in Chicago.[12] However, it was not until the HACD's summer 1943 convention that it became a notable organization. Quite liberal in its political outlook, the group's honorary president was Count Károlyi. By the early forties, Károlyi's friendship with Josef Stalin was well known.

Subsequent OSS documents note that, at least in its early period, the HACD did count conservatives among its members, and that Lugosi outwardly claimed he wanted "for Hungary what we have here [in the United States]."[13] A July 9, 1943 OSS report described Lugosi's ascension to the position of HACD National President:

CONVENTION HALL
TOMORROW
MATINEE AND NITE

(IN PERSON)

BELA LUGOSI

IN THE MAD, FUNNY HIT

ARSENIC
and
OLD LACE

WITH
JEAN ADAIR • JACK WHITING
RUTH McDEVITT • DONALD MACDONALD
MALCOLM BEGGS

SEAT SALE
NOW—At Skaggs

Ticket Phone 3-5922

Prices: Mat., 84c; $1.12,
$1.68, $2.24

Nite, $1.12, $1.68, $2.24,
$2.80 (Inc. Tax)

SERVICE MEN and WOMEN
MATINEE 56c

From the *Tulsa Tribune* of January 29, 1944.

It was rumored that there was at first dissatisfaction among some members with Lugosi's election to the post. However, it appears that for the sake of unity all the members will give him their support. Because he is well known to the American public and because he has not concerned himself with politics in the past, Lugosi is felt to be well qualified for leadership of the present movement.[14]

Not surprisingly, Lugosi's new role gave the OSS ample reasons to watch him even more closely.

OSS documents include excerpts from Lugosi's speech at the summer 1943 conference. To the assembled delegates, he declared:

We must immediately line up all Hungarian power, unity, and enthusiasm behind our Allies; liquidate Hungarian fascism; punish betrayers of the Hungarian nation who have caused innocent people to perish on the battlefields and as martyrs at home; wipe out Hungarian feudalism and imperialism, giving back the land to the people.

... [The HACD should] aid morally and possibly financially the underground movement of our brothers in Hungary, the National Front for Hungarian Independence, ... and to organize a central organization to line up all the democratic forces in the world for Hungary and the Hungarian people under the leadership of Michael Karolyi.[15]

Lugosi received "volcanic applause" and a "standing ovation" for his keynote address, which might have quelled some of the earlier discontent at his election.

To these notes, the OSS recorded its understanding that the HACD offered full support to FDR and the Allied war effort, full support for a democratic Hungary based upon the principles of the Roosevelt-Churchill Atlantic Charter, and total opposition to the Horthy regime.[16] Rather than being initially concerned that the "Dracula Council" (as the HACD quickly became known) was subversive, the OSS instead kept documentation on the growing animosity between it and other Hungarian-American groups.

Their files include excerpts from such publications as the conservative *Amerikai Népszava*, which wrote, "the famed underground united front about which so much has been said has suddenly emerged above the ground. The rocks have split asunder and from among them in horrendous reality there leaped forth Dracula." Its editorial proceeded to dismiss the HACD as a small group that "could not gain support among the Hungarian-Americans."[17]

Actors Jack Whiting and Ann Lincoln in a photo printed in the *Tulsa World* on January 30, 1944.

In August 1943, when Lugosi was on the west coast preparing to open in *Arsenic and Old Lace*, an OSS agent met in New York City with the HACD's secretary, Moses (Mózes) Simon. Simon detailed plans for Lugosi's political lecture tour in October 1943. Though it does not seem to have occurred, it would have taken Lugosi to such locations as Bridgeport, Detroit, Toronto, Cleveland, and Chicago. Simon also mentioned that Lugosi would soon be making recordings for radio transmission to Hungary. He would call on the population to resist Fascism, to cease fighting, and to aid the Allies.[18]

At Károlyi's request, Lugosi also attempted to enlist other key Hungarian-American figures into the HACD, particularly Oscar Jászi and Rustem Vámbéry. Neither Jászi or Vámbéry were Communists, but they had hard left political views.[19] Jászi had been part of Károlyi's brief government before becoming a naturalized US citizen in 1931. By the time of World War II, he was a political science professor at Oberlin College.[20] Rustem Vámbéry was an attorney who had defended Károlyi in a Hungarian court years earlier. When Horthy assumed control of the Hungarian government, Vámbéry fled to the US, just as Lugosi fled to Austria.[21] Like Lugosi, Jászi and Vámbéry rejected any possible compromise with the Horthy government after the war ended.[22]

Despite many shared beliefs, the gulf between them and Lugosi remained wide. Perhaps they

Joseph Taylor Robinson Memorial Auditorium, Little Rock, Ark.

Lugosi and troupe played this venue in Little Rock.

avoided the HACD because their egos clashed with Lugosi's, as well as with each other's. In July 1943, for example, Vámbéry purported to appreciate Lugosi's "histrionic abilities, but I don't think these make him more competent to be the leader of a democratic organization than Jászi."[23]

All that said, it is also possible that the two men may have been sincerely concerned about rumors that the HACD was becoming a hotbed of Communism. As Jászi wrote in a letter in 1943: "I do not see the smallest reason why we should regard a new pseudo-organization, wire-pulled by the Communists, (I have proof of this in my hands), as a new support of the democratic cause."[24]

Jászi did not detail the proof he had, but his view was hardly unique. The FBI began watching Lugosi during the war as well, to the extent that it was intercepting Lugosi's letters to and from Károlyi.[25] But based upon surviving files, the FBI did not scrutinize Lugosi as closely as its counterparts in the OSS.

In October 1943, the OSS produced a lengthy internal report on Hungarian politics in America.[26] While noting that the basic aims of the HACD were similar to those of Vámbéry and Jászi, the report underscored the jealousies between the various factions and the eagerness with which they would mar one another's reputations. A close reading of this particular report suggests that the OSS understood petty differences divided these men and even saw a degree of humor in their bickering.

At the same time, the October report seriously questioned the HACD leadership. There can be no doubt that Lugosi's professional career kept him from being in charge on a daily basis. As a result, it is fair to ask if the leadership was really centered in the hands of Moses Simon, or in one or two other key figures on the council. That was the question, but even though Lugosi was in something of a figurehead position, that does not necessarily mean that he was completely out of the loop, or ill-informed, or without power and influence. His own letters and meetings make clear that – while his exact role is difficult to determine – he was regularly involved with at least some important decisions.

Indeed, Lugosi openly and willingly wrote to the OSS on HACD letterhead on November 3, 1943:

> The rapid march of events in Europe calls upon all of us Americans of Hungarian descent to serve our country in the most effective way. The time has come when every patriotic Hungarian-American should use his influence in Hungary to help the Allies in the war against Germany and the Horthy government.
>
> You must realize that the tens of thousands of Americans of Hungarian descent can wield a tremendous influence with the population of Hungary.
>
> Every available channel through which to reach the Hungarian people must be utilized, such as radio broadcasts, printed material, and so on. These must call upon the people of Hungary to fight with utmost vigor against the Nazi armies. They must be made to understand that the best way to fight for freedom is to fight the Axis and help the Allies.

Published in the *Arkansas Gazette* (Little Rock, AR) on January 30, 1944.

> Who better than Americans of Hungarian descent to talk to them?
>
> It would be greatly encouraging if you would state that a union of Americans of Hungarian descent for the accomplishment of these purposes would be desirable.[27]

Of course the very "rapid march of events" that Lugosi discussed meant that more and more Americans saw the Allied victory as an inevitability. That in turn caused more and more Americans to be concerned about Communists in the Soviet Union and in the United States.

Whether out of jealousy or patriotism or some combination of the two, Lugosi's detractors in the Hungarian-American community seem to have seized on the growing anti-communist

Artwork printed in the *Arkansas Democrat* (Little Rock, AR) on January 30, 1944. *(Courtesy of Jack Dowler)*

mood to decry him. In November 1943, for example, Vámbéry quietly informed the OSS that the "Dracula Council" was in his opinion a Communist organization.[28] But in a subsequent phone call, Vámbéry also admitted that the HACD's attempt to form a trade union could split his own organization.[29] His reasons for denigrating Lugosi were plural, it would seem.

Those who defamed Lugosi also argued the HACD held little influence over most Hungarian-Americans, which may well have been true. That said, it should be noted that members of the HACD's Committee for California included such film celebrities as Albert Dekker, Walter Abel, Steven Székely (aka Steve Sekely), Michael Curtiz (who had directed Lugosi in a number of Hungarian silent films), Jean Hersholt (Lugosi's costar in *Mark of the Vampire* in 1935), and Melchoir (Menyhért) Lengyel (screenwriter of *Ninotchka* in 1939, in which Lugosi had appeared).[30]

On the Lam

So many eyes stared at Lugosi. Some gazed at him through the shadowy world of wartime politics and intrigue; others peered out of the darkness of theatre auditoria. Fans knew little of Lugosi's politics, but many of them read their newspapers carefully for ads publicizing Lugosi film screenings, as well as his rare personal appearances in their own cities and towns.

By January 14, 1944, Lugosi had signed on for the *Arsenic and Old Lace* tour, with the press noting that he would play Jonathan Brewster on the road for twelve weeks.[31] The murderous character is on the lam from the law, and unhappily sports a face modified by plastic surgery, one that of course makes him "look like Bela Lugosi."

Boris Karloff had to leave the in-progress tour after a performance in Salina, Kansas on January 27, 1944; the reason was to return to California for pending film and radio work.[32] At least some of the bookings that would feature Lugosi – including a date in Asheville, North Carolina – were scheduled when Karloff was the star.[33] As a result, playbills in at least a few cities Lugosi visited still featured Karloff artwork.

Lugosi's involvement was hardly surprising, given his fame in the horror genre and his role in *Arsenic* in 1943. In fact, at the time he signed his contract for the 1944 tour, his agents were Richard Kline and Sam Howard, the same two men who had produced the 1943 version in which he starred.[34]

Overall, the timing worked out quite well for Karloff, who was needed at Universal to star in *The Climax* (1944), and for Lugosi, who – despite fighting a flu – finished working on *One Body Too Many* (1944) in January but had no other pending film roles.[35] As a result, Lugosi, with his wife Lillian, travelled to Oklahoma City to take over the Brewster role.

CHUCKLES STILL COME FROM MURDER-COMEDY

'Arsenic And Od Lace' Again Pleases Memphians

"Arsenic and Old Lace," becoming as familiar to Memphians as Main and Madison, returned to Ellis Auditorium for a matinee and night performance yesterday with Bela Lugosi as the featured player, although not necessarily the star.

The small matinee audience and the near capacity audience last night howled in glee as Ruth McDevitt and Jean Adair portrayed the parts of Abby and Martha Brewster, such nice old ladies with but one unfortunate habit—murder.

Published in the *Commercial Appeal* (Memphis, TN) on February 3, 1944.

They left Los Angeles on January 25, presumably by rail, as from Oklahoma City-onward the cast travelled together on the train.[36] As Lillian recalled later in life: "That was a wonderful play to travel with because every night you'd hear another funny line that you had missed the night before. ... It's a fun play to do and it's a fun play to watch and it's fun when people are laughing. It just makes you feel good."[37]

Though it was just another one-night stand on a lengthy tour, Oklahoma City was important because it was the night that Lugosi became the star. On January 29, 1944, he appeared at the city's 2,000-seat Shrine Auditorium for matinee and evening shows. The rest of the players remained the same from the Karloff leg of the tour. Among them were Jean Adair and John Quigg; they had played Martha Brewster and Officer Brophy in the original Broadway cast.

Others in the cast included Jack Whiting (Mortimer Brewster), Ann Lincoln (as Elaine Harper), Henry Sherwood (as Dr. Einstein), Malcolm Lee Beggs (Uncle Teddy), John Marston (Dr. Harper), Don Hershey (Officer Klein), John Beck (Mr. Gibbs), Donald MacDonald (Officer O'Hara), Victor Sutherland (Lt. Rooney), and Ashley Cooper (Mr. Witherspoon).

The *Daily Oklahoman* described Lugosi's search in Oklahoma City for the right wardrobe:

Monday he made a tour of city pawnshops with Jim Boyle, local manager, and Victor Sutherland, stage manager for the company. He bought an aged blue, shiny suit and a second-hand black hat and an old pair of shoes.

The shop owner thought he had a real mental case on his hands when Lugosi refused to look at his 'better merchandise.' The veteran stage and movie star then insisted on a suit two sizes too large in order to provide a proper bag. Then he carefully tied the new suit up in a knot, to give it wrinkles.[38]

The shop owner "about jumped out of the window" until he learned Lugosi's identity, leaving him to conclude, "Actors are funny people."

The same thought might have occurred to journalist Ray Park when he interviewed Lugosi at the city's Biltmore Hotel:

As I tiptoed into the Biltmore, I expect to find beautiful blonds scattered all over the corridor. Well, you can just imagine how I felt when I burst into his room and found that strange, half-human, half-bloodsucking vampire, lying there on the bed with his evil eye fixed on a lovely, delicate little postage stamp.

Yes sir, the terrible Dracula turned out to be a stamp collector. Also, he was wearing red suspenders, his eyes were a mild, kindly blue and his long, smooth-brushed hair was streaked with a middle-aged gray. He could have been somebody's father.

RYMAN AUDITORIUM
THUR. EVE., FEB. 3
BELA LUGOSI
IN THE MAD, FUNNY HIT
ARSENIC
and
OLD LACE
WITH
JEAN ADAIR • JACK WHITING
RUTH McDEVITT • DONALD MACDONALD
MALCOLM BEGGS

PRICES: $1.10, $1.65, $2.20, $2.75 TAX INC. SEATS NOW ON SALE AT RYMAN AUD. BOXOFFICE.

From the *Nashville Tennessean* of February 1, 1944.

Dracula, who also is known as Bela Lugosi, collects stamps everywhere he goes. When he isn't doing that, he is reading and hiking, strange relaxations for him, it would seem, until one realizes that a man who makes his living working as Dracula year after year wouldn't get a whale of a kick out of playing post office on his nights off.

When he's home, his big fun comes from playing with his 6-year-old son. 'You wouldn't believe it, but he is already imitating me.' Lugosi beamed, acting just like a father.

Lugosi also smokes cigars that have had the nicotine taken out of them. He likes, he says, green salads, raw fruit, no sweets, orange juice and milk.

... From a discussion of art and culture, things moved on to the subject of dinner. 'I would sure like a good rare steak,' he said, forgetting all about the green salad and raw fruit, the Dracula apparently coming out in him. 'And would you like to come by my room first?' he continued, forgetting all about the milk and orange juice.[39]

Lugosi also had an impromptu meeting with a cashier in the hotel's coffee shop. Betty Zane Richardson approached him nervously, saying, "Mr. Lugosi, I never did meet a movie star before." His answer: "Is that right?" Later, Richardson enthused that he was "awful nice."[40]

Published in the *Birmingham News* on February 3, 1944.

At the onset of the tour, Lugosi likely read the major news of the day, ranging from war stories to the coverage of Communists at home and abroad.[41] In early January 1944, for example, a *New York Times* editorial reported that Stalin smiled when seated next to Roosevelt, and that the Soviet Union was softening its stance on religion. At the same time, the editorial cautioned that, "it is impossible now to foretell what will be the expansion of Communism in Europe."[42]

Or domestically, for that matter. Predating Joseph McCarthy, US Representative Fred E. Busbey, a virulent anticommunist, vowed to expose the "Reds' grip" on civil service jobs in America.[43] His cause in early 1944 was but one of many, with probes underway into the Communist infiltration of the Fair Employment Practice Committee and also the George

Lugosi as photographed by the _Birmingham News_ for their February 5, 1944 issue.

Washington Carver School in New York.[44]

Reds were thus allies and enemies at the very same time. And it was easy enough to hang the Communist label on left-wingers who supported Roosevelt's New Deal. The _Nation's Business_ for January 1944 admitted: "We suppose that anyone who hates Fascism is a Communist. We're still confused."[45]

Oklahoma and Arkansas

The 4,200-seat Tulsa Convention Hall hosted the tour's second stop in Oklahoma, the troupe giving a single performance on January 30, 1944.[46] After describing how "fun" the play was, the _Tulsa World_ praised Lugosi for giving it the "spark" of a polished performance.[47]

Soon thereafter, _Variety_ described Lugosi's role from a financial standpoint: "It was expected that when Boris Karloff withdrew from _Arsenic_ ... and was replaced by Bela Lugosi, business would drop, but takings last week proved the show's draw just as strong as ever. ... _Arsenic_ started Sunday (30) with better than $5,000 in Tulsa...."[48]

The tour's next stop was Little Rock, Arkansas on February 1, where the troupe presented the play at the 2,609-seat Robinson Auditorium. Built as a WPA project, the auditorium's

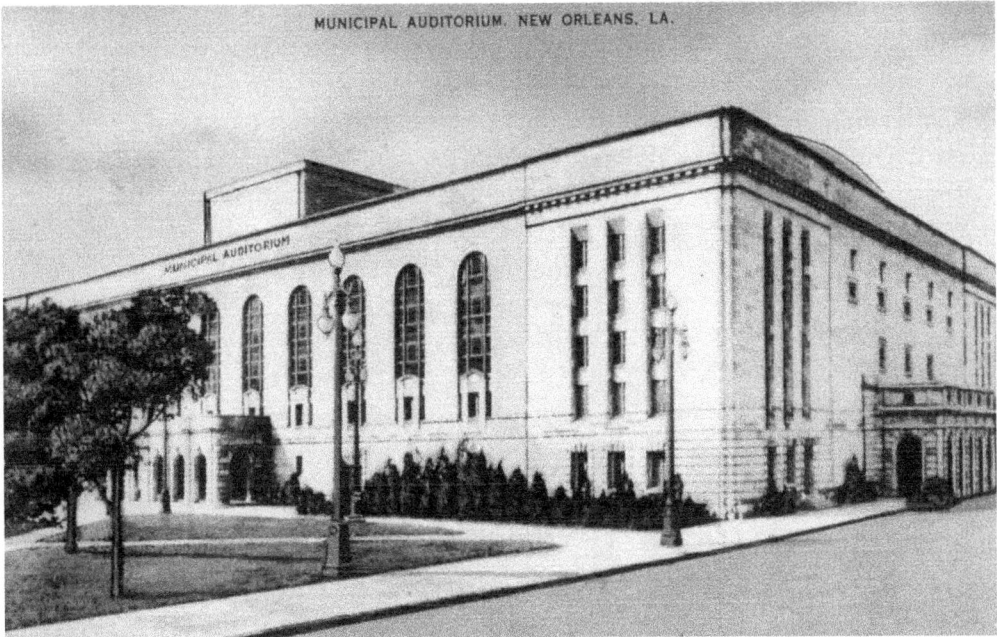

Lugosi and troupe appeared at this venue in New Orleans.

interior combined Art Deco designs with Greek Revival-style columns.[49]   Of the play, the *Arkansas Democrat* praised Malcolm Lee Beggs for outshining the "remainder of an exceptionally good cast."[50] The *Arkansas Gazette* drew attention to Beggs as well, perhaps an indication that he had received the biggest laughs.[51]

Mere hours before Lugosi appeared on the Little Rock stage, the OSS filed a report on an HACD speech in Chicago.[52] That same day, the agency also filed an interview with *Magyar Jövo* editor John Roman, who described his support of the HACD.[53]

Tennessee

On February 2, 1944, the troupe appeared in matinee and evening shows at the Ellis Auditorium in Memphis. Somewhat of a marvel for its time, the Ellis boasted a seating capacity of 12,000, an electrically movable stage, and 30,000 square feet of exhibition space. It was a combination athletic venue, concert auditorium, dance hall, convention center, and farmer's market.[54]

The *Memphis Commercial Appeal* reported, "The small matinee audience and near capacity audience last night howled in glee … Lugosi, as Jonathan Brewster, played the part with all [of] his Dracula-inspired ability."[55] The city's *Press-Scimitar* agreed that it was funny, but ended by saying, "That heavy Hungarian accent of Lugosi's makes it impossible to believe he's a Brooklynite – strange as Brooklynese might be."[56]

On the very same day, Lugosi telegrammed Count Károlyi, proudly informing him that the HACD was starting a drive to set up chapters throughout the US, Central and South America, and Canada.[57]

Then, on February 3, the troupe staged *Arsenic* for a single evening show at Nashville's

Ryman Auditorium; by 1943, the Ryman had begun hosting the famed *Grand Ole Opry*.[58] According to the *Nashville Banner*, the play "brought happy relief from war worries to a crowd which packed the [theatre]."[59]

The *Nashville Tennessean* saw matters quite differently: "Lugosi might have been better received if his vehicle hadn't developed a series of flat tires, bumping along the rocky road of a plot that [wound] its torturous way through a list of murders longer than any arm of the law – those in the play anyhow."[60] It was as if the critic was distressed that *Arsenic*'s policemen were the butt of some jokes.

Alabama and Louisiana

The cast spent February 4, 1944 travelling to their next stop, Birmingham, Alabama's Temple Theatre. With its famed 2,400 pound chandelier, the Temple was primarily a movie theatre, hence its stage being too small to host some live productions.[61]

Prior to appearing in both matinee and evening performances on February 5, Lugosi met with a journalist from the *Birmingham News*. The two spoke twice at the Tutwiler Hotel, once after Lugosi signed autographs for a throng of "high school youths," and then again while eating dinner. Lugosi spoke at length about the HACD's effort to "give to Hungary a democratic form of government and the right to choose her own allies."[62]

Other news that day included complaints that Vice President Henry Wallace was travelling around the country with David Karr, a Communist who had been investigated by the House Committee on Un-American Activities in 1943.[63] Then, on February 6, while the *Arsenic* cast was en route to their next show, newspapers reported that a new group called the Motion Picture Alliance for the Preservation of Ideals had been launched in Hollywood. Its goal was "to combat un-American influences," specifically Communists and Fascists.[64] Members included Norman Taurog, Victor Fleming, King Vidor, and George Waggner, who had produced *The Wolf Man* (1941), *The Ghost of Frankenstein* (1942), and *Frankenstein Meets the Wolf Man* (1943).

A move to Louisiana meant evening shows on February 7 and 8 at New Orleans' Municipal Auditorium, which boasted a seating capacity of nearly 8,000. Newspaper reviews were somewhat mixed:

1890
That was the year

...the first electrocution for crime took place in New York State, that of William Kemmler.

...investigation was opened as to the practicability of bridging the Mississippi at New Orleans.

...the ordinance was passed prohibiting smoking in public conveyances.

...Heligoland was ceded to Germany by Great Britain in return for concessions in Africa.

...Sitting Bull was killed in North Dakota by Indian police.

...one bought perfume under such prosaic names as White Rose, Violet, Lilac, Jessamine, Tuberose, etc.

...every lady wore a "jabot."

...WERLEIN'S WAS FORTY-EIGHT YEARS OLD!

PHILIP WERLEIN, Ltd.
"102 Years of Musical Leadership"
605 CANAL ST.

Be Sure and See
BELA LUGOSI
in
ARSENIC and OLD LACE
MONDAY and TUESDAY, FEB. 7 and 8
MUNICIPAL AUDITORIUM
Tickets at WERLEIN'S

Published in the *New Orleans Times-Picayune* on February 6, 1944.

Orleanians took their arsenic straight last night, and acclaimed the Joseph Kesselring comedy.... Bela Lugosi ... turned in a smooth portrayal but gave the impression of being slightly out of place. – *New Orleans Item*[65]

Bela Lugosi of Dracula fame is featured for his portrayal of Jonathan Brewster, a specialist in esthetic murder... But top honors go to Ruth McDevitt and Jean Adair, who walk off with the show as the two old-maid Brewster sisters.... – *New Orleans Times-Picayune*[66]

Only someone bereft of a sense of humor could fail to enjoy this fast-paced play ... [but] there may be a few weak spots in the cast. – *New Orleans States*[67]

At roughly the same time, the OSS filed more data on the political activities of Hungarian-Americans. But this time the focus was on the conservative American Hungarian Federation, which was seen to be pro-Horthy. The report included mention of radio commentator William S. Gailmor, who denounced the AHF as a "fifth column organization" and who demanded that its "leaders be put behind bars."[68]

In the same report, the OSS noted that the AHF had started a whisper campaign in McKeesport, Pennsylvania in November 1943 in an effort to smear Lugosi, who was set to speak there. They denounced the planned event as a "Jew-meeting," alleging that, "Bela Lugosi, the Jew will come to the Jew-meeting in Jewish ceremonial attire." The report – which clarified that Lugosi was Roman Catholic – claimed, "this is characteristic of Nazi-anti-Semitic propaganda that is carried on by the Federation elements," which included "Hitler-lovers."[69]

From the *New Orleans States* of February 8, 1944.

Published in the *Montgomery Advertiser* on February 7, 1944.

After completing their brief run in Louisiana, the cast used February 9 to return to Alabama for a single evening show at Montgomery's Lanier High School Auditorium on February 10.

Playbill for *Arsenic*'s run in Atlanta. *(Courtesy of Fritz Frising)*

Newspaper publicity recounted Lugosi's biography, which included the anecdote that he had intended to become a "highwayman" before getting into dramatic arts.[70]

That same day, *Daily Variety* published a review of *Voodoo Man* (1944) starring Lugosi, George Zucco, and Carradine: "This nightmarish concoction, engendering some creepy moments, maintains a certain suspense by the sheer insistence of its story development in the face of all credulity or sense of reality."[71] The review came one day after an announcement that Lugosi would soon guest star on Boris Karloff's new radio program, *Creeps by Night.*[72]

Georgia

To begin the Georgia leg of the tour, the cast appeared at Atlanta's 1,790-seat Erlanger Theatre. They were likely appreciative of the extensive dressing rooms, which were among the largest they enjoyed in 1944.[73] The cast staged *Arsenic* three times, a Friday night performance on February 11, and then matinee and evening shows on Saturday, February 12.[74]

One local journalist told readers, "Hollywood producers estimate that Lugosi has been responsible for more bloodcurdling screams than the 1943 income tax form – and, brother, that's a record!"[75] After the first show, the *Atlanta Constitution* reported, "The capacity audience responded whole-heartedly to the clever performance, sparked by Lugosi, Hollywood spook star."[76]

From the *Atlanta Journal* of February 9, 1944.

Capacity audiences resulted in strong box-office receipts. The *New York Times* wrote, "in six performances played last week in New Orleans, Montgomery, and Atlanta, the touring aggregation took in $20,000. This despite the fact that these cities had previously seen Erich von Stroheim in the murder drama."[77]

Then it was off to Savannah, for a trio of shows at the city's Municipal Auditorium: the evening of February 14, and matinee and evening performances on February 15.[78] A near-capacity crowd applauded "enthusiastically" during the first show, with the *Savannah Morning News* adding, "Mr. Lugosi, who appeared shortly after the opening of the first act, received an ovation from the audience. … [He] played the role with an ease and aplomb that showed his years of expertise."[79]

Augusta's 2,690-seat Auditorium (also known as the Bell Auditorium) became the final stop in Georgia. Local businessmen had recently formed a company to present roadshows and name bands in the city.[80] The cast presented a single evening performance staged on February 16, only one day after Savannah.[81] Rain poured down that night, but hardly dampened audience enthusiasm. The *Augusta Chronicle* noted, "When Lugosi came on stage,

Lugosi in *Voodoo Man* (1944),
which *Daily Variety* reviewed
just before the *Arsenic* troupe
played Atlanta.

Artwork used to promote Lugosi in the 1944 tour. *(Courtesy of the Free Library of Philadelphia, Theatre Collection)*

he was met with a round of applause. The entire troupe was vigorously applauded at the final curtain and answered two curtain calls."[82]

The Carolinas

From Georgia, the troupe began an arduous series of eight cities in nine days in the Carolinas, mainly North Carolina. This leg of the tour began at Columbia, South Carolina's Township Auditorium on February 17, 1944.[83] A review in the *Columbia Record* claimed that the audience "heartily approved" the play and added that McDevitt and Adair had "overshadowed" Lugosi.[84] *The State*, another Columbia-based newspaper, described the event as being a "welcome treat" to the assembled crowd of 2,000, but advised its success would have been greater, "had it been presented in a smaller theatre where the listeners would not have had to strain to hear many of the lines ... except those of the 'terror of the screen,' Bela Lugosi."[85]

The next day, the cast gave a single performance at Charlotte's Carolina Theatre, with most of the seats selling out.[86] Originally constructed in 1927 as part of Paramount's Publix theatre chain, the Carolina was designed by eminent Charlotte architect C. C. Hook. Its interior gave the illusion of an open-air Spanish patio with views of a Mediterranean sky.[87]

MUNICIPAL AUDITORIUM
Savannah, Ga., Feb. 14th and 15th, 1944

HOWARD LINDSAY and RUSSEL CROUSE
present

BELA LUGOSI
in

"ARSENIC AND OLD LACE"
A New Comedy by JOSEPH KESSELRING
with

Jean Adair	Jack Whiting	Ruth McDevitt
Malcom Lee Beggs		Donald MacDonald

Staged by BRETAIGNE WINDUST

Setting by RAYMOND SOVEY

CAST
(In the order in which they speak)

ABBY BREWSTER	RUTH McDEVITT
THE REV. DR. HARPER	JOHN MARSTON
TEDDY BREWSTER	MALCOM LEE BEGGS
OFFICER BROPHY	JOHN QUIGG
OFFICER KLEIN	DON HERSHEY
MARTHA BREWSTER	JEAN ADAIR
ELAINE HARPER	ANN LINCOLN
MORTIMER BREWSTER	JACK WHITING
MR. GIBBS	JOHN BECK
JONATHAN BREWSTER	BELA LUGOSI
DR. EINSTEIN	HENRY SHERWOOD
OFFICER O'HARA	DONALD MACDONALD
LIEUTENANT ROONEY	VICTOR SUTHERLAND
MR. WITHERSPOON	ASHLEY COOPER

SYNOPSIS OF SCENES

The entire action of the play takes place in the livingroom of the Brewster home in Brooklyn. Time: the present.

ACT I
An afternoon in September

ACT II
The same night

ACT III
Scene 1. Later that night.
Scene 2. Early the next morning.

Arsenic was well received, but the *Charlotte Observer* believed Jack Whiting's Mortimer Brewster – rather than Lugosi, McDevitt, or Adair – stole the show.[88]

On February 19, the group arrived in Asheville, North Carolina to play the local Auditorium. They arrived on the 11AM train from Charlotte and stayed at the George Washington Hotel.[89] The city's *Citizen-Times* claimed: "The exceptionally responsive audience warmed up immediately to the comedy.... It was a completely satisfied audience, notwithstanding chills and thrills experienced during the more than two hours of the play, which finally applauded Lugosi and the original New York cast to several curtain calls."[90]

February 20 found the group in Greenville, having briefly travelled back to South Carolina.[91] The *Greenville News* did not review the single Monday night performance at the city's 1,118-seat Carolina Theatre, but the paper did publish a large amount of advance publicity. An article on Lugosi claimed, "it is not difficult to imagine him among his beakers and his test tubes carrying on nefarious experiments in a subterranean crypt."[92]

The cast then quickly moved on to their date at the 1,800-seat National Theatre in Greensboro, North Carolina.[93] One show on a Tuesday night, February 22, which the *Greensboro Daily News* called "funny, hilariously so." But there was a minor bit of discomfort, as the same newspaper identified:

> Patrons, if any, who exercised the foresight and clothed themselves in palm beach and lighter raiment got the greatest satisfaction out of the theatre's heating system. Patrons in woolens simply sweltered and applauded weakly. The temperature did not prevent an audience from enjoying a show immensely but the climbing mercury was one of the reasons why the audience rushed for the exits after the first curtain call.[94]

From the *Augusta Chronicle* of February 16, 1944.

By the time the *Daily News* published this review, the cast was already making its way toward the next location, giving two performances (one a matinee) at Raleigh's State Theatre on February 23.[95] The *Raleigh News and Observer* wrote, "Lugosi, as usual, was outstanding. A veteran actor, he gave a smooth performance."[96]

At roughly the same time, major newspapers across America reported that vandals had damaged a trio of churches in New York City: "designs" painted in red resembled hammers and sickles.[97] Meanwhile, in San Francisco, the Communist Party filed a plea of intervention

"Arsenic and Old Lace" Is Offered Columbians Tonight

BELA LUGOSI in "ARSENIC AND OLD LACE"

Published in *The State* (Columbia, SC) on February 17, 1944.

From the *Columbia Record* of February 16, 1944.

to "clear its name of charges it advocates the overthrow of this government by force and violence."[98]

While Lugosi might have read newspapers in his hotel rooms or on the trains, he had little rest. Another day meant another performance. Durham, North Carolina saw *Arsenic* for a single performance on February 24 at the city's 1,016-seat Carolina Theatre. Ads in the *Durham Herald-Sun* promoted what was stated or implied in every other city: Bela Lugosi would be "In Person – On the Stage."[99] He was there ... and then he was gone almost as quickly as he had arrived.

On February 25, the troupe appeared at the State Theatre in Winston-Salem, North Carolina for another one-night stand, this time arriving in town only one hour before curtain call.[100] The troupe even had to stand most of the way on the overcrowded train.[101] According to the city's *Journal*, the audience laughed and clapped "enthusiastically."[102]

Despite the brevity of the booking, the *Twin City Sentinel* managed to nab an interview with Lugosi. To journalist Mary Garber (later a famous sports writer), Lugosi praised Lon Chaney, Sr.'s dedication as an actor as well as Karloff's ability to create horror through makeup. When Garber asked him if he was himself afraid of the dark, Lugosi responded with good humor: "Not afraid ... just cautious."[103]

Heading North

After leaving the Carolinas, the cast staged a matinee and evening performance at the

On The Stage - In Person
BELA LUGOSI in
Arsenic and Old Lace
with
JEAN ADAIR - JACK WHITING
RUTH McDEVITT - DONALD Mc-
DONALD - MALCOLM BEGGS
TONIGHT
One Performance Only
Curtain 8:15 Sharp
Tickets Now On Sale At Box
Office.

CAROLINA THEATRE

Balcony Seats,
Standing
Room Only
Available
$1.10

Published in the *Charlotte Observer* on February 18, 1944.

BELA LUGOSI TO APPEAR TONIGHT IN COMEDY HERE

'Arsenic And Old Lace' Will Be Presented At At Auditorium

"Arsenic and Old Lace," the famous thrill comedy starring the equally famous boogie-man of the stage, radio, and screen, Bela Lugosi.

From the *Asheville Citizen* of February 19, 1944.

1,500-seat Academy of Music in Roanoke, Virginia on February 26, 1944. The *Roanoke Times* described the audience's uproarious laughter and praised McDevitt and Adair's "exceptionally fine" performances. "The entire production was well done," the critic concluded, "and those who have seen previous productions of the play agreed that the cast that played Roanoke last night turned in a better than usual night's work."[104]

Despite crowds and applause, the *Arsenic* roadshow tour was $33.70 in the red in late February. Noting this was an "unusual" problem for the play, *Variety* explained that *Arsenic* had to meet a $4,450 weekly payroll, plus $1,300 for advertising, plus $1,375 for railroad fares and handling. Ticket sales were very good, but not so much as to surpass the expensive costs. Interestingly, though, *Variety* added that the "takings" had been "unaffected" by the shift in stars from Karloff to Lugosi.[105] Put another way, Lugosi wasn't blamed for the downturn in profits.

Whatever the press said, the troupe had to keep moving to maintain its intense schedule. At long last, though, they experienced something of a change. The Ford's Theatre in Baltimore, Maryland staged *Arsenic* from February 27 to March 3, giving Lugosi his first week-long stay in any single city. [106] During that week, famed labor leader John L. Lewis expressed his regret that Communists had come to "dominate" the CIO. Members of its Political Action Committee were "prisoners" of the Reds, he declared.[107]

Advance ticket sales in Baltimore were brisk, and critics were generally kind. While arguing that Lugosi "seemed quite a commonplace killer," the *News-Post* admitted the play was "good entertainment for an evening, even from the standpoint of the several gentlemen who find preliminary 'peace' in the window seat."[108] The *Baltimore Sun* wrote something quite similar:

In its four visits in slightly more than three years … [*Arsenic*] has presented Baltimoreans with the opportunity to compare the fearfulness of three of the theatre's most fearful bogeymen: Boris Karloff, Erich von Stroheim, and now, Bela Lugosi.

Of the three, perhaps Mr. Karloff was the most fearful, despite overtones of conceivable gentlemanliness and even gentleness; Mr. von Stroheim, the most hateful, and Mr. Lugosi, the most comforting.

...Mr. Lugosi is almost too commonplace a killer ... even for those in the $2.21 seats, his sanguinity is perceptibly diminished.

That is not to say that *Arsenic and Old Lace* suffers from Mr. Lugosi's presence ... the dialogue is consistently lively, the suspension is beautifully sustained, and Raymond Sovey's original setting is perfect.[109]

The play went on to gross a "fine" $13,300 in Baltimore, though how much that translated into net profits for the producers is unknown.[110]

The Mason-Dixon Line

The cast proceeded north of the Mason-Dixon line on or about March 4, 1944, having a two-day break prior to their next engagement. That may have been just as well, not only given their need for rest, but also because March 4 was the day on which a different cast enacted two scenes of *Arsenic* on the radio show *Atlantic Spotlight*; the much-publicized broadcast was heard over NBC and, in a transatlantic hookup, over the BBC in Great Britain.[111]

When the tour resumed on March 6, it was another one-night stand, this time at the 1,200-seat Karlton Theatre in Williamsport, Pennsylvania.[112] The city's *Gazette and Bulletin* ran ads for the show, but did not publish a review.[113]

From there, the troupe moved on to a single performance at Allentown's 1,200-seat Lyric Theatre on March 7. While there, Lugosi stayed at the Americus Hotel and gave an interview to the city's *Chronicle*:

A Dracula in disguise – that was Bela Lugosi as he treated

Published in the *Greensboro Daily News* on February 12, 1944.

From the *Raleigh News and Observer* of February 24, 1944.

five-year-old Joyce Clark and her 18-month-old brother, Donald, to some ice cream yesterday in the Americus hotel. Their brother, Charles, aged 3, wouldn't pose with the 'vampire' of movie fame.

'Tonight I k-e-e-l twelve men, just like that,' sneered Bela Lugosi as he snapped his fingers and then tackled a big steak set before him yesterday in the Americus hotel.

For a man contemplating 'murder" Lugosi appeared very much unconcerned about the consequences. 'And why shouldn't I be?' he asked. 'For 15 years I have been murdering and none of the victims have complained.'

... Now Lugosi has but one big ambition, he admitted, and that is to retire on a 'pension' and spend a lot of time with his young wife and six-year-old son, Bela Jr. 'After all, if you had been working for 42 years, wouldn't you want a rest, too?' he asked....[114]

CAROLINA Theatre, Durham, N. C.
ONE NIGHT THUR. FEB. 24th.

In Person --- On The Stage

HOWARD LINDSAY and RUSSEL CROUSE, Authors of "LIFE WITH FATHER" present

BELA LUGOSI
IN PERSON in BROADWAY'S MADDEST, FUNNIEST HIT ...

ARSENIC and OLD LACE

by Joseph Kesselring with
JEAN ADAIR • JACK WHITING • RUTH McDEVITT
DONALD MACDONALD • MALCOLM BEGGS

BOX OFFICE OPEN 11 A. M. to 6 P. M.
(Tickets Will Not Be On Sale Sunday)

PRICES INCLUDING TAX——
Main Floor .... $2.75 and $2.20   Mezzanine $2.20
1st Balcony .... $1.65   Col. Bal. .... $1.65 and $1.10
Send Mail Order or Cashier's Check with Self-Addressed, Stamped
Envelope. NO PERSONAL CHECK ACCEPTED.

From the *Durham Herald-Sun* of February 20, 1944.

Lugosi's thoughts about retirement may have stemmed not only from the relentless tour schedule, but also his hopes to become professionally involved in geopolitics.

Nevertheless, he continued to make time for those fans who were eager to shake his hand. After meeting a young actor at a restaurant in Allentown, Lugosi invited him to sit at his side. The man later recalled how thick Lugosi's glasses were when he signed an autograph, and how Lugosi shed tears when a string combo played a Yiddish song.[115]

Lugosi also impressed a local critic. The *Allentown Evening Chronicle* wrote, "Even for those persons who had seen *Arsenic and Old Lace* before, last night's presentation in the Lyric was thoroughly enjoyable – a tribute to the fine cast. ... Lugosi's portrayal of the maniacal Jonathan Brewster was as convincing as any given on the local stage."[116]

Presumably the cast was travelling by rail to the next engagement when the OSS filed a new report. It confidently described Lugosi as a "former Communist Party member in Hungary."[117] In this case, the information was treated less as a rumor and more as a fact.

Trenton, New Jersey became the next city on the tour's agenda, with the cast playing one evening performance at the War Memorial Auditorium on March 8. Seating a little over 1,800, the venue sported an Italian Renaissance Revival style. Ads promoted Lugosi "In Person" and touted the War Memorial as Trenton's only theatre "devoted to the stage play."[118]

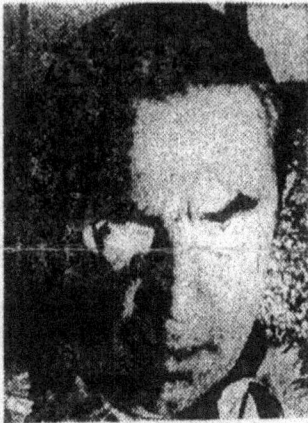

MENACE. Bela Lugosi has made an art of it. Maidens faint and strong men quail at the thought of what this mood forebodes.

SADISTIC GLEE is the actor's mood. You will remember this expression of the famous Vampire Dracula in picture of the same name.

HATE! You can see it in his eyes, the curving eyebrows, slightly open mouth. These expressions add up to menace, a paying commodity in the theatre.

Published in the *Twin City Sentinel* (Winston-Salem, NC) on February 25, 1944.

REAL LUGOSI, genial and delightful. Forget those fearful faces and see the man as he really is. Lugosi heads the cast of "Arsenic and Old Lace" appearing on the stage of State Theatre tonight.
—(Staff Photo by Jim Wommack.)

The play then scored a critical success at Wilmington, Delaware's Playhouse, giving three evening performances between March 9 to 11, as well as one matinee.[119] The *Morning News* assured readers that *Arsenic* was "as full of laughs as ever," while the *Journal-Every Evening* praised Lugosi for being "more reserved" in the role than Karloff and von Stroheim, but "just as cold, bloodless, and cunning."[120]

On March 12, the troupe staged no performances. During their lull, US Representative Martin Dies painted a dark picture of federal bureaus that had become infiltrated by Communists and other subversives. Their goal, he claimed, was to undermine and eventually overthrow the American government: "I shudder at the thought of the fate of our free institutions in the face of this steady and sinister movement toward bureaucracy."[121] The Red threat seemed to be growing ever more dangerous.

At roughly the same time, the OSS filed a 37-page report on the "Free Hungary Movement." It attempted to chronicle all of the various players and organizations, including the HACD and Lugosi. It also noted that Communists subsidized the *Magyar Jövo,* a publication that supported the HACD. Overall, the report concluded that Hungarian political activity in America was divided into three factions: a dominant group of "Revisionist Hungarians"; a clutch of pro-Nazis; and a confederation of Communists and "Fellow Travelers."[122] To their eyes, Lugosi presumably fell into the latter category.

BELA LUGOSI IN PERSON

HOWARD LINDSAY & RUSSEL CROUSE
AUTHORS OF "LIFE WITH FATHER"
present

BELA LUGOSI
IN PERSON

IN

ARSENIC AND OLD LACE

by JOSEPH KESSELRING

"SO FUNNY NONE OF US
WILL EVER FORGET IT"
N.Y. TIMES

with

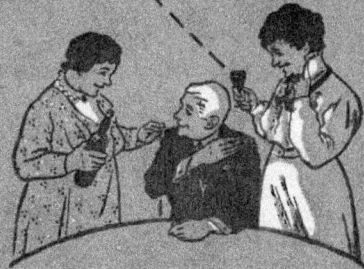

JEAN ADAIR   JACK WHITING   RUTH McDEVITT
MALCOLM BEGGS   DONALD MACDONALD   ANN LINCOLN

ACADEMY OF MUSIC
ROANOKE, VA.
Mat. and Evening, Saturday, February 26
Mail Orders Now. Seat Sale Roanoke Book & Sta. Co.
Mat. 85c, $1.10, $1.65, $2.20; Eve. 85c, $1.10, $1.65, $2.20, $2.75

Playbill cover for Roanoke, Virginia features artwork of Karloff alongside Lugosi's name.

None of that likely mattered in Bridgeport, Connecticut between March 13 and March 15; thanks to producer Albert E. Shea, Lugosi starred in *Arsenic* at the city's Lyric Theatre for three evening performances and one matinee.[123] Fred Russell of the *Bridgeport Post* said the following in his review:

Lugosi is an old-hand at horror stuff and he plays his current role to the hilt with excellent results being properly menacing and sinister at all times. ... The show is unbelievably goofy from start to finish, but it is swell stage fare of the escapist type.[124]

Russell also lauded the other cast members, particularly Malcom Lee Beggs, who "stands out in the role of Teddy."

The troupe then gave a single performance at the High School Auditorium in Pittsfield, Massachusetts on March 16. The show's backers staged it "to raise funds for ... charity work."[125] The town had earlier planned on booking the show *Tropical Revue* for that purpose, but changed its mind because it "proved a little too hot to handle" for perceived local tastes.[126]

Worcester, Massachusetts provided the setting for the next one-night stand: March 17 at the city's Memorial Auditorium, a 3,500-seat venue that featured a Classical Revival style. Its interior featured some of the largest murals of their kind in the United States.[127] Both local reviewers praised the show, and both drew comparisons between Lugosi and Karloff:

An advertisement promoting the Williamsport show as published in the *Lock Haven Express* (Lock Haven, PA) on February 24, 1944.

Time was when we wouldn't expect a Broadway comedy hit to play Worcester even once a season, but here was one making its second appearance. The cast and production are the same, save for Bela Lugosi in the Jonathan Brewster role, played previously by Boris Karloff... Bela Lugosi makes a fine bad egg Brewster. If you want comparisons   with Karloff, I'd say Lugosi's performance isn't quite as clearcut or ominous, but it's plenty dark and gruesome, nevertheless. Lugosi has been in the horror business too long to be stumped by his assignment.... – *Worcester Telegram*[128]

The difference between... Bela Lugosi and... Boris Karloff, will not make theatrical history, but it was just about the only difference between last night's performance at the Auditorium and the one earlier in the season. The difference to Samuel Wasserman was that he probably didn't get quite as many people to come see Mr. Lugosi as came

Lugosi onstage in the 1944 version of *Arsenic and Old Lace*.

A 'KILLER' COMES TO TOWN!
Bela Lugosi Surveys a Satisfyingly Murderous Past

From the *Allentown Evening Chronicle* of March 8, 1944.

to see Mr. Karloff. Nevertheless there was a large enough audience to justify Mr. Wasserman's hopes in re-booking the play. As far as we, personally are concerned, the difference in the art of the two stars will cause no extra excitement either way. We wouldn't care to be haunted by either one of them, but we thought Mr. Lugosi offered a rather meeker brand of horror than Mr. Karloff, and a Brooklyn accent made in Southern Hungary, though perhaps a shade more intelligible than a Brooklyn accent made in Brooklyn, still is lacking in realism. – *Worcester Evening Gazette*[129]

One wonders just how realistic the same critic found Karloff's accent, given that he was English and – based upon surviving examples of his work as Jonathan Brewster – made no effort to sound as if he was from Brooklyn either.

Within 24 hours, Lugosi and his colleagues were in Hartford, Connecticut, giving two performances, matinee and evening, on March 18 at Bushnell Memorial Hall. Less than one year earlier, in May 1943, Lugosi had trod the boards of the very same theatre in a touring version of *Dracula–The Vampire Play*.

According to the *Hartford Times*, *Arsenic* broke the Bushnell's "revival records." And the *Times'* editor believed "that the bloodcurdling Bela is quite the boy." Neither of the city's newspapers reviewed the play, but the *Courant* promised readers in advance that it would be "great."[130] Elsewhere in the city, while Lugosi was onstage, he was also onscreen. The city's State Theatre was then screening *Voodoo Man*.

The City on a Hill

From March 19 to April 1, 1944, *Arsenic* was on display at the 1,700-seat Colonial Theatre in Boston.[131] The day prior to opening, the HACD hosted a meeting in San Francisco, a prelude to a celebration they would hold on March 26.

Near the end of *Arsenic*'s two-week Boston run, at the stroke of midnight on March 30, Lugosi performed on a horror-themed radio show called *Grave Moments* on station WMEX. The episode title was *Ghost of Count Fachelone*.[132] Also during the two weeks in Boston, Lugosi took time to speak with a journalist from the *Boston Globe*, who told readers:

> Bela Lugosi, Jr. can't understand why the sight of his tall, thin, steely-eyed father causes all his boy companions to suddenly stop their play. "It's only Daddy," says Bela soothingly.

> But the other kids know better. They have seen Mr. Lugosi in a series of horror characterizations that have made older and stauncher persons than they blanch with terror.

> They have heard whole theatres of people scream with apprehension when the fear-provoking Lugosi stalks across the screen. He may be 'just Daddy' to their pal, but he's the kind of character people use to scare bad children with.

MONDAY, FEBRUARY 28th
8:35 P. M.
THE ORIGINAL

Don Cossack Chorus
AND DANCERS
SERGE JAROFF
Conducting
$3.30 — $2.75 — $2.20 — $1.65 — $1.10

WEDNESDAY, MARCH 1st
Matinee, 2:30 P. M.—Evening, 8:30 P. M.
MESSRS. SHUBERT present
EVERETT MARSHALL
in the Operatic Success of the 20th Century
THE STUDENT PRINCE
Matinee: $2.75—$1.65—$1.10— .85
Evening: $2.75—$2.20—$1.65—$1.10

WEDNESDAY, MARCH 8th
8:30 P. M.
FAREWELL TOUR !
BELA LUGOSI
IN THE MAD, FUNNY HIT
ARSENIC
and
OLD LACE
$2.75—$2.20—$1.65—$1.10

-- Announcement --
The Oscar Levant Concert Thursday, March 9th, has been cancelled. Will you, who have series or single tickets kindly advise the office this week.
Thank You!

From the *Trenton Times* of February 27, 1944.

Young Bela does impersonations of his father and screams with delight at his own cleverness. He adores mystery pictures and would probably be very happy if he could be in Boston, watching Papa Bela portraying on the stage the sinister and maniacal Jonathan Brewster in *Arsenic and Old Lace* at the Colonial Theatre.

Mr. Lugosi likes the play, in which he has appeared for a brief seven weeks, because people laugh so hard. He enjoys hearing audiences express their mirth as loudly as possible.

The one-night stands which preceded Boston have caused him to lose 11 pounds and he is leaner and more hawk-like than ever. People always recognize him – even at

Excerpt from Office of Strategic Services (declassified) interoffice memo, HU-498. *(Courtesy of the National Archives and Records Administration, College Park, Maryland)*

luncheon at the Ritz-Carlton matronly diners were getting a thrill by surreptitious looks at the famous film and stage "heavy."

He was wearing a quietly-cut blue suit, conservative cuff links and a pleasant expression. But the smile didn't fool the women. They knew that the Hungarian actor must be plotting something dire.

Actually he was drinking double orange juices and discussing his stamp collection. He likes being in Boston because there are 18 stamp dealers listed in town and he intends to visit every one of them. He says that whenever he gets some unexpected money he uses it in the finest investments he knows of... War Bonds. The other half stamps.[133]

Lugosi shared these stories and various words of wisdom at the Ritz-Carlton Hotel, where he and Lillian stayed during the Boston run of the play.

As for the production, critics for the area newspapers had already seen Karloff playing Jonathan Brewster, so their reviews tended to compare the two:

Mr. Lugosi lacks the subtlety of Karloff's villainy, but leaves no doubt when he gets sinister. – *Boston Traveler*[134]

He seems a likely villain and plenty of women in the audience screamed enthusiastically whenever he glared at acrobatic, personable Jack Whiting, the dramatic critic hero. – *Boston Globe*[135]

It doesn't seem possible that anyone could conceivably have missed this waggish parody of murder thrillers, which has to do with a couple of dear old ladies who poison a dozen or so of their gentlemen guests and bury them properly in the cellar, so the chief item of interest this morning concerns the appearance of Bela Lugosi in the role of their sinister nephew, who tries unsuccessfully to make the score 13 to 12 in his favor. And it may promptly be said that Mr. Lugosi amply fulfills the promise of his many film iniquities splendidly. – *Boston Herald*[136]

[Lugosi] must succeed in being all that his colleagues in performance say he is. He must not so much represent as be represented. In all logic a character should not come through under such passive treatment. Mr. Lugosi's Jonathan of the Brewsters of Brooklyn nevertheless takes on force and vitality that way, and a fascinating study in the sinister he becomes. – *Christian Science Monitor*[137]

From the *Boston Herald* of March 21, 1944.

Audiences seem to have been generally pleased, though the play's second week "lost a little ground," grossing only $9,000.[138] Later, the producers admitted that they lost $426.50 on the Boston production.[139] Here again, the blame was placed not on Lugosi, but on the fact that *Arsenic* had already been staged in the city on more than one occasion.

While Lugosi received applause in Massachusetts, the press continued to report on the positives and negatives of Communism. On the one hand, Elmer Davis publicly denied that the Office of War Information (OWI) employed Communists or Fellow Travelers; his statement came only days after a legislator in California argued that local Red political activities were "increasing."[140] On the other hand, news of secret "Communist" cells in Nazi Germany was certainly welcome.[141]

And at least some Hungarian-Americans supportive of Fascism must have paused when the puppet government in Hungary agreed to pay Germany for the maintenance costs of Nazi occupation troops on their own soil. That same government had just allowed eleven trainloads of Jews, journalists, and Communists to be deported from Budapest to concentration camps.[142]

Respite

During the first week of April, the cast enjoyed a much-needed break. Lugosi and Lillian spent most of their time at the Essex House on Central Park South in New York City. Even though he was able to rest, Lugosi was hardly idle.

On Friday, April 7 at 8PM EST, he guest-starred on Kate Smith's radio show, which was broadcast on WABC. Details are few, but it is evident that Smith sang *Ave Maria* that night, and that her other guests included bandleader Count Basie.[143]

At roughly the same time, Lugosi's old friends Lyman and Chamberlain Brown – who were theatrical agents in Manhattan – attempted to entice him into future *Arsenic and Old Lace* performances. They first tried to reach Lugosi via Boston, but finally made contact with him while he was in New York:

> Since *Arsenic and Old Lace* will be available for the summer companies this year, [we're] writing to find out if you'd be interested in doing it in various theatres after your present tour closes.[144]

Lugosi declined their offer, perhaps because he believed that approximately three months on the road in *Arsenic* was enough, and also perhaps because he was eager to return to California, which would get him closer to film work and closer to his son.

The City of Brotherly Love

For *Arsenic* performances beginning on April 9 and ending on April 22, 1944 the cast regrouped in Philadelphia. Lugosi was no stranger to the chosen venue: he had played the Locust Street Theatre less than one year earlier in a touring version of *Dracula–The Vampire Play*.

As with Boston, local critics had already seen *Arsenic*, with the Lugosi production marking the play's fourth appearance in Philadelphia. Nevertheless, the notices were generally positive:

> It's true that Mr. Lugosi's heavy Hungarian accent seems a bit incongruous as a member of the old American family of the Brewsters of Brooklyn, but after all the wicked Jonathan had been around quite a bit, and Mr. Lugosi's hypnotic eye has just

Jean Adair Ruth McDevitt and Bela Lugosi
in ARSENIC and OLD LACE

COLONIAL
THEATRE
— BOSTON —
Direction L. A. B. Amusement Corp.

Jonathan Brewster (Lugosi) and Dr. Einstein (Henry Sherwood) menace Elaine Harper (Ann Lincoln).

the right goofy gleam for the role.

If anything, Mr. Lugosi ... plays the part of the killer escaped from an institution for the criminally insane along even broader lines than Erich von Stroheim and Boris Karloff, his predecessors here as Jonathan Brewster. Which makes even more amusing a play which extracts heaps of hilarity from murder and madness.... – *Philadelphia Inquirer*[145]

The Hollywood horror-expert brings all the creepy virtuosity of his former incarnation in *Dracula* to the role, enacted here in prior productions by Boris Karloff and Eric von Stroheim. – *Philadelphia Record*[146]

Though somewhat muted in its praise, the *Evening Bulletin* agreed that Lugosi ("Hollywood's high priest of horror") was as equally sinister as any of his predecessors in the play.[147]

Variety reported that the Philadelphia run "surprised" the industry with a "lusty" gross of $13,000 for its first week.[148] The play also generated a good deal of local publicity for Lugosi. In some cases, it was not unlike what had been published in other cities. Lugosi offstage was different than on. He collected stamps, he loved his wife, and he missed his son. Lillian shared her view that the couple was "disappointed" Lugosi had not been able to play the lead character in *The Lodger* (1944), a film starring Laird Cregar.[149] As for Lugosi, he made clear that he hated "opinions in women."[150]

But, in a curious article purportedly based on an interview, Elsie Finn of the *Philadelphia Record* resurrected a tale of the type that fan magazines had published over a decade earlier. Her improbable article – about a beautiful Hungarian actress who put a "spell" on Lugosi – smacked similar to a 1929 story printed in *Motion Picture* magazine. In it, journalist Gladys Hall claimed that a Hungarian succubus haunted Lugosi and made him fear going to sleep.[151]

Rather than being scared of the dark, Lugosi seems to have enjoyed the Philadelphia nightlife. To celebrate Lillian's birthday, the couple dined at Jack Lynch's Walton Roof club. Accompanied by Warren O'Hara (the *Arsenic* company's manager) and showgirl Sally Kelly, the couple feasted on wine and liederkranz cheese while watching *Funzafire!* with Benny Meroff.[152]

Lugosi's political life continued as well. On April 9 and April 16, the HACD (in tandem with the National Council of Hungarian American Trade Unionists) published enormous advertisements in the *Washington Post* as part of a membership drive. And Lugosi surely read with great interest about Count Károlyi's involvement in the formation of a Hungarian council in London.[153]

From the *Philadelphia Daily News* of April 10, 1944.

As for the OSS, the agency filed a new report about an HACD meeting held in Chicago on April 16. Due to his *Arsenic* schedule, Lugosi was not present, but he would have been aware that its keynote speech decried Nazi persecution of the Jews.[154]

Meanwhile, the press wrote about various new Red scares. A priest in Baltimore alleged that Communists had infiltrated local shipyards and war factories.[155] A former chief of the Special Studies division of the Federal Communications Commission (FCC) reassured Congress that she had never been affiliated with Communist-front organizations.[156] And the *New York Times* reported on the growing ideological war in Hollywood, with various factions labeling one another as "Fascists" and "Communists."[157]

Newark

The 2,800-seat Mosque Theatre of Newark, New Jersey – which featured flourishes of Middle Eastern, Mediterranean, and Egyptian styles – presented *Arsenic and Old Lace* for the week of April 23, 1944.

During its run, Lugosi gave a speech at a mass meeting in New York held in support of Hungary's liberation.[158] The OSS monitored the event, recording that some 1,200 persons

were present.[159] In one of two separate reports filed, the OSS recorded the essential details of Lugosi's speech:

> Then followed the similarly lively and fiery speech of Bela Lugosi, President of the Hung. Am. Democratic Council, whose theme was: 'How to Help the Hungarian People.' Mr. Lugosi praised Mr. Cordell Hull's message to the Hung. people, calling on them to revolt against the Horthy Quislings. Lugosi also praised the leadership of Count Károlyi, calling him the 'inspiration of the suffering Hungarian people.'

> Then Mr. Lugosi presented a program for action, among which the most important points were: United Nations should recognize Count Károlyi and his movement as representing the Hungarian resistance against the Nazis; American Hungarians should support the Hungarian National Council of Károlyi, just formed in London; the OWI should broadcast the news of this N.Y. meeting to the Hungarian people; a Hungarian Partisan Army should be formed by uniting the already existing Hungarian Partisan forces in Ruthenia and Yugoslavia; when the Hung. Partisan Army is formed, American and Allied 'lend-lease' and other aid should be sent to the Hungarian people by parachute shipments; American-Hungarians must raise money to help the people of Hungary with food, medicines, and other supplies; [and] President Roosevelt's program and his re-election should be supported.[160]

The very same day, William S. Gailmor, the commentator who had earlier denounced the American Hungarian Federation, interviewed Lugosi on his radio program.

As for the Newark performances, local critics pronounced them a success, heaping praise on Lugosi:

> Lugosi is ideally suited for the role of the demoniac mad murderer who returns to the family home after years of absence in the hope of plying his nefarious trade there, only to find himself in competition with his mild-mannered aunts... it is capital entertainment all the way through. – *Newark Star-Ledger*[161]

> Setting forth these amazing folk, before a fine setting and in a production which runs like a chronometer, is a fine cast. Most prominent is Bela Lugosi, whose Transylvanian accent is baffling (considering the Brooklyn location of the play) but who brings a cozy touch of *Dracula* to the proceedings... For a jolly evening among the corpses, *Arsenic and Old Lace* is hereby recommended. – *Newark Evening News*[162]

During the run, which ended on April 30, Lugosi could be spotted outside of the theatre. His film *The Return of the Vampire* played the bottom of a double-bill with *The Heavenly Body* (1944) at the Loew's State in Newark.[163] And the man himself visited the House of Chan restaurant in nearby Manhattan, much to the surprise of other diners.[164]

TALPRA MAGYAR!

ON YOUR FEET HUNGARIANS!

The Horthy Quislings betrayed the people of Hungary to their hereditary enemies—the Germans.

The Hungarian government and the Hungarian people are not the same.

The people want to fight against the Nazis. They want to be in the war for freedom.

It is their government that fights for Hitler.

Many of the people of Hungary are already fighting in the snow capped Carpathian Mountains of the North. They are fighting in the sunny wheat fields of the South—in the ranks of Yugoslavia's People's Army of Liberation under the great Marshal Tito. They are fighting to convert their fertile Danube valley from a Nazi "Lebenstraum" (Living Space) to a Nazi "Todesraum" (Graveyard).

It is a hard fight. You know what happened at Lidice. You know what happens everywhere when civilian patriots stand up against the tanks and machine guns of mechanized Nazi divisions.

Now it is happening to Hungarians. They need your help.

We are Americans. Our fathers came from Hungary—the land of Louis Kossuth who said Hungary must live in liberty like America or die.

We want Hungary to live. The Hungarian people's fight for freedom is our fight—because every country that fights for freedom guarantees the freedom of America.

The Hungarian people now fighting for their freedom will take heart in the knowledge that they are backed to the hilt by citizens of the great United States who were once their countrymen.

We know the tactics of the ruling clique of Hungary. Our fathers escaped from their tyranny. We can and must make certain that the Hungarian people win their liberty in this war and retain it in the peace that follows.

To do this most effectively we have formed the Hungarian American Council for Democracy and the National Council of Hungarian American Trade Unionists. American Hungarians of all religious and political beliefs are included in these organizations.

We are not alone. Free Hungarians are similarly organized in England, Canada, Mexico, Chile, Uruguay, Argentina, Brazil, and Bolivia. They are rallied around the banner of Michael Karolyi, former President of the Hungarian People's Republic, who was exiled from his homeland because he believed in the ideals of Kossuth and Lincoln—and fought for them.

We stand for a speedy United Nations victory and lasting peace.

We stand for the liberation of the people of Hungary and all the oppressed peoples of the world as agreed at Teheran by Roosevelt, Churchill and Stalin.

We stand for a democratic Hungary in a democratic world.

We stand for a Hungary built on a "good neighbor" policy with her neighboring states.

We want to mobilize every American of Hungarian origin for an all out support of the war and its objectives. If you believe in this—join us.

At this critical time, we call on all American friends of democracy—whether they be of Hungarian parentage or not—to help us, support us, fight with us!

Hungarian American Council for Democracy
Bela Lugosi, President.

National Council of Hungarian American Trade Unionists
Julius Emspack, President,
National Secretary-Treasurer, United Electrical, Radio and Machine Workers of America

If you are an American of Hungarian origin— join us!

If you are an American of any other origin— sponsor us!

I join ☐   I sponsor ☐

THE HUNGARIAN AMERICAN COUNCIL FOR DEMOCRACY
23 West 26th Street, New York 10, N. Y.

NAME ....
          PRINT

ADDRESS ....
          PRINT

I want to help by contributing $ ....

Send communications and contributions to:

HUNGARIAN AMERICAN COUNCIL FOR DEMOCRACY
23 WEST 26TH STREET, NEW YORK 10, N. Y.
MUrray Hill 4-3457

Account audited by Martin Schwaeber & Company, Certified Public Accountants

Published in the *Washington Post* on April 16, 1944.

And then there was the film version of *Arsenic and Old Lace*. Just as the Newark opening took place, the press announced that the movie (which had been completed in 1941) would finally get released in American theatres.[165] The delay had occurred due to contractual agreements that it could not be screened until the Broadway version closed, which it did in June of 1944.[166]

In the film, theatre critics had yet a fourth Jonathan Brewster to examine, as the role was played not by Karloff, von Stroheim, or Lugosi, but instead by Raymond Massey. (That said, the movie did feature Jean Adair as Martha Brewster, the same actress who toured with Lugosi in 1944.)

The Tour Ends

At the end of April of 1944, the *New York Times* announced that the "touring company" of *Arsenic and Old Lace* had "close[d] its career" in Newark.[167] The strenuous tour was over.

Variety had indicated that the "2d Co." (as the Lugosi troupe was called) would give performances in Syracuse, Binghamton, and Schenectady, but either that report was in error or plans changed.[168] In the latter two cities, the play was staged, but the only performer from the Lugosi company to appear was Malcolm Beggs.

Why did Newark become the last engagement? Despite its success in many cities, the *Arsenic* tour was not generating big net profits. And the Broadway version did close in June. Both of them going dark may well have been tied to Warner Bros.' need to put *Arsenic* film into circulation.

Sam Wood (President of the Motion Picture Alliance), Clark Gable, and Barbara Stanwyck after attending a meeting discussing the fight against Communism in the Hollywood film industry. Published in the *Los Angeles Times* on April 29, 1944.

It could also be that Lugosi was eager to return to Universal Pictures and appear in one of their upcoming horror movies. In mid-April, the *New York Times* reported that Paul Malvern would have $500,000 to make *The Devil's Brood* at the studio.[169] The film – later produced as *House of Frankenstein* (1944) – went before the cameras without Lugosi. John Carradine played Dracula instead.

The famous vampire was also set to appear in Universal's *Wolf Man Vs. Dracula*, a project that revealed, at least in its core idea, the influence of Columbia's *The Return of the Vampire*. Ford Beebe was set to produce and direct the film at the end of April 1944, with the studio referring to it in June as *Dracula vs. the Wolf Man*.[170] *Daily Variety* announced it was "slated for summer rolling."[171] Bernard Schubert completed a script by July 17, but the studio delayed the project until the autumn.[172] In December of 1944, the PCA analyzed another draft of the script (which returned the Wolf Man's name to first place in the title), but it never went before the cameras.

KALURAH TEMPLE

2 DAYS ONLY
Tuesday and Wednesday
MAY 30 and 31
TUESDAY (Decoration Day) MAT. and EVE.
Wednesday, May 31, Evening Only

The HILARIOUS COMEDY THRILLER

"ARSENIC and OLD LACE"

TICKETS NOW ON SALE AT

WEEKS & DICKINSON
39 Chenango Street
Phone 4-2481

Evenings: 75c, $1.00, $1.50, $2.00—Plus Tax
DECORATION DAY MATINEE: 75c, $1, $1.50—Plus Tax

Only Opportunity to See This Sensational Laugh Hit Now on Final Tour—Fourth Big Year in New York

"Smash stage hit."—Walter Winchell.   "Frightfully funny."—N. Y. Journal-American.

PHONE FOR RESERVATIONS NOW

Published in the *Binghamton Press* on May 27, 1944.

Lugosi purchases a war bond from Rosa Friedman in Pasadena in May 1944.

Whether or not Lugosi's involvement with *The Return of the Vampire* had any effect on Universal's subsequent avoidance of him in 1944 is difficult to substantiate. At any rate, the studio did not hire him again until 1948.

For at least one week (if not upward of two-and-a-half weeks) after the *Arsenic* tour ended, Lugosi remained in the New York area. On May 4, Santiago Grevi interviewed Lugosi on his Brooklyn-based WBYN radio show *Voice of Fighting Spain*.[173] The following day, Lugosi made a return visit to Kate Smith's WABC radio program. This time, he acted in a dramatic sketch on an episode that also featured comedian Harry Savoy and football player-turned active marine Angelo Bertelli. Smith sang several tunes on the show that night, including *Dream a Little Dream of Me* and *Please Don't Talk About Me When I'm Gone*.[174]

Soon thereafter, Lugosi bumped into jazzman Cab Calloway in the theatre district of Midtown Manhattan.[175] Though filmed in different locations, the two men had both appeared in the Paramount comedy *International House* (1933) with W. C. Fields. In it, Calloway sang the song *Reefer Man*. Lugosi had played a Soviet.

The exact date of Lugosi's return to Los Angeles is unknown, though he appeared at a war bond rally in Pasadena on or around May 21, 1944.[176] At roughly the same time (on May 20), Guy Lombardo and His Royal Canadians played Lugosi's "favorite tune" on a *National Barn Dance* radio broadcast devoted largely to patriotic music. The song in question: *I'll Walk Alone*.[177]

Lugosi's new film *Return of the Ape Man*

D. All fascist laws designed to supress minorities, Jews, unions, peasant organizations etc., must be wiped out at once. Democratic rights of the individual must be secured equally for all the people. Freedom of the press, trial by jury must be established as soon as possible.

E. The working man should be guaranteed freedom of organization, the right to work, a fair living standard and social security.

F. Friendly relations must be established with the neighbour nations, free Yugoslavia, Czechoslovakia, Roumania and Austria, and with the great nations who liberated them, the Soviet Union, the United States and other Countries of the United Nations. In turn, we expect that free Hungary will be dealt with by the United Nations as an independent Nation on the basis of the Atlantic Charter.

G. We wish and hope that the Hungarian people will elect a democratic, progressive government representative of all anti-fascist political parties that will lead Hungary towards a better and happier future.

We call upon all Hungarian Americans to adopt this program wholeheartedly and extend a helping hand to the suffering Hungarian people. Let us all stand, united, behind free, democratic, independent Hungary. In this united action let us assure the Hungarian people of our brotherly love and our determination to help them to the limit of our ability in the hard task of reconstruction so they may live in peace, freedom and prosperity as deserved by a people of good will.

                    THE HUNGARIAN AMERICAN DEMOCRATIC COUNCIL

                                   BELA LUGOSI, Chairman

Excerpt from a declassified OSS report on an HACD convention, dated January 10, 1945. *(Courtesy of the National Archives and Records Administration, College Park, Maryland)*

(1944) was released in July 1944; *One Body Too Many* (1944) hit theatres that November. In the autumn of that year, he was cast in *Zombies on Broadway* (1945) and *The Body Snatcher* (1945) at RKO.[178]

During his months on the road in *Arsenic*, Lugosi may or may not have been aware of the extent to which his marriage was under strain. Perhaps the troubles were the accumulation of many years; perhaps they were exacerbated by the arduous tour. But whatever the exact reasons, Lugosi's wife Lillian left him on August 16, 1944.[179] Charging him with being a "cruel and inhuman husband," Lillian sued for divorce and demanded custody of their son.[180] Lugosi would say:

I have courted her with flowers and candy ever since she walked out. ... I've been shaving regularly. That was one of our troubles. I was a careless husband; as a European I expected things too much my own way in the home. American girls don't like that. They want things more 50-50.[181]

Only days after their separation, Lugosi spoke at a political rally in Los Angeles on the

Mr. DeWitt C. Poole,   3 March 1945
Page two

    e. Dr. Kerekes -- "Reactionary." The society of which
he is secretary "was financed by Horthy."

    f. Melchior Lengyel -- "A coffee house playwrite;" "has no
creed and is unimportant;" and "is a parasite."

    g. Michael Curtiz, movie director and his brother, Gabor
Curtiz -- "not at all active in Hungarian-American circles."

    h. "All the Hungarians of Hollywood, except Farago are
skunks. They are worse than reactionaries."

    2. Questioned about the activities of Archduke Felix in Los
Angeles during his recent visit there, he replied that he knew
nothing about them. Asked about his opinion on Otto's prospects,
Lugosi answered, "He has none."

    3. "I favor a Danube federation of one hundred percent
democratic states."

    4. Concerning Hungarian-American reactions to Yalta, he
said, "It's one hundred percent _for!_"

    5. "The Allies should see to it that the Hungarian people
can express their opinions, and they should regard them as allies --
one of the most loyal allies."

    6. According to Lugosi, the society of which he is president,
the Hungarian Democratic Council, and the American Hungarian
Federation of which Dr. Kerekes is secretary "have the masses
of Hungarian-Americans behind them." Only the leaders, he said,
of the latter organization are reactionary. "The influence

Excerpt from a declassified OSS interview with Lugosi, dated March 3, 1945. *(Courtesy of the National Archives and Records Administration, College Park, Maryland)*

BELA LUGOSI IN PERSON

Ballyhoo promoting *The Body Snatcher* (1945).

subject of Nazi persecution of the Jews.[182] The couple reunited shortly before the end of October 1944.[183]

By that time, the OSS filed yet another report, this time on the "Hungarian Situation in Ohio and Michigan." It included quotations from a doctor in the AHF who confidently claimed that Lugosi was a Communist; a clergyman in the Hungarian Reformed Federation of America said the same.

By contrast, a Hungarian monsignor gave a very different opinion to the same agent:

[Lugosi] is one of the finest men.... He is modest and a sympathetic person, and I believe he is a liberal and became interested in the movement which he is heading now because of his liberal views. ... I believe Lugosi is sincere in his pronouncements and beliefs, but he is in the wrong company. His influence among the Hungarians in America is nil. ... However it would be unjust to call Mr. Lugosi a Communist. I believe that the group got him to   become president and he thought he might be a big man. He does not deserve to be pushed around. He is honest, [but] is not a politician, and not a diplomat.[184]

Nevertheless, rumors of Lugosi the Communist soon began to appear in print in English-

language publications. In July, the *New York Post* published an article that claimed members of the "Institute for International Democracy" were "pinks" or "reds."[185] Accompanying photographs depicted Orson Welles, Charlie Chaplin, and Bela Lugosi.

Perhaps as a result of these accusations, J. Edgar Hoover sent a letter to the FBI office in Los Angeles in September 1944 asking them to conduct an "investigation concerning the activities" of Bela Lugosi.[186] That same month, the OSS completed a new, ten-page report on "Hungarian Activities in California." It included the following analysis of the HACD:

[The Los Angeles and San Francisco branches] of the Hungarian-American Council for Democracy are still loosely organized groups and their membership is not believed to be very numerous. One Hungarian-American spokesman in Los Angeles vouched the opinion that the Council is 'generally not taken too seriously among the Hungarian community.'

... Other West Coast Hungarian leaders, especially in Los Angeles, are opposed to the Council because of its general Leftist orientation and of the support given to it by alleged Communists who appear as speakers at all the meetings sponsored by the Council. These claim that the Council is a Communist-front organization which has always followed and supported the pro-Soviet line, and they substantiate their claim by pointing out the fact that the Council derives the bulk of its membership as well as its leadership (in Los Angeles) from the Hungarian American Trade Union Council.[187]

By year's end, another OSS report detailed an HACD meeting in New York City, at which Lugosi was not present. Its anonymous author seems not to have been worried about the HACD, but nevertheless deemed it a "disguised Communist organization. Anyhow, the word 'Communist' is not to be taken very seriously, as far as they are concerned. The members are mostly 'fellow travelers'; they like Roosevelt in America but Stalin in Europe."[188]

Was Lugosi a Communist? There is certainly no evidence that he was during his life in America. By contrast, it seems as if he was exactly what he claimed to be: an extremely liberal Democrat. Though it is impossible to say with certainty, rumors about Lugosi the Communist would seem to be nothing more than that: rumors spread by those who disliked him.

As for Lugosi's wartime activities, particularly during the *Arsenic and Old Lace* tour, they evoke a noir nightmare in which everyone seemed to be watching everyone else, but in which few saw things as they really were. Despite all of the neon marquees and all of the theatre spotlights, too much remained hidden in the shadows and in the fog of war.

Then, while a variety of onlookers watched, Lugosi's Hollywood career faltered after 1945. He was never able to work for the United Nations or any subsequent political organization. Nor did Count Károlyi assume leadership of post-war Hungary. Much to Lugosi's chagrin, the Soviet Union satellized his homeland after occupying it with troops. But here was a world that Lugosi could scarcely have envisioned during the war.

Shortly after the Allied victory, Edgar G. Ulmer's *Detour* (1945) appeared on American theatre screens. Ulmer had earlier directed such movies as *The Black Cat* (1934) with Karloff and Lugosi. But *Detour* was a film noir in which a male lead named Al Roberts (Tom Neal) finds himself at the mercy of events over which he has little control. His ill-fated journey is as psychological as it is geographical.

"That's life," Roberts says. "Whichever way you turn, Fate sticks out a foot to trip you."

(Endnotes)

1   Schrader, Paul. "Notes on *Film Noir.*" *Film Comment* Spring 1972.
2   In the book *Lugosi* (Jefferson, NC: McFarland, 1997), Gary D. Rhodes provided the first chronicle of each city in which Lugosi performed on the 1944 *Arsenic and Old Lace* tour. Additional primary materials have surfaced since that book was published. As a result, it should be noted that the city listings in that book do not include the show in Bridgeport (discussed herein), but do feature a typographical error in the mention of Wilmington, Delaware (incorrectly listed in *Lugosi* as "Willington"), as well as mention of Syracuse, Binghamton, and Schenectady. Despite primary sources that implied otherwise, Lugosi did not actually appear in those three cities.
3   "Looking at Hollywood with Hedda Hopper." *Chicago Tribune* 26 Mar. 1944.
4   Presumably Karloff also made money from the 1943 Kline-Howard production of *Arsenic and Old Lace* that starred Lugosi.
5   Hazen, David W. "Bela Lugosi Famous in Hungary As Actor Before Entering Movies." *The Oregonian* (Portland, OR) 17 Feb. 1936.
6   "Loyalty Pledged by Hungarian Group." *San Bernardino Daily Sun* 28 Nov. 1940.
7   Durant, Alta. "Gab." *Daily Variety* 18 Mar. 1942. The event was held at the Polytechnic High School on 29 Mar. 1942.
8   "Piccadilly Arcade to Reopen." *New York Times* 14 Feb. 1943.
9   OSS FNB HU-368. *A. Heckscher Interview with Bela Lugosi on Hungarian Politics, Statler Hotel, Washington, D. C.* 22 June 1943. [Available in the US Office of Strategic Services, Foreign Nationalities Branch Files, 1942 - 1945 at the National Archives and Records Administration, National Archives at College Park, Maryland.]
10   Ibid.
11   OSS FNB HU-369. A. Heckscher to D. C. Poole. *Report on Prof. T. Kerekes' Approaching Bela Lugosi, with Invitation to quit the Democratic Hungarian Movement, and work with the American Hungarian Federation.* 23 June 1943. [Available in the US Office of Strategic Services, Foreign Nationalities Branch Files, 1942 - 1945.]
12   *Memorandum: Hungarian Politics in the United States.* 1942. [Available in the US Office of Strategic Services, Foreign Nationalities Branch Files, 1942 - 1945.]
13   OSS FNB HU-374. Letter from Rustem Vámbéry, Committee for a New Democratic Hungary, to Alan Cranston, Office of War Information. 3 July 1943. [Available in the US Office of Strategic Services, Foreign Nationalities Branch Files, 1942 - 1945.]
14   OSS INT33 HU-9. *Foreign Nationality Groups in the United States, Number 140, The Hungarian Political Scene in the United States.* 9 July 1943. [Available in the US Office of Strategic Services, Foreign Nationalities Branch Files, 1942 - 1945.]
15   OSS FNB HU-389. Memorandum of Transmittal from James R. Sharp, Foreign Agents Registration Section to Alan Cranston, Office of War Information, DeWitt Poole, Office of Strategic Services, and Miss Rebecca Wellington, Department of State. *Re: The Hungarian-American Committee for Democracy.* 20 July 1943. [Available in the US Office of Strategic Services, Foreign Nationalities Branch Files, 1942 - 1945.]
16   Ibid.
17   Qtd. in Ibid.
18   OSS FNB HU-402. Letter from John Roman to C. W. Blegen, Washington D. C. 1 Aug. 1943. [Available in the US Office of Strategic Services, Foreign Nationalities Branch Files, 1942 - 1945.]
19   Várdy, Steven Béla. "Hungarian Americans During World War II: Their Role in Defending Hungary's Interests." *Ideology, Politics, and Diplomacy in East Central Europe.* Ed. by M. B. B. Biskupski. Rochester, NY: Univ. of Rochester Press, 2003: 134.
20   *Memorandum Digest, Confidential: Free Hungary Movement.* [Available in the US Office of Strategic Services, Foreign Nationalities Branch Files, 1942 - 1945.]

21 Ibid.
22 Várdy, "Hungarian Americans during World War II: Their Role in Defending Hungary's Interests."
23 Qtd. in OSS FNB HU-393. *Summary of Letter from Jászi defining his attitude toward the HACD along with a letter from Vámbéry to Károlyi describing his discussion via phone with Jászi.* 23 July 1943. [Available in the US Office of Strategic Services, Foreign Nationalities Branch Files, 1942 - 1945.]
24 Ibid.
25 These matters are detailed at some length in: Rhodes, Gary D. *Bela Lugosi, Dreams and Nightmares* (Narberth, PA: Collectables, 2007).
26 OSS INT33 HU-11. *Foreign Nationality Groups in the United States, Number 155, Hungarian Politics in the United States Reviewed.* 13 Oct. 1943. [Available in the US Office of Strategic Services, Foreign Nationalities Branch Files, 1942 - 1945.]
27 OSS FNB HU-448. Letter from Bela Lugosi to C. W. Blegen, Office of Strategic Services, Washington D. C. 3 Nov. 1943. [Available in the US Office of Strategic Services, Foreign Nationalities Branch Files, 1942 - 1945.]
28 OSS FNB HU-452. Interoffice Memo from W. I. Wheeler to DeWitt C. Poole. *Subject: 'Dracula' Council Dinner, December 5.* 16 Nov. 1943. [Available in the US Office of Strategic Services, Foreign Nationalities Branch Files, 1942 - 1945.]
29 OSS FNB HU-454. Memorandum from M. I. Wheeler to DeWitt C. Poole, Subject: More Information on #115. 23 Nov. 1943. [Available in the US Office of Strategic Services, Foreign Nationalities Branch Files, 1942 - 1945.]
30 OSS FNB HU-480. *Declaration and Guide to Policy and Action of the Hungarian-American Council for Democracy.* 27 June 1943. [Available in the US Office of Strategic Services, Foreign Nationalities Branch Files, 1942 - 1945.]
31 Zolotow, Sam. "Revised *Sheppey* Due in the Spring." *New York Times* 14 Jan. 1944.
32 "Karloff Quitting *Lace* for Pix and Radio." *Daily Variety* 19 Jan. 1944; "Current Road Shows." *Variety* 19 Jan. 1944.
33 "Inside Stuff – Legit." *Variety* 12 Jan. 1944.
34 See Chapter 11 of this book for more information on Kline and Howard, and Lugosi's 1943 appearances in *Arsenic and Old Lace*.
35 "Hollywood Inside." *Daily Variety* 1 Feb. 1944; "Ill in Pix." *Daily Variety* 13 Jan. 1944.
36 "Screen News Here and in Hollywood." *New York Times* 26 Jan. 1944; "Lugosi Takes *Arsenic.*" *Daily Variety* 26 Jan. 1944.
37 D'Arc, James D. "Oral History Interview Donlevy, Lillian Lugosi, 1912." 20 May 1976. Available at L. Tom Perry Special Collections, Harold B. Lee Library, Brigham Young University, Provo, UT.
38 "Dracula's Odd Clothing Taste Horrifies City Shop Operator." *Daily Oklahoman* (Oklahoma City, OK) 1 Feb. 1944.
39 Park, Ray. "Sissies Should Bolt the Doors; Movies' Dracula Is in Town." *Daily Oklahoman* 29 Jan. 1944.
40 "Boo!" *Daily Oklahoman* 29 Jan. 1944.
41 "Any Blood Donors?" *New York Times* 29 Jan. 1944.
42 "The Spread of Soviet Communism." *New York Times* 3 Jan. 1944.
43 "Vows Exposure of Reds' Grip on Federal Posts." *Chicago Tribune* 6 Jan. 1944.
44 "Boilermakers' Union Claims Communists Influenced FEPC." *Pittsburgh Courier* 15 Jan. 1944; White, Walter. *Chicago Defender* 15 Jan. 1944.
45 "Assignment for 1944." *The Nation's Business* Jan. 1944.
46 "Buildings in the National Register of Historic Places." Available at: http://www.tulsapreservationcommission.org/nationalregister/buildings/index.pl?id=46. Accessed 24 Feb. 2014.
47 Ketcham, George L. "Murder Is Given a Comedy Slant." *Tulsa World* 31 Jan. 1944.
48 "Patrons Like to Be Scared by Lugosi." *Variety* 9 Feb. 1944.
49 "Robinson Center (Little Rock)." Available at: http://en.wikipedia.org/wiki/Robinson_Center_%28Little_Rock%29. Updated 18 November 2013. Accessed 22 Feb. 2014.
50 "Mystery Play Is Presented in Auditorium." *Arkansas Democrat* (Little Rock, AR) 2 Feb. 1944.
51 "*Arsenic and Old Lace* Well Received." *Arkansas Gazette* (Little Rock, AR) 2 Feb. 1944.
52 OSS INT33 HU-14. *Public Meeting Report, OSS, Foreign Nationalities Branch, Number M-142.* 1 Feb. 1944. [Available in the US Office of Strategic Services, Foreign Nationalities Branch Files, 1942 - 1945.]
53 OSS FNB HU-480. Untitled Report of Interview with John Roman. 1 Feb. 1944. [Available in the

US Office of Strategic Services, Foreign Nationalities Branch Files, 1942 - 1945.]

54   "Memphis Ellis Auditorium AKA Memphis Auditorium and Market House." Available at: http://historic-memphis.com/memphis-historic/ellis/ellis.html._ Accessed 22 Feb. 2014.

55   "Chuckles Still Come from Murder-Comedy." *Memphis Commercial Appeal* 3 Feb. 1944.

56   Johnson, Lee. "Two Sweet Old Ladies – Murder Is Their Hobby." *Memphis Press-Scimitar* 2 Feb. 1944.

57   Lugosi, Bela. Telegram to Mihály Károlyi. 2 Feb. 1944.

58   "Ryman Auditorium." Available at: http://en.wikipedia.org/wiki/Ryman_Auditorium. Updated 20 Feb. 2014. Accessed 22 Feb. 2014.

59   Crain, Fitzhugh. "*Arsenic* Gives Relief from War Worries." *Nashville Banner* 4 Feb. 1944.

60   Steber, Bob. "*Arsenic, Lace* Fails to Create Goose Pimples." *Nashville Tennessean* 4 Feb. 1944.

61   "Temple Theatre, Birmingham, Alabama." Available at: http://www.birminghamrewound.com/features/bhamtheaters_part2.htm. Updated 16 Aug. 2006. Accessed 22 Feb. 2014.

62   Caldwell, Lily May. "Boogieman Bela Lugosi Here – But He Really Is a Nice Guy." *Birmingham News* 5 Feb. 1944.

63   "It's Fun for the New Dealers." *Chicago Tribune* 26 Feb. 1944.

64   "Group Formed in Hollywood to Fight Reds." *Chicago Tribune* 6 Feb. 1944.

65   Lester, John. "*Arsenic*; Hilarious Homicide." *New Orleans Item* 8 Feb. 1944.

66   Neff, Emily. "Murder Is Made Funny In Comedy – *Arsenic and Old Lace* Is Hit at Auditorium." *The Times-Picayune* (New Orleans, LA) 9 Feb. 1944.

67   "*Arsenic, Old Lace* Is Hilarious Treat." *New Orleans States* 8 Feb. 1944.

68   OSS FNB HU-485. Letter from Constantine Poulos, Chief, Foreign Language Division to Carl W. Blegen, Foreign Nationalities Branch, OSS. 7 Feb. 1944. Attached report is *American Hungarian Federation, the Fifth Column of Hungarian Fascism in the United States*. 8 Feb. 1944. [Available in the US Office of Strategic Services, Foreign Nationalities Branch Files, 1942 - 1945.]

69   Ibid.

70   "Native of Hungary." *Montgomery Advertiser* 3 Feb. 1944.

71   "Film Preview." *Daily Variety* 10 Feb. 1944.

72   "Karloff *Creepers* Preem on Feb. 15." *Variety* 9 Feb. 1944.

73   "Atlanta Theatre." Available at: http://cinematreasures.org/theaters/4784. Accessed 22 Feb. 2014.

74   Advertisement. *Atlanta Constitution* 4 Feb. 1944.

75   Brawshaw, Rosalyn. "Spook Star Of *Dracula* Is Home-Loving Husband." *Atlanta Journal* 13 Feb. 1944.

76   Jones, Paul. "Lugosi Sparks *Arsenic* Lace." *Atlanta Constitution* 12 Feb. 1944.

77   "Children's Shows Listed for Today." *New York Times* 12 Feb. 1944.

78   "3 Performances of Play Slated." *Savannah Morning News* (Savannah, GA) 6 Feb. 1944; "Thrill Comedy Play Here Next Week." *Savannah Evening Press* (Savannah, GA) 12 Feb. 1944.

79   "Weird Comedy Pleases Crowd." *Savannah Morning News* 15 Feb. 1944.

80   "Augusta Bizmen Want Shows." *Billboard* 19 Feb. 1944.

81   "Critics Praise Stage Comedy." *Augusta Chronicle* (Augusta, GA) 30 Jan. 1944.

82   "*Arsenic and Old Lace* Gets Approval of Audience Here." *Augusta Chronicle* 17 Feb. 1944.

83   "Famed Comedy To Be Given Here Tonight." *Columbia Record* (Columbia, SC) 17 Feb. 1944.

84   "*Arsenic and Old Lace* Wins Acclaim Here." *Columbia Record* 18 Feb. 1944.

85   "Bela Lugosi and Strong Cast Bring *Arsenic* to 2,000 Here." *The State* (Columbia, SC) 18 Feb. 1944.

86   "Few Seats Left for Production of Play Tonight." *Charlotte Observer* (Charlotte, SC) 18 Feb. 1944.

87   "Explore the Carolina Theatre." Available at: http://www.carolinatheater.us/explore.html. Accessed 22 Feb. 2014.

88   "Bela Lugosi Is Starred But Whiting Steals Show." *Charlotte Observer* 19 Feb. 1944.

89   "Bela Lugosi to Appear Tonight in Comedy Here." *Asheville Citizen-Times* (Asheville, NC) 19 Feb. 1944.

90   "Large Audience Sees Lugosi In *Arsenic* Play – Production Affords Many Laughs, Thrills, And Chills." *Asheville Citizen-Times* 20 Feb. 1944.

91   Advertisement. *Greenville News* (Greenville, SC) 9 Feb. 1944.

92   "Lugosi Is Star of Stage Play." *Greenville News* 6 Feb. 1944.

93   "National Theater." Available at: http://cinematreasures.org/theaters/15690. Accessed 22 Feb. 2014.

94   Wagg, T. E. "Audience Here Is Titillated by Stage Hit." *Greensboro Daily News* (Greensboro, NC) 23 Feb. 1944.

95   "Lugosi to Appear in Comedy Here." *Raleigh News and Observer* 20 Feb. 1944.
96   "Insanity Gallops in *Arsenic And [Old Lace]*." *Raleigh News and Observer* 24 Feb. 1944.
97   "Vandals Smear Three Catholic Churches in N. Y." *Chicago Tribune* 19 Feb. 1944.
98   "Communist Party Files Plea to Clear Name of Violence." *Los Angeles Times* 22 Feb. 1944.
99   Advertisement. *Durham Herald-Sun* (Durham, NC) 20 Feb. 1944.
100 Advertisement. *Winston-Salem Journal* (Winston-Salem, NC) 24 Feb. 1944.
101 Garber, Mary. "Lugosi, *Arsenic and Old Lace Star*, Looks Menacing But Is Mild-Mannered." *Twin City Sentinel* (Winston-Salem, NC) 25 Feb. 1944.
102 Wilson, Mary Lib. "Well-Cast Play Brings Laughter and Shrieks." *Winston-Salem Journal* (Winston-Salem, NC) 26 Feb. 1944.
103 Garber, "Lugosi, *Arsenic and Old Lace Star*, Looks Menacing But Is Mild-Mannered."
104 "Audience Likes Play at Academy." *Roanoke Times* (Roanoke, VA) 27 Feb. 1944.
105 "Inside Stuff – Legit." *Variety* 8 Mar. 1944.
106 Johnson, Clint. "*Arsenic* Back; *Rosalinda* To Start Mar. 13." *Baltimore American* 27 Feb. 1944.
107 "Communists Dominate C.I.O., Lewis Declares." *Los Angeles Times* 29 Feb. 1944.
108 "Bela Lugosi In *Arsenic* At Ford's." *Baltimore News-Post* 29 Feb. 1944.
109 "*Arsenic and Old Lace*." *Baltimore Sun* 29 Feb. 1944.
110 "*Arsenic* $13,300, Balto." *Variety* 8 Mar. 1944.
111 "*Arsenic* Across the Sea." *Variety* 8 Mar. 1944.
112 Harer, Mark Peter and Rosenberg-Naparsteck, Ruth. *A Picture of Lycoming County* (Williamsport, PA: Greater Williamsport Art Council, 1978).
113 Advertisement. *Williamsport Gazette and Bulletin* (Williamsport, PA) 28 Feb. 1944.
114 "A 'Killer' Comes to Town! – Bela Lugosi Surveys a Satisfyingly Murderous Past." *Allentown Evening Chronicle* (Allentown, PA) 8 Mar. 1944.
115 Bergen, Ronn. "A Lugosian Memory." *Famous Monsters of Filmland* July 1971.
116 "A 'Killer' Comes To Town! – Bela Lugosi Surveys a Satisfyingly Murderous Past."
117 OSS FNB HU-565. *Daily Report 8334, Free Hungary Movement.* 8 Mar. 1944. [Available in the US Office of Strategic Services, Foreign Nationalities Branch Files, 1942 - 1945.]
118 Advertisement. *Trenton Times* (Trenton, NJ) 8 Mar. 1944.
119 Advertisement. *Wilmington Morning News* (Wilmington, DE) 8 Mar. 1944.
120 "*Arsenic, Old Lace* Pleases on Return." *Wilmington Morning* News 10 Mar. 1944; Frank, William P. "*Arsenic* Still Has Old Kick." *The Journal-Every Evening* (Wilmington, DE) 10 Mar. 1944.
121 "Rep. Dies Warns of Infiltration in U.S. Bureaus." *Chicago Tribune* 13 Mar. 1944.
122 OSS FNB HU-498. Interoffice Memo from Lt. R. G. Gort to Lt. James Kronthal. *Memorandum Digest on Free Hungary Movement.* 12 Mar. 1944. [Available in the US Office of Strategic Services, Foreign Nationalities Branch Files, 1942 - 1945.]
123 Advertisement. *Bridgeport Post* 12 Mar. 1944.
124 Russell, Fred. "Passing Show." *Bridgeport Post* 14 Mar. 1944.
125 "*Arsenic and Old Lace* to Play Here." *Berkshire Evening Herald* (Pittsfield, MA) 2 Mar. 1944.
126 Ibid.
127 "Worcester Memorial Auditorium." Available at: http://en.wikipedia.org/wiki/Worcester_Memorial_Auditorium. Updated 16 Jan. 2014. Accessed 23 Feb. 2014.
128 Moore, Leslie. "*Arsenic and Old Lace* Here with Bela Lugosi." *Worcester Telegram* (Worcester, MA) 18 Mar. 1944.
129 Foxhall, George. "*Arsenic and Old Lace* Back With Bela Lugosi." *Worcester Evening Gazette* (Worcester, MA) 18 Mar. 1944.
130 "In Great Comedy Here Twice Today." *Hartford Courant* 18 Mar. 1944.
131 "Citi Colonial Theatre." Available at: http://boston.broadway.com/venues/theaters/citi-colonial-theatre/. Accessed 23 Feb. 2014.
132 "Radio – Air Attractions." *Boston Globe* 30 Mar. 1944.
133 "Bela Lugosi's Acting Has Made Thousands Blanch With Terror." *Boston Globe* 26 Mar. 1944.
134 Watts, A. E. "Lugosi Now in *Arsenic*." *Boston Traveler* 21 Mar. 1944.
135 "Colonial Theater *"Arsenic and Old Lace*." *Boston Globe* 21 Mar. 1944.
136 Elie, Jr., Rudolph. "The Theater. Colonial. *Arsenic and Old Lace*." *Boston Herald* 21 Mar. 1944.
137 "Bela Lugosi Star of Cast At Colonial." *Christian Science Monitor* 21 Mar. 1944.
138 "*Follow Girls* $44,000, Boston." *Variety* 5 Apr. 1944.
139 "Premiere Tonight of Seaton Comedy." *New York Times* 11 Apr. 1944.
140 "OWI Has No Reds, Says Elmer Davis." *New York Times* 29 Mar. 1944; "Legislator Charges Red

Activity Growing Here." *Los Angeles Times* 24 Mar. 1944.

141 "New Communists Active in Germany." *New York Times* 26 Mar. 1944.

142 "Hungary Reported Paying Nazi Costs." *New York Times* 28 Mar. 1944.

143 Juengst, William. "Radio." *Brooklyn Eagle* 7 Apr. 1944.

144 Brown, Chamberlain and Lyman. Letter to Bela Lugosi. 29 Mar. 1944. [Available in the Chamberlain and Lyman Brown Papers, and Undated, Series II: Correspondence, Box 64, Folder F.9 at the New York Public Library/Lincoln Center for the Performing Arts in New York.]

145 "Lugosi Stars In *Arsenic* At Locust." *Philadelphia Inquirer* 11 Apr. 1944.

146 "*Arsenic and* – Returns Again With Lugosi." *Philadelphia Record* 11 Apr. 1944.

147 "*Arsenic and Old Lace.*" *The Evening Bulletin* (Philadelphia, PA) 11 Apr. 1944.

148 "*Porgy* Tops 21G in 4th Philly Try." *Variety* 19 Apr. 1944.

149 Lee, Laura. "Murder with a Great Big Smile." *The Evening Bulletin* 12 Apr. 1944.

150 Finn, Elsie. "Beauty Hung A Hex Sign On Bela Lugosi!" *Philadelphia Record* 9 Apr. 1944.

151 Hall, Gladys. "The Case of the Man Who Dares Not Fall Asleep." *Motion Picture* Aug. 1929.

152 Gaghan, Jerry. "Cross Town." *Philadelphia Daily News* 22 Apr. 1944.

153 "Karolyi Heads Council." *New York Times* 12 Apr. 1944.

154 OSS FNB HU-521. *Subject: Hungarian Meeting.* 18 Apr. 1944. [Available in the US Office of Strategic Services, Foreign Nationalities Branch Files, 1942 - 1945.]

155 "Communists Active in Md. Shipyards, Priest Declares." *Washington Post* 15 Apr. 1944.

156 "FCC Aide Denies 'Red' Tie." *New York Times* 19 Apr. 1944.

157 Stanley, Fred. "Tempest in Hollywood." *New York Times* 23 Apr. 1944.

158 OSS FNB HU-534. Interoffice Memo, from T/3 Priediger to DeWitt C. Poole, *Subject: Mass Meeting American Hungarians, Manhattan Center.* 23 and 24 Apr. 1944. [Available in the US Office of Strategic Services, Foreign Nationalities Branch Files, 1942 - 1945.]

159 Ibid.

160 OSS FNB HU-545. *Report on Hungarian Anti-Nazi Meeting, Manhattan Center, New York.* 26 Apr. 1944. [Available in the US Office of Strategic Services, Foreign Nationalities Branch Files, 1942 - 1945.]

161 "Good Fun in *Arsenic and Old Lace.*" *Newark Star-Ledger* 26 Apr. 1944.

162 "Jolly Murders At the Mosque." *Newark Evening News* 25 Apr. 1944.

163 Advertisement. *Newark Evening News* 22 Apr. 1944.

164 "House of Chan Ashtray." Available at: http://www.newyorkfirst.com/gifts/house-of-chan-ashtray-339. Accessed 19 Feb. 2014.

165 Schallert, Edwin. "*Arsenic* Showing Set; Judy Gets Gala Break." *Los Angeles Times* 24 Apr. 1944.

166 "Inside Stuff – Legit." *Variety* 7 June 1944.

167 "Mrs. Berg Finishes First Act of Play." *New York Times* 29 Apr. 1944.

168 See, for example: "Current Road Shows." *Variety* 31 May 1944.

169 Stanley, Fred. "Hollywood Flash." *New York Times* 16 Apr. 1944.

170 "Beebe Double Chore." *Daily Variety* 26 Apr. 1944; "Universal Skeds 55 Features in New Yr." *Daily Variety* 12 June 1944; Universal Dishing Up Extra Dose of Chillers." *Daily Variety* 15 June 1944.

171 Ibid.

172 "Short Shorts." *Daily Variety* 17 July 1944; "*Daltons Ride Again* Is Top Budgeter at U." *Daily Variety* 29 Sept. 1944.

173 "Daily Data – From the Hotel de Dial Register." *Brooklyn Eagle* 4 May 1944.

174 Patterson, Pat. "On The Beam." *Mason City Globe-Gazette* (Mason City, IA) 5 May 1944.

175 Eaton, Hal. "Going to Town." *Jamaica Long Island Daily Press* (Jamaica, NY) 20 May 1944.

176 "Peace Investor." *Los Angeles Times* 22 May 1944.

177 "Patriotic Tunes Will Highlight *Barn Dance.*" *Lima News* (Lima, OH) 20 May 1944.

178 "Lugosi Into *Zombie.*" *Daily Variety* 11 Sept. 1944.

179 "Film 'Monster' Is Sued By Wife As 'Inhuman.'" *Binghamton Press* (Binghamton, NY) 18 Aug. 1944.

180 "A.M. Dailies." *Daily Variety* 21 Aug. 1944.

181 "Lugosi Shaves And His Wife Returns." *Hutchinson News-Herald* (Hutchinson, KS) 29 Oct. 1944.

182 "Group Formed to Save Jews from Blood Bath." *Los Angeles Times* 20 Aug. 1944.

183 Durant, Alta. "Gab." *Daily Variety* 30 Oct. 1944.

184 OSS FNB HU-555. *Subject: Hungarian Situation in Ohio and Michigan.* 10 and 11 May 1944. [Available in the US Office of Strategic Services, Foreign Nationalities Branch Files, 1942 - 1945.]

185 "The N. Y. Press This Morning: G.I. Joe and What He Reads." *New York Post, Daily Magazine Section* 17 July 1944.

186 Hoover, J. Edgar. Letter to the Special Agent in Charge. FBI Field office, Los Angeles. 5 Sept. 1944. [Copy exists in Lugosi's FBI file.]

187 OSS FNB HU-627. *Report on Hungarian Activities in California, Los Angeles, California.* 22 Sept. 1944. [Available in the US Office of Strategic Services, Foreign Nationalities Branch Files, 1942 - 1945.]

188 OSS FNB HU-672. Untitled Report, compiled shortly after a 14 Dec. 1944 meeting at the HACD office in New York City. [Available in the US Office of Strategic Services, Foreign Nationalities Branch Files, 1942 - 1945.]

Publicity portrait for *Return of the Ape Man* (1944).

Epilogue

Bela Lugosi's personal appearances from 1931 to 1945 provide crucial insight into his Hollywood career. The same is true of those from the end of World War II until his death in 1956, albeit in a very different manner. Save for the period during 1937 and 1938, Lugosi's personal appearances prior to the war's end augmented a vibrant screen career. Whenever Lugosi appeared live, he was a movie star in the flesh. It was as if he had stepped out of the screen, but still remained larger than life.

After the war, Lugosi's career increasingly relied upon summer stock, off-Broadway plays, vaudeville sketches, nightclub acts, and spook shows. Rather than augment his career, they became his career. His film output dwindled so much as to mean that – by the late 1940s and certainly the 1950s – many viewed him as a former screen star.

Certainly there were a few exceptions, most notably his role as Dracula in *Abbott and Costello Meet Frankenstein* (1948). But in general, Lugosi's personal appearances – drawing as they did on his old horror movies like *Dracula* – engaged not in a dialogue with an ongoing film career, but rather in a conversation with film history.

None of this is to say that Lugosi's presence was not still remarkable. To his costars and his fans, Lugosi in Person remained electric, enigmatic, and unforgettable. Some of this quality was the residual effect of having once been a movie star, one whose name was still prominent thanks to film reissues and television broadcasts of aging movies. But then some of it was his personality, one that transcended the cinema.

Lugosi and Robin Ladd in July 1950.

Consider, for example, Lugosi's summer stock appearance in *Dracula–The Vampire Play* at St. Michael's Theatre in Winooski Park, Vermont. The 21-year-old actress Robin Ladd portrayed Lucy in the 1950 production. Ladd recalled:

Bela's wife gave him cues in Hungarian behind the sets, if he missed an English cue. ... He was very pleasant ... [but he] didn't fool around; [he was] all business. He was somebody that you were rather in awe of. I was in awe of him because he had a professional way. ... He didn't talk much about himself. ... The point is that he was extremely attractive, attractive in his own way.[1]

Ladd added that, while Lugosi largely kept to himself, he was a "totally different person" offstage than on, "very much a gentleman."[2]

For that very same production, student intern Margaret O'Brien worked backstage. She remembered:

It took me a while to realize what was striking me, and it was that he was not just a unique Dracula, but he was an excellent actor. And when we the students, we would visit with him, talk with him, he would talk to us, he was interested in students. Yes, he made it so easy to talk to him. To tell him what you were hoping to do. ... He interacted extremely well. A lot of times the actors after the show would party down in the green room or something like that. But he would be talking on the porch with us! I don't want you to get the wrong impression here. I don't mean this was an everyday occurrence. But I just remember that we would sit on the porch with him. And he wanted to know about what we wanted to do.[3]

O'Brien observed that onstage Lugosi was "terrifying," his use of the cape being so expert that it was "almost another actor." Offstage, Lugosi was "totally different. He was incredibly considerate, low-key, very, very friendly, and just the opposite [of Dracula] obviously."

But while Lugosi in Person held the power to fascinate, Lugosi the Man could not successfully translate the same into a cinematic comeback. Each new personal appearance of the post-war era seems in retrospect to signal his distance from Hollywood, if not always geographical then certainly professional.

At a given point, certainly between 1952 and 1956, the number of Lugosi's personal appearances abated to the degree that he no longer had a career, but rather extremely rare engagements during an era of involuntary semi-retirement.

Lugosi had entered another terrain, an undiscovered country, from whose bourn no traveler returns.

(Endnotes)

1   Qtd. in Lord, William. Email to Bill Kaffenberger. 16 Feb. 2015.
2   Qtd. in Lord, William. Email to Bill Kaffenberger. 3 Jan. 2015
3   Kaffenberger, Bill. Interview with Margaret O'Brien. 14 May 2013.

Lugosi in the stage play *No Traveler Returns* (1945).

Lisa Mitchell in a production of
Lillian Hellman's *The Children's Hour* at The Players Ring Theatre in
West Hollywood, California, 1956.
(Courtesy of Lisa Mitchell)

Afterword

By Lisa Mitchell

Perhaps it was only a delayed adolescence of fevered fandom that made me so crazy about Bela Lugosi in my twenties and thirties. Then again, perhaps not. I have come to believe that I had good reason for being besotted. There was, after all, just something about him. But I sensed it long before becoming an adult zealot. In fact, I felt it before I'd even seen him on the screen in his signature roles. In a reversal of most of the stories in this book, my Lugosi connection didn't culminate with beholding him in person. It began with it.

From 1953 to 1956, between the ages of 13 and 16, I used to see Mister Lugosi on a regular basis, as we lived within three blocks of each other in the same Hollywood neighborhood. I wasn't driving yet and he never drove, so we both went everywhere on foot, which made for many sightings. This was when he was 71 through 73, the last, three, painful years of his life. (His death in 1956 was two months before his 74th birthday.)

As I came home from school or was on my way to a dance class, there he'd be walking along Hollywood Boulevard. When I went shopping at the A&P, he'd pass me slowly wheeling his cart down the aisles. My mother called him "a regular Hollywood character."

No matter where or when I saw him, this tall, thin, old man was always alone; always smoking a cigar. Summer or winter, night or day, I don't remember his wearing anything but open-collared, short-sleeved, bright sports shirts, tan Bermuda shorts and sandals – a uniform that revealed long, skinny arms and legs, networked by protruding veins and stringy muscles. His steel grey hair was combed straight back from a high forehead. Without speaking a word, he magnetized me by locking his gaze to mine. He never smiled, but narrowed his eyes (probably because of the cigar smoke in them) as he looked at me, which made his penetrating stare a little scary but kind of wonderful. It was as though dot-dot-dot lines zapped from his eyes to mine the way they do in comic books. I was fascinated beyond all reason.

"Dracula," my father whispered one night after coming upon Mister Lugosi at the Midnite Delicatessen – the first time for me to see him there but not the last. The Midnite was a neighborhood deli on the south side of Hollywood Boulevard between Western and Serrano that stayed open quite late. My father frequently walked there from our apartment on Garfield Place to get the evening papers and buy some ice cream or a quart of milk. On weekends throughout the school year, and on weeknights during summer vacations, I accompanied him. "Dracula," my father repeated on the way home. "You know. Bela Lugosi."

So, the mysterious man was a Hungarian actor, and the Transylvanian Count was his most famous role. It wasn't easy for me to put him together with the character I saw as a child in *Abbott and Costello Meet Frankenstein* (1948), but I liked the idea. When I heard that he used to be a big star in many horror movies, it sounded right. Eventually, when Dad and I walked into the Midnite and saw Bela, a subtle recognition developed between the three of us. I used to hang around the counter when he was paying for his packages, trying to hear what he was saying to Jack, the man behind the register. Of course, what I was really hoping for was that he would say something to me. He never did … but neither did he stop staring.

He did, however, speak to my father, who was the manager of Price's, a men's shoe store on Hollywood and Ivar, which Lugosi often visited. Mostly he'd just browse around, Dad said, but once he bought a pair of sandals. He seemed to like the atmosphere there and my father invited him to use the store as a rest stop during his long walks anytime he wished. He'd just sit quietly in the back, sort of meditating, my father recalled, that is, staring off into space. Sometimes he'd take out a little notebook that he would read. Once in awhile, he'd engage in some conversation with my father and one of the salesmen. My father said that Lugosi didn't seem to see a bright future for himself and did not like to talk about past glories. When asked about his successful days, he answered quickly and changed the subject.

But, Dad felt, there were times when he wanted "to get things off his chest." He was polite and grateful to my father for listening to his "tales of woe" and thanked him for always making him feel comfortable and welcome. If only he could have known that one day, Bela Lugosi would have his own star on the Hollywood Walk of Fame – right across from where Price's shoe store once stood.

Early in 1955, I saw an already thin man become emaciated. In April, I found out why. Newspapers reported that Bela had courageously committed himself to a county general hospital for treatment to overcome a medically induced drug addiction. By August, he was cured and twenty days after his release, got married for the fifth time. The following August, 1956, his new wife found him dead of a heart attack in their Hollywood apartment on Harold Way.

The young teenager so smitten with Lugosi in his eleventh hour, became, at twenty-eight, a self-proclaimed connoisseur of the professional actor. After seeing *Dracula* (1931), I tracked down such other gems as *The Black Cat*, 1934 ("Supernatural, perhaps. Baloney, perhaps not"), *The Raven*, 1935 ("It's *more* than a hobby"), and began a life-long habit of memorizing his dialog. But as attracted as I was to his horror film persona, I was always knocked out by his versatility. Look at him holding his own with W.C. Fields in *International House* (1933), playing the "good" scientist opposite Boris

Karloff in *The Invisible Ray* (1936), and stealing scenes from Greta Garbo in *Ninotchka* (1939). At one point, I bought a little newsreel of Bela being interviewed on a ship as he arrived in London in 1952. Seeing him smiling, charming, funny, was an antidote to some images of his last days, as were photographs I found showing his happy camaraderie with some Hungarian friends.

I began writing about Lugosi for various publications in my mid-thirties, and though I'm no longer the nutty young woman who planned a trip to Transylvania, to this day, I never fail to marvel at a screen presence like no other. Bela has, indeed, withstood the test of time – mine and the world's. In the old days, there was always a competition among horror fans as to who was the greater star, Karloff or Lugosi. While taking nothing away from the brilliant Boris, today I believe that Lugosi wins, hands down, as new generations fall under his spell.

Film historian James D'Arc, agreed. Discussing Lugosi's appeal in April, 2015, he pinned Bela's staying power to his peculiar "mystique." There was, in Lugosi, "the frayed boundary between the suave and sinister, due, in part, to his thick Hungarian accent, his halting delivery and his lithe good looks." Even when no longer young, Lugosi maintained a "credibility in the myriad parts he played."

When D'Arc said that the Dracula character itself, "while lamenting the state of being undead, was reconciled to making the most of it," I thought of Lugosi's long relationship, for better or worse, with the Count: "It's a living," he'd often say. There was, in fact, a certain nobility in his making "the most of" Dracula by traversing the country with him, appearing wherever he could, a good man, caring for his family.

I have lived in the Hollywood hills now for many years where, on my walks in Beachwood Canyon, I regularly look at two old English brick houses on Westshire Drive where Lugosi once lived in his palmier days. I love seeing them, standing next door to each other (he had lived in both, by turns) because it's as though, after all this time, we are still living in the same neighborhood. I think of the first time I saw them on a dark, shadowy night decades ago. I was standing on the balcony of a friend's house, which was across the street from Lugosi's, and a bat suddenly came out of nowhere and flew straight over to Bela's place. It was the only bat I have ever seen in all my years in Hollywood.

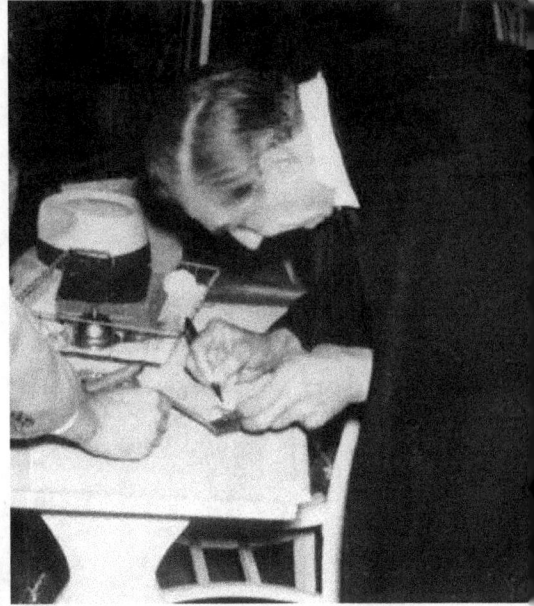

Lisa Mitchell has written for newspapers, magazines, films and television. A former actress, she specializes in writing and lecturing about Hollywood's Golden Age and is the author, with Bruce Torrence, of *The Hollywood Canteen: Where The Greatest Generation Danced With The Most Beautiful Girls In The World* (BearManor Media, 2012).

Lugosi in Tod Browning's film *Dracula* (1931).

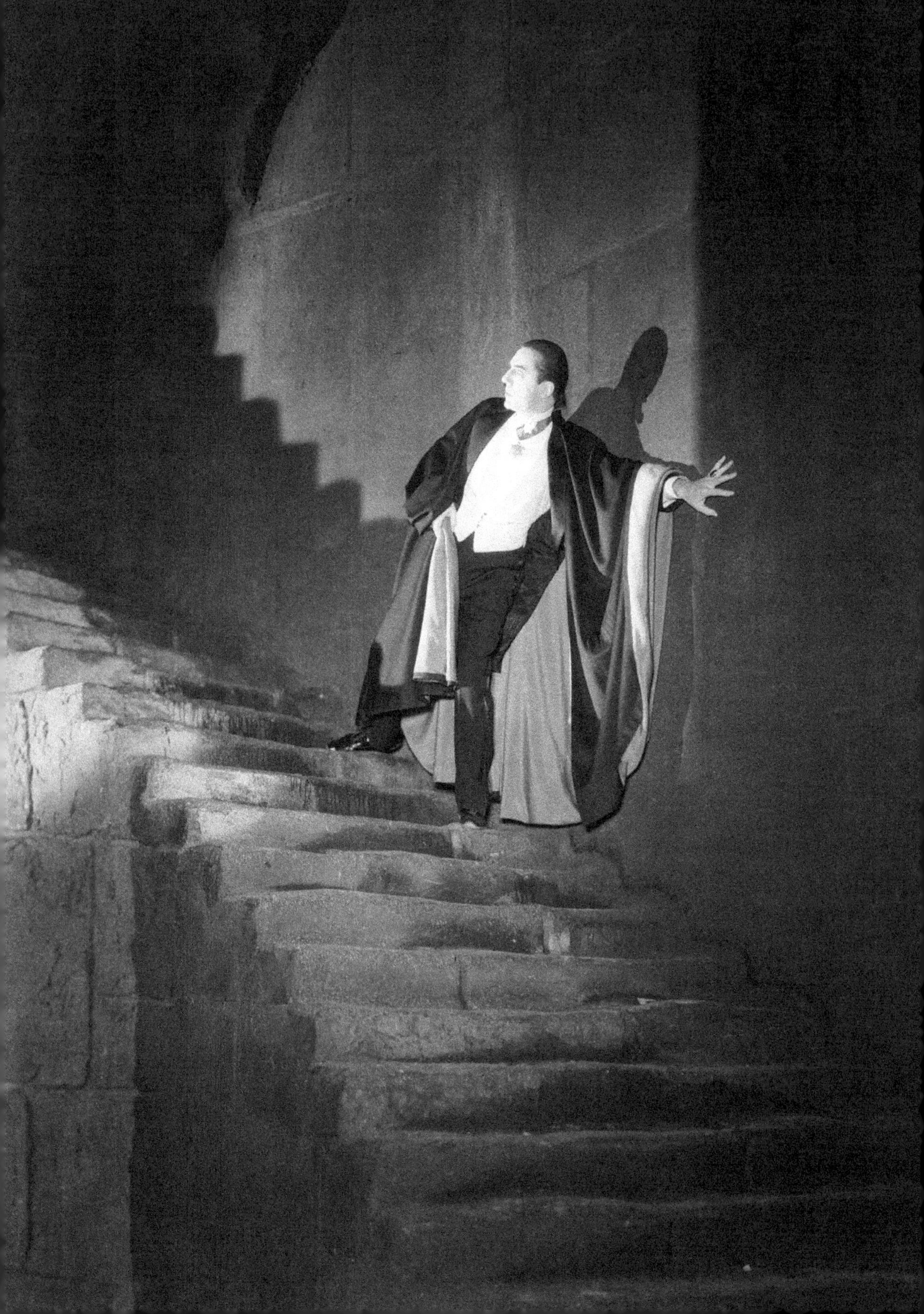

Timeline of Personal Appearances

T he following timeline catalogs Bela Lugosi's personal appearances in North America from the time of the release of *Dracula* in February 1931 until the time of Lugosi's death in August 1956.

These live appearances include movie premieres, vaudeville sketches, variety shows, stage plays, nightclub acts, spook shows, music concerts, sporting events, court dates, wartime rallies, and political speeches. Social events that were covered in the press are listed, as are impromptu public meetings with fans. In addition, cancelled events are also catalogued.

Among the various features of this timeline are new findings for the years from 1945 to 1951, a period previously covered in *No Traveler Returns: The Lost Years of Bela Lugosi* (Bear Manor Media, 2012).

This timeline should be considered a work-in-progress, as new data will likely emerge regarding either the events covered herein or those that have not yet been discovered.

1931

Friday, 3/27: BL attended the Los Angeles premiere of *Dracula* at the Orpheum Theatre (2,000 seats) with future wife Lillian Arch. No advertisements promoted this appearance, which does not seem to have been arranged by Universal Pictures. Likewise, it does not seem that BL appeared onstage.

Friday, 4/17: Along with a number of other Hollywood celebrities, BL attended the premiere of Universal's *Seed* (1931) at the Carthay Circle Theatre (1,518 seats) in Los Angeles.

Saturday, 7/25: BL was one of several special guests at the California Newspaper Publishers Association banquet meeting held at the Fontana Inn in Fontana, CA. Also in attendance was Willy Pogany.

Monday, 7/27: BL attended the "Spirit of Notre Dame"

★★★★★★★★★★★
Attend with
THE STARS!!
TONITE 11:30 P.M.
Lt. HUGH CROWLEY
TRIBUTE BENEFIT
Complete
LOEW'S STATE SHOW
and FOLLOWING STARS
IN PERSON
▼
ROBERT MONTGOMERY
SALLY EILERS
HOOT GIBSON
GEORGE BANCROFT
WALLACE BEERY
TOM MIX
FRANK FAY
BARBARA STANWYCK
JAMES GLEASON
BOB ARMSTRONG
ELISSA LANDI
BELA LUGOSI
BERT HANLON
POLLY MORAN
MINNA GOMBELL
RUBE WOLFE
CHINESE THEATRE STAGE SHOW
PARAMOUNT STAGE SHOW
LUCKY DAY COMPANY
GENE MORGAN
SAM JACK KAUFMAN
10 ARABIAN NIGHTS
ERNY PINCKERT
POLICE BAND
FIREMAN'S BAND
HOLLYWOOD LEGION
FIFE AND DRUM CORPS
and many, many others

◄———————————►
Staged by FANCHON and
SID GRAUMAN
★★★★★★★★★★★

From the *Los Angeles Times*
of January 30, 1932.

Lugosi at an unknown event in the 1930s.

luncheon along with Leo Carrillo, Mae Clarke, George Sidney, Sidney Fox, Ricardo Cortez, James Whale, and others. The luncheon was held in honor of Knute Rockne and the upcoming Universal film about his life. Mrs. Knute Rockne was also present.

Wednesday, 11/11: Along with Michael Curtiz, Carla Laemmle, Paul Lukas, Victor Varconi, Willy Pogany and others, BL attended a joint recital of Antonio Albanese (an Italian piano virtuoso) and Joseph Diskay (a Hungarian tenor) in the Cortile Lido Salon at Hollywood's Knickerbocker Hotel.

Wednesday, 11/25: On this day, the press announced that Preston Duncan had recently entertained over 200 guests with a special reception and tea at his new studio on Vine Street. In attendance were BL, Constance Bennett, Billie Dove, Mary Astor, Ann Harding, Jean Harlow, Thelma Todd, Myrna Loy, Monte Blue, Roland Young, Randolph Scott, Alan Hale and others.

1932

Saturday, 1/30: BL was one of many stars who appeared at Loew's State Theatre (2,422 seats) at an evening benefit for Lt. Hugh Crowley.

Friday, 2/26: BL attended the Western Association of Motion Picture Advertisers (WAMPAS) meeting and show at the Writers Club in Hollywood. The festivities included music, a comedy skit, and a testimonial for Carl Laemmle, Sr. In addition to BL, guests included Louella O. Parsons, Jean Hersholt, Anita Louise, Gloria Stuart, Onslow Stevens, Lupita Tovar, and Paul Kohner.

Murdered Alive
Saturday, 4/2 - Saturday, 4/16: Carthay Circle Theatre (1,500 seats), Los Angeles.

Lugosi at the beach in the 1930s.

Lugosi with unidentified friends in the 1930s.

Rehearsals for the play had started around March 24.

Friday, 4/22 - Thursday, 4/28: RKO Orpheum (2,900 seats), San Francisco.

Saturday, 4/30 - Thursday, 5/5: RKO Orpheum (2,000 seats), Los Angeles.

Wednesday, 5/18: BL spent several days in San Bernardino as a guest of Cornelius "The Count" de Bakcsy and his wife.

Dracula

Sunday, 5/29 - Saturday, 6/4: El Capitan Theatre, Portland, OR. BL in *Dracula–The Vampire Play*.

Tuesday, 9/20: Along with such cast members as Irene Ware, BL appeared onstage at a screening of *Chandu the Magician* (1932) at the Loew's State Theatre (2,422 seats).

Wednesday, 11/23: BL appeared at an "informal Russian salon" hosted in the home of Mr. and Mrs. Peter Terry.

Friday, 12/16: BL and Boris Karloff were among those who dedicated an international Christmas tree at Hollywood's Hotel Christie.

1933

Week of 2/11: At some point during this week, Ferike Boros entertained BL, Willy Pogany and a number of others at Eugene Stark's Hollywood Cafe.

August: At some point during this month, Willy Pogany gave a tea party at his Hollywood hillside home attended by BL, his wife Lillian, Charlie Chaplin, Alice White, Claudette Colbert, Adrienne Ames, and others.

Murder at the Vanities

Monday, 8/28 - Wednesday, 9/6: BL appeared in the off-Broadway tryout of *Murder at the Vanities* at the Garrick Theatre (1,800 seats), Philadelphia, PA.

Lugosi visiting a film set in England in 1935. To his screen right are Margaret Lockwood and Hughie Green.

Tuesday, 9/12 - Sunday, 12/3: BL appeared in *Murder at the Vanities* at the New Amsterdam Theatre (1,702 seats) on Broadway. On November 6, the show switched locations to the Majestic Theatre (1,645 seats), where it remained even after BL left the production on December 3. During the course of the production, BL made local appearances at area restaurants and clubs, one of which was a Mickey Mouse birthday celebration at the Hollywood Restaurant.

Bela Lugosi Vaudeville Tour
Tuesday, 12/5 - Thursday, 12/7: BL premiered his first vaudeville show at Loew's Gates Theatre (2,868 seats), Brooklyn.
Friday, 12/8 - Thursday, 12/14: BL's vaudeville tour moved to the Loew's State Theatre (3,327 seats) on Broadway.
Friday, 12/15 - Thursday, 12/21: BL's vaudeville show at the Loew's Stanley Theatre (3,287 seats) in Baltimore, MD.
Friday, 12/22 - Thursday, 12/28: BL's vaudeville show at the Loew's Fox Theatre (3,433 seats) in Washington, D.C.

1934

Saturday, 2/10: BL was a guest of honor at the Hungarian Artists' Ball held in New York City at the Pennsylvania Hotel.

Lugosi at a soccer game with Victor McLaglen (far right) in the mid-1930s. *(Courtesy of Jack Dowler)*

Wednesday, 3/14: BL and Boris Karloff participated in the "Black Cat Day" at Universal Pictures. Local children presented their black cats for the two actors to judge.

Tuesday, 4/10: BL and Boris Karloff attended a "barn dance" given at Universal City Stage 4 in support of the Motion Picture Theatre Owners of America (MPTOA). Others in attendance were Andy Devine, Alice White, Lillian Bond, Buck Jones and Onslow Stevens.

Thursday, 5/3: BL, Boris Karloff, and Jacqueline Wells appeared at the Hollywood premiere of *The Black Cat* (1934) at the Pantages Theatre (2,703 seats).

Friday 5/18 - Sunday 5/20: BL and Boris Karloff participated in the "Film Stars Frolic" (also known as the "First Annual Fiesta"), which the Screen Actors Guild presented at the Gilmore Stadium in Hollywood. Eddie Cantor led the grand opening parade. Among the stars scheduled to appear were Frederic March, James Cagney, Paul Muni, Lee Tracy, Ralph Bellamy, Stuart Erwin, Richard Arlen, Gloria Stuart, June Collyer, Edmund Lowe and others. More than 50,000 people visited the stadium and the presentation of film stars, circus, rodeo and Mardi Gras-style entertainments.

Saturday, 6/9: BL and Beth Kosik sponsored a program of Hungarian music for a meeting of the International Friendship Alliance at the Melrose Hotel in Los Angeles. Among the scheduled guests was Dr. Theodore Von Karmon of the California Institute of Technology.

September: At some point during this month, BL attended a performance by the Russian tenor/musician Saveli Walevitch.

Sunday, 11/25: BL, Boris Karloff, Gloria Stuart, Buck Jones, and others attended a spaghetti party at the Beverly Hills home of Henry Armetta.

Lugosi and Lillian receive the key to the city. *(Courtesy of Bill Chase)*

1935

Saturday, 1/26: BL was scheduled to appear along with a number of other stars in a benefit show at the Shrine Auditorium (6,442 seats) in Los Angeles in support of the Mt. Sinai Home.

Wednesday, 5/29 - Tuesday, 6/4 (?): BL definitely appeared at the Hollywood Motion Picture Hall of Fame exhibit at the Pacific International Exposition in San Diego on 5/29. While it is uncertain, news reports at the time implied that he was in San Diego for approximately one week.

Thursday, 7/4 - Friday, 7/5: On two consecutive evenings, BL took bows at the New York City premiere of *The Raven* (1935) at the Roxy Theatre (5,886 seats).

Sunday, 9/15: BL and Lillian slipped away from Hollywood to the San Bernardino area for a short visit with their friend Cornelius "The Count" de Bakcsy and his wife.

October: At some point during this month, Lilly Pons hosted a house party at which BL, Boris Karloff and Peter Lorre were present.

Sunday, 11/10: BL attended a reception given by Carl Laemmle, Sr. at the Beverly Wilshire for Hungarian opera singer and film star Marta Eggerth.

Tuesday, 11/26: BL was one of many celebrities attending a private preview of the new Max Factor Building in Hollywood.

Friday, 11/29: BL and Lillian hosted a Hungarian midnight supper in honor of wrestler Sandor Szabo. Other guests included Willy Pogany, Duci de Kerekjarto, Melchior (Menyhért) Lengyel, and Ervin Nyíregyházi.

December: BL became honorary president of the Los Angeles Soccer League. BL was in attendance at numerous soccer games and related functions during the course of his Hollywood career, particularly between 1935 and 1941.

Monday, 12/16: BL rode in the Christmas procession down "Santa Claus Lane" in Los Angeles along with Clyde Beatty and Alan Dinehart.

1936

Saturday, 2/22: BL participated in the Screen Actors Guild ball at the Biltmore Ballroom in Los Angeles. The guest list consisted of over 600 Hollywood personalities, among them Robert Armstrong, Sally Blane, Joseph Cawthorne, Joan Crawford, Marlene Dietrich, Errol Flynn, Preston Foster, Frank Lawton, Francis Lederer, Fredric March, Gloria Swanson, Victor McLaglen, and Fay Wray.

Monday, 2/24: Along with more than 300 other past and present screen personalities, BL attended a thirtieth anniversary celebration for Carl Laemmle, Sr. at Universal Pictures.

Tuesday, 2/25: BL participated in the Screen Actors Guild "Midwinter Labor Frolic," staged at the Shrine Auditorium. BL served on the co-operating committee along with James Cagney, Ralph Morgan, Louis Wilson, and Lucille Webster Gleason.

Monday, 3/16: BL appeared in Municipal Court in Los Angeles as a witness against defendant Mano Glucksman, former executive of a theatre chain in New York City. Glucksman was accused of forging BL's name to a check on a London bank.

Wednesday, 4/22: BL was one of many attendees at yet another gala celebration honoring Carl Laemmle's thirtieth year in show business.

Tuesday, 5/12: BL, Buster Crabbe, and other celebrities presented awards at the Pre-Olympic Track Carnival held at the Whittier College Stadium in Whittier, CA.

Saturday, 6/6: BL and Los Angeles Mayor Shaw opened the Hungarian National Day. The celebration featured a parade with floats.

Sunday, 6/28: BL participated in a Hungarian Day Celebration at the Riverside Breakfast Club. Among the sponsors were Michael Curtiz, Claudette Colbert, Myrna Loy, Wallace Beery, Joe E. Brown, Errol Flynn and Paul Lukas.

Wednesday, 7/1: BL and Rochelle Hudson performed a scene from *Dracula* (presumably the stage play) as part of the Annual Benefit for the Actors' Fund of America. Also known as the *Night of 1,000 Stars*, the show took place at the Pan-Pacific Auditorium and featured

Lugosi and his son circa 1940.

such stars as Clark Gable, Jean Harlow, Charlie Chaplin, Mary Pickford, Warren William, Clarence Muse, Laurel and Hardy, Victor McLaglen, and Bette Davis.

Tuesday, 7/14: BL was the guest speaker at a concert of Hungarian music at the Redlands Bowl near San Bernardino.

Sunday, 7/19: Alongside beauty pageant winner Irene Nagy, BL served as the co-chairperson of Oakland's Hungarian Celebration at the La Honda Bowl. In his additional role as honorary mayor of Oakland, BL led a caravan of cars filled with fellow Hungarians. Among their passengers were Duci de Kerekjarto and Joseph Diskay.

1937

Tovarich

Friday, 3/19 - Saturday, 3/20: Lobero Theatre (604 seats), Santa Barbara.

Monday, 3/22 - Saturday, 4/17: Curran Theatre (1,667 seats), San Francisco. During the run of the play in San Francisco, BL made an appearance at the Tanforan Racetrack's "*Tovarich* Day."

Monday, 4/19 - Saturday, 5/15: Biltmore Theatre (1,654 seats), Los Angeles.

1938

Thursday, 8/11 - Thursday, 8/25: BL made stage appearances at 10PM each night at the Regina Theatre (785 seats) in Beverly Hills in support of its triple bill of *Dracula* (1931), *Frankenstein* (1931) and *The Son of Kong* (1933). The bracketed dates given here are estimates based on contemporary trade publication reports of the time.

Saturday, 12/31: BL was one of many celebrities attending the fifth meeting of the Los Angeles Turf Club at the Santa Anita Raceway.

1939

Thursday, 3/23: BL held a press conference for interviewers at the Waldorf Astoria Hotel in New York City.

Saturday, 5/27: The press reported that BL caused a stir when returning to Los Angeles after his trip to Great Britain. Crowds of fans surrounded him for autographs.

Arthur Treacher, Lugosi, Marjorie Weaver, and Helen Parrish guest star on radio during the *Stardust Cavalcade* tour. Photograph taken in Youngstown, Ohio.

Sunday, 6/18: BL was one of dozens of guests attending a cocktail party given by producer Joe Pasternak in honor of S. Z. "Cuddles" Sakall, Hungarian-born comedian.

Wednesday, 8/9: BL, along with wife Lillian, attended a shower sponsored by the local Hungarian colony in honor of Miss Esther Fellegi's upcoming wedding to John F. McManus. The celebration was held at St. Stephen's Hall in Los Angeles.

Sunday, 8/27: Along with Boris Karloff and various others, BL participated in a Screen Actors Guild Meeting held at the American Legion Stadium.

Sunday, 9/10: BL gave a speech at the "Press Day Festival" held at the Czechoslovak Park in La Crescenta, CA.

Week of 10/8: Along with Allan Rivkin, Dore Schary, and others, BL was a guest speaker at the Overseas Press Club of America's luncheon forum. The exact date has not yet been determined.

Wednesday, 10/25: On this day, *Variety* reported that BL would appear as the headliner in a vaudeville unit at the RKO Keith's State-Lake Theatre (2,734 seats) in Chicago. However, there is no evidence that this show occurred.

Friday, 12/15: BL, along with Karloff, Auer, Nan Grey and John Sutton, made personal appearances at San Francisco's Warfield Theatre in support of the film *Tower of London* (1939).

1940

Sunday, 1/14: Hedda Hopper reported that she had recently interviewed BL and Boris Karloff together at Karloff's home in Coldwater Canyon.

Thursday, 1/18: In front of the press and newsreel cameras, Manly P. Hall allegedly hypnotized BL so that BL would more realistically perform a scene in *Black Friday* (1940).

Thursday, 2/29: BL and Vincent Price made a personal appearance in support of a double bill of *Black Friday* and *The House of the Seven Gables* (1940) at the RKO Palace Theatre (2,451 seats) in Chicago.

Thursday, 3/14: On this day, the Associated Actors and Artists of America held the "Gambol of the Stars" in the Cocoanut Grove at LA's Ambassador Hotel. Along with Boris Karloff and others, BL appeared in a sketch called "How to Maintain Order at a Party". Others participating in the "Gambol" included Edward G. Robinson, Lionel Barrymore, Jack Benny, Mickey Rooney, Ernest Truex, and Eduardo Ciannelli.

Ed Sullivan's Stardust Cavalcade

Saturday, 3/30 - Wednesday, 4/3: Colonial Theatre (1,800 seats), Dayton, OH.

Thursday, 4/4 - Saturday, 4/6: Stanley Theatre (3,719 seats), Pittsburgh, PA.

Sunday, 4/7: Capitol Theatre (2,000 seats), Steubenville, OH.

Monday, 4/8 - Thursday, 4/11: Stanley Theatre (3,719 seats), Pittsburgh, PA. During the Pittsburgh run, BL met with local college professor Dr. Martin I. J. Griffin.

Friday, 4/12 - Monday, 4/15: State Theatre (3,064 seats), Hartford, CT. During the travel time between Pittsburgh and Hartford, BL and the cast created a stir when passing through Grand Central Station in Manhattan.

Thursday, 4/18 - Wednesday, 4/24: Loew's State Theatre (3,327 seats), New York City. BL made a number of informal appearances while in New York, including at the Hurricane Club, the Versailles Club, the Beachcomber, and Sardi's. BL was also on the bill at the American

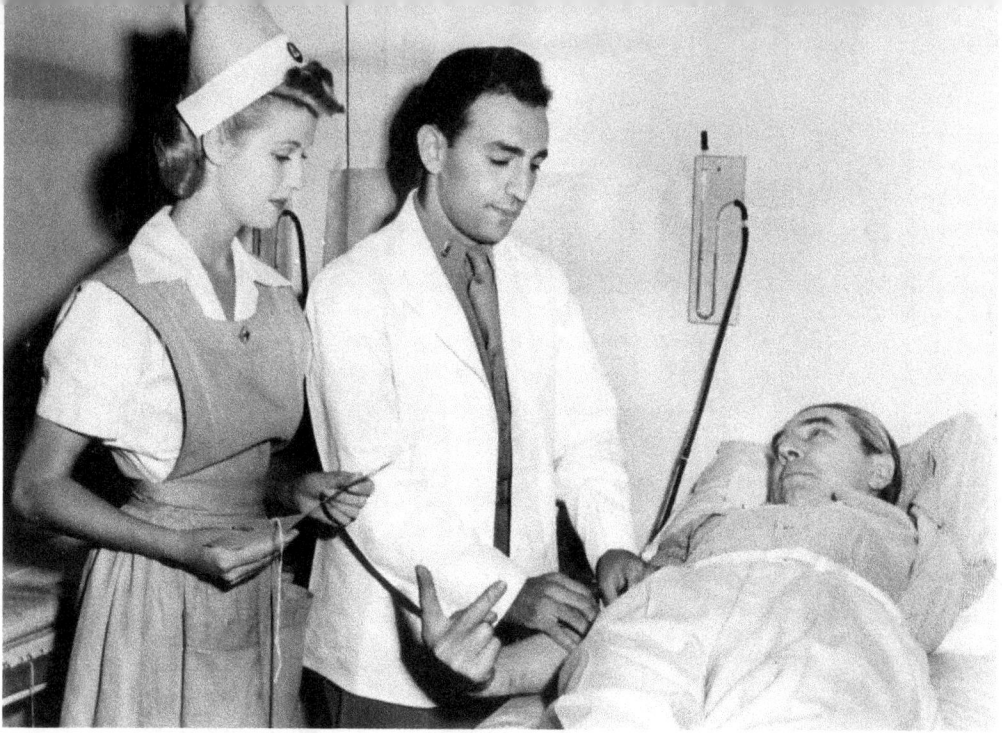

Lugosi prepares to give blood in 1943. *(Courtesy of Jack Dowler)*

Newspaper Publishers Convention (exact date unknown), and was apparently in attendance (on April 21) at the Associated Actors and Artists of America Ball.

Thursday, 4/25: Press gathering and cocktail party at the Hotel Carlton in Washington, D.C.

Friday, 4/26 - Thursday, 5/2: Capitol Theatre (3,432 seats), Washington, D.C.

Friday, 5/3 - Monday, 5/6: Palace Theatre (2,100 seats), Akron, OH.

Tuesday, 5/7 - Wednesday, 5/8: Palace Theatre (2,400 seats), Youngstown, OH.

Thursday, 7/25: BL was an honorary pallbearer at the funeral of John (János) Kurucz, a Hungarian composer. Other honorary pallbearers included Victor Varconi and Steven Székely (aka Steve Sekely).

Tuesday, 9/24: BL likely attended a preview screening of *Spring Parade* (1940) with Deanna Durbin at the Hollywood Pantages Theatre. He was invited, but whether he actually attended is unknown.

Saturday, 9/28: BL gave a speech at the inauguration of Hungaria House in Los Angeles.

Wednesday, 11/13: BL, Boris Karloff, and Helen Parrish attended the Los Angeles premiere of *You'll Find Out* (1940).

Tuesday, 12/10: As part of a Christmas celebration in Los Angeles, BL rode in the "Santa Claus Sleigh" with John Wayne and Russell Gleason.

1941

Thursday 1/16: Along with Suzanne Kaaren, Sidney Blackmer, and others, BL and Lillian attended a wedding reception for Sue Taylor and Arthur Whitney at the Florentine Gardens in LA.

One Night of Horror

Friday, 5/2 - Thursday, 5/8: BL appeared in *One Night of Horror* at the Oriental Theatre (3,250 seats) in Chicago. Structured like a vaudeville bill and paired with the film *Invisible Ghost* (1941), *One Night of Horror* presented BL onstage in a spook show-style sketch.

Saturday, 5/10 - Sunday, 5/11: BL appeared at the Palace Theatre (1,157 seats) in Fort Wayne, Indiana. In large measure, the show was the same as it had been in Chicago; however, it was retitled *Mirth and Horror*. While it seems the brief tour might have continued, BL reportedly fell ill, cut short the Fort Wayne appearance, and returned to Los Angeles.

Lugosi at an unknown event, probably related to his wartime political activities, circa 1944 or 1945.

1942

Wednesday, 1/21: Along with Warren William, Lionel Atwill, Claire Dodd, Nat Pendleton, Maria Ouspenskaya, and Evelyn Ankers, BL appeared at the Vogue Theatre (897 seats) in Los Angeles in support of a double bill screening of *The Wolf Man* (1941) and *The Mad Doctor of Market Street* (1942).

Thursday, 3/26: Along with Lionel Atwill, Evelyn Ankers, and Lon Chaney, Jr., BL appeared at two theatres in the LA area to promote *The Ghost of Frankenstein* (1942): the Pantages (2,812 seats) and the RKO Hillstreet (2,890 seats).

Sunday, 3/29: BL was a guest speaker at a Red Cross benefit sponsored by the United Hungarian-American Defense Federation and held at the Polytechnic High School in LA. Other attendees included Ilona Massey, Joe Pasternak, and Michael Curtiz.

Wednesday, 8/26: Press reports claimed that BL had arrived in Chicago for a four week engagement in *Dracula–The Vampire Play* at the Cohan Grand Opera House. However, the play was cancelled.

Friday, 8/28: BL spoke at the Philharmonic Auditorium in Los Angeles in support of Jews being victimized by the Axis Powers.

Wednesday, 11/25: BL spoke before the United Nations Committee of Southern California, announcing that Hungarian-Americans were loyal to the United States and its efforts to defeat the Axis Powers.

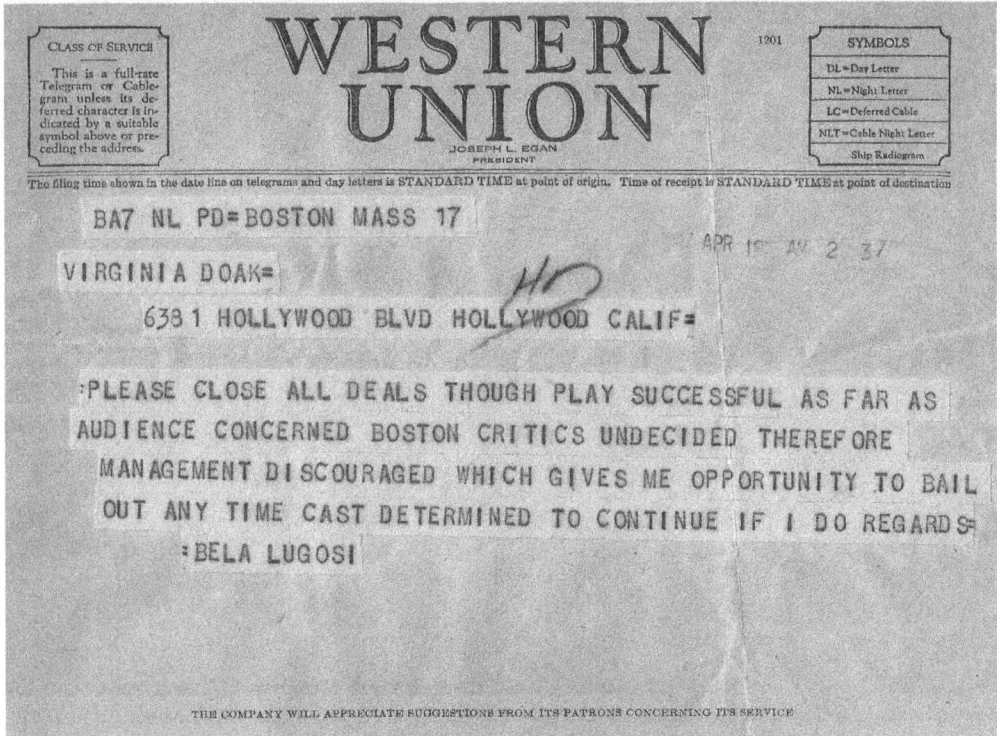

WESTERN UNION

CLASS OF SERVICE

This is a full-rate Telegram or Cablegram unless its deferred character is indicated by a suitable symbol above or preceding the address.

1201

SYMBOLS

DL = Day Letter
NL = Night Letter
LC = Deferred Cable
NLT = Cable Night Letter
Ship Radiogram

JOSEPH L. EGAN
PRESIDENT

The filing time shown in the date line on telegrams and day letters is STANDARD TIME at point of origin. Time of receipt is STANDARD TIME at point of destination.

BA7 NL PD= BOSTON MASS 17

APR 18 AM 2 37

VIRGINIA DOAK=

6381 HOLLYWOOD BLVD HOLLYWOOD CALIF=

:PLEASE CLOSE ALL DEALS THOUGH PLAY SUCCESSFUL AS FAR AS AUDIENCE CONCERNED BOSTON CRITICS UNDECIDED THEREFORE MANAGEMENT DISCOURAGED WHICH GIVES ME OPPORTUNITY TO BAIL OUT ANY TIME CAST DETERMINED TO CONTINUE IF I DO REGARDS=

:BELA LUGOSI

THE COMPANY WILL APPRECIATE SUGGESTIONS FROM ITS PATRONS CONCERNING ITS SERVICE

Lugosi's telegram to his agent here refers to the play *Three Indelicate Ladies* (1947). *(Courtesy of D'Arcy More)*

1943

Wednesday, 3/17: On this day, *Daily Variety* reported that BL would make a personal appearance in support of Monogram's *The Ape Man* (1943) at the Colony Theatre (500 seats) on Hollywood Boulevard. No evidence has yet surfaced to suggest that appearance took place.

Dracula–The Vampire Play

Friday, 4/30: Klein Auditorium (1,400 seats), Bridgeport, CT.

Saturday, 5/1: Bushnell Auditorium (2,800 seats), Hartford, CT.

Monday, 5/3 - Saturday, 5/15: Plymouth Theatre (1,500 seats), Boston, MA.

Sunday, 5/9: Camp Framingham, MA. BL also made a speech to the American soldiers attending this show.

Wednesday, 5/19 - Saturday, 5/29: Locust Street Theatre (1,580 seats), Philadelphia, PA.

Thursday, 5/20: BL gave a speech at the Globe Hoist Company in support of the war effort.

Sunday, 5/23: Fort Meade, MD.

Monday, 5/31 - Saturday, 6/5: Erlanger Theatre (1,500 seats), Buffalo, NY.

Monday, 6/7 - Sunday, 6/13: Hanna Theatre (1,535 seats), Cleveland, OH.

Monday, 6/14 - Saturday, 6/19: Nixon Theatre (2,500 seats), Pittsburgh, PA. While in Pittsburgh, BL was guest of honor at a Verhovay Association Dinner. He and the cast also ate dinner one evening at Emma's Café.

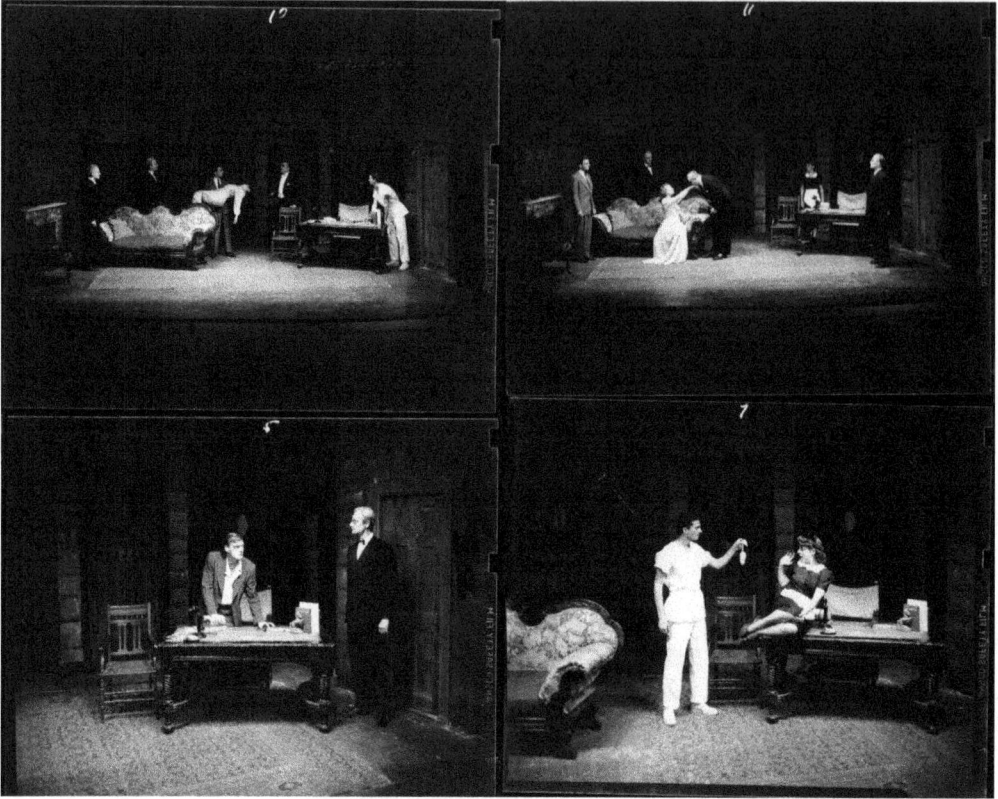

Photographs from Lugosi's appearance in *Dracula–The Vampire Play* in Litchfield, Connecticut in 1947.

Monday, 6/21 - Saturday, 6/26: National Theatre (1,676 seats), Washington, D.C.

Sunday, 6/27: BL gave a speech at the inaugural Conference of the Democratic Hungarians in Chicago, IL.

Bela Lugosi Lecture Tour

October: OSS records indicate that BL had planned to give speeches in Hungarian population centers in support of Hungary and the war effort. The tour would have taken him to New York City on October 3, Bridgeport on October 4, and Detroit on October 6, followed by stops in Toronto, Cleveland, and Chicago. As filming for *Return of the Ape Man* (1944) began on October 6, it is highly unlikely that this tour actually occurred.

Arsenic and Old Lace

Wednesday, 8/4: BL hosted a cocktail party for the press at the Hotel St. Francis in advance of the play's opening.

Thursday, 8/5 - Wednesday, 8/18: Tivoli Theatre (1,385 seats), San Francisco, CA. During the run of the play, BL entertained the troops at local Stage Door Canteen.

Friday, 8/20 - Wednesday, 9/22: Music Box Theatre (980 seats), Los Angeles, CA. BL left the company on September 22, but the play continued until October 24, 1943.

Friday, 9/10: BL donated blood at a Red Cross office in Los Angeles to help support the war effort.

Lugosi swimming in the late 1940s.

Friday, 10/1: The press noted that BL would appear as the "bat boy" at the upcoming Comedians-Leading Men's ball game.

1944
Arsenic and Old Lace
Saturday, 1/29: Shrine Auditorium (2,000 seats), Oklahoma City, OK.
Sunday, 1/30: Convention Hall (4,200 seats), Tulsa, OK.
Tuesday, 2/1: Robinson Auditorium (2,609 seats), Little Rock, AR.
Wednesday, 2/2: Ellis Auditorium (12,000 seats), Memphis, TN.
Thursday, 2/3: Ryman Auditorium (2,362 seats), Nashville, TN.
Saturday, 2/5: Loew's Temple Theatre (3,100 seats), Birmingham, AL.
Monday, 2/7 - Tuesday, 2/8: Municipal Auditorium (8,000 seats), New Orleans, LA.
Thursday, 2/10: Lanier Auditorium (800 seats), Montgomery, AL.
Friday, 2/11 - Saturday, 2/12: Erlanger Theatre (1,790 seats), Atlanta, GA.
Monday, 2/14 - Tuesday, 2/15: City Auditorium, Savannah, GA.
Wednesday, 2/16: Bell Auditorium (2,690 seats), Augusta, GA.
Thursday, 2/17: Columbia Township Auditorium (3,099 seats), Columbia, SC.
Friday, 2/18: Carolina Theatre (1,100 seats), Charlotte, NC.
Saturday, 2/19: The Auditorium (2,341 seats), Asheville, NC.
Monday, 2/21: Carolina Theatre (1,118 seats), Greenville, SC.

Tuesday, 2/22: National Theatre (1,800 seats), Greensboro, NC.

Wednesday, 2/23: State Theatre (1,190 seats), Raleigh, NC.

Thursday, 2/24: Carolina Theatre (1,016 seats), Durham, NC.

Friday 2/25: State Theatre (1,500 seats), Winston-Salem, NC.

Saturday 2/26: Academy of Music (1,500 seats), Roanoke, VA.

Sunday, 2/27 - Friday, 3/3: Ford's Theatre (2,000 seats), Baltimore, MD.

Monday, 3/6: Karlton Theatre (1,200 seats), Williamsport, PA.

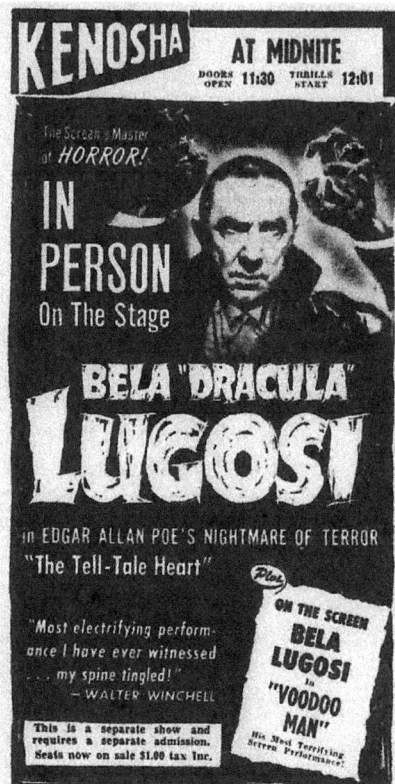

**From the *Kenosha Evening News*
(Kenosha, WI) of November 26, 1947.**

Tuesday, 3/7: Lyric Theatre (1,200 seats), Allentown, PA.

Wednesday, 3/8: War Memorial Auditorium (1,800 seats), Trenton, NJ.

Thursday, 3/9 - Saturday, 3/11: The Playhouse (1,252 seats), Wilmington, DE.

Monday, 3/13 - Wednesday, 3/15: Lyric Theatre (2,165 seats), Bridgeport, CT.

Thursday, 3/16: High School Auditorium, Pittsfield, MA.

Friday, 3/17: Memorial Auditorium (3,500 seats), Worcester, MA.

Saturday, 3/18: Bushnell Hall (2,800 seats), Hartford, CT.

Sunday, 3/19 - Saturday, 4/1: Colonial Theatre (1,700 seats), Boston, MA.

Sunday, 4/9 - Saturday, 4/22: Locust Street Theatre (1,580 seats), Philadelphia, PA. BL and Lillian celebrated her 32nd birthday at the well-known Jack Lynch's Walton Roof club.

Sunday, 4/23 - Sunday, 4/30: Mosque Theatre (2,800 seats), Newark, NJ. These were the final performances of the tour.

Sunday, 4/23: Prior to an evening performance of *Arsenic and Old Lace*, BL gave a speech at a mass meeting at the Manhattan Center in New York. The content concerned support for Hungary during World War II.

Sunday, 5/21: The press reported that BL had attended a War Bond drive at a United Nations event in Pasadena, likely on Saturday, 5/20.

Saturday, 10/28: BL called a press conference at the RKO Studios lot, where he was working on *The Body Snatcher* (1945). The purpose was to announce his marital reconciliation.

1945

No Traveler Returns

Saturday, 2/24: Lobero Theatre (604 seats), Santa Barbara.

Monday, 2/26 - Friday, 3/9: Curran Theatre (1,667 seats) in San Francisco.

Tuesday, 3/13 - Sunday, 3/18: Metropolitan Theatre (1,650 seats), Seattle.

Monday, 4/23 - Saturday, 5/19: BL signed for vaudeville tour of the Midwest, but it was cancelled.

Saturday, 8/4: *Billboard* announced Don Marlowe had written a new vaudeville act for BL. Though it was apparently cancelled, the act was set to premiere at the Loew's State (3,327 seats) in NYC and then go on tour.

1946

Saturday, 5/4: On this date, the *New York Post* reported that BL had been seen at the Trocadero Club along with Marlene Deitrich, Adolph Zukor, Joe Penner, Stu Erwin and a number of other Hollywood personalities.

Friday, 9/13: BL was expected to attend the opening celebration for Anson Bond, publisher of such magazines as *Movie Mystery Magazine*, *Craig Rice Crime Digest* and *Bonded Mysteries*. Others attendees included Alan Ladd, Dick Powell, Humphrey Bogart, Peter Lorre, Sydney Greenstreet, and Boris Karloff.

Friday, 7/19: *Variety* reported that BL would do personal appearances for *Scared to Death* at the Golden Gate Theatre in San Francisco. These events did not occur given the film's delayed release.

Tuesday, 12/17 - Wednesday, 12/18: BL appeared in *That We May Live*, a production at the Los Angeles Shrine Auditorium (6,442 seats). The show was staged in support of a Jewish free state.

NEXT WEEK HERE

OPENING JULY 8th THROUGH **JULY 13th** THURSDAY THRU TUESDAY

MATINEE SATURDAY, JULY 10th

BELA LUGOSI

MASTER CHARACTER ACTOR IN PERSON
(Special permission with Universal-International Pictures)
IN

DRACULA

Classic Masterpiece

The Weirdest Legend Ever Told . . . .
"IT WILL HOLD YOU SPELLBOUND"
N. Y. Tribune

RESERVATIONS TAKEN AT BOX OFFICE OR NOW ON SALE AT MAY CO. BOX OFFICE

NO ADVANCE IN PRICES

$2.40 — $1.80   Matinee $1.80 — $1.00

COMING . . . SYLVIA SIDNEY
→ July 15th thru 20th ←

Advertisement for Lugosi in *Dracula–The Vampire Play* in Denver, Colorado in 1948. *(Courtesy of Lee Harris)*

1947

Friday 2/7 – Saturday 2/8: BL starred in *A Nightmare of Horror*, Orpheum Theatre (1,952 seats), San Diego, CA.

Sunday, 4/6: Along with Mickey Rooney, Victor Mature, Richard Conte and Brian Donlevy, BL participated in the annual Easter Brunch at the Monte Carlo in New York City. The event was to raise funds for the various actors guilds in Manhattan.

Thursday, 4/10: BL made a guest appearance at the Governor's and Celebrities Day, New England Modern Homes Show, Boston, MA.

Three Indelicate Ladies

Thursday, 4/10 - Saturday, 4/12: Shubert Theatre, New Haven, CT.

Monday, 4/14 - Saturday, 4/19: Wilbur Theatre, Boston, MA.

Monday 4/14: BL appeared at a noon luncheon at Dinty Moore's Restaurant followed by an afternoon appearance at a Red Cross show.

Thursday, 4/17: On this day, a newspaper announced that BL would lecture on criminology at Boston University on Monday 4/21. It has not yet been possible to verify that this event occurred.

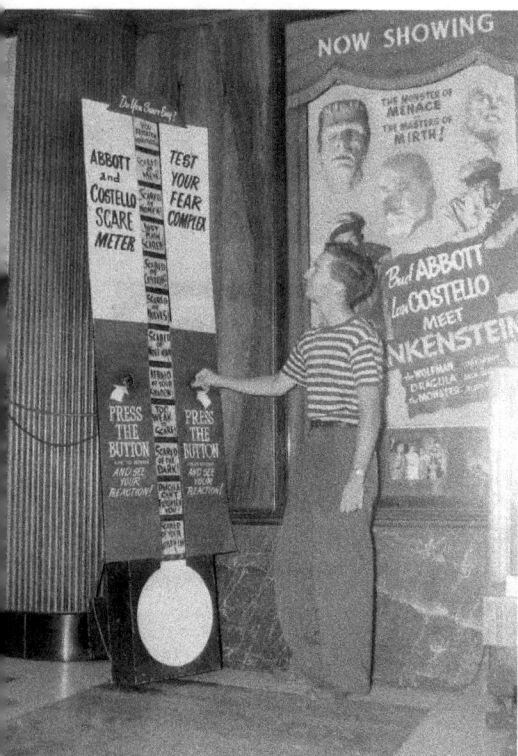

Theatre lobby promotions for *Abbott and Costello Meet Frankenstein* (1948).

Friday 4/18: BL appeared in a midnight show with Joey Faye at The Casino, Boston, MA.

Saturday, 4/26: BL and Lillian attended an International Workers Order (IWO) dinner in New York City given in honor of BL's friend Kalman Marki.

Tuesday, 7/1 - Saturday, 7/5: BL starred in a summer stock version of *Arsenic and Old Lace* at the Bucks County Playhouse, New Hope, PA.

Thursday, 7/3 - Saturday, 7/5: BL made daily personal appearances as part of the "Chamber of Horrors" at the New Hope Street Fair.

Monday, 7/14 - Saturday, 7/19: BL starred in *Dracula–The Vampire Play* at the John Drew Theatre, East Hampton, Long Island, NY.

Monday, 7/21 - Saturday, 7/26: BL starred in *Dracula–The Vampire Play* at the Boston Summer Theatre, New England Mutual Hall, Boston, MA.

Monday, 7/28 - Saturday, 8/2: BL starred in *Dracula–The Vampire Play* at the, Cambridge Summer Theatre, Cambridge, MA.

Monday, 8/4: BL made a personal appearance at the Saratoga Springs Racetrack. A front-page article in the local *Knickerbocker News* (4 Aug. 1947) noted, "At the New Worden in Broadway the wide veranda was filled with men studying the 'bible' of the Saratoga season – the Racing Form. Inside the room clerk reported the most famous guest was Bela Lugosi, the horror man of moving pictures." A week later, the *Knickerbocker News* (11 Aug. 1947) reported that "Lugosi ... had chosen to play a horse named 'Wolf' but that the horse turned out to be as gentle as a lamb, running an indifferent race."

Tuesday, 8/5 - Sunday 8/10: BL starred in *Arsenic and Old Lace* at the Spa Summer Theatre, Saratoga Springs, NY.

Friday, 8/8: BL joined Robert L. Ripley aboard the *Mon Lei*, their shipboard meeting covered by the press.

Saturday, 8/9: BL entertained colleagues involved in the Saratoga Springs version of

Lugosi having fun for the camera, likely in Miami in 1948. *(Courtesy of Ron Adams)*

Arsenic and Old Lace at the famous Delmonico's Restaurant.

Monday, 8/18 - Saturday, 8/23: BL starred in *Dracula–The Vampire Play*, Kenley Deer Lake Theatre, Hamburg, PA.

Friday, 8/22: The *Lock Haven Express* announced that the Kiwanis Club of Lock Haven, PA would book BL for a one night performance of *Dracula–The Vampire Play*. There is no evidence that this performance (tentatively scheduled for 8 Oct. 1947) occurred.

Monday, 8/25 - Saturday, 8/30: BL starred in *Arsenic and Old Lace*, Fairhaven Summer Theatre, Fairhaven, MA.

Tuesday, 9/2 - Sunday, 9/7: BL starred in *Dracula–The Vampire Play*, Litchfield Summer Theatre, Litchfield, CT.

Tuesday 9/23: Don Marlowe announced that he was arranging a version of *Dracula–The Vampire Play* in London for BL. It does not occur.

Sunday, 11/9: BL appeared at the *Continental Varieties* live production in New York.

The Tell-Tale Heart

Wednesday, 11/19 - Thursday, 11/20: BL at the Coronado Theatre (2,556 seats) in Rockford, IL. Two nights of midnight shows. *Dracula* (1931) is on the screen.

Monday, 11/24: BL at the Venetian Theatre (1,935 seats) in Racine, WI. Midnight show. On the screen was *One Body Too Many* (1944).

Wednesday, 11/26: BL at the Kenosha Theatre (2,082 seats) in Kenosha, WI. Midnight show. On the screen was *Voodoo Man* (1944). While in Kenosha, BL made a surprise visit at Frank's Diner, supposedly in full Dracula costume.

Thursday, 11/27: BL at Geneva Theatre (705 seats) in Lake Geneva, WI. Midnight show. *Ghosts Break Loose* is the advertised film; it is likely a retitled version of *Spooks Run Wild* (1941) or *Ghosts on the Loose* (1943).

Thursday, 11/27: BL at the Delavan Theatre (405 seats) in Delavan, WI. Midnight show.

Return of the Ape Man (1944) is on the screen. Delavan is located about a 20 minute drive to the west of Lake Geneva. BL more than likely shuttled between the two towns, with the film being shown first at one theatre with the stage appearance second, and the reverse order at the other theatre.

Wednesday, 12/3: BL scheduled to appear at Capitol Theatre (1,383 seats) in Manitowoc, WI, but this might have been cancelled.

Friday, 12/5: BL scheduled to appear at Park Theatre (864 seats), Waukeesha, WI. Cancelled due to reported illness.

Monday, 12/8: BL scheduled appearance at Vista Theatre (929 seats), Negaunee, MI did not happen due to Lugosi's reported illness.

Tuesday, 12/9: BL scheduled to appear at Delft Theatre (522 seats), Munising, MI. Another cancellation due to illness.

Thursday, 12/11: BL scheduled to appear at Delft Theatre (650 seats), Marquette, MI. Yet another cancellation due to illness. *Dracula* (1931) would have been on the screen.

Saturday, 12/13: BL scheduled appearance at Capitol Theatre (2,244 seats), Madison, WI did not occur, more than likely due to Lugosi's illness.

Tuesday, 12/23: BL scheduled appearance at Hollywood Theatre (944 seats), Eau Claire, WI did not occur, more than likely due to Lugosi's illness. Originally set for two shows, one at 8 p.m. and one at midnight.

Wednesday, 12/10: On this day, *Daily Variety* reported that BL had recently been "barnstorming" the "one-night circuit" with a film print of *Dracula* (1931). The article claims he inserted an eight-minute live recreation of a famous scene onstage, apparently during the film. No additional data has surfaced to confirm that such shows occurred. Given the timing, it is possible this report actually refers to *The Tell-Tale Heart*.

Thursday, 12/18 - Wednesday 12/24: BL costarred with Dr. Bill Neff's *Madhouse of Mystery* show, Adams Theatre (2,037 seats), Newark, NJ.

Thursday, 12/25 - Tuesday, 12/30: BL vaudeville act at Hippodrome Theatre (2,100 seats), Baltimore, MD.

Saturday, 12/27: BL appeared with the Hippodrome cast at the Baltimore Variety Club. Exact date unknown, but more than likely it was either 12/26 or 12/27.

1948

Monday, 5/17 - Saturday, 5/22: BL nightclub act at Tony's Chi Chi Club in Salt Lake City, UT.

Thursday, 7/8 - Tuesday, 7/13: BL starred in *Dracula–The Vampire Play*, Phipps Auditorium, Denver, CO.

Thursday, 7/15: BL was the Guest of Honor at the Philco Dealers Dinner in Burlington, IA.

Monday, 7/19 - Saturday, 7/24: BL starred in *Dracula*, Green Hills Theatre, Reading, PA. BL also made a publicity appearance at a Rotary Club Luncheon, where he gives a speech.

Monday 8/2 - Saturday 8/7: BL starred in *Dracula–The Vampire Play* at the Norwich

FRANKFORD
THEATRE - 4715 Frankford Ave.

SATURDAY EVE., DEC. 30th
CONTINUOUS FROM 7 P. M.

MR. HORROR HIMSELF!   ON OUR STAGE!

BELA LUGOSI IN PERSON
AND COMPANY
with his
HORROR and **MAGIC STAGE SHOW**
13 BLOOD CURDLING SCENES 13

SEE!
BEAUTY and THE MONSTER!
LUGOSI AND THE BLOODY GUILLOTINE!
GHOSTS - GOBLINS - IMPS OF DARKNESS FLY THRU THE AIR!
BEAUTIFUL GIRL BURNED ALIVE!

-and ON SCREEN too!...
BELA LUGOSI in
"THEY CREEP IN THE DARK"

TICKETS NOW ON SALE
AT BOX-OFFICE
ALL SEATS $1.00 INC TAX

From the *Frankford News Gleaner* (Philadelphia, PA) of December 28, 1950.

Playhouse, Norwich, CT. During the week, BL made a live appearance at the local Elk's Fair (on Friday, 8/6) and also attends a Lion's Club Luncheon where he made an impromptu speech.

Monday, 8/9: The *Pittsburgh Press* announced plans for a joint stage appearance by BL, Boris Karloff, and Peter Lorre that would incorporate clips of their films. Nothing comes of these plans.

Monday, 8/9 - Saturday, 8/14: BL starred in *Arsenic and Old Lace*, Sea Cliff Summer Theatre, Sea Cliff, Long Island, NY.

Sunday, 8/15: BL was spotted at the Harrisburg, PA train station on Monday on the way to his next destination.

Friday, 8/20 - Thursday, 8/26: BL appeared in vaudeville, Broadway-Capitol Theatre (3,367 seats), Detroit, MI.

Wednesday, 9/1 - Tuesday, 9/7: BL appeared in vaudeville, Olympia Theatre (2,500 seats), Miami, FL.

Wednesday, 9/1: BL and Lillian were special guests at the Club Bali, Miami, FL.

Friday, 9/3: BL and Lillian were special guests at the Five O'Clock Club, Miami, FL.

Tuesday, 9/14: BL attended a press luncheon in Springfield, MA.

Thursday, 9/16 - Sunday, 9/19: BL in vaudeville, E. M. Loew's Court Square Theatre (1,730 seats), Springfield, MA.

Monday, 9/20 - Wednesday, 9/22: BL nightclub act at the Gray Wolf Tavern, Masury, OH. Originally scheduled to run through 9/26. BL cuts the engagement short on 9/23.

Saturday, 9/25 - Sunday, 9/26: BL in vaudeville at the Steel Pier's Music Hall (2,500 seats), Atlantic City, NJ.

Monday, 10/11: BL in vaudeville, Loew's Bedford Theatre (1,866 seats), Brooklyn, NY. This appearance marked one of the first of a continuing series of vaudeville appearances in the New York City area Loew's circuit.

Tuesday, 10/12: BL in vaudeville, Loew's Triboro Theatre (3,290 seats), Astoria, NY.

Sunday, 10/24: BL in vaudeville, the Valley Arena Gardens (2,000 seats), Holyoke, MA.

Friday, 10/29: BL in vaudeville, Manhasset Theatre (968 seats), Manhasset, NY.

Thursday, 11/4 - Saturday, 11/6: BL in vaudeville, Binghamton Theatre (1,747 seats), Binghamton, NY.

Thursday, 11/4: BL and Lillian were guests of honor at a supper party sponsored by the Southside American Legion in Binghamton, New York.

Monday, 11/15: BL, along with Boris Karloff, Peter Lorre, and others appeared at the *Night of Stars*, Madison Square Garden, NYC. The event was dedicated to the new state of Israel and in support of the United Jewish Appeal of Greater New York.

Monday, 11/22: The *Brooklyn Eagle* announced that BL would begin a vaudeville tour of New York City area RKO circuit theatres starting 11/30. However, that tour did not occur. BL returned to California in late November.

Wednesday, 11/24: BL in vaudville at Loew's Oriental Theatre (2,731 seats), Brooklyn, NY.

1949

January - June: BL entered an extended period of general unemployment, perhaps in order to reconnect with his wife and son. During this time frame, he communicated with several agents in New York City in an effort to arrange a return to Broadway, as well as to line up additional summer stock for the next season.

Frankford 4715 Frankford Ave.
TONIGHT ONLY
Continuous From 7.00 P. M. to 12 Midnight
ON STAGE—IN PERSON
THE ONLY & ORIGINAL DRACULA
BELA LUGOSI
AND HIS EVIL SPIRITS IN
HORROR & MAGIC
STAGE SHOW
SEE BELA LUGOSI Come to Life From His Coffin. Ghosts, Goblins, Vampire Maidens. Voodoo Magic **SEE**
The Bloody Guillotine—Bat Man & The Monster in Death Struggle—It s Spine Tingling! Plus on Screen Bela Lugosi. 'THEY CREEP IN THE DARK'
13 Breathtaking Scenes to Hold You Spellbound **13**
Tickets Now on Sale at Box Office
ALL SEATS $1.00 Tax Inc.

From the *Philadelphia Inquirer* of December 30, 1950.

It seems likely that BL performed in a new incarnation of *A Nightmare of Horror* in San Diego and Los Angeles during this period. Glenn Strange appeared as Frankenstein's Monster, and the show included screenings of *Abbott and Costello Meet Frankenstein* (1948).

Saturday, 4/23: *Billboard* announced that BL would appear in a roadshow version of *Dracula–The Vampire Play* with actor Hampton White. It does not occur.

Tuesday, 7/5: BL met with fellow Hungarian actor Paul Lukas and attends a performance of his play at the Famous Artists Country Playhouse in Fayetteville, NY.

Saturday, 7/9: BL visited a paralyzed war veteran named Vinnie Shelton in Syracuse, NY.

Monday, 711 - Saturday, 7/16: BL starred in *Arsenic and Old Lace* at Famous Artists Country Playhouse, Fayetteville, NY.

Tuesday, 7/26 - Sunday, 7/31: BL starred in *Arsenic and Old Lace*, Lakeside Theatre (400 seats), Lake Hopatcong, Landing, NJ.

Monday, 8/1 - Saturday, 8/6: BL starred in *Arsenic and Old Lace* at Litchfield Summer Theatre, Litchfield, CT.

Horror Stage and Screen Show
TWO BIG SHOWS — 6 P. M. to MIDNIGHT

(Courtesy of D'Arcy More)

From the *Virginian-Pilot* (Norfolk, VA) of March 19, 1951.

Tuesday, 8/9 - Sunday, 8/14: BL starred in *Arsenic and Old Lace* at the Ocean Playhouse (aka Ocean Hall, 1,450 seats) on the Steel Pier, Atlantic City, NJ.

Tuesday, 8/16 - Sunday, 8/21: BL starred in *Arsenic and Old Lace* at Green Hills Theatre, Reading, PA.

Friday, 9/9: BL in vaudeville, Loew's Coney Island Theatre (2,472 seats), Brooklyn, NY.

Friday, 9/16 - Sunday, 9/18: BL in vaudeville, Loew's Melba Theatre (2,156 seats), Brooklyn, NY.

Tuesday, 9/20: BL in vaudeville, Loew's Triboro Theatre (3,290 seats), Astoria, NY.

Friday, 9/23: BL in vaudeville, Loew's Bedford Theatre (1,866 seats), Brooklyn, NY.

Friday, 10/14: BL in vaudeville, Loew's Hillside Theatre (2,653 seats), Jamaica, Queens, NY.

Tuesday, 11/8: BL in vaudeville, Loew's Willard Theatre (2,168 seats), Woodhaven, Queens, NY.

Wednesday, 11/16 - Tuesday, 11/22: BL in vaudeville, Fox Theatre (5,037 seats), St. Louis, MO.

Wednesday, 11/23 - Wednesday, 11/30: BL in vaudeville, Orpheum Theatre (1,659 seats), Wichita, KS.

1950

Monday, 2/13 - Saturday, 2/18: BL nightclub act at the Copa Club, Pittsburgh, PA.

Thursday, 3/2 - Friday, 3/3: BL in vaudeville, Schine's Oswego Theatre (1,805 seats), Oswego, NY.

Wednesday, 3/8: BL in vaudeville, State Theatre (999 seats), Torrington, CT.

Monday, 3/20 - Saturday, 3/25: BL starred in *Dracula–The Vampire Play*, presented by the St. Petersburg Players, Southside Junior High School, St. Petersburg, FL.

Wednesday, 3/23: BL and Lillian were guests at the famous Tramor Cafeteria (Fourth Street South location) in St. Petersburg, FL.

Wednesday, 3/29 - Thursday, 3/30: BL in vaudeville, Schine's Geneva Theatre (1,868 seats),

Geneva, NY.

Thursday, 4/13 - Saturday, 4/15: BL in vaudeville, Rialto Theatre (1,400 seats), Amsterdam, NY.

Friday, 4/21: BL was "Ghost of Honor" at the Mystery Writers of America dinner in Manhattan.

Wednesday, 5/24: BL is Guest of Honor at the Gamut Club Dinner, Manhattan.

Tuesday, 7/4 - Saturday, 7/8: BL stars in *Dracula* at St. Michael's Playhouse, Winooski Park, VT.

The Devil Also Dreams

Monday, 7/24 - Saturday, 7/29: Somerset Theatre, Somerset, MA.

Monday, 7/31 - Saturday, 8/5: Famous Artists Country Playhouse, Rochester, NY.

Monday, 8/7 - Saturday, 8/12: Fayetteville Country Playhouse, Fayetteville, NY

Monday, 8/14 - Saturday, 8/19: Royal Alexandria Theatre, Toronto, Canada.

Monday, 8/21: Capitol Theatre, Ottowa, Canada

Tuesday, 8/22 - Saturday, 8/26: His Majesty's Theatre, Montreal, Canada.

Bela Lugosi Horror and Magic Stage Show

Saturday, 12/16: Producer and booking agent Dave Dietz announced the upcoming *Bela Lugosi Horror and Magic Show* for the NYC area. Though it had to change due to BL's reported illness, the original schedule would have taken him to the following locations in 1950:

Tuesday, 12/26: RKO Capitol Theatre (1,878 seats), Trenton, NJ; **Thursday, 12/28:** RKO Proctor's Palace (2,060 seats), Yonkers, NY; **Friday, 12/29:** RKO Proctor's (2,688 seats), New Rochelle, NY.

The original tour also scheduled BL to appear at the following locations in 1951: **Monday, 1/1:** RKO Alden (1,888 seats), Jamaica, Queens, NY. Three shows; **Wednesday, 1/3:** RKO Alhambra (1,332 seats), Harlem, NY; **Friday, 1/5:** RKO Albee (3,250 seats), Brooklyn, NY; **Saturday, 1/6:** RKO Richmond Hill (2,234 seats), Richmond Hill, NY; **Monday, 1/8:** RKO Strand (1,750 seats), Far Rockaway, NY; **Wednesday, 1/10:** RKO Jefferson (1,787 seats), New York City, NY; **Thursday, 1/11:** RKO Proctor's 125th Street (1,564 seats), Harlem, NY; **Friday 1/12:** RKO Proctor's Palace (2,275 seats), Newark, NJ; **Saturday, 1/13:** RKO Dyker (2,142 seats), Brooklyn, NY; **Friday 1/19:** RKO Fordham (2,353 seats), Bronx, NY; **Saturday, 1/20:** RKO Franklin (2,937 seats), Bronx, NY; **Wednesday, 1/24:** RKO 86th Street (3,131 seats), New York City, NY; **Thursday, 1/25:** Warner's Regent (1,949 seats), Paterson, NJ. [While the Warner's Regent was the named venue, the published schedule is unclear; the venue could have been the RKO Regent (1,771 seats) in Manhattan, as the original tour appeared to be exclusive to RKO Theatres]; **Friday, 1/26:** RKO Kenmore (3,017 seats), Brooklyn, NY; **Sunday 1/28:** RKO Proctor's (1,879 seats), Mt. Vernon, NY; **Tuesday, 1/30:** RKO Bushwick (2,004 seats), 1396 Brooklyn, NY.

Monday, 12/18: The *Trenton Times* publsished an article regarding the "world premiere" of the *Bela Lugosi Horror and Magic Show*. This show and subsequent dates listed in this timelines reflect the revised tour schedule as it actually occurred.

Thursday, 12/21: After arriving in Trenton, NJ for rehearsals for the *Horror and Magic Stage Show*, BL is interviewed by the local press. He received the "key to the city." He was also special guest at the annual "*Trenton Times* Newsboys Christmas Party" during the evening.

Tuesday, 12/26: BL starred in the premiere of the *Bela Lugosi Horror and Magic Stage Show*, RKO Capitol (1,878 seats), Trenton, NJ. Midnight show. On the screen was a reissue of *The Ape Man* (1943) under the title *They Creep in the Dark*. Unless otherwise noted below, this was the movie screened as part of the *Horror and Magic Stage Show* during the tour that actually occurred.

Thursday, 12/28: BL starred in the *Horror and Magic Stage Show* at RKO Proctor's Palace Theatre (2,060 seats), Yonkers, NY.

Friday, 12/29: BL starred in the *Horror and Magic Stage Show* at RKO Proctor's Theatre (2,688 seats), New Rochelle, NY.

Saturday, 12/30: BL starred in the *Horror and Magic Stage Show* at the Frankford Theatre (1,595 seats), Philadelphia, PA.

Sunday, 12/31: BL starred in the *Horror and Magic Stage Show* at the Tower Theatre (3,119 seats), Upper Darby, PA.

1951

Monday, 1/1: BL starred in the *Horror and Magic Stage Show* at RKO Alden Theatre (1,888 seats), Jamaica, Queens, NY. The films screened were *They Creep in the Dark* and *Frankenstein Meets the Wolfman* (1943).

Wednesday, 1/24: BL's *Horror and Magic Stage Show* tour resumed by this date (if not earlier), with an appearance at RKO Jefferson (1,787 seats) in Manhattan.

Friday, 1/26: BL's *Horror and Magic Stage Show* appeared at the RKO Franklin (2,937 seats), Bronx, NY.

Monday, 1/29: The BL *Horror and Magic Stage Show* appeared for one performance at the RKO 86th Street (3,131 seats), in Manhattan. The theatre screened its two current films rather than a BL movie.

Tuesday, 1/30: BL starred in the *Horror and Magic Stage Show* at the RKO Keith's (2,929 seats), Flushing, NY.

Thursday, 2/1: BL appeared in the *Horror and Magic Stage Show* at the RKO Strand (1,750 seats), Far Rockaway, NY.

Saturday, 2/3: BL starred in the *Horror and Magic Stage Show* at the RKO Richmond Hill (2,234 seats), Richmond Hill, NY.

Thursday, 2/8: BL's *Horror and Magic Stage Show* appeared at the RKO Regent Theatre (1,771 seats), Harlem, NY.

Friday, 2/9: BL's *Horror and Magic Stage Show* appeared at Warner's Regent Theatre (1,949 seats), Paterson, NJ. In addition to the stage show and Lugosi's *They Creep in the Dark*, the bill included Olsen and Johnson in *Ghost Catchers* (1944).

Saturday, 2/10: BL starred in the *Horror and Magic Stage Show* at Warner's State Theatre (3,064 seats), Hartford, CT.

Tuesday, 2/13: BL starred in the *Horror and Magic Stage Show* at RKO Bushwick (2,004 seats), Brooklyn, NY.

Saturday, 2/17: BL's *Horror and Magic Stage Show* tour continued with an appearance at RKO Dyker Theatre (2,142 seats), Brooklyn, NY.

Monday, 2/19: BL's *Horror and Magic Stage Show* appeared at the RKO Proctor's 125th Street Theatre (1,564 seats), Harlem, NY. The theatre screened its current two features rather than a Lugosi film.

Tuesday, 2/20: BL's *Horror and Magic Stage Show* at the RKO Proctor's Palace Theatre (2,275 seats), Newark, NJ.

Thursday, 2/22: BL made a live appearance at the National Photographic Show in NYC.

Friday, 2/23: BL's *Horror and Magic Stage Show* at the RKO Kenmore Theatre (3,017 seats), Brooklyn, NY.

Saturday, 2/24: BL's *Horror and Magic Stage Show* at the RKO Greenpoint (1,673 seats), Brooklyn, NY.

Monday, 2/26: BL's *Horror and Magic Stage Show* at the RKO Proctor's (1,879 seats), Mt. Vernon, NY. Advertised films are *They Creep in the Dark* (1943) and *Brighton Strangler* (1945).

Tuesday, 2/27: BL's *Horror and Magic Stage Show* at the RKO Madison (2,760 seats), Ridgewood, Brooklyn, NY.

Monday, 3/5: BL's *Horror and Magic Stage Show* at the Skouras Astoria Theatre (2,560 seats), Astoria, Long Island, NY.

Tuesday, 3/6: BL's *Horror and Magic Stage Show* at the Skouras Boulevard Theatre (1,821 seats), Jackson Heights, Long Island, NY.

During this period, BL's *Horror and Magic Stage Show* might have appeared at the Skouras Jamaica Theatre (1,620 seats), Jamaica, Queens, where – according to a fan who attended it – BL was sandwiched between showings of *The Ape Man* (1943) and *Devil Bat* (1940). Unfortunately, no independent verification has yet surfaced.

Monday, 3/12: BL's *Horror and Magic Stage Show* at the Rivoli Theatre (1,855 seats), Hempstead, Long Island, NY.

Saturday, 3/17: BL's *Horror and Magic Stage Show* at the RKO Stanley Theatre (2,213 seats), Camden, NJ.

Attending a promotional luncheon for *The Black Sleep* in 1956. To Lugosi's screen right are Akim Tamiroff, Tor Johnson, Sally Yarnell, and John Carradine. *(Courtesy of Jack Dowler)*

Tuesday, 3/20: BL's *Horror and Magic Stage Show* at the Norva Theatre (1,637 seats), Norfolk, VA. Unlike the pricing in many of the northeastern towns that hosted the show, the cost of a ticket at the Norva was just 99 cents.

Wednesday, 3/21: BL's *Horror and Magic Stage Show* at the National Theatre (1,393 seats), Richmond, VA. According to theatre manager Bob Fagan, "Lugosi is on tour, having assembled a 13-scene show with a sizable cast. Some of the weird characters who will accompany Lugosi for his appearance here include Dr. Montez, a maker of magic; Igor the monster … the Vampire Maidens who are said to be well versed in voodoo…. Lugosi's show will be climaxed not with the usual spectacle of a girl sawed through the middle, but with something he calls the 'Bloody Guillotine.' He also has one girl whom he regularly 'burns alive.'"

While additional shows may come to light, the Richmond show likely ended the *Horror and Magic Stage Show* tour.

Tuesday, 4/3: BL and Lillian boarded the *Mauritania* to sail to Great Britain, where BL stars in a tour of *Dracula–The Vampire Play*. During that period, BL makes a number of personal appearances.

Tuesday, 12/11: BL and Lillian return to New York City aboard the *Queen Elizabeth*. Passengers of note on board the ship with them were Glynis Johns and Burt Lancaster. After a short stay in New York, the couple returned to their home in California.

1952

Saturday, 7/26: On this day, a newspaper noted that BL had recently been seen at the House of Murphy restaurant in Los Angeles.

1953

Wednesday, 4/16: BL appeared the Paramount Theatre for the Los Angeles premiere of *House of Wax* (1953).

Friday, 10/30: The press reported that MCA had paired BL with Wally Vernon to form a nightclub act. The anticipated opening was to occur at the Tops club in San Diego.

Wednesday, 11/4 - Friday, 11/6: *Variety* announced that BL and Wally Vernon had brought their newly formed act to San Diego for a tryout. Local press reports noted that they were indeed in the city; however, no advertisements promoting the show have surfaced thus far, bringing into question whether it actually occurred.

November: At some point during this month, BL and Dolores Fuller appeared at the Hollywood Historama exhibit, which was held in a four-story building on Hollywood Boulevard. Ed Wood arranged their visit.

Wednesday, 12/31: BL appeared as the special New Years Eve attraction at West Coast Theatre in San Bernardino, California. He gave a speech and signed autographs.

1954

Arsenic and Old Lace

Tuesday, 1/19 - Monday, 1/25: BL starred in *Arsenic and Old Lace* at the Empress Playhouse in St. Louis, Missouri.

The Bela Lugosi Revue

Friday, 2/19 - Thursday, 4/1: BL starred in the *Bela Lugosi Revue* at the Silver Slipper Saloon in Las Vegas, Nevada.

1955

Friday, 4/22: BL appeared before Judge Wallace Ware at Los Angeles County General Hospital. After hearing BL's request to be cured of a narcotics addiction, Ware had BL admitted to the Metropolitan State Hospital at Norwalk, CA.

Thursday, 8/5: With journalists present, BL was released from the Metropolitan State Hospital.

Thursday, 11/3: BL attended the opening of the Carmel Museum Theatre in Carmel, California.

Tuesday, 11/15: BL gave testimony about the dangers of narcotics to US Senator Price Daniel (D-TX) in California.

Sunday, 11/27: The Los Angeles press reported that BL had recently startled customers at Johnny Davis' Cameo Room. Apparently finishing up filming on location at a cemetery in Hollywood, BL unexpectedly went in for a snack while still in makeup. The cemetery footage may well be the same that Ed Wood later edited into *Plan 9 From Outer Space* (1959).

Onstage as Dracula at
an unknown venue.

1956

Thursday, 2/23: Along with John Carradine, Tor Johnson, Lon Chaney Jr. and others from the cast of *The Black Sleep* (1956), BL attended a publicity luncheon for the film at the Tail o' the Cock restaurant in Hollywood.

Wednesday, 6/6 - Thursday, 6/7: Along with Lon Chaney, Jr., Tor Johnson, and John Carradine, BL embarked on a brief publicity tour in support of *The Black Sleep*. The group appeared in San Francisco on June 6, giving a press luncheon before immediately heading to Portland, Oregon. On the afternoon of June 7, the group gave another press luncheon and then appeared onstage that night at Portland's Paramount Theatre. BL allegedly collapsed onstage and had to be taken back to Los Angeles.

Friday, 6/8 - Saturday, 6/9: BL was supposed to appear as an international drug smuggler in the play *The Devil's Paradise* at Hollywood's Troupers Green Room. Mention of the play had been made in the press as early as March of 1956. Despite the fact that a promotional flyer exists, it seems evident that – while rehearsals likely occurred and publicity photographs were definitely taken – the play was not actually staged.

Wednesday, 6/27: BL attended a Los Angeles screening of *The Black Sleep* at the New Fox Theatre. Also present were Vampira (Maila Nurmi), Tor Johnson, Richard Sheffield, and Forrest J Ackerman.

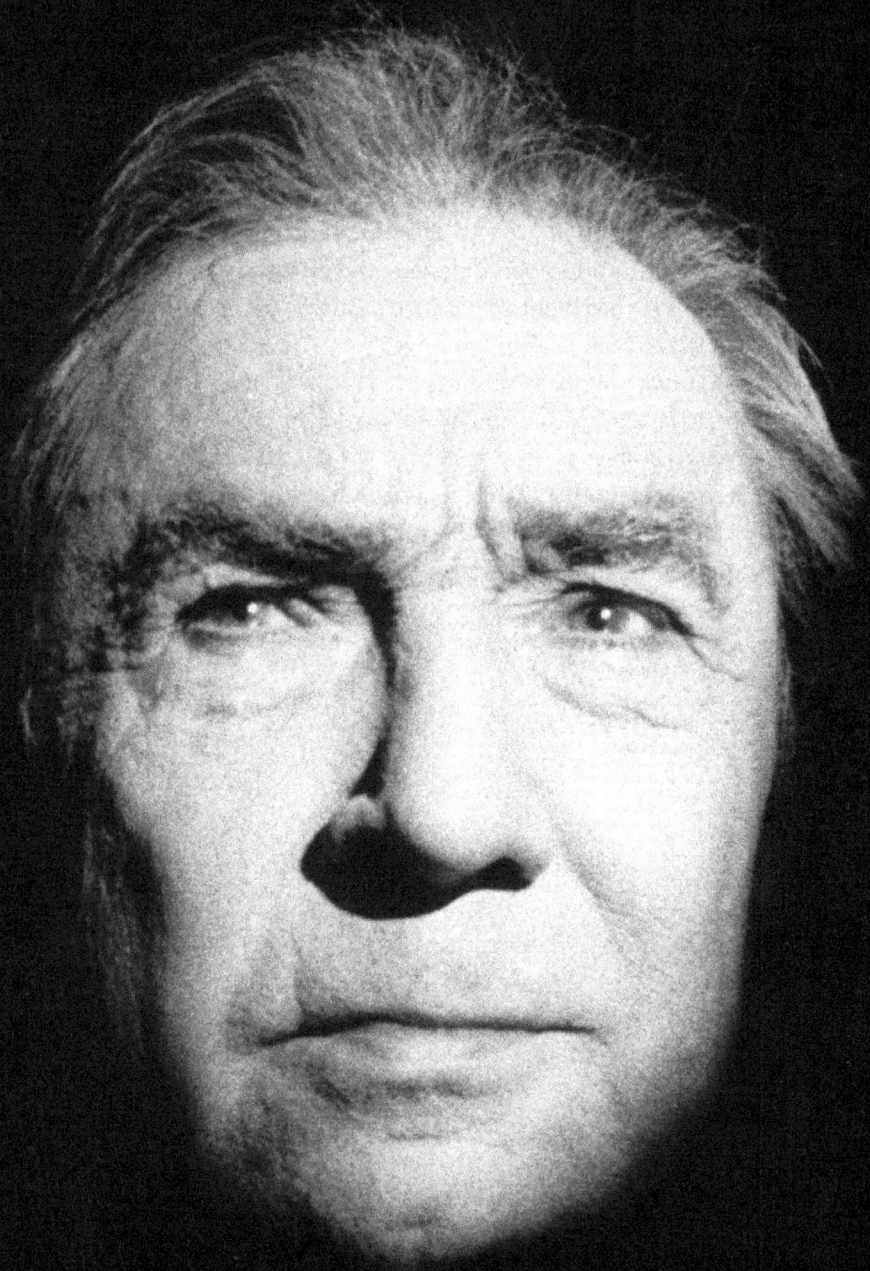

Acknowledgments

The authors would like to extend their gratitude to the various archives, libraries, museums, and universities that kindly offered assistance during the research phase of this book project: The Akron-Summit County Public Library of Ohio, the Alabama Department of Archives and History, the Albright Memorial Library of Scranton, Pennsylvania, the Allentown Public Library of Pennsylvania, the American Heritage Center at the University of Wyoming, the American Radio Archives at the Thousand Oaks Library in California, the American Museum of Vaudeville Collection at the University of Arizona Library, the Andover-Harvard Theological Library of Massachusetts, the Annenberg Rare Book and Manuscript Library at the University of Pennsylvania, the Ardmore Public Library of Oklahoma, the Atlanta Public Library of Georgia, the Bancroft Library at the University of California at Berkeley, the Billy Rose Theatre Division of the New York Public Library, the Birmingham Public Library of Alabama, the Boston Public Library of Massachusetts, the Bridgeport History Center of Connecticut, the Chickasaw Regional Library System of Oklahoma, the Cleveland Public Library of Ohio, the Dayton Metro Library of Ohio, the D.C. Public Library of Washington, D.C., the Department of Special Collections at the University of California at Santa Barbara, the Durham County Library of North Carolina, the Enoch Pratt Free Library of Maryland, the Federal Bureau of Investigation, the Forsyth County Public Library of Winston-Salem, North Carolina, the Framingham Public Library of Massachusetts, the Free Library of Philadelphia, the Georgia Heritage Room of the Augusta-Richmond County Public Library of Georgia, the Georgia Historical Society of Savannah, Georgia, the Greenville County Library System of South Carolina, the Harry Ransom Center at the University of Texas at Austin, the Hartford Public Library of Connecticut, the Hillman Library at the University of Pittsburgh, the Historical Society of Pennsylvania, the Howard Gottleib Archival Research Center at Boston University in Massachusetts, the Immigration and Naturalization Service, the Institute of Contemporary History and Wiener Library Ltd. Of London, England, the Kiplinger Research Library of Washington D.C., the Library of Congress of Washington, D.C., the Library of Virginia, the Live Oak Public Libraries of Savannah, Georgia, the Margaret Herrick Library of the Academy of Motion Picture Arts and Sciences, the Media History Digital Library, the Museum of Performance and Design of San Francisco, California, the National Archives of the United States, the New York State

Historical Association, the Newark Public Library of New Jersey, the Oregon Historical Society of Portland, Oregon, the Pasadena Playouse of California, the Pennsylvania Department of Education - Bureau of State Library, the Peter White Public Library of Marquette, Michigan, the Pickering Educational Resources Library at Boston University, the Public Library of Charlotte and Mecklenburg County in Charlotte, North Carolina, the Public Library of Winston-Salem-North Carolina, the Public Library of Youngstown and Mahoning County of Ohio, the Richland County Public Library of Columbia, South Carolina, St. Michael's College of Colchester, Vermont, the San Diego Public Library of California, the Santa Barbara Public Library of California, the Screen Actors Guild, the Syracuse University Archives of New York, the Tennessee State Library and Archives of Nashville, Tennessee, the Trenton Free Public Library of New Jersey, the University of Central Oklahoma, the University of Iowa Library of Iowa City, Iowa, the Wisconsin Center for Film and Theatre Research, the Worcester Public Library of Massachusetts.

In addition, the authors would like to express their appreciation to the following individuals who have helped make this book possible: Tom Anker, Jerry Armellino, Ellen Bailey, Gyöngyi Balogh, Marty Baumann, Scott Berman, the late Richard Bojarski, Tom Brannan, Olaf Brill, Larissa Brookes, Duane Brower, Joe Busam, Bart Bush, Jeff Carlson, Allison Carmola, Mario Chacon, Wiliene Chitwood, William Cronauer, Richard Daub, Michael J. David, Kate Deeks, Frank J. Dello Stritto, Dorothy Demarest, Patricia Dew, the late David Durston, Robert Ray and Ruth Edgington, Robert Edgington Jr., Michael Engel, Scott Essman, the late Philip R. Evans, the late William K. Everson, Elena Filios, Fabian Fuerste, Lawrence Fultz, Jr., Shawna Gandy, Raymond Glew, Cheri Goldner, Julio Gonzalez, the late Richard Gordon, the late Gordon R. Guy, Steve Haberman, G. D. Hamann, Warren G. Harris, Betsy L. Hendrix, Suzette Hinson, David J. Hogan, Suzanne Horton, Durham Hunt, Roger Hurlburt, the late Alan Jefferys, the late Steve Jochsberger, Steve Kaplan, Amy Kastigar, Constance Kelly, Anthony Kerr, Nancy Kersey, Eugene Kirschenbaum, Robin Ladd, Rosemary Lands, Sierra Lepine, Frank Liquori, Bill Lord, Steve McFarland, Lauren Martino, Jeremy Megraw, Peter Michaels, Jean-Claude Michel, Mark A. Miller, Deborah A. Mitchell, Lynn Naron, Randy Nesseler, Scott Nollen, John Norris, Eniko Numerasz, Jim Nye, Chris O'Brien, Margaret O'Brien, Dennis Payne, Victor Pierce, William Pirola, William V. Rauscher, Mike Ravnitzky, Robert Rees, Kate Reeve, Jeffrey Roberts, Barbara L. Rothschild, Becky Scarborough, Bruce Scivally, the late Richard Sheffield, Joseph Shemtov, Margaret Sides, Zoran Sinobad, Barb Smith, Don G. Smith, George R. Snell, John Soister, Lynette Suckow, Graham Sutton, Kirsten Tanaka, Brian Taves, Maurice Terenzio, Mario Toland, Nadine Turner, Elizabeth Van Tuyl, John Ulakovic, Dr. Steven Béla Várdy, the late Stratton Walling, Jon Wang, Jennifer West, the late Robert Wise, Clay Withrow, Laraine Worby, Valerie Yaros, and Gregory Zatirka.

The authors would also like to offer their deepest thanks to a number of individuals who gave so much of their time and support that they proved crucial to this book's completion: Ron Adams, Leonardo D'Aurizio, Matthew E. Banks, Buddy Barnett, Doug Bentin, Damon Blalock, Kevin Brownlow, Bob Burns, Bill Chase, George Chastain, Ned Comstock, Michael Copner, Kristin Dewey, Jack Dowler, Edward "Eric" Eaton, John Ellis, Theodore Estes, Michael

Ferguson, Phillip Fortune, Beau Foutz, Fritz Frising, Christopher R. Gauthier, Robert Guffey, Lee Harris, Cortlundt Hull, Josh Hume, Elena Kaffenberger, Dr. Michael Lee, Bela G. Lugosi, Mark Martucci, Susan D. Mazza, Jerry McCoy, D'Arcy More, David Nahmod, Constantine Nasr, Henry Nicolella, Ben Ohmart, Paul J. Phillips, Gerald Schnitzer, Samuel M. Sherman, Dr. Robert Singer, Anthony Slide, Carter Smith, Lynne Lugosi Sparks, Billy Stagner, David Stenn, Cezar Del Valle, David Wentink, and Glenn P. White.

Marcus O'Brien, Linda Rice, and Ann Croft have been particularly helpful in making the foreword to this book happen; likewise, we extend our deepest thanks to Lisa Mitchell for writing the afterword. Robert Cremer, Donald F. Glut, and Bela G. Lugosi have also performed a kind and valuable service in providing commentary for the back cover.

Tom Weaver, Gregory William Mank, and Dr. Robert J. Kiss deserve an extended round of applause for their assistance with proofreading and insightful commentary on our rough drafts. Likewise, we acknowledge the crucial contribution of Michael Kronenberg, who devoted much time to creating this book's stunning layout design.

Author Biographies

Gary D. Rhodes, Ph.D. currently serves as Postgraduate Director for Film Studies at The Queen's University in Belfast, Northern Ireland. He is the author of such books as *Lugosi* (McFarland, 1997), *White Zombie: Anatomy of a Horror Film* (McFarland, 2002), *Emerald Illusions: The Irish in Early American Cinema* (IAP, 2012), *The Perils of Moviegoing in America* (Continuum, 2012), and *Tod Browning's Dracula* (Tomahawk, 2014), as well as the editor of such anthologies as *Horror at the Drive-In* (McFarland, 2001), *Edgar G. Ulmer: Detour on Poverty Row* (Lexington, 2008), and *The Films of Joseph H. Lewis* (Wayne State, 2012). Rhodes is also the writer-director of such documentary films as *Lugosi: Hollywood's Dracula* (1997), *Chair* (2000), and *Banned in Oklahoma* (2004).

William M. (Bill) Kaffenberger, in addition to his writing credentials, works as a freelance actor, musician and Bela Lugosi researcher. He has appeared in such productions as Spielberg's *Lincoln* (2012) and Colonial Williamsburg's *War of 1812* (2011) as well as in *House of Cards* (2014) and *Veep* (2014). He also co-produced and provided original music for *Hi There Horror Movie Fans* (2011), a documentary about Virginia horror movie host The Bowman Body. Kaffenberger has contributed Lugosi research to a number of books and magazine articles. He sings and plays guitar in Richmond, Virginia's Americana group, The Totally Unrehearsed Band, and also has several music CDs to his credit.

Gary D. Rhodes and William Kaffenberger coauthored the book *No Traveler Returns: The Lost Years of Bela Lugosi* (Bear Manor, 2012).

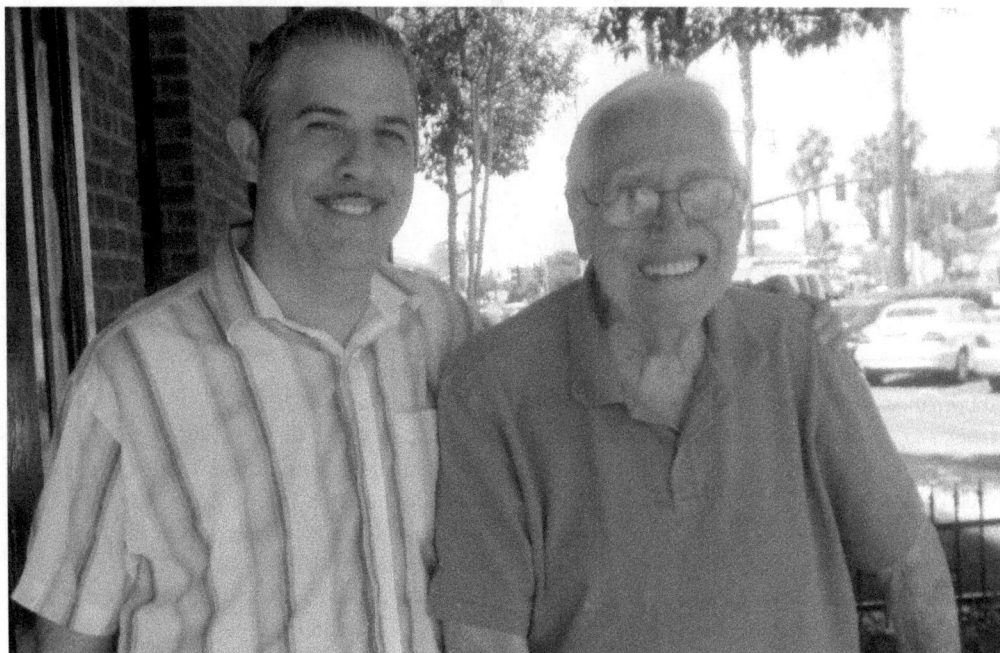

Gary D. Rhodes with Lugosi screenwriter Gerald Schnitzer

William M. (Bill) Kaffenberger

Index

www.ingramcontent.com/pod-product-compliance
Lightning Source LLC
Chambersburg PA
CBHW050402110426

42812CB00006BA/1773